Handbook of Artificial Intelligence Applications for Industrial Sustainability

The subject of Artificial Intelligence (AI) is continuing on its journey of affecting each and every individual and will keep on this path in the times to come. This handbook is a collection of topics on the application of artificial intelligence applications for sustainability in different areas. It provides an insight into the various uses of concepts and practical examples for different domains all in one place, which makes it unique and important for the potential reader.

Handbook of Artificial Intelligence Applications for Industrial Sustainability: Concepts and Practical Examples examines the influence of AI and how it can be used in several industries to improve corporate performance, reduce security concerns, improve customer experience, and ultimately generate value for customers and maximize profits. The handbook offers practical examples, concepts, and applications that provide an easy understanding and implementation process. It provides AI applications in many fields, such as sustainable credit decisions, cyber security and fraud prevention, warehouse management, and much more.

This handbook will provide insight to customers, managers, professionals, engineers, researchers, and students on the various uses of AI and sustainability in different domains. All of this needed information compiled into one handbook makes it unique and important for the engineering, business, and computer science communities.

Technology Innovations: Strategies for Business Sustainability and Growth

Series Editors: Gurinder Singh, Vikas Garg, Richa Goel, and Elizabeth Maw

The aim of this book series is to understand the latest technologies that are emerging and changing the entire outlook of management and how the emerging technologies are influencing the communication and day to day activities of the organization. The goal is to cover how technologies such as AI, blockchain technology, data analytics, multimedia, etc. affect the organization and the impact they have on management. The books will include tried and tested approaches, solutions, and case studies. The books will focus on how the latest technologies have changed the outlook of management and offer solutions to various problems that occur because of the impact of these emerging technologies.

If you are interested in writing or editing a book for the series or would like more information, please contact Cindy Carelli, cindy.carelli@taylorandfrancis.com.

Handbook of Artificial Intelligence Applications for Industrial Sustainability: Concepts and Practical Examples
Edited by Vikas Garg, Richa Goel, Pooja Tiwari, and Esra S. Döngül

Handbook of Artificial Intelligence Applications for Industrial Sustainability

Concepts and Practical Examples

Edited by
Vikas Garg, Richa Goel, Pooja Tiwari, and
Esra S. Döngül

CRC Press
Taylor & Francis Group
Boca Raton London New York

CRC Press is an imprint of the
Taylor & Francis Group, an **informa** business

Designed cover image: Shutterstock

First edition published 2024
by CRC Press
6000 Broken Sound Parkway NW, Suite 300, Boca Raton, FL 33487-2742

and by CRC Press
4 Park Square, Milton Park, Abingdon, Oxon, OX14 4RN

CRC Press is an imprint of Taylor & Francis Group, LLC

© 2024 selection and editorial matter, Vikas Garg, Richa Goel, Pooja Tiwari, and Esra S. Döngül; individual chapters, the contributors

ISBN: 978-1-032-38761-1 (hbk)
ISBN: 978-1-032-39088-8 (pbk)
ISBN: 978-1-003-34835-1 (ebk)

DOI: 10.1201/9781003348351

Typeset in Times New Roman
by Newgen Publishing UK

Contents

Foreword

Handbook of Artificial Intelligence Applications for Industrial Sustainability: Concepts and Practical Examples is a comprehensive reference source that will provide personalized, accessible and well-designed experiences. Systems that use artificial intelligence (AI) are already revolutionizing industries and ingraining themselves into every aspect of our everyday life. All industries will benefit from using AI and sustainable development to create a better planet that meets present demands without endangering future generations as a result of climate change or other significant issues. We are only at the beginning of the alliance between artificial intelligence and a sustainable economy, which will, among other things, help us construct more effectively, use resources responsibly, and lessen and manage the trash we produce.

Covering topics that include examination of artificial intelligence applications of enterprises in terms of sustainability in the marketing, sustainable green fashion industry, e-commerce industry, banking services, HRM, artificial intelligence models in pattern recognition, concepts challenges and applications, agricultural sector, sustainable education, workforce analytics, talent management, fraud detection, cyber security will have the potential to contribute to sustainability in two ways: directly by making certain processes more sustainable, and indirectly by encouraging people to live more environmentally friendly lives.

I assume that this book is anticipated to be highly valuable for a wide range of readers with a variety of interests, and it is not limited to academics, postgraduate students, and research associates, but also to corporate executives, entrepreneurs, and other professionals and masses in all fields who can improve and expand their knowledge with the learning of the basic trends and activities in this book. As artificial intelligence applications is a new field which has the potential to transform entire industries and can revolutionize any industry as and when required thus in the next years, it will have an influence on every single person on the planet.

This book offers a valuable guide to the intellectual and practical work and calls for need to rethink and examines the consequences for future management of innovation. I am pleased to write this foreword as the editors of this book has given full hearted effort for a great solution and innovation. All chapters in this book have been selected based on peer review where reviewers were very much expert in the sector.

Dr. Michela Floris
University of Cagliari, Italy

Preface

HANDBOOK OF ARTIFICIAL INTELLIGENCE APPLICATIONS FOR INDUSTRIAL SUSTAINABILITY: CONCEPTS AND PRACTICAL EXAMPLES

Artificial intelligence (AI) systems today are already transforming industries and becoming an indispensable part of our daily lives. The fourth industrial revolution, often known as Industry 4.0 practises, has been ushered in thanks to recent advances and breakthroughs in AI-based methodologies. AI-based techniques have a favorable effect on sustainability, and manufacturing organizations can see this at the system, product, and process levels. Adopting AI-based industrial solutions enhances system performance, productivity, and decision-making. The implementation of AI-based approaches in manufacturing organizations is still constrained due to employees' knowledge and digital abilities, despite sustainability and other advantages. Due to the digitalization of manufacturing processes, intelligent sensors, and supply chain operations, industries are currently struggling to deal with the large volume, wide variety, and rapid influx of data.

In order to reach their goals of increasing product uniformity, productivity, and lowering operational costs, industries are collaborating with people and robots. Intelligent automation systems interact with many machines in hyperconnected manufacturing processes in smart industries by capturing and deciphering all forms of data. Modern production could be fundamentally changed by intelligent automation platforms. AI is utilized in factories to enable the predictive management of sensitive industrial machinery to predict asset failure in Industry 4.0. AI gives appropriate information to take decision-making and alert personnel of potential faults.

To produce accurate predictions and make better use of their resources, businesses need to have stronger analytical capabilities. Market managers can also get ideas for modernizing their business models to reflect the evolving manufacturing industry. The intense usage of AI frameworks in the modern day requires that digital data be compatible as the foundation for new business models and monetization. Businesses need to be completely aware of their desire and level of digitalization to make the best decisions. Hospitals, biological sciences, immobilization, education, manufacturing, and other sectors have all seen significant advancements as a result of AI. A wired, intelligent, and smart society will be made possible by the rapid growth of AI in the next years.

This book presents key theoretical frameworks as well as the most recent empirical research findings in the field. It uncovers new and innovative features AI applications and how it can help in promoting industrial sustainability for raising economic efficiency at both micro and macro levels and provides a deeper understanding of the relevant aspects of artificial intelligence impacting efficacy for better output. Covering topics such as Artificial Intelligence, corporate sustainability, robotic process automation, e-commerce, FinTech, talent management, analytics, pattern recognition, and many more. It is an ideal resource for researchers, academicians, policymakers, business professionals, companies, and students. Numerous practical aspects of artificial intelligence that enhance industry skills as well as decision-making are gaining momentum.

This book is a solid step forward. The theme of the book is very much inter–disciplinary in nature. Although focused on the stakeholder strategies, the book will be great use for the people in corporate, business professionals, sociology, political science, public administration, mass media and communication, information system, development studies as well to the business studies. The models discussed in the book will have a huge replication and practice potential across the world and the field is one of the most important growing fields across the globe. On the other hand, this book will serve as an excellent reference source to the practitioners working in the field of stakeholders and their strategies.

This book is laid out in a reader friendly format where important information duly analysed is highlighted thus facilitating easy understanding of the content. The book provides resources to the readers thus providing an opportunity for further detailed studies. The case studies will provide a tried and tested approach to resolution of typical problems in area of study. The key concepts and summarized content of the chapters will enable the reader to absorb contents at glance

Chapter 1 discusses the examination of Artificial Intelligence applications in enterprises and their market sustainability. It is important for businesses to follow the developing technologies to survive. They also need to integrate these innovations into their own systems. No expense should be spared to win in the sectoral struggle, which takes place in an intensely competitive environment and continues under difficult conditions. This is essential for enterprises to survive and be sustainable. For the financial sustainability of enterprises, it is necessary to create a climate of trust, not to lose customers, and to protect their brand values and reputations. However, to be one step ahead during the struggle, strong systemic projects and knowledge pools are also needed. In the globalizing world, in digitalized markets, businesses can now easily buy and sell goods in international markets. For this reason, it is understood that businesses should use artificial intelligence applications, but they should act carefully.

Chapter 2 deals with Artificial Intelligence models in pattern recognition, concepts challenges, and applications. Pattern recognition is a complicated process that involves analyzing the data that is being inputted, removing patterns from the data, attempting to compare the patterns to specific standards, and then employing the findings to guide the actions that the system will take in the future. Developing a pattern recognizer that any machine can utilize has been the subject of investigation for about a decade. On the other hand, Artificial Intelligence (AI) is promising as an effective alternative to traditional modelling methods. Moreover, AI-based solutions are viable options for determining engineering design variables when testing is impossible, resulting in substantial savings in human time and testing effort. AI can also expedite decision-making, minimize errors, and boost computational effectiveness. As a result, AI and patten recognition have recently attracted a lot of interest and are emerging as a new category of intelligent structural engineering solutions.

Chapter 3 explores efficient techniques for disease prediction from medical data using Artificial Intelligence and machine learning. The healthcare system of today is one of the most vulnerable systems to cyber-attacks. It is because the healthcare system handles sensitive data like payments, the history of a patient as well as private patient information, and the list goes on. When it comes to cyberattacks, healthcare systems cause significant harm to both organizations and patients. Due to the increased demands for high-quality healthcare and the increasing cost of care, ubiquitous healthcare is seen as a technology-based solution to tackle global health problems. Particularly, the recent advancements in the field of the Internet of Things have led to the creation of the Internet of Medical Things (IoMT). Although these inexpensive and widespread sensing devices could transform reactive healthcare into preventative the privacy and security concerns associated with these devices are often ignored. In this paper, security and privacy issues and threats, as well as the requirements and research directions for the future in the area of IoMT are examined, giving an overview of most recent methods.

Chapter 4 covers topics on the way forward towards sustainable and circular fashion–understanding the role and contribution of Artificial Intelligence (AI) Today, it's a well-established fact that the fashion industry and especially the fast-fashion segment has been a key natural resource devourer. Resultantly, it has also been a key contributor to the disastrous changes in environment and decay of biodiversity. This research endeavors to bring out practical recommendations for how the fashion brands and retailers can leverage the AI technologies for refining their processes and enhance the value proposition and brand credibility among their target audience.

Chapter 5 discusses sustainable human resources management in the age of Artificial Intelligence. Today's industry is undergoing a rapid transformation due to rapidly growing digital technologies and Artificial intelligence (AI) based solutions. With this transformation, the developments in intelligent automation create new problems that businesses will face, and make it necessary to develop capabilities that can fight with all competitors in the world. In the age of artificial intelligence starting with Industry 4.0 and Society 5.0, it is of great importance how to ensure sustainable Human Resources management and how Human Resources departments and policies will be affected by these changes. In addition, with the technological developments experienced, it is based on a human–and environment-oriented approach for social, environmental and economic sustainability to better meet industrial and technological targets without compromising socio-economic conditions and environmental performance. Therefore, establishing smart and environmentally friendly organizations comes to the forefront.

Chapter 6 covers performance analysis of fraud detection using Artificial Intelligence. Fraud exists in all walks of life and detecting and preventing fraud represents an important research question relevant to many stakeholders in society. So to solve that problem, technologies like Artificial Intelligence (AI) and machine learning are playing great roles. Utilizing AI to distinguish fraud has helped organizations in working on internal security and improvement in corporate activities. Artificial Intelligence has in this way arisen as a critical apparatus for keeping away from monetary violations because of its expanded proficiency. This study is focused to perform the performance analysis of the research constituents that contributed to the field of fraud detection using AI. The Biblioshiny app is used to perform the analysis on the extracted documents from the web of the science database. This study will help scholars and practitioners to understand the past and present research trends in this field.

Chapter 7 deals with the impact of Artificial Intelligence (AI) on sustainable education and its prominent effect on differently-abled students. This study with its insightful literature reviews aims at emphasizing the importance that AI has in modern education and its ability to facilitate differently abled children in the field of education to create a more inclusive future. Thus, we can say that the emergence of AI can facilitate and revolutionize how we view the world for future generations, it has the potential to decrease inequality by reassuring the inclusion of minor communities in our society. The availability of e-learning and resources online has also helped education, research, and skill development for countless at a lower cost and higher flexibility. The main aim of nations worldwide should be the sustainable development of education for future generations and merging it with AI seems a possible solution for the future.

Chapter 8 discusses the implementation of Artificial Intelligence for sustainable practices in agriculture sector. In the last decades, farming has seen many transformational changes. Technological changes take place in agriculture which help to control the practices of farming like livestock and crop management with the help of agriculture gadgets. Artificial Intelligence based techniques are being used in agriculture for the progress of farming. Self-automated agriculture systems are developed for crop management. The present chapter aims to explore the acceptance of farmers towards the implementation of artificial intelligence in agriculture.

Chapter 9 explores how Artificial Intelligence is transforming human resources: the Future of workforce analytics. AI has transformed the workplace and changed how human resources are managed erstwhile. Organizations need to engage in advanced data analysis to provide actionable insights to the HR teams in organizations. As 'AI' is becoming the new mantra everywhere. The use of big data to provide information and pieces of evidence regarding the operation of the complete system is a key strategic component of HR metrics and workforce analysis. The present book chapter aims to understand how to strengthen Human Resources Management (HRM) using Artificial Intelligence (AI) technology. Workforce analytics is a strategic imperative; the chapter explores and discusses the potential of an AI-powered workforce analytics framework in organizations.

Chapter 10 deals with Artificial Intelligence and personalized banking services: the impact and importance. AI has the potential to transform almost every aspect of banking, from customer service and account maintenance to risk management and fraud detection. AI can automate routine tasks, such as monitoring credit card accounts for unusual activity or detecting when an ATM has been tampered with. This chapter explains how AI can be used to create sustainable personalized banking experiences. With customers demanding more from their banks than ever before, it's no surprise that digital-only banks are experiencing such explosive growth.

Chapter 11 covers e-commerce and trade: the role of Artificial Intelligence. The integration of this e-business (IT) strategy with quickly advancing, extensively used, and extremely affordable information technology causes organizations to struggle. As a result, businesses are compelled to continuously modify their business plans to satisfy shifting customer demands. Depending on the context, AI can take the form of systems, tools, techniques, or algorithms. Big data can be used to target client demands through customized offers, giving businesses a competitive advantage. The demand for online commerce is also anticipated to increase globally due to reasons like rising mobile and smartphone adoption. Online sales have increased dramatically as a result of changing customer behavior and the availability of trustworthy, affordable technologies for secure transactions.

Chapter 12 explores fraud detection using machine learning: an Artificial Intelligence approach. Experts use fraud detection and decision support systems to examine fraud instances, which are becoming more and more of a concern in online banking and retailing. These professionals encounter the black-box dilemma and lack confidence in AI predictions for fraud with the introduction of Artificial Intelligence (AI) for decision support. There are number of fraud issues in the modern world. The credit card fraud detection technology was introduced to identify fraudulent actions. The primary focus of this study is how Artificial Intelligence (AI) and machine learning systems have the capability to be integrated into the claims processing, customer service, and fraud detection.

Chapter 13 discusses robotic process automation–the emerging technology. This research aimed at to assess the impact of Artificial Intelligence (AI) on the processes between a bank and its B2B customers. Nowadays AI has been progressing at an accelerated pace that motivated to study how this rapidly improving technology might impact e-business processes. The main objective of the research was to identify the impact and its significance from bank's perspective and or customer's perspective hence to prepare both banks and their customers for the inevitable changes ahead.

Chapter 14 covers a study to determine the relationship between human resource management in Artificial Intelligence era: a balance between human resource and AI. This study will examine the three aspects related to Human Resource management and its relation or association and effect with Artificial Intelligence (AI). In first part there will be the introduction of Human Resource management and Artificial Intelligence and in second part we will be discussing the introduction of Artificial Intelligence (AI) in the area of Human Resources and its effect on employment and overall existence of Human Resource in the last part will be discussing the way to develop the strategies to bring out the balance between the Human Resource and AI with talent management technique so that promptness of machines as well as trust, commitment and decision making power of humans can survive simultaneously.

Chapter 15 explores the impact of Artificial Intelligence on sustainable green fashion industry. COVID-19 has been a wake-up call to recognize that the economy, environment and human health are intrinsically linked. We are already seeing a shift in mentality to produce less and demonstrate more environmental awareness. The global fashion industry is expected to grow from $1.5 trillion in 2020 to approximately $2.25 trillion in 2025, indicating continued growth in demand. New technological developments are used for the transition to a green economy and to promote an environmentally conscious fashion movement. Artificial Intelligence (AI) has become an integral part of the fashion industry, which is often an accelerator of waste. With the help of artificial intelligence, decisions in the fashion industry can be implemented quickly and efficiently and all processes within the fashion industry can be fully planned without insignificant costs and pollution. The impact of Artificial Intelligence on fashion will make this industry smarter and smarter in understanding customers' feelings and fashion tastes.

Chapter 16 discusses understanding artificial intelligence for industrial sustainability: adoption of emerging AI technologies in reshaping e-business and trade. AI is becoming a significant engine behind the growth of e-commerce. This chapter simply described the current state of AI technology application in the field of e-commerce and its future prospects. This chapter only summarises the prospects for AI technology and the current state of e-commerce development. It also examines how AI technology is used in the field of e-business.

Chapter 17 explores leveraging Artificial Intelligence for sustainable talent management in companies. As 'sustainability' is becoming a new success mantra, developing sustainable talent management architecture is now a strategic imperative for organizations. This chapter explores and discusses the potential of an AI-powered sustainable talent management framework in organizations. Prima facie, the authors inspect the potential applications of artificial intelligence in talent management. The study extends to understanding the potential of AI-based talent analytics and its way forward in Human Resource Management. In short, this chapter offers a framework which integrates technology, talent and people for organizational sustainable competitive advantage.

Thus, this book intends to give a quality publication with unique insights and methods of application for current scholars and users. This book offers a great overview of how Artificial Intelligence (AI) transforms organizations and organizes sustainable innovation.

Acknowledgment

First and foremost, we want to express our gratitude to our Almighty God. We learned how genuine this talent of writing is while putting this book together. You gave us the courage to follow our aspirations and trust in our passions. We could not have done it without your belief in us. Our sincere and heartfelt gratitude to our family members who have been a pillar of support for us during the laborious process of finishing this book.

The editors would like to express their gratitude to everyone who contributed to this project, especially the authors and reviewers who participated in the review process. This book would not have been possible without their help.

First, and foremost, the editors like to express their gratitude to all the contributors. the chapter writers, whose time and skills were generously donated to this book, deserve our appreciation. Second, the editors would like to thank the reviewers for their substantial contributions to the quality, coherence, and presentation of information in the chapters.

We greatly appreciate the fact that many of the writers also acted as referees. Those who provided comprehensive and critical feedback on a few chapters encouraged us to clarify concepts, investigate specific aspects of insight work, and explain the rationales for certain recommendations. We, also like to thank many people who have helped us learn and practice both the art and science of networking throughout the years.

Vikas Garg, Richa Goel, Pooja Tiwari, and Esra Sipahi Döngül

About the Editors

Dr. Vikas Garg, is assistant director of the Executive Programs Management Domain at Amity University, Uttar Pradesh, India. He has an almost 20+ years of experience and has more than 10 PhD scholars currently under his guidance. He has published numerous research papers in various Scopus–and ABDC-indexed international and national journals. He is acting as associate editor of the *Journal of Sustainable Finance and Investment,* (indexed in the WoS and Scopus). He is also acting as the book series editor for Taylor & Francis Group for three books series: Technology Innovations: Strategies for Business Sustainability and Growth; Emerging Trends in Technology in Management and Commerce; and Electronic Commerce Management for Business. He has been working with new innovative ideas in the field of patents and copyrights. He has been the lead organizer in conducting various international conferences, workshops, and case study competitions, including those affiliated with IEEE. He has been conferred with many national and international awards for being best academician, researcher, and employee.

Dr. Richa Goel is an associate professor in Economics and International Business at Symbiosis Centre for Management Studies, Noida, Symbiosis International (Deemed) University, Pune, India. She is a gold medalist in her masters of economics with dual specialization at master level accompanied with an MBA in HR and also with dual specialization at graduate level with gold medalist in economics also with bachelor of law. She is PhD in management where she had worked for almost 6 years in the area of diversity management. She has a journey of almost 21+ years in academics. She is consistently striving to create a challenging and engaging learning environment where students become lifelong scholars and learners. Imparting lectures using different teaching strategies, she is an avid teacher, researcher, and mentor. She has to her credit numerous publications in UGC, Scopus, and ABDC journals accompanied with hundreds of research participation in international/national conferences including FDP, MDP, and symposiums. She is serving as a member of review committee for conferences and journals and acting as associate editor of the *Journal of Sustainable Finance and Investment*, which is abstracted and indexed in the *Chartered Association of Business Schools Academic Journal Guide* (2018 edition) and Scopus (print ISSN: 2043-0795; online ISSN: 2043-0809).

Dr. Pooja Tiwari is working as an associate professor in School of Business Studies, Sharda University. Dr. Tiwari has more than 15 years of experience in teaching and research. She holds a doctorate degree from Gautam Buddha Univeristy, Greater Noida. She has published 15 research papers in Scopus indexed journal and one in SCI indexed journal. She has also published numerous research papers in UGC indexed journals and has 14 copyrights in her name. She has presented and participated in many National and International conferences (IIT, IIMs Conferences). Dr Pooja has also written chapters in books published by Taylor & Francis Group, IGI, Springer, Emerald. Her teaching engagements have been in talent management, employee relations and labour laws, performance management, human resource management and international human resource management.

Dr. Esra S. Döngül graduated from Istanbul Gelisim University Business Administration Doctorate Program. Her expert areas of management, business, corporate social responsibility, organization. She has a strong background in research activities in management and organization areas. She has published many articles in the field and has also attended and presented at numerous international conferences. She is associate editor of Heliyon/Elsevier Scopus indexed journal. Also, she has good skills in meta-analysis, artificial intelligence applications, statistical analysis, and administrative applications. Her brilliant personal strengths are extremely self-motivated. She is currently working at the Aksaray University in Aksaray, Turkey.

1 Artificial Intelligence Application for Enterprise Sustainability

Erkin Artantas
Korkut Ata University
Osmaniye, Turkey

Hakan Gursoy
HG Training and Consultancy
Ankara, Turkey

1.1 INTRODUCTION

It is important for businesses to follow developing technologies to survive. They also need to integrate technological innovations into their own systems. No expense should be spared to win during the sectoral struggle, which occurs in an intensely competitive environment and continues under difficult conditions. This is essential for enterprises to survive and be sustainable. For the financial sustainability of enterprises, it is necessary to create a climate of trust, mainly to not lose customers, and to protect their brand values and reputations. For enterprises or businesses to reach their goals and objectives, a strong leader and management team is needed to guide the enterprises or businesses, respectively. Of course, strong leaders and their teams will bring in success to the business. However, to be one step ahead during the struggle, strong systemic projects and knowledge pools are also needed. In this globalizing world, businesses in digitalized markets can now easily buy and sell goods in international markets. In this structure, which has now turned into digitalization, enterprises need to use applications that can establish quality communication with other enterprises and to convey that they offer goods and services, that can increase their customers, and that can enhance productivity and efficiency. One such application is the artificial intelligence (AI) application, which is gaining increasing importance today. AI applications affect the role of enterprises in marketing strategies and customer behavior at a high level, and this scenario will persist. Enterprises will experience change and transformation in these matters to market financial services and gain financial power. The role of managers is also very important in this change, and now managers are aware of the importance of AI in terms of communication with consumers. Of course, these applications cannot be easily applied, and their operation

DOI: 10.1201/9781003348351-1

may be challenging. However, these diverse situations can be quickly resolved by forming appropriate teams and providing training on AI. Thanks to qualified managers and teams with knowledge of AI applications, critical steps will be taken in the way of communication of enterprises with customers. Good communication with customers will significantly attract customers to the enterprises amidst the competitive market. This chapter discusses about AI applications, which has currently gained more momentum and adds value for enterprises.

1.2   RESEARCH FINDINGS AND RESULTS

AI-based studies have now been adopted by managers in almost every field and in every sector and have started to be used rapidly. As illustrated in Figure 1.1, researchers have started using AI applications to conduct research in various field, and the utility or value of their application is being assessed. It is our belief that research will continue in the future.

In this study, 47 studies on AI were included in the scope of work, and the findings and results of the researchers conducting these AI-based studies were analyzed, which is presented in the following paragraph.

In his research, Alawaad examined the extent of AI use in the marketing sector and assessed the results. Particularly, the use of AI has had great impact in the field of public relations and marketing, wherein it increases the value of branding in its journey with consumers and plays an important role in the generation of new ideas. Additionally, the applications and programs used have had significant impact on the marketing departments and the transactions they perform (2021).

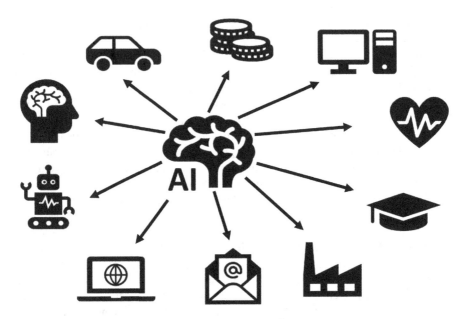

FIGURE 1.1   Areas where artificial intelligence is used[1].

According to Ameen et al., AI has a structural framework that can play a significant role in creativity in the field of marketing in the future. In this direction, they examined 156 research articles in their study. They reported that constant renewal of and change in technology led to the use of AI technologies. In addition, AI applications can help solve many problems in terms of employees' relationships with each other. These applications will also facilitate the provision of important functional standards in the recruitment and training of personnel for businesses. With such AI programs to be implemented, contributions to customer acquisition will increase in the journey with consumers in line with effective marketing strategies (2022).

One of the sectors where AI technologies are being used is the medical field. Amish et al. examined the use of AI in the digitalized environment and for many purposes in the medical field, such as booking appointments, maintaining records, reporting, and preparing prescriptions that are ready to use at any time. The authors reported that AI is used in these fields and that different algorithms have been created in different units of the medical field. According to the researchers, the important thing was that people work in harmony with the machines and that people were trained on the applications. It was important to strike a delicate balance because, otherwise, the benefits of AI applications could cause harm (2019).

AI can be used for purposes that generally deceive consumers by influencing their behavior toward making choices. Andre et al. reported that by using all tactics and techniques together with technology, consumers' choice perceptions can be played with and their welfare levels can be affected. In fact, these perceptions were carried out before, but the severity of the perception would increase with AI applications. It is obvious that it will benefit consumers in marketing departments, automation systems, and many other areas. However, it was also important to take necessary measures to protect consumer rights (2018).

Bag et al. examined the creation of AI tools for businesses in South Africa. In their research, three issues were discussed in terms of business-to-business (B2B) user, foreign market, and customer information. In the B2B process, AI tools have been used to achieve positive results in all aspects of the decision-making stages. The authors reported that it is inevitable for businesses to use AI in competitive environments and that AI applications have positive effects and contributions to businesses (2021).

Basri conducted research on enterprises. In his research, he examined the effects of AI on social media. His results have shown that the use of AI in small and medium enterprises (SMEs) is necessary because of the pressure of technology. Again, it has been shown that the use of AI-supported social media provides increasing levels of increase in the profitability of SMEs, an increase in the number of customers with the classification of information, and an effective business management performance (2020).

AI applications, which is known to have human-like intelligence, have recently attracted a lot of attention from governments and businesses. It has become possible to use these applications in many fields, spanning from the field of economy to the field of health and from the field of security to social media. It has now advanced so much that the use of AI has progressed from acquiring and transmitting data to recognizing sounds. It has led to developments from the music industry to customer services, from smart home systems to assistant services, and from online commerce to social media. Its use continued to grow with a rapid and increasing momentum (Bhattacharjee, 2019).

There is deep sense of co-operation in the field of marketing with the use of AI-based machine programs. All data transferred to AI machines are evaluated in the field of marketing. Again, information coming from AI machines will return to data user people. Training and specialization of personnel are of particular importance for the correct use of this information. If these applications are not used correctly, danger alarms will start to sound in the field of AI. The most obvious difference between traditional technical data and AI data is that AI is closed and uncertain. Where and how or for what purpose the information will be used is also a trap (Bruyn, 2020).

Capatina et al. conducted research on the type of software to be used to learn about consumer expectations about the increasing use of AI in social media platforms. They formed the research population from social media experts in France, Italy, and Romania. Monitoring, emotion, and image analysis skills, wherein each factor was tested separately in three countries, were perceived as effective. It was emphasized that the feedback of the data determined by the experts is Important. In the developing and constantly renewing digitalized technology world, it has been evaluated that AI software needs continuous and renewed talented personnel and solutions and will be effective in strategic decision-making (2020).

In his research, Chen examined the effects of AI use on companies' performance. He has worked with 250 people who are experts in their fields, including marketing, product development, advertising, and brand managers, among others. Research results have shown that AI affects the performance of companies in many areas from product development to sales capabilities, from brand value to advertising, from pricing to customer acquisition (2019).

It is a fact that AI will transform the course of marketing in the near future. It is clear that it will be effective in determining the strategies to be applied in marketing and in the field of communication with customers. Instead of replacing managers, AI programs will become more efficient in the hands of knowledgeable and educated managers. It has been seen that AI applications are important and beneficial for governments and businesses. However, we would like to emphasize once again that it is important to comply with ethical rules about the confidentiality of data, and where and how it will be used (Davenport et al., 2020).

Today, the use of AI has become important for solving many problems. AI, which consists of a mixture of humans and machines, continues to take important steps. Devang et al., in their research, reported that the Indian government has recently given importance to AI applications and programs, and they have been encouraging research on this subject. With such efforts from the government, it has become mandatory to focus on and apply AI tools in businesses. These applications will play an effective role in improving business performance and strategies (2019).

Many governments have now started to use AI programs in many areas, ranging from the automotive to the industrial sector, from defense industry systems to commercial activities. They are taking very strong and important steps in the use of AI tools. However, the known and unknown uncertainties have not yet been resolved. Many data arrangements can be made regarding the precautions to be taken against competitors with AI. Evaluation of possible risks and exercising precautions can be realized. Continuous knowledge renewal development can be beneficial in the long term (Dietterich, 2017).

The e-commerce sector, whose volume is growing with increasing momentum, closely follows technological developments while preparing its marketing plans. However, I wonder to what extent AI applications contribute to the preparation of these plans. The results of Fayed's research show that AI applications used by organizations contribute to compiling and analyzing information about what competitors are doing and environmental factors. It can be clearly seen that AI has strategic effects in guiding market targets and plans (2021).

AI systems and machines play a communicating role between businesses and consumers. AI has a direct effect in the context of business and customer relationships, which are the most important place of marketing. It appears that smart robots that use AI applications play a major role in determining consumer needs. In fact, rather than determining consumer needs, management of consumer needs with perception management is the fore (Grandinetti, 2020).

Technological advances emerge day by day, and the technology constantly renews itself. This situation has led to developments in taking important strategic steps in terms of marketing between consumers and producers (AI). The developments and advances in the AI fields were causing great changes in the marketing sector. AI provided support to businesses in every aspect, starting from customer communication to savings measures as well as from cost calculation to product quality. Businesses benefited from the ability of robotic AI to compile and analyze data. However, there was uncertainty about issues such as data security, and caution was required (Grewal et al., 2020).

Will AI improve human intelligence, or will anticipated concerns come true and war may eventually break out? These questions were confusing. Would the information obtained in this way be used unethically and illegally against competitors? To what kind of end will the "self-driving cars" that people make using AI to achieve comfort with their own hands? Or what would be the situation of a person who plays chess in his own phone and is certain to be defeated in the future? The results of Haenlein and Kaplan's research showed that all these uncertainties brought along concerns about AI (2019).

The use of AI by businesses is essential. It is important that business managers should choose the appropriate AI application. First, the use of AI determined for B2B marketing should be known by the employees, and appropriate training on AI should be given. In this way, businesses will be able to struggle with the problems they will encounter in the future and solve the problems more easily. In addition, they will have had used an effective tool in creating business value, customer relations, decision making, and portfolio. Managers will have realized the change and transformation by switching from the traditional model to the digital model in their operational practices in areas such as product, supply, and workflow (Han et al., 2021).

It is obvious that the use of AI applications is inevitable and provides many benefits for businesses. However, the issue discussed by the authors mostly includes ethical issues about how to use AI, that is, whether it can be used in accordance with business ethics. In addition, the fact that it will increase consumption as it will manage customer perception toward sales in the field of marketing is another issue discussed. Whether it will be beneficial or harmful will continue to be discussed. Necessary steps must be taken for these situations, such as to prevent bad consequences. If these steps are taken and legal studies are carried out, then it is obvious that climate change, environmental activities, and other activities that will increase and support the welfare of society will be beneficial (Hermann, 2022).

We do not know exactly what will happen in the future with regard to AI, but the facts are clear, and it is certain that AI robots and algorithms will shape our lives. For instance, it will be different for a person to sort the photos saved on their mobile phone and for the machine to find them and bring them back. The superiority of AI algorithms is obvious. From self-driving cars to other digital innovations, the younger generation is ready for anything that will make incredible dreams come true. Their vision is always straightforward. The power of AI in solving problems and producing solutions is indisputable. In fact, people have started using AI applications in their lives with digital devices and social media applications that they use knowingly or unknowingly. What is important is what needs to be done to prevent abuses in this area. In addition to states and businesses, most importantly, all people have great duties in regulating and complying with moral rules (Hildebrand, 2019).

The limited AI applications developed to date have been used for many goals and purposes in the field of marketing. His thinking and emotional intelligence were limited. However, AI applications have made great progress today in fulfilling these skills. As expected, AI will be able to respond to the demands of marketers on many issues from customer relations to sales. However, the fact that AI will replace humans in thinking and emotion may bring an unfavorable scenario. Despite ongoing research, there are many uncertainties on this issue (Huang and Rust, 2021).

The popular trend of recent times in different sectors, ranging from the medical field to the industrial field, is moving toward AI use. Finally, AI has made a rapid entry into the field of marketing and is started to be used in businesses. The research results of Jarek and Mazurek showed that AI is effective both in the field of marketing and for managers. Businesses use AI in their operational activities, from customer relations to sales strategies, resulting in profitability. In terms of employees in the marketing departments, providing training and imparting knowledge of AI use to the teams will provide significant support in solution-oriented strategy implementations. AI applications used in many areas of marketing will also create positive energy in business management (2019).

AI is used in the marketing sector with voice-sensitive smart voice assistants and serves customers. Marketing professionals will be more effective when they learn where and how to evaluate the information from these assistants. However, as in other AI applications, how the data are evaluated, confidentiality, and confidence building are an important questions in the field where voice communication assistants are used (Jones, 2018).

One of the important dynamics of innovation trends in the field of marketing in terms of businesses has been the use of AI applications. Research has shown that consumers' preferences, attitudes, and behaviors play an important role in determining which goods and services they need. Many voice assistant robots such as "Siri" have already started competing with each other. Marketers know the value of AI tools and use it in all areas of marketing (Kalicanin et al., 2019).

Within the scope of B2B marketing, AI applications play a very important and effective role, especially in the sector of digital marketing. Research shows that AI can eliminate the deficiencies in B2B marketing research. AI can be used successfully as a guide and solution producer in B2B applications (Keegan et al., 2022).

Khanna et al. reported that AI has many benefits that support businesses in their activities. It provides great convenience in the classification and storage of data, cost calculation, functionality and standardization, different sales methods, and increase in operational efficiency. As with all other technologies, AI applications may have shortcomings, and therefore, caution should be exercised when using AI applications and precautionary measures should be taken against adverse situations (2020).

Khatri investigated whether AI applications used in the sector of digitizing marketing affect consumer behavior. In his research, he reported that AI is greatly important for determining the most appropriate time for and the most suitable options for businesses to reach consumers and that it has the most effective role in determining the needs of consumers. Some difficulties may be encountered when using AI in the sector of digital marketing, but the significance of AI brings many advantages in the sector of digital marketing (2021).

Kolbjørnsrud et al. interviewed 1,770 executives and 37 digital transaction executives from 14 different countries on how they could be successful in using AI. The authors analyzed the results of these meetings and presented them to the reader. The fact that AI made all functions in order automatically was important in the measures and decisions to be taken by the managers. Managers had to adapt to this issue. Because most of them wanted AI support. AI should have been used for supporting purposes rather than for replacing managers who exercised judgment and discretion. As a matter of fact, the vast majority of managers said that these practices would help them gain trust when making decisions. It was not correct to compare machines with humans here because the adoption of strategies could only occur with human strategies and approaches. On the contrary, it would be beneficial for managers to undergo training on this subject and prepare themselves according to AI programs. Technological innovations are increasing rapidly day by day and the use of AI would be inevitable (2016).

Copella et al. approached the subject of AI from three different angles. The first approach was how AI will affect the economic level of countries, and whether it will increase the economic inequality between countries and affect it both positively and negatively. Second, the authors discussed the issue in the context of enterprises. Businesses have started to integrate AI with their own systems in the field of marketing and have started to use it globally in practice. Third, they examined the use of AI in terms of consumers. In this context, AI has also been used to analyze consumer behaviors in their own cultural environment. However, ethical and privacy concerns still make themselves felt. However, AI applications, which foresee the cooperation of humans and machines, will be able to act in harmony with the systems of enterprises when used properly. As a natural consequence of this, businesses will frequently use these AI applications in harmony with their systems in the future (2021).

One of the important issues that businesses focus on is content marketing. AI support is needed to effectively use content marketing, especially smart content marketing. Today, smart content marketing applications continue to be developed thanks to AI technologies in many Internet channels. Consumers are now aware of this situation and have paid more attention to AI technology. These studies, which will be carried out using AI technologies, will continue to be developed and implemented at an increasing rate (Kose and Sert, 2017).

In fact, marketers involved in the production of AI tools constitute a small proportion. Most marketers are recognized as AI users. They see AI applications as an intermediary in the marketing of goods and services. For them, it will be very beneficial in terms of increasing the product supply and sales in line with the needs of the consumer. However, it is not clear how fair the ethical and empathetic approaches of those in power will be. In addition, since machines cannot replace humans in terms of human emotions, it will be more beneficial to develop and use AI algorithms in this direction. Again, AI applications will not be possible to fully meet the needs of customers in terms of this emotional approach (Kozinets and Gretzel, 2021).

Kuhl et al. conducted research on social media. In this context, they included more than 1000 German tweets in the scope of the evaluation. They used different models and coding. According to the results of their analysis, the models could possibly respond to requests and problems and tendencies of the consumers to a large extent. The categories are well defined, and once the information is entered, the necessary information will be obtained. However, as much data as the requested information, that is, the entered definitions, will be obtained. Even though limited, problems related to automated data in line with the consumer need to be obtained for the future can be solved (2020).

According to Lai and Yu, students should be familiar with AI applications because this will contribute to their vision within the scope of digital marketing. In this way, having knowledge and education will make their lives easier in the future. They will gain skills in research, development, sales, marketing, and management and will be able to establish their own business life (2021).

In this globalizing world, industrial and digital innovations occur revolutionary. Now AI applications are coming into use rapidly and are preparing to mark the future. It seems that this effect will be greater than the other innovations. Now the machines will respond and perform the evaluation for us. Even if these AI technologies do not make decisions for us, it is obvious that the decisions to be taken will also be effective. However, the fact that people will be replaced by machines brings along the worry of unemployment; however, there are two types of people: on the one hand, people who are concerned about the possible risks of AI applications, and, on the other hand, people who claim that these worries are unnecessary. However, the risk should still be considered and appropriate measures should be taken (Makridakis, 2017).

Programs called "expert systems" are used for AI applications used in the marketing sector. These programs are used in analytical and evaluation processes. While creating databases, the incomes, profits, market situations, etc. of the enterprises should be evaluated. The customer portfolio, wishes, and preferences, are to be obtained by considering important strategic data such as the needs of the consumers as well as the needs of the consumers' data are to be considered (Markic et al., 2015).

Mauro et al., in their research, described about the importance of machine learning and the future activities it will bring. Machine learning occupies a major place in the use of AI-based applications, especially in recent years. Algorithms consisting of a combination of human and machine intelligence play a major role in creating a data source about financial values, consumer preferences, customer experience, and opinions. AI-based robotic smart systems will continue to be used in many areas of marketing (2022).

Micu et al. conducted research on how AI systems are applied in social media applications. As it is known, social media platforms have become an important channel used by many people. Easy access to the customer portfolio in social media applications, which are used so heavily, has made this channel attractive. The work of experts in this medium, which is seen as a major marketing area, would increase its market share. Here, AI applications and the data to be collected from this channel with a large customer portfolio would make great contributions to product and service marketing (2018).

Mikalef et al. investigated the interaction of AI dynamics in businesses in Norway in terms of B2B marketing. Businesses have started applying AI-based applications to achieve B2B marketing purposes for their commercial activities. Although they encounter difficulties during implementation, value generation of AI-based programs and applications in the workflow processes of perception, transformation, and capture leads to preference (2021).

Managers of businesses are aware of AI and are aware of the event to use it in their businesses. Mogaji and Nguyen conducted research on financial marketing with bank executives in several different countries. When evaluated in terms of bank managers, managers want to be informed about the available methods and the methods they will apply and what opportunities or difficulties they will encounter in terms of customer relations. However, for this, they need to be trained and equipped in AI. Not only themselves but also their teammates will need to have the same knowledge. In terms of customers, the results obtained from AI applications should be analyzed, and the returns should be evaluated. In addition, the activities for the modernization of AI applications should be continued according to the developing situations (2021).

As can be seen, AI is causing tremendous transformation in all kinds of people's lives. It is obvious that technological developments are used in the business world, in the provision of communication, and in the fields of education and training. Today, it is used as a system in many digital machines for recognition, speech, chat, data security, and fast access to information. They may even be less costlier than the human factor. From the medical sector to the fields of politicians, these machines are effectively used in data collection and analysis. However, in addition to its social benefits, its disadvantages and harms should be considered (Mohammad, 2021).

In the globalizing world, the use of AI in the field of digital marketing has started to find an area of use with increasing momentum. It plays a major role in increasing the efficiency of data storage and use in the commercial activities of companies. It is already widely used in digital platforms and provides great advantages for digital markets. Companies have an important role in reaching consumers and in their relations with customer portfolio creation. In B2B sales and marketing, AI provides great transformation and change in creating brand values, increasing company reputation, and productivity, and generating ideas about sustainability (Murgai, 2018).

Mustak et al. (2020), in their research, systematically and comprehensively examined the topic of AI. The main topics they examined were customer relations, satisfaction, loyalty, feelings, and trust from the perspective of consumers as well as opportunities in terms of business can be listed as brand management, market performance, and voice communication. Judging by the results they obtained, it was seen that AI was an effective tool if used correctly. This comprehensive study indicated that AI would be very effective and will continue to be used in the future. It provided information on AI for researchers. However, researchers had to systematically examine AI applications and continue their research in a versatile manner (2020).

It is seen that AI applications have a feature that will revolutionize the transportation sector in the rapidly developing technological world. Self-powered or self-driving cars, in the future, seem to change the actions of people and their lives. AI applications, which are integrated into many fields, will help people in matters such as minimizing accidents and traveling convenience. Countries that apply these technological developments to their industries will be superior over others. However, we must say again that it is essential to comply with the legal procedures applied by the states and to act ethically by giving importance to the confidentiality of confidential information (Nadikattu, 2020).

Palanivelu and Vasanthi (2020) examined the effects of AI on the marketing industry. When the research is evaluated according to the data obtained from the participants, it has been concluded that AI applications are tools that attract great attention and demand in the business world with each passing day, and it started to be used in finance and business management functions and contributes to the productivity of businesses. Again, it has been seen that the issue that consumers focus on the most is ethical rules. Feedback should be obtained by meeting more consumers on AI, and research on this topic should be continued (2020).

AI has both "business-to-consumer" (B2C) and B2B effects. Paschen et al., in their research, headed on the effects of AI on B2B marketing. In particular, B2B marketing managers want to use the advantages of AI in the light of developing technologies. Because AI applications are an important argument that B2B marketing managers can use to transform any data they obtain. For example, it can provide the opportunity to easily use AI in a foreign market in a competitive environment by compiling information about the market and customers. In the era of digitalization, managers will particularly want to use AI for determining the market strategies of their businesses (2018).

Pillai et al. (2020) conducted research on the use of AI applications in retail stores. For the study, they conducted a survey of 1250 consumers. The results of the research showed that, in automated retail stores, they have seen that consumers generally have an important beneficial effect on the perception of convenience and usefulness in terms of innovation and optimism, and they give negative reactions to the perception of trust. These results show that consumers welcome AI applications in the light of technological developments but are cautious about trust due to uncertainty (2020).

AI applications also provide significant benefits in the hospitality industry today. In this industry, AI has implications for the functionality of businesses, from customer acquisition and advertising services to reduce costs and operational activities. AI-based applications will provide great convenience to both the managers of the hospitality industry and the consumers who will benefit from this industry. It is important to develop AI applications by adopting technological innovations in terms of providing quality service not only to managers but also to employees, marketers, and customers in this field. Perhaps the duty of the managers here will be to focus on programs that are suitable for their own strategies for these applications (Pongsakorn, 2022).

1.3 DESIGN AND METHOD

The following is the scope of the study: In a process where today's technologies are rapidly becoming digitalized, the importance of AI applications for businesses is discussed. It has also been observed in this process how the managers will benefit from AI in the marketing strategies and operational activities they will implement. The introduction consists of the results of the findings obtained by the researchers, followed by the design and method and the results and suggestions.

The model pattern used in this study is shown in Figure 1.2. First, the "supportive research" method was used for this study in terms of purpose. The purpose of this method is the researcher's attempt to present his own ideas with information, documents, and evidence obtained during the research he conducted on the same subject. The researcher meticulously compiles the data from reliable sources and includes these studies in the scope of the research after ensuring that they are correct. For this reason, the authors compiled all the publications belonging to the researchers included in the research in the alphabetical order in the results section of the findings obtained by the researchers. To find the sources, the "documentary source compilation" (Seyidoglu, 2009) method was used. While using this method, first, indices in the reliable category were found by the academic community. Then, by scanning

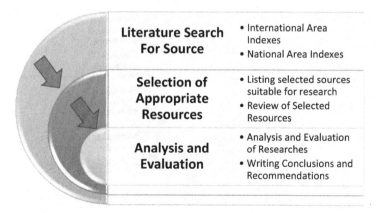

FIGURE 1.2 Model design of this research[2].

these indexes, the authors' articles and theses, academic publications as after these sources were classified, the publications that were considered not suitable for the research were excluded from the scope. As a review result, analysis, and assessment of the publications included in the research, the authors wrote the findings, discussion, and conclusion and recommendations sections to reflect their own ideas and opinions. To add updated information in the study, the research articles of the researchers that were generally published in the last 5 years were included in the scope, excluding only a few of them.

1.4 FINDINGS AND DISCUSSION

The findings obtained in the research suggest that, in general, digitalization has been made in line with technological developments. The findings highlight that businesses should use some of the suitable applications, one of which is AI-based applications, a popular topic of recent years, to ensure their sustainability and continue their existence in this digital world.

Already, businesses operating in many fields ranging from the healthcare field to the automotive sector, from social platforms to the digital industry, and from the finance sector to the education sector have started to use AI applications. Managers have realized this and are taking the necessary steps. Because it is seen that AI applications indisputably support managers in many issues from operational decisions to marketing strategies. In addition, various positive contributions of the AI tools to the reduction of costs, the regulation of administrative functions, and the activities of the employees of the enterprise cannot be ignored. Of course, in addition to this, it also provides very important benefits in terms of creating a customer

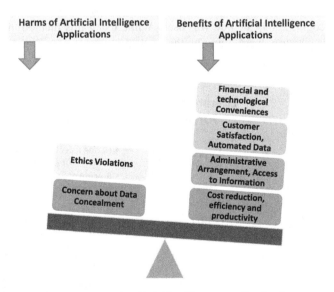

FIGURE 1.3   Benefits and harms of artificial intelligence applications[3].

portfolio, developing customer relations, gaining customers, and creating a brand and reputation. It contributes to businesses in every way such as productivity, efficiency, and quality customer service. Already, social media platforms continue to be used extensively in many areas including audio and video. Especially in today's world, where economic crises are experienced, businesses have to do everything they can for sustainability when competitive conditions are considered. Managers who cannot follow and catch the development and change and integrate it into their business will be on the verge of extinction. For this reason, AI applications are important in this respect and will continue to gain importance and expand the field of application with increasing momentum. However, there will obviously be some problems and risks here. Research on this topic has assessed whether people who obtain unlimited information after using these applications will use it negatively. For this reason, it is a natural practice to approach these practices with respect to ethical violations such as not respecting the confidentiality of data. In other words, generally these problems occur with AI applications as with other applications. Some measures should be taken to eliminate insecurity. Of course, it is necessary for businesses to take the necessary measures to relieve consumers in this regard. I wonder whether it will be more effective to deal with this more comprehensively with laws or measures to be enacted by states, or whether it will be more effective for states, businesses, and consumers. It is also not known whether joint measures by all stakeholders will be more effective. Therefore, answers to all questions of obscurity must be sought.

1.5 CONCLUSION AND RECOMMENDATIONS

At this point, the data obtained from the results of the researchers' work suggest that the use of AI applications by businesses is increasing. AI applications are used for the following purposes: to provide good health service in the field of medicine, to determine the customer portfolio in the human resources department, in the sales-marketing-shipping departments of e-commerce sites for online shopping, in the automation systems of industrial productions, in the advertising and research departments of social media platforms, and to examine the marketing strategies and customer behaviors of all sectors and units. Briefly, AI tools have started being used in all sectors and units. From a marketing perspective, AI applications provide information about the markets, customer/consumer portfolio, and competitors; reduce costs, and streamline the business processes in a positive way. Briefly, these applications will also be of great benefit in identifying and monitoring purposes. However, while AI offers the advantage of automatically analyzing all data, it is considered that it is inconvenient to replace human thinking ability. If this is the case, businesses should give due importance to their training on AI instead of changing their managers. In addition, this job is not limited to just the manager. At the same time, the person who will work with the managers must undergo this training and specialize in AI applications. Another issue is that businesses should not avoid the costs related to AI and give due importance to infrastructure and investment planning. The fact that technological applications such as AI applications are important for businesses to continue their existence and sustainability has emerged. However, it should be considered that AI applications may bring along unethical concerns that may reveal their security and privacy for both businesses and consumers. In particular, it will be essential to gain the trust of consumers, who are indispensable for businesses, by taking measures to eliminate their concerns. For this reason, it is essential for businesses to use AI applications as well as to be sensitive and careful about these issues. While dealing with the issue of the laws or measures to be enacted by the states, governments, businesses, and consumers. We believe that measures should be taken jointly by all stakeholders. In addition, we consider that the problems related to AI applications can be overcome if the person using AI applications is trained and equipped. Another issue is the thought that adequate multi-dimensional and comprehensive research on AI applications is lacking. We believe that more and more up-to-date research presented in this study, such as the studies of valuable researchers, will be useful to the literature, which will guide people who carry out AI studies.

NOTES

1   Figure created by the authors.
2   The authors created the model design.
3   The authors created the shape of artificial intelligence benefits and harms.

REFERENCES

Alawaad, A.H. (2021). The role of artificial intelligence (AI) in public relations and product marketing in modern organizations. Turkish Journal of Computer and Mathematics Education, 12(14): 3180–3187.

Ameen, N., Sharma, D.G., Tarba, S., Rao, A. and Chopra, R. (2022). Toward advancing theory on creativity in marketing and artificial intelligence. Wiley Online Library, Psychology & Marketing, 39(9): 1802–1825.

Amisha, M.P., Pathania, M., Rathaur, V.K. (2019). Overview of artificial intelligence in medicine. Journal of Family Medicine and Primary Care, 8(7): 2328–2331

Andre, Q., Carmon, Z., Wertenbroch, K., Crum, A., Frank, D., Goldstein, W., Huber, J., Boven, V.L., Weber, B., Yang, H. (2018). Consumer choice and autonomy in the age of artificial intelligence and big data. Customer Needs and Solutions, 5: 28–37.

Bag, S., Gupta, S., Kumar, A., Sivarajah, U. (2021). An integrated artificial intelligence framework for knowledge creation and B2B marketing rational decision making for improving firm performance. Industrial Marketing Management, 92: 178–189. https://doi.org/10.1016/j.indmarman.2020.12.001

Basri, W. (2020). Examining the impact of artificial intelligence (AI)-assisted social media marketing on the performance of small and medium enterprises: toward effective business management in the Saudi Arabian context. International Journal of Computational Intelligence Systems, 13(1): 142–152. https://doi.org/10.2991/ijcis.d.200127.002

Bhattacharjee, S. (2019). Metamorphic transformation: critically understanding artificial intelligence in marketing. Asia Pacific Journal of Multidisciplinary Research, 7(4): 61–70. Available at SSRN: https://ssrn.com/abstract=4088282

Bruyn, A., Viswanathan, V., Beh, Y.S., Brock, K-U.J., Wangenheim, V.F. (2020). Artificial intelligence and marketing: pitfalls and opportunities. Journal of Interactive Marketing,

51: 91–105. Available at: www.sciencedirect.com/science/article/pii/S1094996820300 888 Manuscript_fb6476a7086a93460d1e1224e562f9d5

Capatina, A., Kachour, M., Lichy, J., Micu, A., Micu, A.E., Codignola, F. (2020). Matching the future capabilities of an artificial intelligence-based software for social media marketing with potential users expectations. Technological Forecasting & Social Change, 151: 1–11, 119794.

Chen, J. (2019). The augmenting effects of artificial intelligence on marketing performance. Doctoral program in business administration, The University of Texas at El Paso, Open Access Theses & Dissertations. 1976. https://digitalcommons.utep.edu/open_etd/1976

Davenport, T., Guha, A., Grewal, D., Bressgott, T. (2020). How artificial intelligence will change the future of marketing. Journal of the Academy of Marketing Science, 48: 24–42.

Devang, V., Chintan, S., Gunjan, T., Rai, K. (2019). Applications of artificial intelligence in marketing. Annals of Dunarea de Jos University of Galati Fascicle, Economics and Applied Informatics, 25(1): 28–36. https://doi.org/10.35219/eai158404094

Dietterich, T.G. (2017). Steps toward robust artificial intelligence. AI Magazine, 38(3): 3–24.

Fayed, E.A. (2021). Artificial intelligence for marketing plan: the case for e-marketing companies. Marketing and Management of Innovations, 1: 81–95. https://doi.org/10.21272/mmi.2021.1-07

Grandinetti, R. (2020). How artificial intelligence can change the core of marketing theory. Innovative Marketing (LLC "Consulting Publishing Company "Business Perspectives"), 16(2), 91–103. doi:10.21511/im.16(2).2020.08

Grewal, D., Hulland, J., Kopalle, K.P., Karahanna, E. (2020). The future of technology and marketing: a multidisciplinary perspective. Journal of the Academy of Marketing Science, 48: 1–8. https://doi.org/10.1007/s11747-019-00711-4

Haenlein, M., Kaplan, A. (2019). A brief history of artificial intelligence: on the past, present, and future of artificial intelligence. California Management Review, 61(4): 1–10. The Regents of the University of California 2019 Article reuse guidelines: sagepub.com/journals-permissions. https://doi.org/10.1177/0008125619864925.

Han, R., Lam, K.S.H., Zhan, Y., Wang, Y., Dwivedi, K.Y., Tan, H.K. (2021). Artificial intelligence in business-to-business marketing: a bibliometric analysis of current research status, development and future directions. (Emerald Insight). Journals Industrial Management & Data Systems, 121(12): 2467–2497.

Hermann, E. (2022). Leveraging artificial intelligence in marketing for social good—an ethical perspective. Journal of Business Ethics (Springer), 179: 43–61.

Hildebrand, C. (2019). The machine age of marketing: how artificial intelligence changes the way people think, act, and decide. NIM Marketing Intelligence Review, 11(2): 10–17.

Huang, H.M., Rust, T.H. (2021). A Strategic framework for artificial intelligence in marketing. Journal of the Academy of Marketing Science, 49:30–50.

Jarek, K., Mazurek, G. (2019). Marketing and artificial intelligence. Central European Business Review, 8(2): 46–55. https://doi.org/10.18267/j.cebr.213.

Jones, K.V. (2018). Voice-activated change: marketing in the age of artificial intelligence and virtual assistants. Published in Journal of Brand Strategy, 7(3): 239–251.

Kalicanin, K., Colovic, M., Niegus, A., Mitic, V. (2019). Benefits of artificial intelligence and machine learning in marketing. Data Science & Digital Broadcasting Systems, in Sinteza 2019, International Scientific Conference on Information Technology and Data Related Research, Belgrade, Singidunum University, Serbia. 472–477. https://doi.org/10.15308/Sinteza-2019-472-477.

Keegan, J.B., Dennehy, D., Naudé, P. (2022). Implementing artificial intelligence in traditional B2B marketing practices: an activity theory perspective. P Nature Public

Health Emergency Collection, Epub ahead of print, 1–15. https://doi.org/10.1007/s10 796-022-10294-1.

Khanna, V., Ahuja, R., Popli, H. (2020). Role of artificial intelligence in pharmaceutical marketing: a comprehensive review. Journal of Advanced Scientific Research, 11(3): 54–61. https://sciensage.info/index.php/JASR/article/view/506

Khatri, M. (2021). How digital marketing along with artificial intelligence is transforming consumer behaviour? International Journal for Research in Applied Science & Engineering Technology (IJRASET), 9(7): 523–527. https://doi.org/10.22214/ijraset.2021.36287.

Kolbjørnsrud, V., Amico, R., Thomas, J.R. (2016). How artificial intelligence will redefine management. Harvard Business Review, 2: 1–6.

Kopalle, K.P., Gangwar, M., Kaplan, A., Ramachandran, D., Reinartz, W., Rindfleisch, A. (2021). Examining artificial intelligence (AI) technologies in marketing via a global lens: current trends and future research opportunities. International Journal of Research in Marketing, 39: 522–540.

Kose, U., Sert, S. (2017). Improving content marketing processes with the approaches by artificial intelligence. Ecoforum, 6(1): 1–8.

Kozinets, V.R., Gretzel, U. (2021). Commentary: artificial intelligence: the marketer's dilemma. Journal of Marketing, 85(1) 156–159. https://doi.org/10.1177/0022242920972933

Kühl, N., Mühlthaler, M., Goutier, M. (2020). Supporting customer-oriented marketing with artificial intelligence: automatically quantifying customer needs from social media. Electronic Markets, 30: 351–367. https://link.springer.com/article/10.1007/s12 525-019-00351-0

Lai, Z., Yu, L. (2021). Research on digital marketing communication talent cultivation in the era of artificial intelligence. Journal of Physics: Conference Series 1757 012040 IOP Publishing. https://doi.org/10.1088/1742-6596/1757/1/012040

Makridakis, S. (2017). The forthcoming artificial intelligence (ai) revolution: its impact on society and firms. Futures, 90: 46–60.

Markić, B., Bijakšić, S., Šantić, M. (2015). Artificial intelligence in determination of marketing customer strategy. Informatol. 48: 39–47.

Mauro, A., Sestino, A., Bacconi, A. (2022). Machine learning and artificial intelligence use in marketing: a general taxonomy. Italian Journal of Marketing, https://doi.org/10.1007/s43039-022-00057-w

Micu, A., Capatina, A., Micu, A.E. (2018). Exploring artificial intelligence techniques' applicability in social media marketing. Journal of Emerging Trends in Marketing and Management, 1(1): 156–165.

Mikalef, P., Conboy, K., Krogstie, J. (2021). Artificial intelligence as an enabler of b2b marketing: a dynamic capabilities micro-foundations approach. Industrial Marketing Management, 98: 80–92.

Mogaji, E., Nguyen, P.N. (2021). Managers' understanding of artificial intelligence in relation to marketing financial services: insights from a cross-country study. International Journal of Bank Marketing, 40(6): 1–49.

Mohammad, S.M. (2021). Artificial intelligence in information technology. Available at SSRN: https://ssrn.com/abstract=3625444 or http://dx.doi.org/10.2139/ssrn.3625444

Murgai, A. (2018). Transforming digital marketing with artificial intelligence. International Journal of Latest Technology in Engineering, Management & Applied Science (IJLTEMAS), 7(4): 259–262. www.ijltemas.in/digital-library/volume-vii-issue-iv.php

Mustak, M., Salminen, J., Pl'e, L., Wirtz, J. (2020). Artificial intelligence in marketing: topic modeling, scientometric analysis, and research agenda. Journal of Business Research, 124: 389–404. https://doi.org/10.1016/j.jbusres.2020.10.044

Nadikattu, R.R. (2020). New ways in artificial intelligence. International Journal of Computer Trends and Technology (IJCTT), 67(12): 89–94. Available at SSRN: https://ssrn.com/abstract=3629063 or http://dx.doi.org/10.2139/ssrn.3629063

Palanivelu, V.R., Vasanthi, B. (2020). Role of artificial intelligence in business transformation. International Journal of Advanced Science and Technology, 29(4): 392–400.

Paschen, J., Kietzmann, J., Kietzmann, C.T. (2018). Artificial intelligence (ai) and its implications for market knowledge in B2B marketing. Journal of Business & Industrial Marketing, 34(1): 1–10. https://doi.org/10.1108/JBIM-10-2018-0295

Pillai, R., Sivathanu, B., Dwivedi, K.Y. (2020). Shopping intention at AI-powered automated retail stores (AIPARS). Journal of Retailing and Consumer Services, 57: 1–45. https://doi.org/10.1016/j.jretconser.2020.102207

Pongsakorn, L. (2022). Artificial intelligence (ai) in the hospitality industry: a review article. International Journal of Computing Sciences Research. Advance online publication. 6(6): 1–12. https://doi.org/10.25147/ijcsr.2017.001.1.103

Seyidoglu, H. (2009). Scientific Research and Writing Handbook. Improved 10th Edition. Istanbul: Güzem Can Publications.

2 Artificial Intelligence Models in Pattern Recognition

Mohammed Rashad Baker
Software Department, College of Computer Science and
Information Technology, University of Kirkuk
Kirkuk, Iraq

Umesh Solanki
TAPMI School of Business, Manipal University Jaipur
Jaipur, Rajasthan, India

2.1 INTRODUCTION

Pattern recognition investigates how machines scan their environment, learn to characterize patterns of particular interest from the underlying background, and draw logical inferences regarding the kinds of patterns. The things being looked at are sorted into the appropriate category during the pattern recognition process. The process of pattern recognition involves analyzing incoming data to recognize recurring patterns. The objective of exploratory pattern recognition is to recognize data patterns in general, whereas the first step of descriptive pattern recognition is to classify the patterns that have been recognized and discovered. Consequently, pattern recognition addresses each discussed case, and various pattern recognition methods rely on the data type and use case. As a result, pattern recognition does not involve a single method but rather a comprehensive collection of various methodologies, with only frequently tangentially connected information. Intelligent systems typically need to be able to recognize patterns to function correctly. Words or other text, photos, or audio files can be used as data inputs for pattern recognition. Therefore, pattern recognition encompasses a broader scope than computer vision, which concentrates on recognizing images (Shaker et al., 2022).

Finding patterns from data is a critical challenge with a long and fruitful history (Fayyad et al., 1996). For example, early in the twentieth century, the development and validation of quantum physics were greatly aided by the finding of regularities in atomic spectra. Pattern recognition involves the use of methods and algorithms to identify individual data patterns, after which the patterns are used to perform operations such as categorizing the data (Baker & Akcayol, 2017; Raj et al., 2015).

DOI: 10.1201/9781003348351-2

The scientific field of pattern recognition aims to categorize or classify items into various groups or subgroups. According to the application, these items could be waveforms of signals, pictures, or other measures requiring classification and are known as "patterns." Before the sixtieth of the last century, theoretical statistics research was the primary source of pattern recognition (Ding & Shi, 2005). The growth of computers led to the need for pattern recognition in practical applications, as it did for everything else, creating new demands for theoretical advancements. The requirement for information processing and retrieval is growing as our society transitions from an industrial state to a post-industrial state. Industrial production automation is also becoming increasingly critical. This tendency has elevated pattern recognition to the cutting edge of current engineering research and applications. Many machine intelligence systems created for decision-making include pattern recognition as a core component (Tien, 2017). For most potential implementations, pattern recognition problems are thought to be easier to solve when the variables are changed into a new parameter set.

For example, as for character recognition, the representations of the characters are frequently translated and altered such that each character fits within a box of a specific size (Mellouli et al., 2019). The position and size of all characters inside each class are now the same, making it considerably more straightforward for a pattern recognition algorithm to differentiate between classes.

Note that the same preprocessing methods must be applied to new test data as to the training data. To accelerate computing, preprocessing may also be conducted. Suppose the objective is real-time face recognition in a high-resolution video stream, for instance. In that case, the computer must process many pixels per second, and delivering them straight to a complicated pattern recognition algorithm may be practically impossible (Canedo & Neves, 2019). Instead, the objective is to identify fast-to-compute characteristics that preserve useful discriminatory information, allowing faces to be discriminated against by nonfaces. These features are then fed to the algorithm for pattern recognition as inputs. In particular, mean values of the picture intensity throughout a rectangular segment can be evaluated quite efficiently. Such features can be rather successful for rapid face detection (Kortli et al., 2020). This preprocessing is a form of dimensionality reduction, as the amount of such characteristics is fewer than the number of pixels. Care must be taken during preprocessing because the information is frequently destroyed; if this information is necessary to solve the problem, then the system might not work as well as it should.

Several application areas including healthcare, business, computer vision, and AI have fundamental issues regarding machine-based and automatically detected pattern recognition, description, categorization, and grouping. In such cases, pattern recognition is used to solve these problems. Pattern recognition is essential for machine vision (Kong et al., 2020). A machine vision system gathers images using a camera and analyzes them to generate descriptions of the images captured. Typical manufacturing applications of machine vision systems include automated visual inspection and assembly line automation. Character recognition is another essential aspect of pattern recognition, which has significant implications for automation and data processing. Optical character recognition (OCR) technologies are currently commercially accessible and are essentially commonplace. The "front end" of an OCR system consists of a light source, a scan lens, a paper conveyance, and a detector (Chaudhuri et al., 2017). Another major application of pattern recognition is a computer-aided diagnosis designed to assist medical professionals when making diagnostic judgments (Baker et al., 2022). The doctors will make the final judge for a definitive diagnosis (Aslantaş et al., 2016). Speech recognition is another area where much time and money have been spent on research and development because speech represents the most natural way for people to share information and talk to each other (Hassan et al., 2021). Scientists, engineers, and science fiction writers have been trying for a long time to make smart machines that can understand what individuals say. Pattern recognition is also very effective in data mining and finding new information in databases (Baker & Akcayol, 2022). Data mining is very interesting for a wide range of uses including financial and market analysis (Budhathoki et al., 2018), meaning extraction from the text (Alamoodi et al., 2022) and retrieving webpages (Gozudeli et al., 2014) and gamification (Qader et al., 2022).

In unsupervised pattern recognition, one of the biggest problems is defining "similarity" between two feature vectors and choosing the right way to measure it. Another critical thing to consider is choosing an algorithmic strategy to group the vectors based on the similarity measure (Hruschka et al., 2009). In general, different ways of using algorithms can produce different results, which an expert needs to investigate. Semi-supervised learning/pattern recognition for developing a classification system has the same goals as those of supervised learning/pattern recognition. However, the designer also has a set of patterns whose class origin is unknown, in addition to the training patterns called "labeled data." Semi-supervised pattern recognition might become useful when the person designing the system possesses only a tiny quantity of labeled data. In these situations, it can be helpful to improve the system's design by obtaining additional details from the unlabeled samples about the overall structure of the data at hand (Kang et al., 2021). Clustering tasks also involve the use of semi-supervised learning. In this case, must-links and cannot-links made from labeled data are used as constraints. In other words, the clustering process is limited only to adding specific points in the same group or keeping them away from being in the same group. Semi-supervised learning gives the clustering algorithm some information it already knows (Grira et al., 2008).

This chapter deals with pattern recognition in industrial and research settings in many fields. First, we will delve into specifics regarding the ideas of pattern recognition. We will start with a literature review of recent studies, after which we will discuss the most critical AI methods for pattern recognition. Then, we will discuss its challenges and how we can overcome them. Next, we will discuss the combination of AI and pattern recognition and how it will be used to resolve real-world applications.

2.2 THEORETICAL APPROACHES TO PATTERN RECOGNITION

Pattern recognition can be classified into three types, namely, statistical, structural, and neural types, based on the mechanism utilized to classify the input. Image, sound, voice, and speech pattern recognition are the different types of processed data.

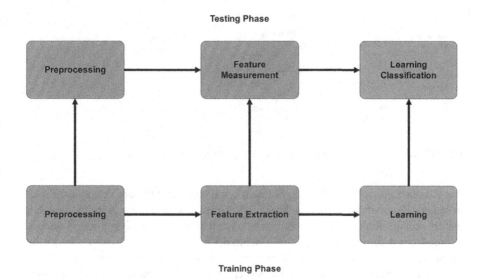

FIGURE 2.1 Statistical pattern recognition.

2.2.1 STATISTICAL CLASSIFICATION

Various industrial recognition systems have been successfully designed using statistical pattern recognition (Jain et al., 2000a). A pattern is expressed as a d-dimensional feature vector by a set of d features or qualities. Decision thresholds are established between pattern classes according to the statistical decision theory. The two methods by which the recognition system operates are training or learning and categorization or testing. Figure 2.1 demonstrates the statistical pattern recognition elements.

The preprocessing module must first distinguish the pattern of interest from the surrounding patterns, remove noise, inherently the pattern, and carry out other operations to define a subset of the pattern (Shanthi & Duraiswamy, 2010). In the training mode, the feature extraction module picks the important features for expressing patterns, and the classifier is trained to partition the feature space. A designer can use the feedback path to enhance preprocessing, feature extraction, and feature selection operations. Based on the observed features, the trained assignment of the training sample to a particular pattern class for evaluation in the classification mode. Several approaches are utilized to construct classifiers for statistical pattern recognition based on the data provided on conditional class intensities (Vailaya et al., 2001).

2.2.2 STRUCTURAL PATTERN RECOGNITION

Structural pattern recognition uses symbolic, nominal qualities with varying cardinality to represent each object (Ahmed et al., 2021). It enables the representation of pattern structures that consider more intricate interrelationships between qualities than

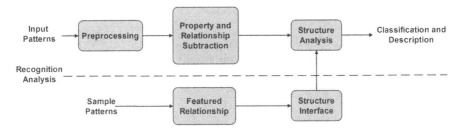

FIGURE 2.2   Block diagram of a structural pattern recognition system.

that is achievable with the flat, fixed-dimensional numerical feature vectors employed in statistical classification. When there is an evident structure in the patterns, syntactic pattern recognition can be utilized instead of statistical pattern recognition. Symbolic strings from a formal language are a method for presenting such structure. In this instance, the differences in class hierarchies are stored as different grammar.

In pattern recognition, the formal structure of a given pattern is reduced (geometric and rule sequence). Usually, the set's numerical values provide more details than pattern information. Connected features are identified and classified to facilitate significant structural characteristics. Synthesis of raw descriptive identification with formal syntax or grammar yields a pattern. Patterns include corner, edge, and other angles. Typically, complicated hierarchical patterns are defined by the structural method's formulation of simpler subpatterns. Each pattern's components are considered as a composition according to the structural technique. Figure 2.2 depicts a system for recognizing structural patterns.

The structural method is predicated on the recursive explanation of large patterns in terms of simpler patterns, just as sentences are constructed by stringing words together and words are constructed by stringing letters together. Using a set of pattern primitives (the simplest subpatterns) and their relationships, this methodology results in an investigated pattern's classification and structural description (Fu, 2018).

Pattern primitives should be significantly simpler to distinguish than patterns themselves. Graphs are another method for representing relationships wherein nodes are connected if their associated subpatterns are related. A piece can be designated as belonging to a class if its diagram is closely associated with model graphs of the class. Typically, patterns are formed hierarchically from simpler subpatterns. This aids in splitting the recognition problem into simpler subtasks by requiring the identification of subpatterns before the true patterns. Structured methods give descriptions of objects that may be helpful in and of themselves. For instance, syntactic pattern recognition could be utilized to identify the items in an image. In addition, structural approaches are effective at locating a mapping of correspondence between two photographs of an object (Pinheiro et al., 2020). In face recognition, under natural conditions, similar features will be mapped in different places and/or may be obscured due to camera angle and perspective. A method for graph matching will produce the optimum correspondence (Bianchi et al., 2022).

2.2.3 Neural Network Pattern Recognition

The pattern recognition methods presented thus far are focused on direct machine computation. Mathematical and statistical principles underpin direct computations. In addition to these techniques, the neural approach to pattern recognition is also explored, as are subjects linked to neural networks (Shanmuganathan, 2016).

Artificial neural networks imitate the real brain's organic neural network, and all nodes in this network are connected, which enables huge parallel distribution. The input units acquire diverse forms and patterns of information based on an inner weighting mechanism, and the neural network strives to learn from the data to generate a single result (Oleinik, 2019). Neural networks provide the advantages of adaptable learning, self-organization, and fault tolerance. Pattern recognition applications utilize neural networks because of their exceptional abilities. An artificial neural network undergoes an initial training phase in which it learns to recognize patterns in the data presented (Bharti, 2021). Figure 2.3 illustrates the basic structure of a feed-forward neural network.

Essential feed-forward networks are frequently used for pattern recognition. The absence of incoming feedback is called feed-forward; by giving feedback to the input data, neural networks could learn from their mistakes in the same way as humans do. This feedback would recreate the input patterns and make them error-free, enhancing neural networks' performance. It is quite challenging to design neural networks of this type. These networks are regarded as auto-associative neural networks (Guerrisi et al., 2022). Using back-propagation methods, this complexity of network construction can be circumvented. Through this supervised stage, the network analyzes their

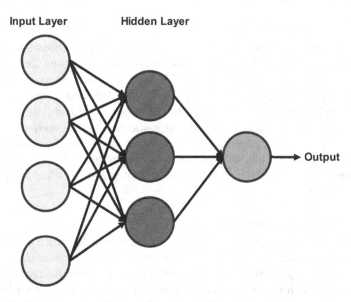

FIGURE 2.3   Basic structure of a feed-forward neural network.

output to the intended output, or the desired output. Local minima are among the primary issues with backpropagation algorithms.

2.2.4   MODELS USED IN PATTERN RECOGNITION

There are many models used in pattern recognition. The following are the most critical used models:

2.2.4.1   Linear Discriminant Analysis

Linear discriminant analysis (LDA) is used to identify the linear synthesis of characteristics that distinguish or describe two or more groups of objects or occurrences (Huang et al., 2002). The synthesis results can be utilized as a classifier or to reduce dimensionality before subsequent classification. The standard LDA can cause a lot of trouble whenever the amount of observations is lower than the feature space. It is recommended that a principal component analysis (PCA) be performed before the LDA to avoid this (Balakrishnama & Ganapathiraju, 1998).

2.2.4.2   Naive Bayes Classifier

It is part of Bayesian statistics that depends on the Bayes theorem. This straightforward probabilistic and statistical classifier makes reasonable (naive) independent constraints and uses the maximum posterior hypothesis (Sharma & Kaur, 2013). Being statistical, it can estimate the possibility that a given sample could belong to a specified class. As naive Bayes implies that an attribute's effect on a class is independent of other characteristics, its starting probability model is an independent feature model (Mahdi et al., 2021).

2.2.4.3   Logistic Regression

In statistical analysis, logistic regression is used to make predictions about a binary result, such as yes or no, from a series of observations; it is used for determining the coefficients of a logistic model. Logistic regression parameters are established according to the data set, typically through maximum likelihood estimation. Artificial neural networks and logistic regression have various functional forms; hence, the former is recognized as a parametric method, while the latter is occasionally referred to as a semi-parametric or nonparametric method (Valentin et al., 2001). This distinction is crucial because, unlike the parameters of a neural network, the contribution of logistic regression's parameters (coefficients and intercept) can often be understood (weights) (Tu, 1996).

2.2.4.4   Multilayer Perceptron

Multilayer perceptron networks map inputs to outputs and determine whether or not information expressed by a vector of integers belongs to a particular class (Alsmadi et al., 2009). It is a predictive model that uses a linear predictor function to combine several weights with the feature vector. It derives its predictions from a linear prediction function that combines a collection of weights with the vector (Freund & Schapire, 1998).

2.2.4.5 Support Vector Machines

Support vector machines (SVMs) are a form of pattern classifier that depends on a revolutionary statistical learning method introduced by Vapnik and his team (Boser et al., 1992). SVMs strive to reduce the misclassification's upper bound by optimizing the margin between the hyperplane. SVM training generates a nonprobabilistic binary linear classifier from a series of training examples labelled for one of two categories (Rivas et al., 2019). SVM links training instances to points across space to maximize the category gap. New samples are mapped into the gap and predicted to correspond to a category (Liu et al., 2017).

2.2.4.6 Boosting

Using boosting models, a learner could be transformed into a strong learner by modifying the weights assigned to the learners. The learner is a method whose behavior is marginally superior to chance. Based on this concept, several enhancements have been developed to boost performance. Modified boosting techniques include AdaBoost, Gradient Boosting, and XGBoost (Uzir et al., 2016).

While boosting is not analytically limited, most algorithms repeatedly learn weak classifiers concerning distribution and combine them to form a final robust classifier. They are weighted according to the poor learners' accuracy when joined together. Reweighting is the process of readjusting data weights following the addition of a weak student. Input data that are incorrectly categorized are given greater weight, whereas correctly classified instances lose weight. Thus, poor learners of the future concentrate more on the cases that their predecessors misclassified.

2.2.4.7 Random Forests

Random forests are an ensemble learning technique that can be used to handle classification, regression, and other problems. They construct numerous decision trees during the training period. A random forest returns the class that most trees select for classification problems. For regression problems, the average or middle prediction of all the different trees is given back (Ho, 1995). Random forests fix the tendency of decision trees to fit their training set too well. On average, random forests perform better than decision trees, but they are less accurate than gradient-boosted trees. Nevertheless, data attributes can affect their performance (Piryonesi & El-Diraby, 2020).

2.2.4.8 K-Means

It is a signal-processing vector quantization technique that seeks to partition in observations into k clusters for each observation corresponding to the cluster's nearest mean (center or centroid), which serves as the prototype (Phorasim & Yu, 2017). K-means employ an iterative refinement technique and cluster centers to describe the data. Yet, it identifies clusters with similar geographic extent, while other k-means variation, such as the Gaussian mixture model, permits a variety of cluster forms.

The unsupervised k-means model is related to the k-nearest neighbor classification, a supervised machine learning approach commonly used for classification that, due to the name, is frequently confused with k-means. The nearest centroid classifier uses the k-means cluster centers and applies the one-nearest neighbor classifier to each of them to classify new data into clusters (Aamir & Ali Zaidi, 2021).

2.2.4.9   Ensemble Averaging

Ensemble averaging creates numerous models and integrates them to achieve the desired outcome instead of developing a single model. Typically, a collection of models outperforms anyone, as the algorithms' errors are average. Ensemble averaging is a specialized committee machine; it maintains less-suitable networks but gives them less weight than standard network construction (Hashem, 1997). Two characteristics of artificial neural networks support the concept of ensemble averaging: The first characteristic is that the bias can be reduced in any network by making the variance bigger; the second characteristic is that reducing variance in a collection of networks is possible without introducing bias (Naftaly et al., 1997).

Ensemble averaging generates a collection of connectivity with a minimal bias and a high variance. It combines them to create a network with minimal bias and low variance. Thus, there is a quick fix to the bias-variance issue (Geman et al., 1992).

2.2.4.10   Principal Component Analysis

PCA is a computational method that decreases data dimensionality while keeping most of the data set's variation (Jolliffe, 2002). It is accomplished by determining directions, known as principal components, in which the variability in the data is most significant. Each instance can be described by a few numbers rather than values for hundreds of variables by employing a few components. Samples can then be plotted, allowing for the visual assessment of differences and similarities between samples and determining whether they can be categorized.

Exploratory data analysis and predictive modeling use PCA. It lowers the number of dimensions by projecting each single value onto the top several main components. This makes the data less complex while keeping the variance. The first main component increases the amount of variation in the data.

For either purpose, the principal components are covariance matrix eigenvectors. Principal components are often computed utilizing eigen decomposition or the breakdown of absolute values of the data matrix. PCA solves the eigenvectors of a certain matrix and uses a more domain-specific design. PCA generates a new orthogonal position that accurately characterizes the variance within a single dataset (Hsu et al., 2009).

2.2.4.11   Recurrent Neural Network

Recurrent neural network allows feedback from some regions to influence consecutive input to the same nodes. This gives it temporal dynamics. Recurrent neural networks use internal model memory to process variable-length input sequences (Abiodun et al., 2018). This makes them useful for networked handwriting and speech recognition (Chachlakis et al., 2019).

2.3 REAL-WORLD/INDUSTRIAL APPLICATION OF PATTERN RECOGNITION

This section provides a more in-depth overview of various pattern recognition application areas, with only four domains being considered. Because public relations encompasses a variety of subfields of research, the decision to focus on these four subfields was made because they cover the broadest range of research subfields possible, thereby highlighting the interdisciplinary nature of pattern recognition applications. Below are some of the important fields in which pattern recognition finds application.

2.3.1 ROBOTICS

Robots and robotics have come a long way in recent years. This engineering subfield is now being considered among the most lucrative of all engineering specializations. Today's robots are intelligent, allowing improved communication and providing a more productive work environment. The study of design, building, operation, and applications of robots is known as robotics. Robotics is applied to create devices that could aid and support people in everyday life while also ensuring the safety of people involved (Okarma, 2020).

The advancements that have been made in information engineering are utilized in robotics. The employment of robots in hazardous areas, such as the examination of radioactive materials and detection, has become commonplace in today's world (Munich et al., 2006). The robot must have senses such as touch, vision, and insight to help accomplish its duty.

2.3.2 COMPUTER VISION

The field of computer vision applies the mathematical and theoretical foundations of artificial systems designed to derive information from pictures. The image data may appear in various formats including video streams and views captured by cameras (Ho & Oh, 2007). Image sensors are essential to the operation of computer vision systems. These sensors are designed to detect electromagnetic radiation, which is commonly manifested in the form of visible light or infrared lights.

In computer vision, computers and other machines are designed to give deep understanding from the digital images or movies fed into them to automate functions generally performed by the human visual system. Image pattern recognition is one of the various methods used in this process. Image pattern recognition is the area of study that focuses on improving images by adjusting many parameters and characteristics of the images.

In reality, image pattern recognition involves recognizing patterns in photographs. In most cases, an image pattern recognition system includes a camera that obtains the image samples to be classified, an image preprocessor that enhances the images, a feature extraction process that retrieves distinguishing characteristics from the images to facilitate validation, and categorization that organizes the input images according to the extracted features or characteristics (Zhang et al., 2020). Because of the utilization of deep neural networks, image identification has become increasingly accurate.

This approach to machine learning attempts to model itself after how a human brain processes information. In this manner, computers are instructed to learn to distinguish various visual features inside an image.

As an example of the application of machine learning, if the sensor were to detect a face and then the gender of the person. A sensor could use the information from a face to classify gender. The resulting image will be analyzed and features will be extracted before being labeled male or female (Mitchell Waldrop, 2019).

2.3.3 BIOMEDICAL AND BIOLOGY

Biomedical science fields include those whose primary emphasis is public health and illness biology. The interaction between biology and pattern recognition has a long and complicated history. Biological research can be viewed as an explosive proliferation of big data, presenting excellent prospects for research such as precision medicine (Saracci, 2018).

The fields of biological sciences are unsuitable for dealing with massive amounts of data that must be organized, minimized, evaluated, and processed in various ways. Most computer-based systems are created using artificial neural network approaches (Pérez-Pérez et al., 2021). Clinical decision support systems were the earliest practical AI applications that concentrated on diagnosing a patient's illness based on his symptoms and demographic information.

Pattern recognition has also proven beneficial in computer-aided detection (CAD), identifying prominent features in medical imaging. CAD systems aid physicians in the analysis of medical images. Some hospitals, for instance, use CAD to assist in mammography, adenoma detection in the polyps, and lung cancer detection. CAD is typically used to highlight suspect constructions and sections.

Preprocessing usually focuses on classifying identified structures or regions through noise reduction or noise enhancement, followed by feature selection and classification. CAD systems are based on exceedingly complex picture patterns. It is used in, for example, mammography screening for breast cancer. The following figure explains the procedure of CAD to determine its role and sampling for mammography images (Patel, 2021).

Content-based image retrieval is another system that looks for patterns, which is a different and additional way to find images in addition to using keywords and metadata (Munjal & Bhatia, 2019).

2.3.4 SPEECH RECOGNITION

Words spoke aloud, and other sounds, such as music or the calls of birds, can be identified with the help of pattern recognition. Voice-activated devices such as handsfree phones and automotive navigation systems use pattern recognition software and hardware. Text-to-voice and voice-to-text applications are among the most practical benefits of speech recognition algorithms. These applications allow visually impaired individuals to hear written text and others to convert their voices into text (Hassan et al., 2021). Voice assistants do the same thing; they offer support at all times to millions of people who utilize websites and mobile applications.

2.3.5 OIL AND GAS

The oil and gas business is another field that uses pattern recognition systems in its daily operations. In today's world, pattern recognition systems are responsible for conducting research on minerals, energy sources, and their distribution patterns over a wide variety of geographical terrains (Li et al., 2021).

2.3.6 IDENTIFICATION OF FINGERPRINTS

The technology that can recognize fingerprints is currently the most popular option in the biometrics market. The process of recognizing and matching fingerprints has been carried out with various strategies, the most common of which is pattern recognition (Reichenbach et al., 2019).

2.3.7 FINANCIAL INDUSTRY SERVICES

Pattern recognition systems assist financial companies' data recognition regarding trends in financial markets (Granados & Garcia-Bedoya, 2022). They execute the job required to identify critical insights; they are competent to accomplish the task, may avert financial collapses, and save society from monetary difficulties. This technology can also be used in the process of expanding enterprises and making investments. Cyber surveillance is one of the applications in which these systems help in identifying hazards in a timely manner and taking steps to mitigate them is (Bhaumik et al., 2021).

2.3.8 NATURAL LANGUAGE PROCESSING

Pattern recognition techniques are widely used in the field of natural language processing (NLP) to construct robust software systems that can effectively analyze and understand human language (Larabi Marie-Sainte et al., 2019). These techniques involve the identification and classification of patterns in data, which can be used to inform decision-making and improve the accuracy and efficiency of NLP systems.

In addition to their use in NLP, pattern recognition techniques have a range of other applications in the fields of computer science and communications. For example, they can be used to analyze and classify data in speech recognition systems, image and video analyses, and other areas where large amounts of data must be processed and analyzed.

Overall, the use of pattern recognition techniques in NLP and other fields has played a crucial role in the development of robust software systems that can effectively analyze and understand complex data (Alamoodi et al., 2022).

2.3.9 Handwriting Recognition

A machine can receive and analyze legibly handwritten input from paper documents, pictures, touch screens, and other devices. Optical scans and intelligent word recognition can be used offline to detect the image of the written text on paper. Alternatively, a pen-based computer screen interface, for example, can detect the motion of the pen tip online. This process is typically simpler because of the greater availability of hints (Chachlakis et al., 2019). A handwriting recognition system manages to format, performs accurate separation of words into characters, and determines the most plausible words.

2.3.10 Credit Scoring

A credit score is a numeric expression of a person's dependability as determined by a review of their credit reports. It is generally derived from a credit report, which normally contains information from credit bureaus (Jain et al., 2000b). Lenders such as banks and credit card firms use credit ratings to assess the potential risk of consumer borrowing money or reduce bad debt losses. Lenders use credit scores to assess loan eligibility, interest rates, and credit limitations. Lenders also use credit ratings to assess which consumers are most likely to generate the highest revenue (DeYoung et al., 2008).

Credit scoring extends beyond banks; other corporations adopt the same strategies including cell phone companies, insurance providers, landlords, and government agencies. Digital finance organizations including online lenders utilize alternative data sources to assess borrowers' credit (Moretto et al., 2019).

2.3.11 Anomaly Detection

In data analysis, anomaly detection is a crucial tool that helps identify trends, patterns, and behaviors that may not be immediately apparent. In many fields, such as how odd behaviors during a card transaction could point to fraud (Baker et al., 2022), an unusual network traffic pattern might signal that a computer has been compromised or is being attacked, such as through the use of viruses and denial of service assaults (Bhuyan et al., 2014) and many others, anomaly detection is a crucial technique for detecting anomalies.

Overall, the role of anomaly detection in data analysis is crucial in helping organizations to better understand their data and make more informed decisions. By identifying unusual trends, patterns, and behaviors, anomaly detection can help organizations identify and address potential issues before they become major problems.

2.3.12 Supporting Healthcare Professionals and Protecting Patients

Artificial intelligence and machine learning have proven valuable tools in the fight against COVID-19 and other pandemics. These technologies can enable mechanization to help contain and control outbreaks, and they can support and protect healthcare professionals, as they work to diagnose and treat patients (Chen & See, 2020).

Artificial intelligence and machine learning can also be used to analyze patterns in mental health and stress levels during pandemics. By detecting and analyzing these patterns, healthcare professionals can better understand the psychological effects of such crises and develop strategies to support people affected. Overall, artificial intelligence and machine learning play a vital role in the fight against COVID-19 and other pandemics, helping to ensure the safety and well-being of patients and healthcare professionals alike (Solanki et al., 2021).

2.4 CONCLUSION

This chapter provides an introduction to pattern recognition. This chapter demonstrated that powerful approaches exist, yet, caution must be exercised when developing strong and consistent classifiers. In this instance, plug-and-play seems to be the optimal method for the unskilled user, who should thus utilize traditional statistical techniques. Machines and neural networks have equal potential to perform pattern recognition. Computers utilize standard arithmetic techniques to determine whether a pattern matches an established model. This procedure is straightforward, indicating either yes or no. It cannot tolerate chaotic patterns. Neural networks, by contrast, can tolerate noise and, if adequately trained, respond appropriately to unknown patterns. Neural networks may not be able to perform miracles. Yet, when built with a proper design and trained with good data, these networks will produce excellent results in pattern recognition and other commercial and scientific applications.

Pattern recognition systems that run on computers have better performance than human senses. It is possible that human understanding would not be able to discern patterns because of age-related vision loss or because the data are not accurate enough. The automated systems then show themselves to be the factor that is advantageous in a variety of facets of life. Pattern recognition applications are on the cusp of expanding, and we have recently made a step toward equipping our systems with pattern recognition technology so that we can apply it to every facet of our nation and meet its requirements. Pattern analysis and argumentation use the prototype to locate answers to issues in various aspects and domains and, in doing so, analyze pertinent patterns.

REFERENCES

Aamir, M., Ali Zaidi, S. M. (2021). Clustering based semi-supervised machine learning for DDoS attack classification. Journal of King Saud University–Computer and Information Sciences, 33(4): 436–446. https://doi.org/10.1016/j.jksuci.2019.02.003

Abiodun, O.I., Jantan, A., Omolara, A.E., Dada, K.V., Mohamed, N.A.E., Arshad, H. (2018). State-of-the-art in artificial neural network applications: a survey. Heliyon, 4 (11). https://doi.org/10.1016/j.heliyon.2018.e00938

Ahmed, S., Basha, S., Arumugam, S., Kodabagi, M. (2021). *Pattern Recognition: An Introduction*. MileStone Research Publications.

Alamoodi, A.H., Baker, M.R., Albahri, O.S., Zaidan, B.B., Zaidan, A.A., Wong, W.-K., Garfan, S., Albahri, A.S., Alonso, M.A., Jasim, A.N., Baqer, M.J. (2022). Public sentiment analysis and topic modeling regarding COVID-19's three waves of total lockdown: a case study on movement control order in Malaysia. KSII Transactions on Internet and Information Systems, 16(7): 2169–2190.

Alsmadi, M.K., Omar, K. Bin, Noah, S.A., Almarashdah, I. (2009). Performance comparison of multi-layer perceptron (back propagation, delta rule and perceptron) algorithms in neural networks. 2009 IEEE International Advance Computing Conference, IACC 2009: 296–299. https://doi.org/10.1109/IADCC.2009.4809024

Aslantaş, A., Dandil, E., Sağlam, S., Çakiroğlu, M. (2016). CADBOSS: A computer-aided diagnosis system for whole-body bone scintigraphy scans. Journal of Cancer Research and Therapeutics, 12(2): 787–792. https://doi.org/10.4103/0973-1482.150422

Baker, M.R., Akcayol, M.A. (2017). Priority queue based estimation of importance of web pages for web crawlers. International Journal of Computer and Electrical Engineering (IJCEE), 9(1): 330–342. https://doi.org/10.17706/ijcee.2017.9.1.330-342

Baker, M.R., Akcayol, M.A. (2022). A novel web ranking algorithm based on pages multi-attribute. International Journal of Information Technology (Singapore), 14(2): 739–749. https://doi.org/10.1007/s41870-021-00833-5

Baker, M.R., Mahmood, Z.N., Shaker, E.H. (2022). Ensemble learning with supervised machine learning models to predict credit card fraud transactions. Revue d'Intelligence Artificielle, 36(4): 509–518.

Baker, M.R., Padmaja, D.L., Puviarasi, R., Mann, S., Panduro-Ramirez, J., Tiwari, M., Samori, I.A. (2022). Implementing critical machine learning (ml) approaches for generating robust discriminative neuroimaging representations using structural equation model (SEM). Computational and Mathematical Methods in Medicine, 2022: 12. https://doi.org/10.1155/2022/6501975

Balakrishnama, S., Ganapathiraju, A. (1998). Linear discriminant analysis–a brief tutorial. Institute for Signal and Information Processing, 18: 1–8.

Bharti, P. (2021). Detection and classification of liver diseases using ultrasound images. International Research Journal of Engineering and Technology (IRJET), 8(7): 1568–1573.

Bhaumik, S., Jana, P., Mohanta, P.P. (2021). Event and activity recognition in video surveillance for cyber-physical systems. Advances in Science, Technology and Innovation (pp. 51–68). Germany: Springer Nature. https://doi.org/10.1007/978-3-030-66222-6_4

Bhuyan, M.H., Kashyap, H.J., Bhattacharyya, D.K., Kalita, J.K. (2014). Detecting distributed denial of service attacks: methods, tools and future directions. Computer Journal, 57(4), 537–556. https://doi.org/10.1093/comjnl/bxt031

Bianchi, E.L., Sakib, N., Woolsey, C., Hebdon, M. (2022). Bridge inspection component registration for damage evolution. Structural Health Monitoring, 0(0), 1–24. https://doi.org/10.1177/14759217221083647

Boser, B.E., Guyon, I.M., Vapnik, V.N. (1992). Training algorithm for optimal margin classifiers. Proceedings of the Fifth Annual ACM Workshop on Computational Learning Theory, 144–152. https://doi.org/10.1145/130385.130401

Budhathoki, D.R., Dasgupta, D., Jain, P. (2018). Big data framework for finding patterns in multi-market trading data. Lecture Notes in Computer Science (Including Subseries Lecture Notes in Artificial Intelligence and Lecture Notes in Bioinformatics), 10968 LNCS, 237–250. https://doi.org/10.1007/978-3-319-94301-5_18

Canedo, D., Neves, A.J.R. (2019). Facial expression recognition using computer vision: a systematic review. In: Applied Sciences (Switzerland) (Vol. 9, Issue 21). https://doi.org/10.3390/app9214678

Chachlakis, D.G., Prater-Bennette, A., Markopoulos, P.P. (2019). L1-norm tucker tensor decomposition. IEEE Access, 7: 178454–178465. https://doi.org/10.1109/ACCESS.2019.2955134

Chaudhuri, A., Mandaviya, K., Badelia, P., Ghosh, S.K. (2017). Optical character recognition systems. In: Studies in Fuzziness and Soft Computing (Vol. 352, pp. 9–41). Springer Verlag. https://doi.org/10.1007/978-3-319-50252-6_2

Chen, J., See, K.C. (2020). Artificial intelligence for COVID-19: rapid review. Journal of Medical Internet Research, 22(10). https://doi.org/10.2196/21476

DeYoung, R., Glennon, D., Nigro, P. (2008). Borrower-lender distance, credit scoring, and loan performance: evidence from informational-opaque small business borrowers. Journal of Financial Intermediation, 17(1): 113–143. https://doi.org/10.1016/j.jfi.2007.07.002

Ding, S.F., Shi, Z.Z. (2005). Studies on incidence pattern recognition based on information entropy. Journal of Information Science, 31(6): 497–502. https://doi.org/10.1177/01655 51505057012

Fayyad, U., Piatetsky-Shapiro, G., Smyth, P. (1996). The KDD process for extracting useful knowledge from volumes of data. Communications of the ACM, 39(11): 27–34. https://doi.org/10.1145/240455.240464

Freund, Y., Schapire, R.E. (1998). Large margin classification using the perceptron algorithm. Proceedings of the Annual ACM Conference on Computational Learning Theory, 209–217. https://doi.org/10.1145/279943.279985

Fu, K.S. (2018). Introduction to pattern processing. In: *Special Computer Architectures for Pattern Processing*. Boca Raton, Florida: CRC Press. https://doi.org/10.1201/9781351076784-3

Geman, S., Bienenstock, E., Doursat, R. (1992). Neural networks and the bias/variance dilemma. Neural Computation, 4(1): 1–58. https://doi.org/10.1162/neco.1992.4.1.1

Gozudeli, Y., Yildiz, O., Karacan, H., Baker, M.R., Minnet, A., Kalender, M., Ozay, O., Akcayol, M.A. (2014). Extraction of automatic search result records using content density algorithm based on node similarity. In: G. Balint, B. Antala, C. Carty, J.-M. A. Mabieme, I. B. Amar, & A. Kaplanova (Eds.), *International Conference on Data Mining, Internet Computing, and Big Data* (pp. 69–75). Uniwersytet Śląski. Wydział Matematyki, Fizyki i Chemii. https://doi.org/10.2/JQUERY.MIN.JS

Granados, O., Garcia-Bedoya, O. (2022). Deep learning-based facial recognition on hybrid architecture for financial services. In: *Internet of Things* (pp. 51–70). Deutschland GmbH: Springer Science and Business Media. https://doi.org/10.1007/978-3-030-80821-1_3

Grira, N., Crucianu, M., Boujemaa, N. (2008). Active semi-supervised fuzzy clustering. Pattern Recognition, 41(5): 1834–1844. https://doi.org/10.1016/j.patcog.2007.10.004

Guerrisi, G., Del Frate, F., Schiavon, G. (2022). Satellite on-board change detection via auto-associative neural networks. Remote Sensing, 14(12). https://doi.org/10.3390/rs1 4122735

Hashem, S. (1997). Optimal linear combinations of neural networks. Neural Networks, 10(4): 599–614. https://doi.org/10.1016/S0893-6080(96)00098-6

Hassan, M.D., Nejdet Nasret, A., Baker, M.R., Mahmood, S. (2021). Enhancement automatic speech recognition by deep neural networks. Periodicals of Engineering and Natural Sciences, 9(4): 921–927.

Ho, T.K. (1995). Random decision forests. Proceedings of the International Conference on Document Analysis and Recognition, ICDAR, 1: 278–282. https://doi.org/10.1109/ICDAR.1995.598994

Ho, Y.S., Oh, K.J. (2007). Overview of multi-view video coding. 2007 14th International Workshop on Systems, Signals and Image Processing and 6th EURASIP Conference Focused on Speech and Image Processing, Multimedia Communications and Services, 5–12. https://doi.org/10.1109/IWSSIP.2007.4381085

Hruschka, E.R., Campello, R.J.G.B., Freitas, A.A., de Carvalho, A.C.P.L.F. (2009). A survey of evolutionary algorithms for clustering. IEEE Transactions on Systems, Man and Cybernetics Part C: Applications and Reviews, 39(2): 133–155. https://doi.org/10.1109/TSMCC.2008.2007252

Hsu, D., Kakade, S.M., Zhang, T. (2009). A spectral algorithm for learning hidden Markov models. COLT 2009–The 22nd Conference on Learning Theory.

Huang, R., Liu, Q., Lu, H., Ma, S. (2002). Solving the small sample size problem of LDA. Proceedings–International Conference on Pattern Recognition, 16(3): 29–32. https://doi.org/10.1109/icpr.2002.1047787

Jain, A.K., Duin, R.P.W., Mao, J. (2000a). Statistical pattern recognition: a review. IEEE Transactions on Pattern Analysis and Machine Intelligence, 22(1): 4–37. https://doi.org/10.1109/34.824819

Jain, A.K., Duin, R.P.W., Mao, J. (2000b). Statistical pattern recognition: a review. IEEE Transactions on Pattern Analysis and Machine Intelligence, 22(1): 4–37. https://doi.org/10.1109/34.824819

Jolliffe, I.T. (2002). Principal component analysis for special types of data. In: *Principal Component Analysis*. New York: Springer. https://doi.org/10.1007/978-1-4757-1904-8_11

Kang, Z., Peng, C., Cheng, Q., Liu, X., Peng, X., Xu, Z., Tian, L. (2021). Structured graph learning for clustering and semi-supervised classification. Pattern Recognition, 110, 107627. https://doi.org/10.1016/j.patcog.2020.107627

Kong, Q., Cao, Y., Iqbal, T., Wang, Y., Wang, W., Plumbley, M.D. (2020). PANNs: large-scale pretrained audio neural networks for audio pattern recognition. IEEE/ACM Transactions on Audio Speech and Language Processing, 28: 2880–2894. https://doi.org/10.1109/TASLP.2020.3030497

Kortli, Y., Jridi, M., Al Falou, A., Atri, M. (2020). Face recognition systems: a survey. In: *Sensors (Switzerland)* (Vol. 20, Issue 2, p. 342). https://doi.org/10.3390/s20020342

Larabi Marie-Sainte, S., Alalyani, N., Alotaibi, S., Ghouzali, S., Abunadi, I. (2019). Arabic natural language processing and machine learning-based systems. IEEE Access, 7, 7011–7020. https://doi.org/10.1109/ACCESS.2018.2890076

Li, H., Yu, H., Cao, N., Tian, H., Cheng, S. (2021). Applications of artificial intelligence in oil and gas development. Archives of Computational Methods in Engineering 28(3): 937–949. https://doi.org/10.1007/s11831-020-09402-8

Liu, P., Choo, K.K.R., Wang, L., Huang, F. (2017). SVM or deep learning? A comparative study on remote sensing image classification. Soft Computing, 21(23): 7053–7065. https://doi.org/10.1007/s00500-016-2247-2

Mahdi, M.N., Zabil, M.H.M., Ahmad, A.R., Ismail, R., Yusoff, Y., Cheng, L.K., Mohd Azmi, M.S., Bin Natiq, H., Naidu, H.H. (2021). Software project management using machine learning technique-a review. Applied Sciences (Switzerland), 11(11): 5183. https://doi.org/10.3390/app11115183

Mellouli, D., Hamdani, T.M., Sanchez-Medina, J.J., Ayed, M., Alimi, A.M. (2019). Morphological convolutional neural network architecture for digit recognition. IEEE Transactions on Neural Networks and Learning Systems, 30(9): 2876–2885. https://doi.org/10.1109/TNNLS.2018.2890334

Mitchell Waldrop, M. (2019). What are the limits of deep learning? Proceedings of the National Academy of Sciences of the United States of America, 116(4): 1074–1077. https://doi.org/10.1073/pnas.1821594116

Moretto, A., Grassi, L., Caniato, F., Giorgino, M., Ronchi, S. (2019). Supply chain finance: from traditional to supply chain credit rating. Journal of Purchasing and Supply Management, 25(2): 197–217. https://doi.org/10.1016/j.pursup.2018.06.004

Munich, M.E., Pirjanian, P., Di Bernardo, E., Goncalves, L., Karlsson, N., and Lowe, D. (2006). Application of visual pattern recognition to robotics and automation. IEEE Robotics and Automation Magazine, 13(3): 72–77. https://doi.org/10.1109/MRA.2006.1678141

Munjal, M.N., Bhatia, S. (2019). A novel technique for effective image gallery search using content based image retrieval system. Proceedings of the International Conference on Machine Learning, Big Data, Cloud and Parallel Computing: Trends, Prespectives and Prospects, COMITCon 2019: 25–29. https://doi.org/10.1109/COMITCon.2019.8862206

Naftaly, U., Intrator, N., Horn, D. (1997). Optimal ensemble averaging of neural networks. Network: Computation in Neural Systems, 8(3): 283–296. https://doi.org/10.1088/0954-898x_8_3_004

Okarma, K. (2020). Applications of computer vision in automation and robotics. In: *Applied Sciences (Switzerland)* (Vol. 10, Issue 19, p. 6783). Multidisciplinary Digital Publishing Institute. https://doi.org/10.3390/app10196783

Oleinik, A. (2019). What are neural networks not good at? On artificial creativity. Big Data and Society, 6(1): 1–13. https://doi.org/10.1177/2053951719839433

Patel, R. (2021). Predicting invasive ductal carcinoma using a reinforcement sample learning strategy using deep learning. ArXiv Preprint, 2105: 12564.

Pérez-Pérez, E.J., López-Estrada, F.R., Valencia-Palomo, G., Torres, L., Puig, V., Mina-Antonio, J.D. (2021). Leak diagnosis in pipelines using a combined artificial neural network approach. Control Engineering Practice, 107: 104677. https://doi.org/10.1016/j.conengprac.2020.104677

Phorasim, P., Yu, L. (2017). Movies recommendation system using collaborative filtering and k-means. International Journal of Advanced Computer Research, 7(29): 52–59. https://doi.org/10.19101/IJACR.2017.729004

Pinheiro, P.O., Almahairi, A., Benmalek, R.Y., Golemo, F., Courville, A. (2020). Unsupervised learning of dense visual representations. Advances in Neural Information Processing Systems 33 (NeurIPS 2020), 4489–4500.

Piryonesi, S.M., El-Diraby, T.E. (2020). Role of data analytics in infrastructure asset management: overcoming data size and quality problems. Journal of Transportation Engineering, Part B: Pavements, 146(2): 04020022. https://doi.org/10.1061/jpeodx.0000175

Qader, B.A., Jihad, K.H., Baker, M.R. (2022). Evolving and training of neural network to play DAMA board game using NEAT algorithm. Informatica (Slovenia), 46(5): 29–37. https://doi.org/10.31449/inf.v46i5.3897

Raj, M.P., Swaminarayan, P.R., Saini, J.R., Parmar, D.K. (2015). Applications of pattern recognition algorithms in agriculture: a review. International Journal of Advanced Networking and Applications, 6(5): 2495–2502.

Reichenbach, S.E., Zini, C.A., Nicolli, K.P., Welke, J.E., Cordero, C., Tao, Q. (2019). Benchmarking machine learning methods for comprehensive chemical fingerprinting and pattern recognition. Journal of Chromatography A, 1595: 158–167. https://doi.org/10.1016/j.chroma.2019.02.027

Rivas, P., Decusatis, C., Oakley, M., Antaki, A., Blaskey, N., Lafalce, S., Stone, S. (2019). Machine learning for DDoS attack classification using hive plots. *2019* IEEE 10th Annual Ubiquitous Computing, Electronics and Mobile Communication Conference, UEMCON 2019, 0401–0407. https://doi.org/10.1109/UEMCON47517.2019.8993021

Saracci, R. (2018). Epidemiology in wonderland: big data and precision medicine. European Journal of Epidemiology, 33(3): 245–257. https://doi.org/10.1007/s10654-018-0385-9

Sarker, S., Jamal, L., Ahmed, S.F., Irtisam, N. (2021). Robotics and artificial intelligence in healthcare during COVID-19 pandemic: a systematic review. Robotics and Autonomous Systems, 22(10): e21476. https://doi.org/10.1016/j.robot.2021.103902

Shaker, E., Baker, M., Mahmood, Z. (2022). The impact of image enhancement and transfer learning techniques on marine habitat mapping. Gazi University Journal of Science, 36(2): 592–606. https://doi.org/10.35378/gujs.973082

Shanmuganathan, S. (2016). Artificial neural network modelling: an introduction. In: *Studies in Computational Intelligence* (Vol. 628, pp. 1–14). Berlin: Springer Verlag. https://doi.org/10.1007/978-3-319-28495-8_1

Shanthi, N., Duraiswamy, K. (2010). A novel SVM-based handwritten Tamil character recognition system. Pattern Analysis and Applications, 13(2): 173–180. https://doi.org/10.1007/s10044-009-0147-0

Sharma, P., Kaur, M. (2013). Classification in pattern recognition: a review. International Journal of Advanced Research in Computer Science and Software Engineering, 3(4): 298–306.

Solanki, V., Solanki, U., Baliyan, A., Kukreja, V., Lamba, V., Kumar Sahoo, B. (2021). Importance of artificial intelligence and machine learning in fighting with COVID-19 epidemic. 2021 5th International Conference on Information Systems and Computer Networks, ISCON 2021. https://doi.org/10.1109/ISCON52037.2021.9702316

Tien, J.M. (2017). Internet of things, real-time decision making, and artificial intelligence. Annals of Data Science, 4(2): 149–178. https://doi.org/10.1007/s40745-017-0112-5

Tu, J.V. (1996). Advantages and disadvantages of using artificial neural networks versus logistic regression for predicting medical outcomes. Journal of Clinical Epidemiology, 49(11): 1225–1231. https://doi.org/10.1016/S0895-4356(96)00002-9

Uzir, N., Banerjee, S., Santhanam, R., Raman, S. (2016). Experimenting XGBoost algorithm for prediction and classification of different datasets. International Journal of Control Theory and Applications, 9(40): 651–662.

Vailaya, A., Figueiredo, M.A.T., Jain, A.K., Zhang, H.J. (2001). Image classification for content-based indexing. IEEE Transactions on Image Processing, 10(1): 117–130. https://doi.org/10.1109/83.892448

Valentin, L., Hagen, B., Tingulstad, S., Eik-Nes, S. (2001). Comparison of "pattern recognition" and logistic regression models for discrimination between benign and malignant pelvic masses: a prospective cross validation. Ultrasound in Obstetrics and Gynecology, 18(4): 357–365. https://doi.org/10.1046/j.0960-7692.2001.00500.x

Zhang, Y., Wang, Y., Liu, X.Y., Mi, S., Zhang, M.L. (2020). Large-scale multi-label classification using unknown streaming images: large-scale multi-label classification using unknown streaming images. Pattern Recognition, 99: 107100. https://doi.org/10.1016/j.patcog.2019.107100

3 Efficient Techniques for Disease Prediction from Medical Data

Bhupendra Kumar
School of Business (Finance)
Galgotias University, Greater Noida, India

Namita Rajput
Professor, Department of Commerce, Sri Aurobindo
College, University of Delhi, Delhi, India

3.1 INTRODUCTION

Data mining methods have aided medical research by simplifying the data processing procedure, allowing a medical professional to make an informed choice about commencing the appropriate therapy. Consequently, it may spare the patient from unnecessary delays caused by various tests that must be performed before deciding on a treatment plan [1]. This chapter focuses on the application of data mining methods such as decision trees, Naive Bayes, random forests, and regression analysis for diagnosing cancer and brain tumors by utilizing machine learning using Kaggle standard datasets. The detection performance measurements employing data mining approaches are completely adequate. The accuracy values for a cancer diagnosis on the standard dataset are 93.86%, 95.61%, 95.80%, and 98.25%, respectively, by utilizing tree structure, naive Bayes, randomized forest, and logistic regression. Overall accuracy values for the diagnosis of a brain tumor on the standard dataset are 97.21%, 97.21%, 99.04%, and 98.14%, respectively, utilizing decision tree, naive Bayes, randomized forest, and logistic regression [2].

3.2 OBJECTIVES

The research aimed to fulfill the following objectives:

- To explain the utility of machine learning in disease prediction
- To study the usefulness of data mining in disease prediction

DOI: 10.1201/9781003348351-3

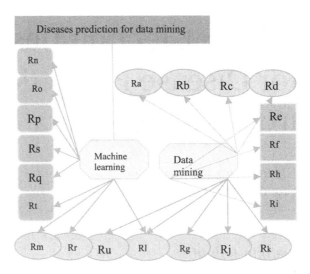

FIGURE 3.1   Effective techniques for disease prediction from medical data using data mining and machine learning.

- What are the techniques of data mining in disease prediction by mining medical data?
- To study the fundamentals of data mining
- To study issues and difficulties in disease prediction
- To study algorithms in machine learning using medical data
- To study the future application areas of machine learning and data mining in the healthcare sector

3.3 METHODOLOGY

The widespread use of computer-based technologies in the healthcare business has resulted in an influx of electronic data. Medical practitioners are struggling to effectively assess symptoms and detect illnesses at an initial point because of massive amounts of data. Furthermore, standard supervised machine learning (ML) technologies have shown tremendous promise in outperforming currently available disease diagnostic methods and assisting medical practitioners in the early identification of high-risk disorders. The goal of this research is to identify patterns in disease diagnosis using different kinds of supervised ML by examining performance indicators. Naive Bayes, decision tree, and K-nearest neighbor (KNN) waste is most often discussed in supervised ML techniques. According to the data, the support vector machine (SVM) is indeed the most appropriate method for diagnosing renal diseases and Parkinson's disease. The logistic regression method can predict cardiac diseases quite effectively. Finally, random forest or the convolutional neural network can precisely predict breast diseases and common diseases.

3.4   MACHINE LEARNING IN DISEASE PREDICTION

Healthcare is always a big concern in any technological advancement that the human race makes. This recent coronavirus onslaught, which has partially devastated the economy, is a good instance of the increasing need for health insurance. In areas where the virus has spread, it is always advisable to monitor people by using remote health monitoring tools. ML algorithms are particularly susceptible to mistakes [3]. First, it is dependent on the quality or selection of datasets, which would be critical for making accurate and impartial conclusions. Second, ML algorithms rely largely on the appropriate selection of characteristics derived from the dataset, thus proving challenging, time intensive, and computationally demanding. These issues impede the learning model's effectiveness and result in catastrophic mistakes that risk patients' lives.

By contrast, normal statistical approaches, job experience, and medical physicians' intuition contributed to unfavorable biases and inaccuracies in recognizing disease-related risks [4]. With the massive increase in health-related electronic data, physicians are finding it difficult to effectively diagnose diseases at an early stage. As a result, powerful computational approaches such as MLX techniques were developed to identify relevant patterns or hidden information in data that may be utilized to make vital decisions. As a result, the load on medical personnel was reduced, while patient survival rates improved.

Standards of ML for disease prediction are shown in Table 3.1:

Percent (%)	Standards of Machine Learning for Disease Prediction
12%–20%	Speed and audio with efficient accuracy
25%–30%	Analytics and computer vision
40%–60%	Content generation and deep learning with natural language processing

3.5   DATA MINING IN DISEASE PREDICTION

Significant advances in information technology have resulted in an overabundance of data in healthcare bioinformatics.

Public healthcare informatics data comprise information about the hospital, patient, disease, or treatment cost. These massive amounts of data are created from many sources and formats [5].

It may include extraneous qualities and missing data. The use of data mining tools to extract insights from enormous amounts of disease-related data is a critical strategy. There are several methods in which data mining may be used to gain insights from large collections of disease-related data. It is possible to use data mining techniques such as classification, clustering, or rule mining to analyze the data to extract relevant information from it. Among the most fundamental data mining applications in the healthcare system include predicting future treatment outcomes using previous information accumulated from clinical conditions, disease diagnosis using patient data, analysis treatment costs and resource demand, pre-processing of additive noise, missing information, and minimizing the time for waiting for disease diagnosis. Data mining tools including Weka, RapidMiner, and Orange are being used to analyze and predict improved outcomes in healthcare data [6]. New and contemporary data mining methods and technologies are employed in disease diagnosis or healthcare bioinformatics to enhance healthcare services while decreasing disease diagnosis time.

3.6 TECHNIQUES FOR DATA MINING

3.6.1 TECHNIQUES FOR DATA MINING

In disease data analysis, data mining methods such as classification, clustering, and association rules are commonly employed.

3.6.1.1 Classification

Classification is a data mining process that is based on ML. Classification is the process of categorizing each piece of information in a batch of data into a specific preset set of categories or classes. It classifies data based on mathematical approaches including decision trees, linear programming, neural networks, or statistics [7].

Modern categorization approaches provide further sophisticated strategies for disease prediction. The SVM, discriminant analysis, network-based decision trees, and linear and nonlinear regression are examples of classification approaches.

3.6.1.2 Clustering

Clustering is a data mining approach that uses an automated technique to create clusters of items with similar characteristics. Clustering establishes classes and places things in the classes when the category is not preset. K-means, Fuzzy Cleans, Rough Cleans, Rough-Fuzzy Cleans, Robust Rough-Fuzzy Cleans, and hierarchical or Gaussian mixture are examples of clustering approaches [8].

3.6.1.3 Mining for Association Rules

Association rule mining is a well-known and well-studied approach for discovering intriguing relationships between various types of data in huge datasets. Its goal is to detect well-built rules revealed in databases by using various techniques of

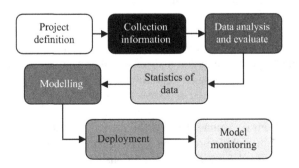

FIGURE 3.2   Risk prediction using machine learning.

significance dependent on the set of input data [9]. The data mining procedure of discovering rules, frequent patterns, connections, correlations, and other causal structures among groups of items that may control relationships and causality objects among sets of things is known as association rule mining. Client purchasing behaviors are discovered by identifying relationships and correlations here between various things in their "shopping basket." Basket's data analysis, cross-marketing, and catalog design are some of the most common uses of association rule mining. The data mining methods described above may be utilized to diagnose diseases [10].

3.7 FUNDAMENTALS OF DATA MINING

3.7.1 DATA MINING FUNDAMENTALS

Data mining is the technique of computationally deriving unknown information from massive amounts of data. It is critical to extract meaningful information from massive datasets and provide decision-making outcomes for disease diagnosis and treatment. By evaluating and forecasting different diseases, data mining can be utilized to obtain knowledge. Healthcare data mining offers enormous potential for uncovering hidden patterns within medical sector datasets [11]. Several data mining methods are accessible, with their applicability determined by the healthcare information. Applications of data mining in healthcare coverage have high promise and efficacy. Data mining automates the procedure of locating predictive data in massive datasets. Data mining relies heavily on disease prediction.

A variety of tests must be performed on the patient to diagnose a condition. However, the use of data mining technologies may reduce the total number of tests required. Performance and time are affected significantly by this reduced test set [12].

Data mining in healthcare is critical because it enables physicians to identify which characteristics such as age, weight, symptoms, and so forth are most important for determining a diagnosis. This one will allow physicians to identify the condition more quickly.

The process of discovering relevant information and patterns within data is often known as knowledge discovery using databases. Data mining may be used to discover knowledge in datasets [13].

3.8 ISSUES AND DIFFICULTIES IN DISEASE PREDICTION

Use of data mining mostly in the medical industry is a difficult challenge in the medical profession. Data mining in medical research starts with a theory, and outcomes are altered to meet the hypothesis. This varies from the typical data mining approach, which begins with datasets and no obvious hypothesis. Patterns and themes in datasets are mostly concerned with conventional data mining, but they have not gained significance in medical data mining. Clinical decisions are often made based on the doctor's intuition [14]. Unwanted prejudice, mistakes, and exorbitant medical costs have an effect on the quality of care provided to individuals. Data mining has the potential to provide a knowledge-rich environment. It has the potential to enhance the significance of clinical decisions.

The three-ML supervised learning techniques are used in the analysis of the cardiovascular disease dataset [15]. This algorithm's classification performance should be examined. This research should be expanded to predict heart disease with fewer features. In the surveys, cardiovascular disease is forecasted using a frequent pattern data mining approach. The author presented a method that employs a search restriction to reduce the number of constraints. In the future, this research should be expanded by using fuzz learning models to determine the precision of time in a bid to reduce the number of rules. There is a survey in which the author introduced a novel approach for categorization that uses a weighted association rule. This study may be expanded in the future by using the association rule concealing approach in data mining [16]. The author presented the smallest group of variables for heart disease predictions in his survey. This study may be developed and improved in the future for the automated prediction of heart diseases. Real-world data of healthcare agencies and organizations should indeed be obtained to compare the optimal accuracy including all data mining techniques. In the investigation, the author anticipates the characteristics of a diabetes patient developing a cardiac disease. As a result of using the Weka tool, the Bayes model was capable of correctly identifying 74% of the input examples. This study will be expanded in the future by including additional data mining approaches [17].

3.9   ALGORITHM OF MACHINE LEARNING IN MEDICAL DATA

Medical diagnoses are becoming more dependent on ML. Patient survival rates have increased remarkably as a result of advances in disease classification and detection techniques, which provide data that aid medical professionals in the early detection of life-threatening disorders. Using data from the UCI repository, we anticipate disease development using a variety of categorization methods (heart diseases, breast cancer, and diabetes), each with its advantages. P-value testing was used to select features with each dataset using backward modeling. The use of ML to diagnose diseases at an early stage is supported by the study's results.

3.9.1 K-NEAREST NEIGHBOR

KNN is used for disease prediction by the user in the healthcare sector. In this approach, the user may anticipate whether or not the sickness will be detected. In the proposed method, the disease is classified into numerous groups that indicate whichever disease will occur based on symptoms. With each regression and categorization problem, the KNN rule is used. The KNN algorithm is constructed on the feature similarity method.

3.9.2 NAIVE BAYES

Naive Bayes, a supervised learning method, is a simple yet very effective rule for prognosticative modeling. The "naive" assumption permits decomposing joint probability into a composite of marginal probabilities. Naive Bayes is the name given to this basic Bayesian classifier. The Naive Bayes classifier posits that the presence of one character in a class is independent of the presence of another. It is simple to construct and beneficial for huge datasets [18].

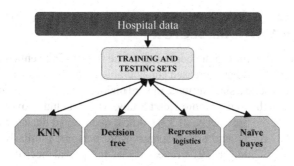

FIGURE 3.3   Algorithm and systemic architecture in machine learning.

3.9.3 REGRESSION IN LOGISTICS

Logistic regression is a supervised learning classification technique used to estimate the likelihood of a disease target variable. Because the nature of an objective or variable is separated, there are only two viable groups.

In simple terms, the variables are binary by nature, with information represented as either 1 (for success/yes) or 0 (for failure/no). A logistic regression model predicts (y=1) as a function of x.

3.9.4 DECISION TREE

A decision tree is a framework that may be used to effectively split a big collection of data into smaller sets of records by using a series of basic decision trees.

The membership of the resultant sets increases more similar to one another with each consecutive division. A decision tree model comprises a set of rules for splitting a big diverse community into shorter, more homogeneous (mutually exclusive) groups about a certain aim.

The variable is often categorical, and the decision tree has been used to either calculate the likelihood that a particular record belongs to each of the categories or classify the record by designating it to the most probable class (or category) [19].

The decision tree in this disease prediction system categorizes symptoms and decreases dataset difficulties.

Table 2 presents information and points for decision-making for patient's health.

Information for decision-making for patient's health	Explanations
Prediction of disease	Machine learning and artificial intelligence help in the prediction of the next-generation viral mutation
Structure analysis	Characteristics and functional sites of the viral genomes
Drug purposing and repurposing	Data mining of drugs with an existing history of drugs for further disease treatment
Novel drug development	Processing allows for efficiencies of the whole drug lifecycle

3.10　FUTURE OF MACHINE LEARNING AND DATA MINING IN THE HEALTHCARE SECTOR

From the twentieth century to the beginning of the twenty-first century, the incidence of type 2 diabetes (T2D) has increased considerably globally because of modification in people's lifestyle, and a slack attitude toward maintaining a balanced diet along with regular exercise. In the San Antonio Heart Study, which included over 5,000 patients during 1987-1996, the prevalence of T2D almost quadrupled during 7 and 8 years in both Mexican Americans and non-Hispanic white persons. Similarly, a nationwide study conducted in China in 2013 revealed that the prevalence of T2D was 10%. Furthermore, as cardiovascular disease (CVD) is directly associated with T2D, there has been an increase in the incidence of CVD globally in recent years. There is strong evidence that T2D is significantly related to higher all-cause mortality and CVD mortality [20]. Furthermore, a homeostasis model evaluation of insulin resistance shows a strong correlation between the risk of CVD and T2D development. Diabetes and its complications account for 12% of worldwide health spending, according to a World Diabetes Federation annual report. To lower this enormous expense, reliable illness prediction is required, as well as an efficient prognostic system that enables prospective patients to receive early therapies before developing more serious diseases.

3.11　CONCLUSION

The use of several ML algorithms allows early diagnosis of numerous ailments such as diseases of the heart, kidney, breast, and brain. SVM, random forest, and algorithms were always the three most commonly utilized prediction algorithms reported in the literature, while accuracy has become the most frequently used performance metric. Predictions of common diseases were most accurately made using the convolutional neural network model. However, owing to its reliability in processing large, complex, and unstructured data, the SVM model demonstrated greater accuracy in most cases of renal diseases and Parkinson's disease. For its potential to expand effectively for big datasets and its sensitivity to overfitting, random forest has demonstrated a greater advantage in the likelihood of accurate disease classification and overall breast cancer prediction. Finally, the logistic regression algorithm is the most accurate model in predicting heart disease. More complicated ML algorithms will be required in the future to enhance disease prediction efficiency. Furthermore, learning models should indeed be adjusted more often after the training period to possibly improve performance. Furthermore, datasets should be increased on diverse demographics to minimize overfitting and improve model accuracy. Furthermore, more appropriate feature selection approaches should be utilized to improve learning models' performance.

REFERENCES

[1]　"Analysis and Prediction of Heart Disease Using Machine Learning and Data Mining Techniques", Canadian Journal of Medicine, 2021. Available: 10.33844/cjm.2021.60500.

[2]   A. Jain, A. K. Pandey, (2019), "Modeling and Optimizing of Different Quality Characteristics in Electrical Discharge Drilling of Titanium Alloy (Grade-5) Sheet" Material Today Proceedings, 18, 182–191 https://doi.org/10.1016/j.matpr.2019.06.292

[3]   "Comparative Study of Data Mining Techniques on Heart Disease Prediction System: a case study for the", International Journal of Science and Research (IJSR), vol. 5, no. 5, pp. 1564–1571, 2016. Available: 10.21275/v5i5.nov163704.

[4]   C. Catal, "Software mining and fault prediction", Wiley Interdisciplinary Reviews: Data Mining and Knowledge Discovery, vol. 2, no. 5, pp. 420–426, 2012. Available: 10.1002/widm.1067.

[5]   V. Poornima and D. Gladis, "Analysis and Prediction of Heart Disease Aid of Various Data Mining Techniques: A Survey", International Journal of Business Intelligence and Data Mining, vol. 1, no. 1, p. 1, 2018. Available: 10.1504/ijbidm.2018.10014620.

[6]   A. Jain, A.K. Yadav & Y. Shrivastava (2019), "Modelling and Optimization of Different Quality Characteristics in Electric Discharge Drilling of Titanium Alloy Sheet" Material Today Proceedings, 21, 1680–1684 https://doi.org/10.1016/j.matpr.2019.12.010

[7]   "Intelligent Cardiovascular disease prediction using Data mining Techniques", International Journal of Pharmaceutical Research, vol. 10, no. 4, 2018. Available: 10.31838/ijpr/2018.10.04.150.

[8]   A. Jain, A. K. Pandey, (2019), "Modeling and Optimizing of Different Quality Characteristics in Electrical Discharge Drilling of Titanium Alloy (Grade-5) Sheet" Material Today Proceedings, 18, 182–191 https://doi.org/10.1016/j.matpr.2019.06.292

[9]   V. Panwar, D.K. Sharma, K.V.P. Kumar, A. Jain & C. Thakar, (2021), "Experimental Investigations and Optimization of Surface Roughness in Turning of EN 36 Alloy Steel Using Response Surface Methodology and Genetic Algorithm" Materials Today: Proceedings, https://Doi.Org/10.1016/J.Matpr.2021.03.642

[10] A. Jain, C. S. Kumar, Y. Shrivastava, (2021), "Fabrication and Machining of Fiber Matrix Composite through Electric Discharge Machining: A short review" Material Today Proceedings https://doi.org/10.1016/j.matpr.2021.07.288

[11] "A Review: Prediction on Chronic Kidney Disease using Data Mining Methods", International Journal of Pharmaceutical Research, vol. 12, no. 1, 2020. Available: 10.31838/ijpr/2020.sp1.213.

[12] V. Panwar, D.K. Sharma, K.V.P. Kumar, A. Jain & C. Thakar, (2021), "Experimental Investigations and Optimization of Surface Roughness in Turning of EN 36 Alloy Steel Using Response Surface Methodology and Genetic Algorithm" Materials Today: Proceedings, https://Doi.Org/10.1016/J.Matpr.2021.03.642

[13] "Heart Disease Prediction with Data Mining Clustering Algorithms", International Journal of Computing, Communication and Instrumentation Engineering, vol. 4, no. 1, 2017. Available: 10.15242/ijccie. dir1116009.

[14] A. Jain, A. K. Pandey, (2019), "Multiple Quality Optimizations In Electrical Discharge Drilling Of Mild Steel Sheet" Material Today Proceedings, 8, 7252–7261 https://doi.org/10.1016/j.matpr.2017.07.054

[15] "Data Mining Apriori Algorithm for Heart Disease Prediction", International Journal of Computing, Communication and Instrumentation Engineering, vol. 4, no. 1, 2017. Available: 10.15242/ijccie.dir1116010.

[16] E. Saleh and M. Bin Abd Kadir, "Prediction of Chronic Kidney Disease Using Data Mining Techniques", SSRN Electronic Journal, 2022. Available: 10.2139/ssrn.4022160.

[17] "Data Mining Classification Algorithms for Heart Disease Prediction", International Journal of Computing, Communication and Instrumentation Engineering, vol. 4, no. 1, 2017. Available: 10.15242/ijccie.dir1116008.

[18] N. Briones and V. Dinu, "Data mining of high-density genomic variant data for prediction of Alzheimer's disease risk", BMC Medical Genetics, vol. 13, no. 1, 2012. Available: 10.1186/1471-2350-13-7.

[19] R.Anupriya, P.Saranya and R.Deepika, "Mining Health Data in Multimodal Data Series for Disease Prediction", International Journal of Scientific Research in Computer Science and Engineering, vol. 6, no. 2, pp. 96–99, 2018. Available: 10.26438/ijsrcse/v6i2.9699.

[20] N.–and D. Mittal, "HEALTHCARE DATA ANALYSIS USING DATA MINING TECHNIQUES FOR DISEASE PREDICTION", Indian Journal of Computer Science and Engineering, vol. 12, no. 5, pp. 1224–1237, 2021. Available: 10.21817/indices/2021/v12i5/211205047.

4 Understanding the Contribution of Artificial Intelligence

Neelam Raut
WPU School of Business
Dr. Vishwanath Karad MIT World Peace University,
Pune, India

Prashant Chaudhary
WPU School of Business
Dr. Vishwanath Karad MIT World Peace University,
Pune, India

Harshali Patil
WPU School of Business
Dr. Vishwanath Karad MIT World Peace University,
Pune, India

Prabha Kiran
Westminster International University
Tashkent, Uzbekistan

4.1 INTRODUCTION

Sustainability refers to the nature, ability, and quality to survive over a sustained and continued interlude of time. Digital technologies are increasingly becoming a dependable means that have proven the potential to drive the fashion industry toward an environmentally conscious and responsible way of conducting the business activities and functions. This research study essentially endeavors to understand the role and contribution of AI technologies in the growth of sustainable and circular fashion. The phrase "artificial intelligence" (AI) is a generic one that refers to the use of various digital technologies to simulate intelligent decisions and actions with the smallest possible amount of human intervention or involvement. AI essentially

DOI: 10.1201/9781003348351-4

enables these digital applications, tools, and technologies to perform functions such as self-monitoring, interpretation, diagnosis, and analysis on their own (Ahmed et al., 2022; Hamet & Tremblay, 2017). Since the twentieth century, the fashion industry is increasingly globalized with the evolution of global supply chains. Fashion clothing and collections are often designed in one country, manufactured in another, and sold worldwide at an ever-increasing pace (Geissdoerfer et al., 2018; Koszewska et al., 2020; Lüdeke-Freund et al., 2019).

Fashion clothing, especially fast fashion clothing, has always been perceived as disposable, and this trend has been further accentuated over the years owing to various favorable macro- and micro-economic factors. Factors such as liberalization of trade policies, increasing preference for branded cloths, growing middle class and upper middle class across the world with higher disposable income, growth of e-commerce, and the emergence of the "fast fashion" phenomenon, among others, are driving the phenomenal growth of production and consumption. The trends of fast fashion and growing consumerism are essentially making it difficult to contain such squandering consumption and expenses (Bhalla, 2022). The fashion industry is supposed to be responsible for 2%-8% of the emissions of greenhouse gases. The manufacturing of polyester fabrics from fossil fuels leads to the release of plastic microfibers into the environment, which has a profoundly adverse effect on climate, biodiversity, and nature (Nations Environment Programme (UNEP, 2021). India being one of the largest global hubs of fast fashion garments is also among the top five apparel manufacturing markets exporting to the US and Europe. While, on the one hand, the demand for fashion is also growing, on the other hand, India was ranked at the bottom position on a number of indicators of the Environmental Performance Index (EPI) of 2022. The report further stated that, if the current trends continue, then China, US, India, and Russia are expected to account for over 50% of enduring global greenhouse gas emissions by 2050 (Bavadam, 2022; Roy, 2022).

Nevertheless, the sustainable and ethical fashion has also emerged as a growing phenomenon to increasing consumer awareness and sensitivity toward climate change and the consequent growing inclination toward ethical fashion for sustainability. Ethical fashion refers to the ethical and sustainable production processes and business practices. It also involves the use of clothes made of recycled clothes/fabrics, clothes manufactured from sustainably grown cotton, and purchasing second-hand fashion items can essentially reduce the carbon footprint significantly. Technologies such as AI, 3D mobile body scanning, big data and analytics, augmented reality (AR), virtual reality (VR), AR/VR dressing rooms, virtual display in the metaverse, machine learning, blockchain technology, and radiofrequency identification devices (RFID), among others, are catalyzing this process (Medri, 2021). According to the report published by Ellen MacArthur Foundation Charity (2017), these are the proven ways to reduce the related emissions' effect of clothing by almost 44%, which was also endorsed by the United Nations (UN) Environment Programme (UNEP).

4.2   SCOPE AND OBJECTIVES OF THE STUDY

This research majorly focuses on understanding the role and application of AI in the evolution and development of sustainable and circular fashion. AI refers to the ability of robots to simulate human thinking in a variety of ways, which includes reasoning, analysis, decision-making, and communication. Experts have compared the functioning of AI with the development of reasoning ability of young infants, which develops with each exposure, every puzzle solved, and each new word learned. In the similar manner, AI can learn endlessly and collect a limitless number of impressions, data points, and values of all types without any human demands or constraints (Dauvergne, 2020).

Hence, the purpose of this secondary research study is to investigate the role and application AI and AI-powered technologies and tools for bring sustainability in the fashion business. The rationale behind undertaking this study was based on findings that showed the significant contribution of the fashion sector to environmental damage and climate change. The objective was to investigate how the different components of the fashion ecosystem, such as retailers, fashion designers, fashion brands, and other stake holders, can utilize AI to bring sustainability and support to this global cause. The overarching objective of this study is to examine the use and applicability of AI as a technological tool to offer sustainable solutions for dealing with environment-related problems with special reference to fashion retailing. Another objective is to provide the groundwork for future studies on how business requirements will match with UN Sustainable Development Goals and what AI's future role will be.

4.3   LITERATURE REVIEW

Industry 5.0 essentially conceptualizes express evolution in the technology, business formats, business processes, consumer behavior, and businesses' effect on the ecological environment. The philosophy and business approach of circular economy has gained traction in recent years as a way of mitigating the climate change, depletion of natural resources, pollution, waste generation, and global warming, which are the outcomes of linear systems (Ki et al., 2020; Research and Markets, 2022). The business models in circular economy are essentially based on the development and implementation of closed systems where resources are utilized responsibly, resource flows are optimized, and recurring closed loop of circulation of resources is formed, which subsequently reduced carbon footprint and/or eliminated the adverse effects on the environment (Geissdoerfer et al., 2017). The circular business approach formats and models essentially bring significant environmental, social, and economic benefits and can be implemented in a wide range of business settings (Bocken et al., 2016; Bolesnikov et al., 2022). With these developments, the fashion industry has received various concepts or terms for sustainable and circular fashion, which are ethical fashion, green fashion, and eco-fashion. To conclude, sustainable fashion refers to a type of fashion that is environmentally beneficial in its design, production, distribution, and use (Hansen & Bøgh, 2021; Hassan et al., 2022).

Being one of the most important sectors globally; fashion contributes to the sizeable fraction of the global business, trade, gross domestic product (GDP), and economy. The fashion business accounts for nearly 2% of the global GDP with 3 trillion dollars in annual economic output. According to the forecasts, the global fashion market is expected to increase from $1.5 trillion in 2020 to over $2.25 trillion in 2025, demonstrating a persistent increase in demand (Akram et al., 2022; Ikram, 2022). Accounting for almost 10% of the global carbon dioxide emission, fashion has a serious environmental footprint. This has been further exacerbated by the fast fashion business model, which promotes the frequent purchase of nondurable and low-priced items, having a very short lifespan because of frequently changing trends. Swiftly changing fashion trends, shifting consumer taste, low prices, high discounts, credit facilities, impulsive buying, and both free delivery and returns all encourage customers to purchase multiple options with the intention to return items. This has led to the amplification in the incidence of return, and subsequently, approximately 30% of online purchases are returned (Dissanayake, 2020; The Conversation, 2022).

4.4   ROLE AND APPLICATION OF TECHNOLOGIES AND TOOLS POWERED BY ARTIFICIAL INTELLIGENCE

The ecological ecosystem and humanity are going through a phase that calls for decisive actions and focused efforts toward the protection of the environment and ecosystem, as we are facing a planetary emergency that has been caused due to interrelated issues such as biodiversity loss, pollution, climate change, global warming, land degradation, human rights violations, water catastrophe, ozone layer depletion, recurring deadly pandemics, and many more. Every sector of the economy, including the fashion industry, now uses AI under certain capacity. When we examine the fashion value chain closely, we find that practically every area uses AI, starting from product development to robotic manufacturing (Lerman et al., 2022; Luce, 2018). As customers' preferred method of buying steadily moves toward online retailers, it really does not seem to be a better time to apply AI-based solutions to the fashion and retail sectors' sustainability objectives (Edwin Cheng et al., 2021).

The use of AI-powered tools and a technology used for trend forecasting, inventory tracking, and supply chain management is leading to reduced returns, diminished overproduction, and elimination of waste. For instance, technologies such as VR and magic mirror allow the customers to try on outfits virtually and make the right purchase decision that leads to reduced returns and subsequently reduces the carbon footprint due to the returns (Altenbuchner et al., 2018; Jacometti, 2019; Pedersen et al., 2019).

The fashion industry is undergoing a significant paradigm shift from an experience-based business model to a highly data-driven business model (Zou & Wong, 2021), and AI aids in speeding up the entire process by having an impact in areas such as trend analysis, fashion recommendation, supply chain management, sales forecasting, and digital shopping, among others (Camacho-Otero et al., 2020; Geissdoerfer et al., 2020; Wazarkar et al., 2020). Fashion brands and retailers are also using technologies such as real-time fashion systems for creating personalization and customization mechanisms. The emphasis is to successfully adapt the design of apparels and garments to the behavior and interests of users (Lee, 2021). Levi's recently launched a virtual stylist called Levi's Indigo through its website and social media platforms. This digital platform assists the online shoppers for finding the apparels and other accessories that are best suited to their preference, style, taste, and size. Tommy Hilfiger launched a project called "Reimagine Retail" in collaboration with the Fashion Institute of Technology and technology major IBM to enhance its designs through AI applications. Additionally, fashion-related business activities such as Virtual Try-On or visiting showrooms and attending fashion weeks were mostly an online event during the epidemic and continued even after the pandemic (Mohammadi & Kalhor, 2021; Silvestri, 2020). AI algorithms may be used to distinguish garment kinds and details, which can simplify and minimize the cost of predicting trends (Shi & Lewis, 2020). AI-based voice assistants (smart speakers) are also being used by fashion retailers and fashion brands for suggesting appropriate options to their customers based on their past purchases, tastes, and preferences, which eventually reduce the chances of returns. These insights can also be leveraged by the designers, manufactures, and retailers for astute merchandise management. Such merchandise planning is often in sync with the latest fashion trends and is tailored to consumers' expectations. For the development of such AI tools, web crawlers, data clustering subsystems, and metadata sifting create the appropriate solutions within the required time that meet the demands of the client (Kotouza et al., 2020). The research study conducted by Nadkarni et al. (2011) delved deep into understanding the advantages of clustering algorithms, which allow AI to digest massive amounts of data at once and generate possibilities for designers to work with. Similar data clustering approaches might be used to generate fashion suggestions, thus improving the accessibility and effectiveness of consumer decision-making while also lowering waste from erroneous or uninformed decision-making—uncontrolled and unplanned purchases (Moreno, 2019; Yilmaz et al., 2022).

According to the report published by Markets and Markets, global spending on AI in the fashion industry would increase by 40.8%, from 229 million USD in 2019 to 1260 million USD in 2024. Because of the growing impact of social media on fashion businesses, the use of AI in fashion solutions is anticipated to increase (MarketsandMarkets, 2019).

4.5 FINDINGS

The encouragement of overconsumption by fast fashion brands and retailers is mainly done through promotion of hedonic lifestyle, influencer marketing, Masstige marketing, and celebrity endorsements (Chaudhary, 2022; Chaudhary & Sharma, 2022), ultimately resulting in irresponsible consumption of resources and its resultant harmful impacts on the ecology and environment (Narke, 2022). The latest innovations in digital technology and retailer's tryst with digital transformation strategies are transforming fashion retail (Chaudhary, 2016). The forward-thinking and progressive fashion retailers and brands are capitalizing on these trends with their sustainability initiative focused on value and convenience. These priorities of fashion brands and retailers are also supported by consumers' sustainability attitudes, purchase preferences, buying behaviors, awareness about climate change, and the consequent changes in consumer sensitivity and sensibility. For instance, the focus of

Indian consumers' sustainable behaviors has found to be on the frugality and simplicity (Mintel Consulting, 2022; Richard Cope, 2022).

There exist a few internal and external challenges that consumers and designers perceive when incorporating sustainable fashion options. Nevertheless, when information about ecological risks is available, consumers are inclined to change their purchasing behavior to avoid purchasing clothes whose production is more harmful to the environment and purchase clothes whose production is less harmful to the environment (Bolesnikov et al., 2022; Hur & Cassidy, 2019). In addition to various technologies, the emerging retail formats and business approaches such as omni-channel retailing, pop-up shops, E-retailing, direct to consumer channels, and ownership to usership are driving factors for sustainability in fashion retailing (Chaudhary et al., 2021; Karangutkar & Chaudhary, 2017). All these measures led the global ethical fashion market to reach to a value of nearly $6000 million in 2020 with a compound annual growth rate (CAGR) of approximately 6% since 2014. Going forward with a CAGR of approximately 9.7%, the ethical fashion market has been expected to grow from nearly $6000 million in 2020 to nearly $10000 million by 2024. It is further expected to grow to approximately $15000 million by 2030 from approximately $10000 million in 2025 at a CAGR of around 9.0% (Research and Markets, 2022).

4.6 CONCLUSION

As the e-commerce model and the omni-channel approach scaled up, the focus of fashion brands and retailers has moved to improving the overall shopping experience across the channels and touch-points (Chaudhary et al., 2021). This also involves the In the fashion business, the application of AI ranges from designing to inventory planning and from sales to personalization and personalized product recommendations. For instance, the integration of real-time data analysis, RFID, and AI has automated various crucial processes such as merchandise planning, assortment planning, private label brand strategy, and inventory management to a significant extent. Fashion brands such as Zara, Levi's, H&M, Poshmark, Tommy Hilfiger, Stitch Fix, Nordstrom Vestiaire Collective, and many others continue to invest in integrating AI-based technologies, automation, 3D printing, and big data for fashion design and styling, virtual merchandising, supply chain management, and retail management to outperform competition, steer clear of excess inventory, and bring sustainability. Hence, AI-powered technologies aid fashion brands and retailers for creating customized ensembles, personalized looks, and outfit choices. New age technologies combined with AI are currently helping fashion retailers to predict the returns before order placement and subsequently customize targeted marketing based on the customer returns profile. AI facilitates real-time appraisal of the customer's basket that is precisely correlated with their individual profile based on preferences such as style, fit, price-points, preferred brands, order value, and previous purchases. This subsequently helps fashion brands and retailers to assess the prediction of probability of the merchandise being returned with an improved level of accuracy.

All these factors indirectly lead to sustainability, as they help customers to make better buying decisions and retailers to offer better shopping experience. These consumer-centric technologies powered by AI have a significant potential to reduce the returns and consequently decrease the carbon footprint.

4.7 MANAGERIAL IMPLICATIONS

AI has a significant effect on every aspect of the fashion business, starting from manufacturing and consumption-oriented design to disposal. This is indeed the ideal time to bring in ideas about utilizing AI to promote and practice sustainability in the business of fashion and fashion retailing, across the entire value chain. This sector needs to embrace AI-powered tools and technologies and contribute to the goals of the Paris Agreement. The fashion industry should focus on social and environmental issues by ensuring sustainable production and encouraging sustainable consumption. Creating resilient infrastructure through innovation will enable sustainable consumption and production. By integrating digital technologies such as the Internet of Things, enterprise resource planning, AI, blockchain, customer relationship management, AR, RFID, simulated three-dimensional visual, and VR, a robust infrastructure with innovation may be achieved by virtue of its use of natural language processing to interact with customers; AI-powered chatbots and smart assistants need to be deployed for providing augmented customer service and experience. Use of state-of-the-art digital technologies such as AI for styling, designing, manufacturing, retailing, selling, supply chain, buying, and last mile logistics along with other measures such as reusing, repurposing, or upcycling are the definitive ways ahead for bringing sustainability into the business of fast fashion.

REFERENCES

Ahmed, I., Jeon, G., & Piccialli, F. (2022). From Artificial Intelligence to Explainable Artificial Intelligence in Industry 4.0: A Survey on What, How, and Where. *IEEE Transactions on Industrial Informatics, 18*(8), 5031–5042. https://doi.org/10.1109/TII.2022.3146552

Akram, S. V., Malik, P. K., Singh, R., Gehlot, A., Juyal, A., Ghafoor, K. Z., & Shrestha, S. (2022). Implementation of Digitalized Technologies for Fashion Industry 4.0: Opportunities and Challenges. *Scientific Programming, 2022*, 1–17. https://doi.org/10.1155/2022/7523246

Altenbuchner, C., Vogel, S., & Larcher, M. (2018). Social, economic and environmental impacts of organic cotton production on the livelihood of smallholder farmers in Odisha, India. *Renewable Agriculture and Food Systems, 33*(4), 373–385. https://doi.org/10.1017/S174217051700014X

Bavadam, L. (2022, August 25). India ranks at the bottom in a list of 180 countries in the 2022 Environmental Performance Index. *Frintline.* https://frontline.thehindu.com/dispatches/india-ranks-at-the-bottom-in-a-list-180-countries-in-the-2022-environmental-performance-index/article65497256.ece

Bhalla, K. (2022, June 29). Impulse buys, fast fashion end up in landfills and stay intact for 200 years. *Business Insider India.* www.businessinsider.in/retail/news/impulse-buys-fast-fashion-end-up-in-landfills-and-stay-intact-for-200-years/articleshow/92533424.cms

Bocken, N. M. P., de Pauw, I., Bakker, C., & van der Grinten, B. (2016). Product design and business model strategies for a circular economy. *Journal of Industrial and Production Engineering, 33*(5), 308–320. https://doi.org/10.1080/21681015.2016.1172124

Bolesnikov, M., Popović Stijačić, M., Keswani, A. B., & Brkljač, N. (2022). Perception of Innovative Usage of AI in Optimizing Customer Purchasing Experience within the Sustainable Fashion Industry. *Sustainability, 14*(16), 10082. https://doi.org/10.3390/su141610082

Camacho-Otero, J., Pettersen, I. N., & Boks, C. (2020). Consumer engagement in the circular economy: Exploring clothes swapping in emerging economies from a social practice perspective. *Sustainable Development, 28*(1), 279–293. https://doi.org/10.1002/sd.2002

Chaudhary, P. (2016). *Retail Marketing in the Modern Age* (1st ed.). SAGE Publishing.

Chaudhary, P. (2022). Online Influencer Marketing–An Effective Marketing Technique for Strategic Branding, Resonating Communication and Customer Engagement. *Management Dynamics (Perspective Section), 22*(1). https://managementdynamics.rese archcommons.org/journal/vol22/iss1/4/

Chaudhary, P., & Sharma, S. (2022). Private Label Fashion Brands: Through the Lens of Masstige Marketing Theory. *Indian Journal of Marketing, 52*(6), 1–8. https://doi.org/10.17010/ijom/2022/v52/i6/169833

Chaudhary, P., Singh, A., & Sharma, S. (2021). Understanding the antecedents of omni-channel shopping by customers with reference to fashion category: The Indian millennials' perspective. *Young Consumers, 23*(2), 304–320. https://doi.org/10.1108/YC-05-2021-1327

Dauvergne, P. (2020). *AI in the Wild: Sustainability in the Age of Artificial Intelligence*. The MIT Press Penguin Random house.

Dissanayake, D. G. K. (2020). Does Mass Customization Enable Sustainability in the Fashion Industry? In R. Beltramo, A. Romani, & P. Cantore (Eds.), *Fashion Industry—An Itinerary Between Feelings and Technology*. IntechOpen. https://doi.org/10.5772/intechopen.88281

Edwin Cheng, T. C., Kamble, S. S., Belhadi, A., Ndubisi, N. O., Lai, K., & Kharat, M. G. (2021). Linkages between big data analytics, circular economy, sustainable supply chain flexibility, and sustainable performance in manufacturing firms. *International Journal of Production Research*, 1–15. https://doi.org/10.1080/00207543.2021.1906971

Ellen MacArthur Foundation. (2017). *A New Textiles Economy: Redesigning Fashion's Future*. Ellen MacArthur Foundation. https://ellenmacarthurfoundation.org/a-new-textiles-economy

Geissdoerfer, M., Morioka, S. N., de Carvalho, M. M., & Evans, S. (2018). Business models and supply chains for the circular economy. *Journal of Cleaner Production, 190*, 712–721. https://doi.org/10.1016/j.jclepro.2018.04.159

Geissdoerfer, M., Pieroni, M. P. P., Pigosso, D. C. A., & Soufani, K. (2020). Circular business models: A review. *Journal of Cleaner Production, 277*, 123741. https://doi.org/10.1016/j.jclepro.2020.123741

Geissdoerfer, M., Savaget, P., Bocken, N. M. P., & Hultink, E. J. (2017). The Circular Economy–A new sustainability paradigm? *Journal of Cleaner Production, 143*, 757–768. https://doi.org/10.1016/j.jclepro.2016.12.048

Hamet, P., & Tremblay, J. (2017). Artificial intelligence in medicine. *Metabolism, 69*, S36–S40. https://doi.org/10.1016/j.metabol.2017.01.011

Hansen, E. B., & Bøgh, S. (2021). Artificial intelligence and internet of things in small and medium-sized enterprises: A survey. *Journal of Manufacturing Systems, 58*, 362–372. https://doi.org/10.1016/j.jmsy.2020.08.009

Hassan, S. H., Yeap, J. A. L., & Al-Kumaim, N. H. (2022). Sustainable Fashion Consumption: Advocating Philanthropic and Economic Motives in Clothing Disposal Behaviour. *Sustainability, 14*(3), 1875. https://doi.org/10.3390/su14031875

Hur, E., & Cassidy, T. (2019). Perceptions and attitudes towards sustainable fashion design: Challenges and opportunities for implementing sustainability in fashion.

International Journal of Fashion Design, Technology and Education, 12(2), 208–217. https://doi.org/10.1080/17543266.2019.1572789

Ikram, M. (2022). Transition toward green economy: Technological Innovation's role in the fashion industry. *Current Opinion in Green and Sustainable Chemistry, 37*, 100657. https://doi.org/10.1016/j.cogsc.2022.100657

Jacometti, V. (2019). Circular Economy and Waste in the Fashion Industry. *Laws, 8*(4), 27. https://doi.org/10.3390/laws8040027

Karangutkar, S., & Chaudhary, P. (2017). Transforming the brick-and-mortar fashion retailing–The Omni-channel Way. *ELK Asia Pacific Journal Of Marketing And Retail Management, 8*(4), 129–147. https://doi.org/10.16962/EAPJMRM/issn. 2349-2317/ 2015

Ki, C. (Chloe), Chong, S. M., & Ha-Brookshire, J. E. (2020). How fashion can achieve sustainable development through a circular economy and stakeholder engagement: A systematic literature review. *Corporate Social Responsibility and Environmental Management, 27*(6), 2401–2424. https://doi.org/10.1002/csr.1970

Koszewska, M., Rahman, O., & Dyczewski, B. (2020). Circular Fashion–Consumers' Attitudes in Cross-National Study: Poland and Canada. *Autex Research Journal, 20*(3), 327–337. https://doi.org/10.2478/aut-2020-0029

Kotouza, M. Th., Tsarouchis, S., Kyprianidis, A.-C., Chrysopoulos, A. C., & Mitkas, P. A. (2020). Towards Fashion Recommendation: An AI System for Clothing Data Retrieval and Analysis. In I. Maglogiannis, L. Iliadis, & E. Pimenidis (Eds.), *Artificial Intelligence Applications and Innovations* (Vol. 584, pp. 433–444). Springer International Publishing. https://doi.org/10.1007/978-3-030-49186-4_36

Lee, Y. K. (2021). Transformation of the Innovative and Sustainable Supply Chain with Upcoming Real-Time Fashion Systems. *Sustainability, 13*(3), 1081. https://doi.org/ 10.3390/su13031081

Lerman, L. V., Benitez, G. B., Müller, J. M., de Sousa, P. R., & Frank, A. G. (2022). Smart green supply chain management: A configurational approach to enhance green performance through digital transformation. *Supply Chain Management: An International Journal, 27*(7), 147–176. https://doi.org/10.1108/SCM-02-2022-0059

Luce, L. (2018). *Artificial Intelligence for Fashion: How AI is Revolutionizing the Fashion Industry* (1st ed. edition). Apress.

Lüdeke-Freund, F., Gold, S., & Bocken, N. M. P. (2019). A Review and Typology of Circular Economy Business Model Patterns. *Journal of Industrial Ecology, 23*(1), 36–61. https:// doi.org/10.1111/jiec.12763

MarketsandMarkets. (2019). *AI in Fashion Market worth $1,260 million by 2024.* MarketsandMarkets. www.marketsandmarkets.com/PressReleases/ai-in-fashion.asp

Medri, A. G. (2021, October 1). Digital technologies for timeless sustainable fashion. *United Nations Development Programme.* https://tinyurl.com/4krykp79

Mintel Consulting. (2022). *Mintel Consulting 2022 Sustainability Barometer* [Corporate Report]. Mintel Consulting. www.mintel.com/press-centre/mintel-consulting-2022-sus tainability-barometer

Mohammadi, S. O., & Kalhor, A. (2021). Smart Fashion: A Review of AI Applications in Virtual Try-On & Fashion Synthesis. *Journal of Artificial Intelligence and Capsule Networks, 3*(4), 284–304. https://doi.org/10.36548/jaicn.2021.4.002

Moreno, C. C. (2019). Natural Language Processing, or How to Communicate With Your Computer. *Journal of the American College of Radiology, 16*(11), 1585–1586. https:// doi.org/10.1016/j.jacr.2019.07.007

Nadkarni, P. M., Ohno-Machado, L., & Chapman, W. W. (2011). Natural language processing: An introduction. *Journal of the American Medical Informatics Association, 18*(5), 544–551. https://doi.org/10.1136/amiajnl-2011-000464

Narke, M. (2022, June 29). *Impulse buys, fast fashion end up in landfills and stay intact for 200 years* [Business Insider India]. www.businessinsider.in/retail/news/impulse-buys-fast-fashion-end-up-in-landfills-and-stay-intact-for-200-years/articleshow/92533 424.cms

Nations Environment Programme (UNEP). (2021). *Putting the brakes on fast fashion.* Nations Environment Programme (UNEP). https://tinyurl.com/322cm4xt

Pedersen, E. R. G., Earley, R., & Andersen, K. R. (2019). From singular to plural: Exploring organisational complexities and circular business model design. *Journal of Fashion Marketing and Management: An International Journal, 23*(3), 308–326. https://doi.org/10.1108/JFMM-04-2018-0062

Research and Markets. (2022). *Global Ethical Fashion Market Opportunities and Strategies Report 2022-2030: Recycling And Upcycling, Increased Transparency Through Storytelling, Animal-Free Leather, Vegan Fashion.* Research and Markets.

Richard Cope. (2022, August 19). *Indian consumers' sustainable behaviour focuses on simplicity and frugality: Report* [Brand Equity–The Economic Times]. https://brandequity.economictimes.indiatimes.com/news/research/indian-consumers-sustainable-behaviour-focuses-on-simplicity-and-frugality-report/93658160

Roy, E. (2022, June 11). Explained: What is the environment index, and why has India questioned it? *The Indian Express.* https://indianexpress.com/article/explained/environment-index-and-india-7963597/

Shi, M., & Lewis, V. D. (2020). Using Artificial Intelligence to Analyze Fashion Trends. *ArXiv, abs/2005.00986.*

Silvestri, B. (2020). The Future of Fashion: How the Quest for Digitization and the Use of Artificial Intelligence and Extended Reality Will Reshape the Fashion Industry After COVID-19. *ZoneModa Journal, V. 10 N. 2,* 61–73 Paginazione. https://doi.org/10.6092/ISSN.2611-0563/11803

The Conversation. (2022, August 12). Fast fashion: Why your online returns may end up in landfill–and what can be done about it. *The Indian Express.* https://indianexpress.com/article/lifestyle/fashion/fast-fashion-why-your-online-returns-may-end-up-in-landfill-and-what-can-be-done-about-it-8080073/

Wazarkar, S., Patil, S., & Kumar V C, S. (2020). A Bibliometric Survey of Fashion Analysis using Artificial Intelligence. *Library Philosophy and Practice, 2020.*

Yilmaz, Y., Jurado Nunez, A., Ariaeinejad, A., Lee, M., Sherbino, J., & Chan, T. M. (2022). Harnessing Natural Language Processing to Support Decisions Around Workplace-Based Assessment: Machine Learning Study of Competency-Based Medical Education. *JMIR Medical Education, 8*(2), e30537. https://doi.org/10.2196/30537

Zou, X., & Wong, W. K. (2021). fAshIon after fashion: A Report of AI in Fashion. *ArXiv, abs/2105.03050.*

5 Artificial Intelligence and Sustainable Green Fashion Industry

Aditi Dhama
Amity University, Greater Noida (U.P.), India

Avneet Kaur
Amity University, Greater Noida (U.P.), India

Esra S. Döngül
Faculty of Health Sciences,
Department of Social Work, Aksaray University
Aksaray, Türkiye

Neha Singh
Department of Fashion and Textile Design
Swami Vivekanand Subharti University, Meerut (U.P.), India

5.1 INTRODUCTION

Fashion is considered one of the most valuable industries in the world. The Indian fashion industry has always been a prominent market recognized for its innovative approach and staying abreast with the trend. The pandemic has disrupted it at considerable levels, but the industry was prompt enough to cope with the changes. While this was a global issue, the pandemic brought to the forefront what sustainable fashion truly is and how every single person has a role to play in striving for a more sustainable industry. The industry is now treading on the path of recovery and is all set to revamp in 2022!

However, this industry has remained quite traditional for decades creating a huge impact on our planet from multiple aspects. From fiber production, to design, production, delivery, usage, and after-use disposal, every stage in its value chain has contributed to the sustainability crisis.

DOI: 10.1201/9781003348351-5

Some tremendous and sustainable changes that resulted in the remarkable growth of the fashion industry are as follows:

- The West will no longer play the leading role in fashion sales, and more than half of the world's apparel sales will come from emerging countries in Asia-Pacific, Latin America, and other regions.
- The advent of digital technologies such as mobile Internet, advanced analytics, virtual and augmented reality, advanced robotics, and artificial intelligence (AI) are fundamentally transforming the industry and fixing the stage for a strong trend toward a crucial phase of digital adoption by mainstream consumers; these processes are designed to match specific trends in customer and business behaviors.
- The massive use of data analytics, growing infinite computing power, and accessibility to advanced algorithms and key analytics lead to a huge increase in the use of AI.

Sustainability is a major issue in textiles and fashion. This has prompted considerable interest in academia and industry as part of an effort to reduce negative environmental impact. The below listed ways are all examples of sustainable efforts.

- Use of biodegradable materials
- Efficient energy use
- Slow fashion
- Purchase of used clothing and consumption reduction
- The most sustainable approach to apparel production is to plan ahead of time in supply chain by creating designs that are environmentally conscious

With this in mind, the majority of fashion brands have formally proposed sustainable plans that include lowering carbon footprints and using sustainable materials such as organic cotton or recycled materials. In this regard, this chapter addresses the importance of applying AI in the fashion industry as the best way to achieve sustainability, as well as an industry example of such implementation.

According to the Artificial Intelligence High Level Group of the European Commission (2019): "Artificial intelligence (AI) refers to systems that display intelligent behavior by analyzing their environment and taking corrective actions—with some degree of autonomy—to achieve specific goals. AI-based systems can be purely software-based, acting in the virtual world (e.g., voice assistants, image analysis software, search engines, speech and face recognition systems), or AI can be embedded in hardware devices (e.g., advanced robots, autonomous cars, drones or Internet of Things applications)."

AI has swept across various industries, potentially disrupting businesses through creative technologies, more effective operational procedures, and access to consumer and industry insights that provide a prospective competitive edge.

Initially, AI automation did not seem appealing for fashion executives to utilize in an industry founded on creative ability and expression. However, as we enter the hyper-digital age, these applications can transform businesses and generate significant industry growth and revenues compared with competitors using traditional methods. Consequently, the worldwide investment of fashion and retail industries in AI technology is predicted to reach $7.3 billion per year by 2023.

AI will become the future state of all fashion things. The fashion industry is geared up to use AI in various areas of its functioning ranging from manufacturing, marketing, and selling products to understanding consumer behavior, creating awareness, developing a product, and tracking demand.

In the coming years, the technology will maximize users' shopping experience, improve sales systems, and enhance the sales process through intelligent automation. Chatbots and touchscreens are being used in stores to improve customer experience and customized product suggestions. It is becoming a common sight to find some form of AI chat technology on fashion websites that is being used to enhance customer experience. A great successful fashion requires the right combination of designs and patterns to design a costume, making it attractive among customers. AI can do that, apart from detecting demand trends and projecting the new trends while reducing the forecasting error. The future product design will be so much driven by AI that it would emerge as the designer itself. Year 2022 and coming years are going to see exponential growth in tech usage and development in the fashion industry revolving around AI, virtual reality and augmented reality, blockchain, and mobile commerce.

Schneider [30] estimates that, by 2022, AI will manage up to 85% of all business-to-consumer interactions. The fashion industry is at a turning point. The McKinsey Global Fashion Index (2022) forecasts that the industry's sales growth increased from $1.5 trillion in 2020 to approximately $2.25 trillion by 2025, indicating continued growth in demand [19].

According to McKinsey [19], 85% of retailers plan to invest in AI in 2023 and 2024, and AI in the fashion industry is being used to reinvent design, merchandising and marketing and also to achieve significant speed. AI in retail is set to be worth $19 billion by 2027, and the pandemic has been the opportune time for the companies to speed up its adoption.

This chapter comprises the following sections:

5.2 Artificial Intelligence for Sustainable Material
5.3 Artificial Intelligence for Design Process
5.4 Artificial Intelligence for Predictive Analysis and Demand Forecasting
5.5 Artificial Intelligence for Operations Automation
5.6 Artificial Intelligence for Product, Inventory, and Supply chain Management
5.7 Artificial Intelligence for Customer Experience Enhancement Online and In-Store

5.2 ARTIFICIAL INTELLIGENCE FOR SUSTAINABLE MATERIAL

In the near future, sustainability will be a dominant trend in the fashion business. Consumers are growing more environmentally sensitive, which has prompted

FIGURE 5.1   Blending artificial intelligence in the fashion industry.

companies to implement eco-friendly practices. While international fashion houses and shops have begun to choose the sustainable path, more will soon do the same. Some of the well-liked initiatives the industry are being launched to follow the sustainability route, including the use of organic textiles and natural dyes, recycling, and upcycling. Additionally, the participants are concentrating on preventing waste at the end of the lifecycle and making it possible to use carbon credits to offset transportation expenses.

Since ages, the fashion industry is being called "culprit" or "polluted" owing to the use of raw material such as leather in excess of global supply or the use of an enormous amount of water to dye fabrics and the production of large waste of fabrics because of rapidly changing fashion trends every week, month, or year. Ranging from two seasons per year, fashion groups, such as BAGAAR, are pushing customers to six seasons per year as if it is inevitable [4]. According to Paul Dillinger, vice president and head of global product innovation and premium collection design at Levi Strauss & Co, six of ten garments we produce end up in landfill or are incinerated within the very first year of production [23].

Some textiles and materials are simply more toxic to the environment than others. AI helps by "looking" at a design, identifying the required materials to make that particular item, and then finding similar textiles that manufacturers can use that are less onerous on the environment. Furthermore, the use of 3D modeling has helped manufacturers streamline their greening processes significantly. This AI-enhanced technology can be used to find alternatives to synthetic material, while still allowing the original vision of the item to be created. You are able to model how it will crease and how the fabric will fall, and you can even work out how much "give" the fabric has to determine sizing better.

To become more sustainable, the fashion industry should embrace new types of fabrics and material that are more sustainable, and biotechnology may play a bigger role into this. Shrilk, a material made from discarded shrimp shells and silk proteins, is very strong and much lighter than aluminum; some more biodegradable materials such as viscose, Tencel, or lyocell use less energy and water than cotton (BAGAAR)

[4]. In addition, some high-end brands have even switched to produce sustainable garments from recycled fabrics or organic materials such as orange peel, mushrooms, or even seaweed [27].

Finally, AI can lead the industry to more sustainable developments by optimizing retailers' business models, thereby making the products less wasteful through the following ways:

- Better demands and sales forecast: the waste products are minimized by reducing over production and following optimal distribution of goods.
- By building more effective and transparent supply chain management:

  AI can not only contribute to better supply chain management but also help provide information on what raw materials are to be used and where to source the labor from. The role played by AI-embedded blockchain technology in tracking provenance of manufactured goods has gained attention.

- AI can also help produce goods according to customer personalized shopping experience by knowing more about customer preferences and taste. This will help reduce waste and number of unsold goods [8].

5.3 ARTIFICIAL INTELLIGENCE FOR DESIGN PROCESS

AI-based fashion design solutions have somehow been overlooked. They do, however, have a huge amount of potential for a sector that is quickly automating its design and presentation processes both now and, most likely, in the future.

When combined with other technologies, AI use in fashion design can assist stores in accelerating time to market and producing custom-fitted apparel. Fashion merchants may weave, cut, and form patterns of new clothing designs using AI and technologies such as direct panel on loom, thereby reducing or eliminating waste and hastening time to market. AI may also aid in the creation of wholly new design combinations based on consumer tastes, popular fashion trends, and upcycling materials that are readily available (for example, converting elephant pants to skinny ones).

An AI engine then collects predictive indicators on fashion and buying trends, sales data from websites, and customer opinions to create a dynamic mood board that is used by human designers to create garments and accessories [17,18].

In 2017, Amazon announced the ability to train a Generative Adversarial Network from the family of generative models for garment design. These models can create images of clothing and can be useful as a starting point for designers. Amazon's elementary AI fashion designer learns a specific fashion style from images and can generate new items in similar styles from scratch [26]. IBM has partnered with Tommy Hilfiger and the Fashion Institute of Technology Infor Design and Tech Lab on a project called "Reimagine Retail" to show how AI can empower design teams by improving and reducing overall lead times and empowering their creative discovery Analysis and Augmentation, recalling insights from thousands of images and videos using computer vision. Designers can also see how to incorporate on-trend colors, key patterns, and style [29]

Shimmy Technologies, a Brooklyn-based apparel and tech startup, has integrated AI to speed up the swimwear design process. Swimwear is notoriously difficult to measure, and tailors have to measure multiple times. Shimmy has partnered with IBM's Watson AI to develop a system where tailors create a 3D model of a design when they submit a measurement to the computer. Using AI, Shimmy reduced designers' work time by 20% [26].

Stitch Fix, the $1 billion online styling services company, uses genetic algorithms to design new clothing styles for its clothes. Based on customer feedback on items such as color, sleeve shape, and hem length, new styles are created by recombining and possibly slightly altering attributes of existing styles. These new styles are then evaluated and approved by human stylists before they reach clients [26].

Overall, machine learning and computer vision technologies can be used to design the new must-have fashion products that match the continuous evolution of customer preferences .Particular effort is being devoted to the development of electronic textiles, known as smart fabrics, which incorporate digital components to provide users with a variety of benefits, ranging from tailored fits to adaptability to weather, drug release, temperature regulation, heart rate monitoring, muscle vibration, and even self-cleaning [4,13].

NEUE, a Swedish fashion tech company that had developed a chip containing sensors and processors that enabled electroluminescent fabric to be controlled, worked with New York's Fashion Institute of Technology to design a garment and accessory that... shown on the red carpet was Harper's Bazaar Icons event [7]

Smart textiles are very closely linked to Internet of Things (IoT) developments. A particularly interesting application of smart fashion techniques is Live: Scape BLOOM, an IoT-connected dress whose floral embellishment changes mode over time in response to real-time meteorological data streams. Live: Scape BLOOM uses traditional textile fabrics, jewelry beads and embellishments, electronic components, a Wi-Fi development kit, servo motors, and custom software [20].

This dress shows the possibilities for wearable, IoT-connected forms as smart fashion. Nanophotonics for AI can extend the concept to future applications in health, communication, and lifestyle.

5.4 ARTIFICIAL INTELLIGENCE FOR PREDICTIVE ANALYTICS AND DEMAND FORECASTING

Trend forecasting is an area that focuses on projecting a market's future. Thus, the area of the fashion industry that projects new fashion trends—colors, styling methods, fabric textures, and so on—that will pique consumer interest is known as fashion forecasting. Product designers use trend projections from fashion forecasters to create new clothes and accessories for businesses.

One of the many methods to include machine learning in systems for forecasting in the fashion industry is the prediction of AI fashion trends. The ability of AI to accurately estimate demand and identify patterns in consumer purchasing behavior is also crucial.

The term "predictive analytics" encompasses a cluster of techniques ranging from statistics to machine learning that use historical data to make predictions using models. A model in predictive analytics is an algorithm that uses the past to predict the future. In the fashion industry, one of the most common uses of predictive analytics is sizing to match a customer to the size that best fits them for a particular garment [15].

The principle of demand and sales forecasting is basically the use of available data for previous interactions of customers with the company's business environment—searches and purchases. AI makes conclusions regarding the demand changes and seasonality of sales, for example.

Consequently, retailers may use prediction in AI to forecast the demand for their particular products at a specific time. It helps to manage stock more effectively and increase sales overall.

Through automated product tagging, AI analyzes market performance on a per-attribute level. Buyers are informed not only on the products that are performing well but also on detailed attributes such as color, prints, sleeves, necklines, and more.

Additionally, instead of looking at trends and product performance as a snapshot at the end of each season, AI provides real-time data to observe shifting trends and stock performance as they are happening. Hence, buying and merchandising teams can adopt a proactive strategy to address consumer demand as it arises and always stay relevant.

According to a 2016 Body Labs Retail Survey, $62.4 billion worth of clothing and footwear is returned each year for incorrect size or fit [11].

Fit Analytics returns a best fit recommendation based on information provided by customers (height, weight, age and preferred fit) through the Fit Finder interface. Fit Finder supports more than 500 million recommendations every month and is used by many fashion brands such as The North Face, As Screen on Screen (ASOS), and Tommy Hilfiger and also by startups such as Amaro, the hottest digital native brand in Brazil. Fit Analytics helped Amaro increase their conversion rate by 2% and decrease their response rate by 4% (FitAnalytics.com).

Predictive analytics could also be helpful to

- Find out which customers are more likely to make a purchase and which customers are more likely to leave the platform (analysis of the number of visits to product pages, frequency of newsletter opens, and other such factors)
- Fight fraud and detect suspicious transactions. Predictive analytics also provides demand forecasts for consumer goods and services.

This is particularly important for the fashion industry, as accurate forecasts can reduce stock levels and product waste. Deep learning algorithms based on neural networks provide significant help in demand forecasting. For example, Long-Short-Term-Memory models are used for time-series forecasts, or a transfer learning model, which is useful for forecasts with small datasets. AI could also be particularly helpful for tracking fashion trends. While humans might find it particularly difficult to answer questions, such as "How many people were wearing white T-shirts in New York today compared with that 2 years ago?," it is easy for AI to compare millions of images from different social media and provide an answer [32].

5.5   ARTIFICIAL INTELLIGENCE FOR OPERATIONS AUTOMATION

AI is used beyond just predicting sales. It directly enhances the production of fashion items by participating in manufacturing, operation, and service automation. AI helps in process operations automations in several ways such as by simplification of delivering customer support, complete automation of data entry tasks, automation of supply chain processes, optimatization in shipments, and enhancements and automation of forecasting.

According to Luce [15], the word "robot" is quite common in the fashion industry. However, there is no clear definition for it. For some, describing a robot as a programmable machine that performs complex actions is simple enough. For others, a robot is truly the physical embodiment of AI operating in the physical world [15].

In the fashion industry, especially in factories, industrial robots are used for sewing and supply chain management. Such is the case with SoftWear Automation, an Atlanta-based robotics company focused on sewing robots. According to its CEO, the use of sewing robots has significant benefits in reducing costs, shifting production, reducing waste and, therefore, environmental impact, and increasing manufacturing flexibility [15]. However, beyond the factory, robots are used in the fashion industry in the warehouse for picking and packing operations.

Kiva systems are an example of robotic automation in warehousing. Companies such as Saks Fifth Avenue and The Gap and Gilt Group use Kiva Systems. Kiva was acquired by Amazon in 2012 and renamed as "Amazon Robotics." For example, Nike is an investor in GRABIT, which offers electro-adhesion-based gripping products for robotics and material handling applications in logistics [29]. Robots are also being used to improve customer service: Zara, for example, is using robots to speed up the in-store pick-up process. Customers who have ordered online can scan or enter a code at the store, and the robots will search for the order and take it to a dropbox where customers can pick it up [16].

5.6   PRODUCT, INVENTORY, AND SUPPLY CHAIN MANAGEMENT

Despite the application of technology and intelligence to improve supply chain management, many supply chains have never performed so poorly. In general, supply chains experience a surplus of some products and a shortage of others due to the inability to predict demand [9]. The fashion supply chain is no exception. To effectively manage a supply chain, it is important to understand the nature of the demand for the products that a company supplies.

According to Fisher [9] and as shown in Figure 5.4, product demand depends on many aspects such as product life cycle, product variety, and other factors and can fall into one of two categories: primarily functional or primarily innovative.

TABLE 5.1
Functional Versus Innovative Products: Difference in Demand

	Functional (Predictable Demand)	Innovative (Unpredictable Demand)
Product life cycle	More than 2 years	3 months to 1 year
Contribution margin	6%–21%	24%–64%
Product variety	Low (10–20 variants per category)	High (often millions of variants per category)
Average margin of error in the forecast	10.5%	50%–100%
Average stock out rate	1.5%–2%	15%–40%
Average forced end-of-season markdown as a percentage of full price	0.5%	10%–25%
Lead time required for made-to-order products	6 months to 1 year	2–3 days to 2 weeks

Note: This contribution margin equals price minus variable costs divided by price and is expressed as percentage.

Each category implies different types of supply chains. Demand forecasting for the fashion industry becomes a particular challenge because of the changing nature of the industry itself. In fact, the product life cycle is becoming shorter and shorter (short fashion). Zara is a case in point. Zara customers soon learned from experience that there would be something new in Zara stores every week and that 70% of the range would change every 2 weeks [23]. Therefore, it is particularly important to correctly forecast the amount of inventory to be manufactured and managed to avoid declining margins when products are discounted or outright losses when the products are not sold. For example, in March 2018, H&M reported a decline in sales for the final quarter of 2017 and told shareholders that it was sitting on a huge $4.3 billion stack of unsold clothing [25].

For this reason, applications of AI for supply chain management in the fashion industry are becoming increasingly common. These applications range from the use of machine learning to trend and demand forecasting to inventory management. The use of AI tools for demand forecasting allows retailers to reduce forecast errors by up to 50% while reducing inventory levels by 20%–50%, making them sell older inventory as quickly as possible [14].

Farfetch, the world's leading online marketplace for luxury goods, is driving AI at Farfetch's partners (1,500 boutiques and ≥200 brands) to improve supply chain transparency by linking their online inventory to inventory in their physical stores and services such as click-and-collect and offer in-store returns [12].

Fashion retailers are also using RFID (radio frequency identification) for real-time inventory tracking, as well as IoT and robotics to improve inventory management and streamline the supply chain. Otto, the largest online retailer of consumer fashion and lifestyle products in Germany, uses a deep learning algorithm to predict with 90%

accuracy what customers will buy before they place the order. This forecasting ability has enabled Otto to implement a warehouse management system that automatically purchases goods from a third-party source [33].

Overall, the use of AI in supply chain management also helps reduce click-to-ship cycle time and dropout rate [34]. Finally, AI is also used for warehouse management and operative purchasing. Indeed, improvements in AI and navigation technologies are enabling automated guided vehicles to move materials between buildings. Until recently, they required physical routing mechanisms such as wires or rails. Furthermore, chatbots can be used in operational purchasing, as they reduce transaction costs and sales cycle time [3].

5.7 ARTIFICIAL INTELLIGENCE FOR CUSTOMER EXPERIENCE ENHANCEMENT ONLINE AND IN-STORE

Today's consumers have more places and ways to shop in the market than ever before. Looking into the competitive scenario resulting in shorter attention spans, if you want to give better online experience to customers, you need to quickly grab their attention and make their shopping experience a pleasant and easy one. Figure 5.5 shows various AI-based tools to give today's customers a unique and customized experience.

5.7.1 CHATBOTS OR ARTIFICIAL INTELLIGENCE SMART ASSISTANTS

The growing scope and granularity of personalization in online fashion could not be managed without AI applications. The chatbots or intelligent AI assistants are the

FIGURE 5.2   Customer experience enhancement online and in-store.

most popular services for personalized online shopping. These are virtual machines that interact with customers through chat, answer customer service queries, help users navigate assortments online and in-store, recommend clothing and accessories that best suit a particular customer, as if they were human shopping assistants working 24 hours a day. From helping as a personal stylist to responding service queries, many retail brands use chatbots to help customers navigate the shopping journey. Moreover, there is a reason to believe that chatbots increase conversions by being more readily available to provide information. Chatbots are further divided into two categories: scripted and artificially intelligent. Scripted chatbots can only follow a given set of rules. This means that they can answer only the questions they are programmed to answer. Instead, AI-based chatbots are able to interpret human speech and find answers to nonpredefined questions.

In addition, there are specialized chatbots specific for retail applications. Chatbots use natural language processing, which allows marketing activities to be tailored based on linguistic context, such as through emails, social media posts, customer service contacts, and product reviews.

ASOS, an online fashion company, increased purchases by 300% through the use of a chatbot, while Levis, a pioneer in using chatbots and working with AI companies such as mode.ai, is using them to help customers find the perfect jeans suiting them [5,21]. Dior also uses a chatbot known as "Dior Insider" to interact with customers through Facebook Messenger. This service offers the ability to use slideshows and links to the site, which greatly simplifies the shopping experience.

Natural language understanding, a subset of natural language processing techniques, helps in understanding human language. In particular, it allows to conduct sentiment analysis, that is, to understand how the customer, who interacts through the chatbot, feels about a certain topic or product [15].

Previous research reported that ensuring customer satisfaction through live chat is higher (73%) than that through phone or e-mail[6]. Chatbots could become particularly sophisticated when used in combination with other technologies. For example, Nike, in partnership with advertising agency R/GA, uses IoT data to operate an AI assistance service, namely Nike on Demand, encouraging users to maintain a regular training pattern.

5.7.2 IMAGE SEARCH

Personalized shopping is also achieved through AI applications based on computer vision and augmented and virtual reality. In fact, fashion is probably one of the industries that relies the most on imagery. Image search usually refers to finding images through a text input. Search engines such as Google have introduced this possibility since 2001.

5.7.3 REVERSE IMAGE

Reverse image search is the process of using an image to find another image.

5.7.4 Visual Search

Visual search is a subset of reverse image search, referring to the ability to find and search for elements in an image. This would make it possible, for example, to search for a similar pair of shoes in an image. While computer vision enables objects to be seen, machine learning and, in particular, neural networks enable them to be recognized.

The combination of computer vision and neural networks leads to interesting use of AI in the fashion industry [15]. Online fashion retailer ASOS has developed a visual search application that turns a customer's smartphone camera into a recognition tool. The customer can photograph a product, and the ASOS application will identify the object's shape, color, and pattern and match it to its own inventory and find similar products.

For an online-only platform like ASOS, this application is an extremely important e-commerce tool [1]. Many retail brands such as John Lewis, Shoes.com, Nordstrom, Hook, and Urban Outfitters use visual search to enhance customer shopping experience. Specifically, Pinterest offers a visual search tool called Lens that allows users to take a picture of an item and search for related items online or in a Pinterest library.

The granularity of personalization has taken a significant step forward with the Sephora Virtual Artist, which combines AI-based facial simulation technology (ModiFace AI technology) with augmented reality to allow potential customers to try on cosmetic products such as lipsticks, highlighter palettes, and eye shadows at the Sephora app or website. Sephora has thus utilized digital transformation to conquer the pole position as the world's leading specialty retailer for beauty care [24].

5.8 SUBSCRIPTION SERVICES AND RECOMMENDATIONS ENGINES

The wealth of data that digital technologies provide in retail enables highly personalized experiences for customers. An interesting business model that uses data to retain customers is the subscription model, characterized by regular and recurring payments for the repeated provision of a good or service [22].

This model has been used to deliver newspapers or goods for years, but digital transformation has expanded the range of applications and spawned a variety of subscription models, namely pay-as-you-go, annual subscription fee paid at once and also different choices and surprises what they receive (chosen by the provider or preselected by the customer). Figure 5.3 shows various subscription services and recommendation engines for customers.

5.8.1 Brand Subscriptions

Brand subscriptions offer branded products that are kept secret until they reach the customer. Causebox is an example of brand subscriptions.

5.8.2 Targeted Subscriptions

Targeted subscriptions ask customers a series of questions before products are shipped, mainly to understand their product preferences. This model is used by

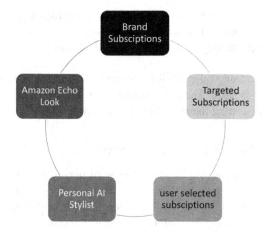

FIGURE 5.3   Subscription services and recommendation engines.

brands such as Stitch Fix. Specialized algorithms and personal stylists are used to target the customers based on the information gathered through the survey and customer feedback.

5.8.2.1   User-Selected Subscriptions

In this case, customers are offered some options, and only the selected products are delivered. Customers still have the option to buy or return. There will be a fee for the round-trip shipping cost if the customer does not buy.

5.8.2.2   Consumable Subscriptions

It offers customers the same product that is used every day (e.g., socks, underwear) at a selected frequency (once a month).

5.8.3   Rental Subscriptions

Rent the Runway offered women the opportunity to rent clothes [31]. They charge a monthly fee, and then women have the choice of what they want to borrow and then return. Rent the Runway customers are also willing to share information about their clothing, body type, and clothing fit and mention the reason for wearing it [15]. Global fashion rentals in 2023 will be worth $1.9 billion. In Italy, a start-up in Milan DressYouCan offers this type of service [10].

Merchandising personalization is also being achieved by retailers through AI-powered recommendation engines. They offer personalized merchandise recommendations based on customer data and are often suggested with phrases such as "You might also like" or "Customers also bought." Recommendation engines help users filter out massive amounts of information they do not need. There are two types of recommendation engines: collaborative filtering and content filtering. The first one uses information from a large dataset of customer purchases and other behaviors to gauge what customers want. The second uses customer actions and preferences. If a customer visits a page and buys only black shoes, then similar items will be suggested to them during their visit.

Nordstrom uses, among other things, recommendation engines. They are similar to what Netflix uses in store. These recommendation engines increase the likelihood of conversion by suggesting the right item to customers.

5.8.4 PERSONAL ARTIFICIAL INTELLIGENCE STYLIST

Having a personal stylist would be the pinnacle of personalization, but it would be prohibitive for an average person. AI makes this possible by creating a personal virtual AI stylist. This product is the culmination of the technologies presented thus far: natural language processing, natural language understanding, computer vision, neural networks, and several types of machine learning. We already know virtual assistants with automatic speech recognition such as Apple's Siri, Google's Google Home and Google Assistant, and Amazon's Alexa. The Virtual Style Assistant is a step forward because it emphasizes the use of images, the ability to take photos, image recognition, and visual search abilities, as well as recommendation engines and access to fashion products.

5.8.5 AMAZON'S ECHO LOOK

Amazon's Echo Look is the best-known example of a virtual style assistant [15]. This hands-free camera aims to give users feedback on their outfit choices. Using voice commands, Echo Look takes a picture of the outfit and suggests its merits based on trends and professional opinions of stylists. It can also provide personalized recommendations for better combinations of items based on the outfits available in the user's personal wardrobe or items available on Amazon. This service is provided by the Style Check function. Differing attitudes toward clothing choices, cultural differences between nations, and concerns about bedroom privacy make it difficult to estimate the true penetration rate of this type of product.

5.9 CUSTOMER EXPERIENCE ENHANCEMENT IN-STORE

Personalization is essential for the success of a business. Because of considerable data innovation, there is an amount of customer data available to be accessed and studied. When integrated with business data, deep learning technologies such as AI and machine learning enable fashion firms to follow individual client buying behavior.

Marketers increasingly leverage growing technology's knowledge and computational skills to comprehend shoppers' expectations and influence their experience based on purchases, favorite colors, textures, and other style preferences.

Digital technologies are also improving the in-store customer experience. Luxury fashion brands use smart mirror technologies in combination with their physical stores.

A smart mirror is a two-way mirror with an electronic display behind it. They are computers supported by a wide range of technologies, from depth-sensing hardware to software equipped with advanced computer vision algorithms [15].

The mirrors allow users not only to see how they look in a garment of different colors but also to switch the type of clothing and compare different outfits side by side. In this way, the shopping experience becomes much more pleasant and easier. Additionally, these mirrors allow customers to share images with people outside the store, who can take the images or videos home and purchase the items without having to queue at the checkout. Smart mirrors also help sellers to bridge the gap between online retail and brick-and-mortar stores.

iMirror does just that by providing an immersive shopping experience, wherein it allows customers to discover personalized offers.

Macy's also complements its physical store offering with a smartphone-based in-store assistant powered by IBM Watson's Macy's on call AI technology that allows customers to talk to digital assistants when they are in store.

In Farfetch's Store of the Future, AI technology enables better offline engagement. It features automatic customer recognition when the shopper arrives at the store and tools such as connected clothing racks, interactive holograms, and connected mirrors are used. Connected clothing racks offer a combination of RFID and ultrasound. RFID detects the product, and ultrasound detects the movement. Therefore, when a customer takes clothes off the shelf, the image of the clothes is sent to the customer's app, which creates a wish list in the store. Interactive holograms allow customers to create and order custom shoes in different leather colors. Connected mirrors allow the customers to select garments of different sizes and colors, request delivery of those items to the dressing room, and pay on behalf of them without leaving the dressing room [2].

5.10 CONCLUSION

One of the most lucrative sectors of the global economy has always been fashion. Everyone wears clothing, and the majority prefers the greatest possible fashion. Everything in a fashion industry, from the factories to the stores, will be improved by applying AI tools. Making AI part of our regular buying experience helps the business discover what customers like and dislike so that the retailers can ensure that the customer receives precisely what they want. By 2023, AI is predicted to have a $7.3 billion global market share in the fashion business. Accurate fashion trend forecasting will aid businesses in both the sale of already produced clothing and the development of fresh designs. The consumer is the most important factor, and AI assists in providing the customer with exactly what they want or in determining what they want. This guarantees that customers are satisfied and encourages them to return each season to improve their seasonal appearance.

Although some claim that technology will lead to everyone's doom, there is still opportunity for advancement in the fashion sector. The fashion business is the one industry that is earning money the quickest in the entire planet. Everyone wears clothing, and the majority prefers the greatest possible fashion. In the current environment, there are several ways AI is influencing the global fashion business to improve its performance, such as through product personalization or improved designing. These technologies have enormous financial potential and also aid in lessening the bad effects on the environment, as seen by the significant growth in investments made in them by several top fashion firms.

Smart mirrors, futuristic fitting rooms, and digital assistants in-store are only a few examples of the technologies that AI is catering to in the fashion sector to fulfil its purpose precisely for the shops as well as for the customers. Making AI part of our regular buying experience helps the business discover what customers like and dislike so that they can ensure that the customer receives precisely what they want. Accurate fashion trend forecasting will aid businesses in both the sale of the already produced clothing and the development of fresh designs. The consumer is the most important factor, and AI assists in providing the customer with exactly what they want or in determining what they want. This guarantees that customers are satisfied and encourages them to return each season to improve their seasonal appearance.

The fashion sector can make choices swiftly and effectively with the use of AI, and all processes may be thoroughly organized without incurring unnecessary expenses or pollution. AI's effects on fashion will make this sector ever-smarter in its comprehension of consumer emotions and fashion preferences and keep increasing. AI has become a crucial component of technology in the garment and fashion industries, as it gives ever-more-effective solutions to eliminate waste during cloth production. Most facets of the fashion business are changing as a result of technological advancements, from the original sketches through the fashion shows to the personalized online purchasing experience. Consumer experiences with customer service are being improved by automation and predictive modeling, while the fashion industry takes innovative steps to eliminate waste through digital fashion.

REFERENCES

[1] Boyd, C. (2017, July 15). Five ways fashion brands are using AI for personalization. Retrieved from www.clickz.com/five-ways-fashion-brands-are-using-ai-for personalization/112558/

[2] B.D.C. (2019, August 1). Farfetch Launches Its "Store of the Future". Retrieved from www.bdc-retail.com/uk/farfetch-store-of-the-future/

[3] Bharadwaj, R. (2019, July 21). Artificial Intelligence in Supply Chain Management–Current Possibilities and applications.Retrieved fromhttps://emerj.com/ai-sector-overviews/artificial-intelligence-in-supply-chain-management-current-possibilities-and-applications/

[4] BAGAAR (2022, August 12). Digital leading the way to a more sustainable textile & fashion industry. Retrieved from www.bagaar.be/insights/digital-leading-the-way-to-a-more-sustainable-textile-fashion-industry

[5] Catchoom (2018, July 9). Top 10 coolest AI trends in fashion e-commerce. Retrieved from https://catchoom.com/blog/top-10-coolest-ai-trends-in-fashion-ecommerce-merchandising-cx/

[6] Chery J.(2021,July 19). UNBXD. Evolution of Commerce: How AI is disrupting the Fashion industry. Retrieved from http://unbxd.com/blog/ai-fashion-industry

[7]   Cadogan, D. (2022, August 28). What the future holds for AI in fashion design. Retrieved from www.dazeddigital.com/fashion/article/41476/1/what-the-future-holds-for-ai-in-fashion-design

[8]   de Freitas, R. (2021, August 16). Artificial Intelligence and the Sustainable Revolution. Fashion Roundtable. Retrieved from www.fashionroundtable.co.uk/news/2018/8/30/artificial-intelligence-and-the-sustainable-revolution-in-fashion

[9]   Fisher, M. I. (1997, August 11). What is the Right Supply Chain for Your Product. Harvard Business. Retrieved from http://mba.teipir.gr/files/Fisher_What_is_the_right_SC_for_your_product.pdf

[10] Giovinazzo, E. (2019, July 25). "Fashion renting" in Italia". Business Insider. Retrieved from https://it.businessinsider.com/vestiti-e-accessori-non-si-comprano-piu-adesso-si-affittano-il-fashion-renting-e-esploso-anche-in-italia/

[11] Ilyashov, A. (2021, August 23). How All Your Clothing Returns Have Created a Ghost Economy. Retrieved from www.refinery29.com/en-us/2021/06/113662/body-labs-clothingsizing-fit-survey

[12] Intelligence Node (2021. September 1). Seven ways AI innovations make life easier for fashion companies. Retrieved from www.intelligencenode.com/blog/fashion-artificial-intelligence-ux/

[13] Intelistyle (2022, August 17). How Artificial Intelligence Is Set To Change The Next Decade of Fashion. Retrieved from www.intelistyle.com/how-artificial-intelligence-is-set-to-change-the-next-decade-of-fashion-with-paul-kruszewski/

[14] Kellet, S. (2019, September 3). How to use Artificial Intelligence in Online Fashion Retailer. Retrieved from https://exponea.com/blog/impact-artificial-intelligence-online-fashion-retail/

[15] Luce, L. (2018). Artificial Intelligence for Fashion. New York: A press–Springer Nature

[16] Musarir, D. (2022, July 27). How artificial intelligence is transforming the fashion industry. NS Business. Retrieved from www.compelo.com/the-adaptation-of-artificial-intelligence-within-the-business-of-fashion/

[17] Marchetti, F. (2021, August 23). How A.I. is shaping fashion.Retrieved from www.cnbc.com/video/2021/03/06/yoox-net-a-porters-federico-marchetti-on-how-ai-is-shaping-fashion.html

[18] Mazza, V. (2018, August 26). Artificial Intelligence and Fashion: Between Innovation and Creativity. Lexology. Retrieved from www.lexology.com/library/detail.aspx?g=12304e5f-33db-4615-998c-1b27b17e3427

[19] McKinsey & Company (2022, Septembe 5). The State of Fashion 2022: A year of awakening. Retrieved from www.mckinsey.com/industries/retail/our-insights/state-of-fashion-technology-report-2022

[20] McMillan, C. (2019). Live: Scape BLOOM: Connecting Smart Fashion to the IoT Ecology, in Artificial Intelligence on Fashion and Textiles, Wong 2019.

[21] OECD (2019, July 21). Artificial Intelligence in Society. Paris: OECD Publishing. Retrieved from www.oecd.org/publications/artificial-intelligence-in-society-eedfee77- en.htm

[22] OECD (2019, July 21). Going Digital: Shaping Policies, Improving Lives. Paris: OECD Publishing. Retrieved from https://doi.org/10.1787/9789264312012-en

[23] Pich, M., Van der Heyden, L. & Harle, N. (2020, Septembe 3). Marks & Spencer and Zara: Process Competition in the Textile Apparel Industry. INSEAD Case Studies Retrieved from https://cases.insead.edu/publishing/case?code=9693

[24] Rayome A. D. (2019, August 8). How Sephora is leveraging AR and AI to transform retail and help customer buy cosmetics. TechRepublic. Retrieved from https://steepnews24.files.wordpress.com/2018/02/sephora_cover_story_final

[25] Rudenko, O. (2018). The 2018 Apparel Industry Overproduction Report and Infographic

[26] Ramirez, R. (2021, August 6). Artificial Intelligence and the Apparel Industry. The Innovation Issue, ASI. Retrieved from www.asicentral.com/news/web-exclusive/september-2021/artificial-intelligence-and-the-apparel-industry/

[27] Ricci, C. (2021, July 27). How Technology Is Helping the fashion Industry to Advance. WTVOX. Retrieved from https://wtvox.com/fashion-innovation/how-technology-is-helping-the-fashion-industry-to-advance/

[28] Sennaar, K. (2019, August 11). AI in fashion-Present and Future Applications. Retrieved from https://emerj.com/ai-sector-overviews/ai-in-fashion-applications/

[29] Segura, A. (2018, July 13). 3D Printing. The Fashion Retailer. Retrieved from https://fashionretail.blog/2018/05/28/3d-printing-in-fashion/

[30] Schneider, C. (2021, July 25). 10 Reasons Why AI-powered, Automated Customer Service Is the Future. Retrieved from www.ibm.com/blogs/watson/2021/10/10-reasons-ai-powered-automated-customer-service-future/

[31] Schwartz, A. (2021, July 21). Costume Change: Rent the Runway wants to lend you your look. The New Yorker. Retrieved from www.newyorker.com/magazine/2021/10/22/rent-the-runway-wants-to-lend-you-your-look

[32] Thomassey, S. &Zeng, X. (2018). Artificial Intelligence for Fashion Industry in the Big Data Era (editors). Springer

[33] The Economist (2017, August 3). How Germany's Otto uses artificial intelligence. Retrieved from www.economist.com/business/2017/04/12/how-germanys-otto-uses-artificial-intelligence

[34] Weiß, M. (2016, June 30). What Does It Mean Strategically that Amazon Robots Cut "Click to Ship" Time from 1h to 15 Minutes? The Future Retail. Retrieved from https://earlymoves.com/2016/06/21/what-does-it-mean-strategically-that-amazon-robots-cut-click-to-ship-time-from-1h-to-15-minutes/

6 Artificial Intelligence for Sustainable Human Resource Management

Şerife Uğuz Arsu
Aksaray University, Aksaray, Türkiye

6.1 INTRODUCTION

In today's globalizing world, industrial revolutions and rapidly advancing technological changes lead to radical changes in human life and business life. The fact that these changes also cause transformations in the workforce draws attention to concepts such as machine learning, Internet of things and services, smart factories, cloud computing, and augmented reality. This situation pins the importance of artificial intelligence in human resources management, such as attracting, hiring, and retaining candidates, talent acquisition and talent management, and sustainable human resources (HR) in the era of artificial intelligence.

Artificial intelligence, which is widely used in almost every field and is no longer used in the sector, is a very powerful tool. In this respect, being aware of artificial intelligence applications is very important for both businesses and the world economy. With increasing changes in the nature of jobs, muscle-based physical work has drastically disappeared, brain-based jobs are growing, and labor-based industries are being replaced by knowledge-based industries. In a world that has become a global village where people interact through technology and innovation, artificial intelligence is helping businesses perform any function more effectively and efficiently (Garg, Srivastav & Gupta, 2018, p. 113).

Thanks to the rapid development in artificial intelligence and innovative technologies, the interactions between businesses, employees, and customers are also fundamentally changing, and the automation of human resource management (HRM) activities is intensifying. Accordingly, technology-supported HRM is also growing rapidly and has attracted great attention in the international business literature. However, in the HR method, smart automation technologies and technological developments bring challenges along with opportunities. These technological advances are a growing force to traditional HR functions; deep learning algorithms provide a variety of benefits for businesses, such as promoting more productive coordination and collaboration with smart objects and the Internet of things, and opportunities to manage employees, improve firm performance, improve HRM functions and reduce costs, while at the same time providing significant technological and ethical

DOI: 10.1201/9781003348351-6

challenges and job opportunities. It also brings disadvantages such as specific obso-lescence (Malik, Budhwar, Patel & Srikanth, 2022, s. 1148; Larivière et al., 2017; Cooke, Wood, Wang & Veen, 2019; Vrontis, Christofi, Pereira, Tarba, Makrides & Trichina, 2021).

However, with artificial intelligence information and communication technology, the concept of green HR has emerged to protect environmental resources, which has improved the business and increased efficiency while ensuring environmental sustainability (Garg, Srivastav & Gupta, 2018, p. 113). In this regard, this section examines the relationship between artificial intelligence and sustainable HRM, which is frequently encountered in both national and international literature. To deepen the theoretical foundations of artificial intelligence in the HRM literature at the theoret-ical level, artificial intelligence is examined from the perspective of HRM, following which the benefits of artificial intelligence are mentioned, and HR are sustainable HR. The use of technology and artificial intelligence in the transformation of HR into resources is mentioned, artificial intelligence applications are mentioned, and the issue of sustainable HRM in the era of artificial intelligence of enterprises is examined with all its conceptual aspects. The section ends with the conclusion.

6.2 ARTIFICIAL INTELLIGENCE

Artificial intelligence refers to the development of intelligent machines or computerized systems that can learn activities as humans do, react as humans do, and perform activities and tasks for many tasks in the business world (Malik, Budhwar, Patel & Srikanth, 2022). Briefly, artificial intelligence is defined as the ability of a computer system to perceive, reason, and react to the environment (Hughes et al., 2019). The main research and application areas of artificial intelligence that can be applied in industries worldwide are robotics and autonomous vehicles, Internet of things, machine learning, and deep learning (Bhave, Teo & Dalal, 2020; Bughin et al., 2017).

Although the pace of advances in artificial intelligence has been mixed, uncer-tain, and unpredictable, there have been significant advances compared with the scen-ario 60 years ago (Stone et al., 2016). The report, the results of which are shown in Figure 6.1 and prepared by Bughin et al. (2017), examines the industries that use artificial intelligence, the investments made in artificial intelligence, how these tech-nologies are used by companies that start using them across sectors, how much they are adopted, and the potential to be a major disruptor.

According to the report, investments in artificial intelligence, dominated by digital giants such as Google and Baidu, are growing rapidly. The adoption of artificial intelligence outside the technology sector has been shown to be an early and often experimental stage. The survey, which was conducted in 10 countries and 14 sectors, shows that only 20% of the firms are currently using artificial intelligence–related technology at scale or in a core part of their business. Many firms have stated that they are unsure of their business situation or return on investment. Among the sectors that adopt and use artificial intelligence, it has been seen that the sectors that are at the top of the digitalization Index, such as financial services or high technology and

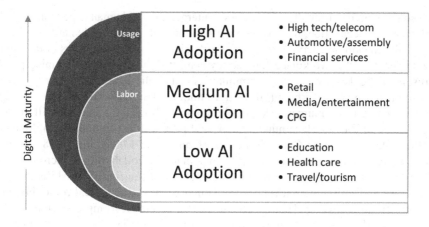

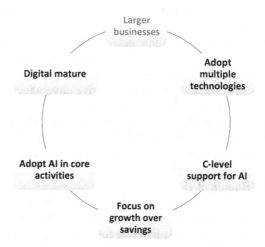

FIGURE 6.1   Adoption of artificial intelligence by companies and industries.

Source: Bughin et al., 2017.

telecom, are also at the top of the artificial intelligence adopters. Again, automakers use artificial intelligence to develop self-driving vehicles and improve operations, for example, while financial service firms use artificial intelligence for customer experience-related functions (Bughin et al., 2017).

As for the use of artificial intelligence technologies, in eight areas primarily focused on by the One Hundred Years of Research on Artificial Intelligence (AI100) Committee, there have been significant advances, especially in the last 15 years in areas such as healthcare, transportation, service robots, workplace and employment, education, low-resource and developing societies, public safety, and entertainment. With such advances in artificial intelligence, in each of these areas, for example, the social and societal risks of reduced interpersonal interactions in the field of entertainment, the difficulty of seamlessly interacting with human experts in the field of health and education, the challenge of building safe and reliable hardware in the field of transport and service robots, the difficulty of overcoming fears of marginalizing people in the workplace and employment, and the difficulty of gaining public trust in the field of low-resource communities and public safety (Stone et al., 2016).

In all these areas, although there are opinions that artificial intelligence, capable of performing human tasks, thinking and feeling like a human, will change the nature of jobs, replace human labor, and pose a threat to human employment (Huang & Rust, 2018; Cano-Kollmann, Hannigan & Mudambic, 2018, pp. 91–92); it creates many opportunities in human–machine collaboration, facilitates services and sales and business activities, benefits in acquiring these skills through expertise and training, as it relates to mathematical skills, logical reasoning, and information processing (Huang & Rust, 2018); creates learning opportunities for employees through simulations and training with artificial intelligence computer intermediaries; and improves employees' skills and improves their performance (Marinova et al., 2016; Singh, Brady, Arnold & Brown, 2016; Bell, Kanar & Kozlowski, 2008).

In the same way, it is seen that enterprises that adopt and use artificial intelligence determine a successful business rationale, establish the right data ecosystem, create appropriate artificial intelligence tools, and adapt it to capabilities, culture, and workflow processes, creating competitive advantages. However, it also poses a number of intersecting challenges between firms, developers, the government, and workers. To benefit from artificial intelligence instead of competing with artificial intelligence, the workforce needs to be re-skilled; cities and countries that are serious about becoming a global hub for artificial intelligence development need to join the global competition to attract artificial intelligence capabilities and investments (Bughin et al., 2017).

Its importance is gradually increasing in issues such as the potential to accelerate changes in profit pools, market share and revenue with the adoption of artificial intelligence in business processes, improve forecasting and sourcing in retail, electrical utilities, manufacturing, healthcare and education, optimize and automate operations, develop targeted marketing and pricing, improve user experience, creating competitive advantage, reducing employee costs, increasing customer participation, job satisfaction, and employee experience (Faliagka et al., 2014; Bughin et al., 2017; Guenole & Feinzig, 2018). This interest has led to the proliferation of studies on artificial intelligence in HRM in the recent call for articles in leading HRM journals. This increasing interest in artificial intelligence-oriented HRM has spread to the subfunctional areas of HRM such as talent acquisition and management, recruitment and retention, video interviews, training and career development, the use of artificial intelligence in talent forecasting, and coaching (Malik et al., 2022). At the same time, with regard to HRM, human–artificial intelligence collaboration and interaction, hiring, the field of AI research encompasses job switching, training, and decision-making (Vrontis et al., 2021). In this regard, one of the areas affected by artificial intelligence is HRM. Therefore, the examination of the interactions between artificial intelligence and HRM is also important in terms of both national and international literature.

6.3 ARTIFICIAL INTELLIGENCE AND HUMAN RESOURCES MANAGEMENT

Rapid technological advances, industrial revolutions, artificial intelligence, and smart automations provide a new, smart, and digital context for HR practices with higher quality HRM data, providing strong HRM ownership for businesses. Thanks to technological developments such as electronic HR, HR cloud computing, HR data mining, HR application for mobile technologies, HR big data, social media, analytics, clouds of traditional terminology, e-recruitment, e-learning, e-competence management, HR has changed the communication and HRM applications and incorporating social robots into HRM applications (Bondarouk & Brewster, 2016).

Therefore, according to Guenole & Feinzig (2018), the inclusion of artificial intelligence in HRM and the main reasons for the application of artificial intelligence capabilities in HRM as used today to increase business operations and consumer solutions is

- **To solve urgent business challenges:** According to Guenole & Feinzig (2018), the inclusion and application of artificial intelligence in HRM today are mainly to increase business operations and consumer solutions.
- **To attract and develop new skills:** To cope with the disruptions constantly occurring in the business world, artificial intelligence applications enable businesses to respond faster to opportunities and to continuously innovate and find effective ways to compete and facilitates HR departments to gain and develop step-by-step employee skills with the changing market demand.
- **To improve employee experience:** Thanks to artificial intelligence, it ensures that everything is tailored and presented to employees who expect a personalized experience rather than a standard one, in a way that works for them from the beginning to the end of the process.
- **To provide strong decision support:** Today, when the speed of change and the production of information are very high, business decisions are taken analytically, and the amount of information is very large, artificial intelligence is used in enterprises to make sense of all these and to offer suggestions. In this way, managers and employees can access the information they need, exactly when they need it.
- **To use HR budgets as efficiently as possible:** Artificial intelligence enables HR to be more efficient with the funding it provides, and HR expenditures to have a higher value for employees without reducing service levels. It also reinvests artificial intelligence HR savings into greater artificial intelligence deployment, helping to continuously develop strategic skills, increase the ability to provide exceptional decision support for employees, solve HR's business challenges, and create positive work experiences.

For the reasons listed above, artificial intelligence is used in various fields in HRM today. The areas of use of artificial intelligence in HRM are as follows (Malik et al., 2022; Guenole & Feinzig, 2018; Bogle & Sankaranarayanan, 2012; Tambe et al., 2019; Upadhyay & Khandelwal, 2018; Garg, Srivastav & Gupta, 2018; Maity, 2019; McColl & Michelotti, 2019; Jantan, Hamdan & Othman, 2010):

Attracting Candidates/Improving Candidate Experience: Artificial intelligence is used to find potential candidates who have the necessary skills for a particular position even before job seekers post a job and encourages candidates to apply for jobs if they are eligible. The use of chatbots for such purposes offers the opportunity to ask the candidates questions that are interpreted and answered. At the same time, it ensures that potential candidates who will apply for a job have information about the organization they will apply for before applying, while for businesses, it also ensures that job seekers are converted into job applicants. For example, IBM, which receives 7000 job applications and resumes per day, has reduced the time from job application to interview with the utility of chatbots, which has significantly shortened the time to hire and greatly improved the matching of candidates with the appropriate jobs.

Talent Acquisition/Recruitment/Efficient and Effective Recruitment: One of the biggest challenges faced by professionals in HRM is managing an organization's capabilities, especially providing the right person for the right job at the right time. In this sense, artificial intelligence is a new building block in the recruitment industry. In job seekers' applications on organizations' websites or job search sites, websites have the potential to use artificial intelligence to filter, identify, and match the most suitable candidate for the required job, and in these cases, artificial intelligence is used. It is possible to see which candidates are better for recruitment, and this can be used to select candidates in the future. For existing employees of an organization, algorithms are mainly used to advise employees on the actions they can take. Thanks to artificial intelligence, it is possible to predict how much time it will take to fill a job demand based on historical data. In this way, artificial intelligence can also be used to make accurate predictions of future performance based on the information collected during the job application process about the job applicant and to determine the match between the candidate's resume and job demand.

Video Calls: A video call is another artificial intelligence–based technology for recruitment and selection, which is one of the basic HRM functions. Businesses now use web-based video interviews instead of face-to-face interviews in candidate screenings and psychometric analyses for candidates.

Talent Management/Motivation Enhancement: With "talent alerts" that support the executive effectiveness of artificial intelligence, first-level managers can be notified about team members, and managers can use these alerts to make decisions about their employees in "participation analysis" applications, a technology that can analyze social media content from within the company. A talent management can be made by learning in advance who will be promoted or who will leave the job, or the social media comments posted about the organization.

Here's Retention/Smarter Fare Planning: To make optimal base wage decisions, a deep understanding of employee skills, the appropriateness of these skills, and the rate of progression toward those skills is needed. In this regard, with artificial intelligence–based wage support, decision support is provided by examining multiple variables, and the preparations that last for wage cycles can be reduced to only a few hours, and the prejudices that may occur in this process are minimized by wage determination skills.

Development and Training/Personalized Learning: Development and training needs for employees have shifted from collective "mass skill development" in the early twentieth century to personalized and individual training requirements in today's world. By integrating employee and learning data from various sources with the open learning platform, it ensures that learning can take place anywhere and anytime by bringing together all relevant content for access from any device, continuously promotes the development of employees' skills by offering personalized learning recommendations tailored to their personal learning history, and to support various needs and interests in learning content through content channels. Artificial intelligence helps people acquire strategic skills for businesses by making learning easily accessible, when and where needed.

Growth/Career Development: Utilizing artificial intelligence, bringing a good level of opportunity for employee career development to everyone in the organization is likely to benefit both employees with increased motivation and engagement, and the organization itself benefits through improved employee job performance overall.

Service: Artificial Intelligence for 24/7 Employee Engagement: Chatbots, which are an artificial intelligence technology with the widest range of applications, have wide usability in terms of both employee interaction and HR issues and functions.

Considering the usage areas of artificial intelligence listed above, businesses have now started to adopt and use the functionality of artificial intelligence in HRM in their business processes. However, little is still known about the use of artificial intelligence in HRM, whether it affects potential candidates' likelihood of being part of the hiring process and applying for a job, or what job candidates' reactions will be to organizations using artificial intelligence to uncover characteristics in terms of job suitability and performance and predict likely behaviors (Van Esch, Black & Ferolie, 2019). In this regard, there are many different opinions on the effects of artificial intelligence on HRM. While artificial intelligence provides numerous advantages to HRM employment, there are opinions that the adoption of HRM will have negative effects on the business, worker, and workplace. Researchers have pointed out to limitations such as "the complexity of the HR phenomenon, ethical and legal constraints, small data, and employee reactions to artificial intelligence management" (Bhave, Teo & Dalal, 2020; Malik, Budhwar, Patel & Srikanth, 2022; Tambe, Cappelli & Yakubovich, 2019; Hughes, Robert, Frady & Arroyos, 2019). According to Cooke et al. (2019), artificial intelligence technologies can simulate actual working conditions for recruitment and evaluation, allowing HR employees to check job applications and employee backgrounds and develop compensation packages for specific positions. According to Tambe et al. (2019), there are gaps between the potential and reality of artificial intelligence on HR. The use of artificial intelligence in HRM. The complexity of the HR phenomenon presents challenges such as the constraints imposed by small datasets, accountability questions associated with fairness and other ethical and legal constraints, and possible adverse employee responses to management decisions through data-driven algorithms. However, according to Hughes et al. (2019), artificial intelligence enables organizations to capture and process the data in real time with higher levels of employee engagement, significant savings in HRM costs through interactive artificial intelligence applications, and advances in

artificial intelligence, all of which enable organizations to incorporate the latest information into their decision-making processes even in the most complex and dynamic
competitive markets. Again, in the recruitment process, organizations can categorize
employees and make selections according to job screening requirements using information such as age, body image, economic class, gender, health status, race, and
sexual orientation related to job candidates. Although this raises ethical concerns,
it is said that personal values are of relative importance with regard to recruitment,
and artificial intelligence–powered recruitment platforms are less biased and more
objective than humans, while at the same time being able to predict likely behaviors
in terms of job suitability and performance (Vanderstukken, Van den Broeck &
Proost, 2016; Van Esch et al., 2019).

In line with this view, it is also suggested that machine learning can greatly help
HR practitioners and firms by transforming the selection process into a more systematic process by eliminating the biases of recruiters and the methods of influencing
candidates to deflect the selection process. As expected, the advantages that artificial intelligence provides to HRM employment constitute a positive development
for HRM. In the context of these positive and negative views, the model presented in
Figure 6.1 shows the use of intelligent automation technologies (artificial intelligence
and robotics) in HRM that transforms recruitment, training and job performance
practices, changes the decision-making processes of organizations, raises job change
issues, enables the cooperation between robots, artificial intelligence technologies
and employees, and offers learning opportunities for employees, and their effects and
consequences on employees and organizations. (Vrontis et al., 2021).

According to the model, the results of artificial intelligence at the individual level
revealed the effects of technology on the nature of work such as changes in duties and
qualifications and employee well-being; organizational-level results operationally,
productivity, and general performance results and transformational transformations
in terms of business making and business models. Research shows that artificial intelligence has potential in the future of HRM.

6.4   SUSTAINABLE HUMAN RESOURCES MANAGEMENT IN THE
ERA OF ARTIFICIAL INTELLIGENCE

Today, in the era of industrialization and artificial intelligence where millions of
organizations work worldwide, businesses are producing enormous amounts of
waste, which is potentially dangerous for humans and pollutes the environment
negatively. At the same time, increasing environmental concerns and environmental
problems for reasons such as globalization, climate change, population increases in
certain regions of the world, aging in some regions, increase in resource scarcity, and
decrease in biodiversity, as well as economic, social, and social models not finding
solutions to these problems, the need for environmentally sensitive activities at the
individual, organizational, and social levels is at the forefront. Subtracts, especially
when the sustainability and HRM literature is examined, demographic trends, intensive work, internationalization, globalization and diversity, emerging developments
in the labor market, and developments in employment policies have also contributed

to the development of sustainable HRM. Therefore, businesses are trying to solve environmental problems and are looking for an economically viable strategy. To implement a new strategy, HR constitutes a basic function for each enterprise (Ehnert, 2009: 94–95; Tuul & Bing, 2020; Acar & Özutku, 2022).

Therefore, the fact that sustainability studies cannot be evaluated independently of HR makes it necessary for businesses to organize personal efforts for sustainability. This requirement brings HR practices suitable for green management to the forefront. Actually, with the developments in the field of HR and the fact that HR managers benefiting from different disciplines started to develop green HR practices, new strategies, new systems, and new learning methods, applications were evaluated within HR (Uçar & Işık, 2019; Kesen, 2016, p.556). In 1996, Wehremeyer first introduced a new method of combining environmental management with HRM to solve environmental problems, and the term "green HR" was used to refer to the contribution of HR policies and practices to the environmental problem, two key elements in the form of environmentally friendly HR practices and knowledge capital protection in general (Tuul & Bing, 2020; Sharma, 2016).

In addition to developments related to green HR, artificial intelligence finds its application in every aspect of our lives, such as health, safety, productivity, and economy, with its growing applications in schools, homes, and hospitals and making rapid changes and improvements in our lives. The fact that artificial intelligence technologies, whose utility has spread over such a wide area, affect almost every sector causes technology companies such as IBM, Google, Apple, Microsoft, and Facebook to spend heavily to explore artificial intelligence applications (Stone et al., 2016). Therefore, in today's age of artificial intelligence, artificial intelligence technologies affect many areas and sectors, including HRM applications and processes. In addition, considering the ongoing debate on artificial intelligence and the ongoing research on its positive and negative effects, many businesses, HRM experts, and industry leaders are turning to establishing smart and environmentally friendly organizations. Thus, this situation, which aims to protect environmental resources and ensure environmental sustainability, has brought the concept of green HR to the agenda in the field of HRM.

Green HRM is the use of HR policies to increase environmental sustainability by supporting the efficient and sustainable use of green resources in business organizations (Sharma, 2016; Garg, Srivastav & Gupta, 2018, p. 113). Artificial intelligence is an emerging field in the field of HR technology that can replace green HRM processes or increase their effectiveness. Artificial intelligence, which provides a stage that can support all the functions of HR from recruitment and selection, job retention, training, development and performance management, and wages, helps businesses turn green in all these functions. Artificial intelligence can be used by organizations to select and screen job seekers, without using much resources for employees' commitment and career development, thus reducing the overall environmental impact (Garg, Srivastav & Gupta, 2018, p. 113). Figure 6.2 shows the green WBS (work breakdown structures) areas where artificial intelligence helps in the model developed by Garg et al. (2018).

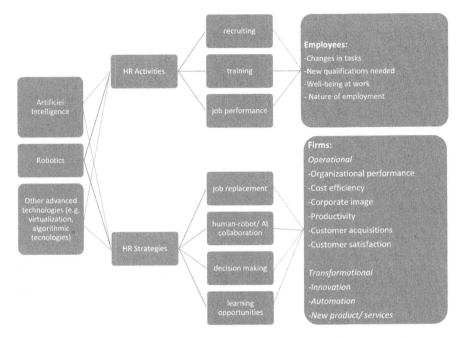

FIGURE 6.2   Effects of artificial intelligence on human resources management.

Source: Vrontis et al., 2021.

According to the model, artificial intelligence directly supports HR practices in the following green HRM areas (Garg et al., 2018). Accordingly, in "Hire," artificial intelligence also saves time by helping to parse and scan resumes. "Performance evaluation" also helps evaluate the performance of employees on a daily basis with artificial intelligence, advanced software, and data analytics. Thanks to artificial intelligence in "operations," various applications are being made available to produce instant solutions for employees and customers, and chat rooms and chat boards have been created to solve employee queries. In terms of "workforce," because companies particularly want to hire innovative and creative people, artificial intelligence saves them time by facilitating the work of recruiters in this process. Again, digitally conducting the green recruitment and selection process through an online application form, online interviews or phone interviews also helps reduce paper waste, fuel consumption, and interview travel (Tuul & Bing, 2020). Green recruitment also uses artificial intelligence, which creates job descriptions and matching resumes, for example, to find and interview candidates to fill vacant positions in Russia, for the food and beverage manufacturer PepsiCo, which has more than $1 billion in retail sales annually. Artificial intelligence software can automatically scan resumes on job sites and search for candidates with the right qualifications and make thousands of phone calls at the same time, thus minimizing the environmental impact of job interview travels and helping the company practice green HRM (Garg, Srivastav & Gupta, 2018, p. 113).

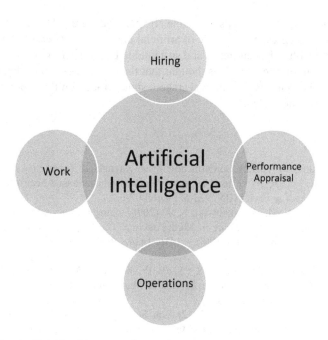

FIGURE 6.3   Artificial intelligence and green human resources management relations.

Source: Garg et al., 2018.

6.5   RESULTS

Artificial intelligence automation uses artificial intelligence applications in training, recruitment, and decision-making to create the vehicle driving the transformation of HRM. Although there are still many more ways to discover and a number of challenges to be addressed, it is important to recognize that artificial intelligence has potential in the future of HRM (Vrontis et al., 2021). This shows that artificial intelligence will also make positive contributions in terms of green HR. Green HR includes specific HR policies and practices associated with three sustainability pillars: environmental, social, and economic balance. In this regard, businesses and employers can identify employee participation and contribution to environmental management programs and the benefits of adherence to environmental performance, such as moving toward creating green products. Unions and employees can also help businesses adopt green HRM policies and practices that help protect workers' health and well-being. Finally, academics and researchers can contribute to the field by doing more research on additional data that can create a knowledge base and literature about green management in general (Sharma, 2016). All these are important in terms of protecting the environment and natural resources for future generations. The future of green HRM looks promising for employers, employees, practitioners, academics, and all stakeholders of HRM. Therefore, particularly in today's age of artificial intelligence, it is seen that there is a need to fill the literature gap on research and environmental management teaching, such as professional sustainable HR practices, green HR in environmental management strategies, and the role of artificial intelligence. Therefore, the relationship between artificial intelligence and sustainable HRM is still in the literature with parts that remain in the dark. It is thought that there are more topics that need to be revealed in this relationship, and researchers should touch on these points to reveal this relationship more clearly.

REFERENCES

Acar, S. & Özutku, H. (2022). Sürdürülebilir İnsan Kaynakları Yönetimi. Ünüvar, İ. (Eds.) içinde Sosyal, Beşeri ve İdari Bilimler Alanında Uluslararası Araştırmalar IX. (153–172), Eğitim Yayınevi, ISBN: 978-625-8468-07-6.

Bell, B. S., Kanar, A. M., & Kozlowski, S. W. (2008). Current Issues and Future Directions in Simulation-Based Training in North America. The International Journal of Human Resource Management, 19(8), 1416–1434. https://doi.org/10.1080/0958519080 2200173.

Bhave, D. P., Teo, L. H., & Dalal, R. S. (2020). Privacy at Work: A Review and a Research Agenda for a Contested Terrain. Journal of Management, 46(1), 127–164. https://doi.org/10.1177/0149206319878254.

Bogle, S. & Sankaranarayanan, S. (2012). Job Search Sustem in Android Environment– Application of Intelligent Agents. International Journal of Information Sciences and Techniques (IJIST), 2 (3), 1–17.

Bondarouk, T., & Brewster, C. (2016). Conceptualising the Future of HRM and Technology Research. The International Journal of Human Resource Management, 27(21), 2652–2671. https://doi.org/10.1080/09585192.2016.1232296.

Bughin, J., Hazan, E., Ramaswamy, S., Chui, M., Allas, T., Dahlstrom, P., Henke, N., & Trench, M. (2017). Artificial Intelligence: The Next Digital Frontier? McKinsey Global Institute. McKinsey & Company. www.calpers.ca.gov/docs/board-agendas/201801/full/day1/06-technology-background.pdf. [Erişim Tarihi: 31.08.2022].

Cano-Kollmann, M., Hannigan, T. J., & Mudambi, R. (2018). Global Innovation Networks– Organizations and People. Journal of International Management, 24(2), 87–92. https://doi.org/10.1016/j.intman.2017.09.008.

Cooke, F. L., Wood, G., Wang, M., & Veen, A. (2019). How Far has International HRM Travelled? A systematic Review of Literature on Multinational Corporations (2000–2014). Human Resource Management Review, 29(1), 59–75. https://doi.org/10.1016/j.hrmr.2018.05.001.

Ehnert, I. (2009). Sustainable Human Resource Management A Conceptual and Exploratory Analysis from a Paradox Perspective. London, New York: Springer.

Faliagka, E., Iliadis, L., Karydis, I., Rigou, M., Sioutas, S., Tsakalidis, A., & Tzimas, G. (2014). Online Consistent Ranking on E-recruitment: Seeking the Truth Behind a Wellformed CV. Artificial Intelligence Review, 42(3), 515–528. https://doi.org/10.1007/s10462-013-9414-y.

Garg, V., Srivastav, S. & Gupta, A. (2018). Application of Artificial Intelligence for Sustaining Green Human Resource Management. International Conference on Automation and Computational Engineering (ICACE–2018), DOI: 10.1109/ICACE.2018.8686988.

Guenole, N., & Feinzig, S. (2018). The Business Case for AI in HR: With Insights and Tips on Getting Started. IBM Smarter Workforce Institute, IBM. www.ibm.com/downloads/cas/AGKXJX6M. [Erişim Tarihi: 31.08.2022].

Huang, M. H., & Rust, R. T. (2018). Artificial Intelligence in Service. Journal of Service Research, 21(2), 155–172. https://doi.org/10.1177/1094670517752459.

Hughes, C., Robert, L., Frady, K., & Arroyos, A. (2019). Managing People and Technology in the Workplace. In C. Hughes, L. Robert, K. Frady, & A. Arroyos (Eds.), Managing Technology and Middle-and Low-skilled Employees (pp. 61–68). Emerald Publishing Limited. https://doi.org/10.1108/978-1-78973-077-720191005.

Jantan, H., Hamdan, A., & Othman, Z. (2010). Human Talent Prediction in HRM Using C 4.5 Classification Algorithms. International Journal on Computer Science and Engineering, 2(8), 2526–2534. ISSN: 0975-3397.

Kesen, M. (2016). İşletme Yönetiminde Sürdürülebilir İnsan Kaynakları Yönetiminin Yeri ve Önemi. İnsan ve Toplum Bilimleri Araştırmaları Dergisi, 5(3), 554–573.

Lin, R., Gal, Y., Kraus, S., & Mazliah, Y. (2014). Training with Automated Agents Improves People's Behavior in Negotiation and Coordination Tasks. Decision Support Systems, 60, 1–9. https://doi.org/10.1016/j.dss.2013.05.015.

Maity, S. (2019). Identifying Opportunities for Artificial Intelligence in The Evolution of Training and Development Practices. Journal of Management Development, 38(8), 651–663. DOI 10.1108/JMD-03-2019-0069.

Malik, A., Budhwar, P., Patel, C. & Srikanth, N. R. (2022). May the Bots Be with You! Delivering HR Cost-effectiveness and Individualised Employee Experiences in an MNE. The International Journal of Human Resource Management, 33 (6), 1148–1178 https://doi.org/10.1080/09585192.2020.1859582.

Marinova, D., de Ruyter, K., Huang, M. H., Meuter, M. L., & Challagalla, G. (2017). Getting Smart: Learning from Technology-Empowered Frontline Interactions. Journal of Service Research, 20(1), 29–42. https://doi.org/10.1177/1094670516679273.

McColl, R., & Michelotti, M. (2019). Sorry, Could You Repeat The Question? Exploring Video-Interview Recruitment Practice in HRM. Human Resource Management Journal, 29(4), 637–656. https://doi.org/10.1111/1748-8583.12249.

Sharma, K (2016). Conceptualization of Green HRM and Green HRM Practices: Commitment to Environment Sustainability. International Journal of Advanced Scientific Research and Management, (1),8, 74–81.

Singh, J., Brady, M., Arnold, T., & Brown, T. (2017). The Emergent Field of Organizational Frontlines. Journal of Service Research, 20(1), 3–11. https://doi.org/10.1177/10946 70516681513.

Stavrou, E. T., Charalambous, C., & Spiliotis, S. (2007). Human Resource Management and Performance: A Neural Network Analysis. European Journal of Operational Research, 181(1), 453–467. https://doi.org/10.1016/j.ejor.2006.06.006.

Stone, P., Brooks, R., Brynjolfsson, E., Calo, R., Etzioni, O., Hager, G., Hirschberg, J., Kalyanakrishnan, S., Kamar, E., Kraus, S., Leyton-Brown, K., Parkes, D., Press, W., Saxenian, A., Shah, J., Tambe, M., & Teller, A. (2016). Artificial intelligence and life in 2030. One hundred year study on artificial intelligence: Report of the 2015–2016 Study Panel, Stanford University, Stanford, CA. https://ai100.stanford.edu/sites/ g/files/sbiybj18871/files/media/file/ai100report10032016fnl_singles.pdf. [Erişim Tarihi: 22.08.2022].

Tambe, P., Cappelli, P., & Yakubovich, V. (2019). Artificial Intelligence in Human Resources Management: Challenges and a Path Forward. California Management Review, 61(4), 15–42. https://doi.org/10.1177/0008125619867910.

Tuul, O. & Bing, S. J. (2020). Green human resouce management: a Theoretical review. Proceedings of the Mongolian Academy of Sciences, 60 (02), DOI: 10.5564/pmas. v60i2.1357.

Uçar, Z. & Işık, M. (2019). Yeşil İnsan Kaynakları Yönetimi ve Uygulamaları. Orçun, Ç. & Sezgin, O. B. (Eds.) içinde Yeşil İşletmecilik (215–238), Ekin Kitabevi Yayınları.

Upadhyay, A. K., & Khandelwal, K. (2018). Applying Artificial Intelligence: Implications for Recruitment. Strategic HR Review, 17(5), 255–258. https://doi.org/10.1108/SHR-07-2018-0051.

Vanderstukken, A., Van den Broeck, A. & Proost, K. (2016). A., & Proost, K. (2016). For Love or for Money: Intrinsic and Extrinsic Value Congruence in Recruitment. International Journal of Selection and Assessment, 24(1), 34–41. doi:10.1111/ijsa.1212710.1111/ijsa.12127.

Van Esch, P., Black, J. S., & Ferolie, J. (2019). Marketing AI Recruitment: The Next Phase in Job Application and Selection. Computers in Human Behavior, 90, 215–222. https://doi.org/10.1016/j.chb.2018.09.009.

Vrontis, D., Christofi, M., Pereira, V., Tarba, S., Makrides, A. & Trichina, E. (2021). Artificial Intelligence, Robotics, Advanced Technologies and Human Resource Management: A Systematic Review. The International Journal of Human Resource Management. https://doi.org/10.1080/09585192.2020.1871398.

7 Relation of Human Resource Management and Artificial Intelligence

Shriniwas Singh
Bharat Institute of Technology (BIT), Meerut, India

Nisha Singh
Swami Vivekanand Subharti University
Meerut, India

Princi Gupta
JERC University, Jaipur, India

7.1 INTRODUCTION

With the introduction of artificial intelligence (AI), there has been a drastic transformation in the field of organization and its behavior as well as in the history of human resource management (HRM). The main objective of AI is that automated machine will perform the tactical tasks of humans to reduce the overburden of task and stress and to speed up the tasks. Many shifts or changes have occurred in the organization in terms of legal aspects, cultural aspects, economical aspects, and many more, but the shift from men to machine is very alarming because, if a correct ratio will not be considered, then it will adversely affect the mindset of employees and the whole HRM will become hampered. This is implicated particularly for fields such as engineering, industrial organization, and HRM.

Briefly, the main objective of analyzing the interaction between machine and men is to bifurcate the tasks between them to enhance the productivity and efficiency of the organization. The main aim of this chapter is to analyze which work is to be allocated to machine and which to men. Avery important point to be considered with regard to the association of AI and HRM is that when we fix the ratio of men and machine in the organization, we should always remember that some aspects in the organization can never be handled by the machine for tasks for which we need men; for example, if we have human resources in an organization, then there will be stress in the organization and that stress will obviously affect the working efficiency of the organization, thus hampering the performance. The stress prevailing in the organization will

DOI: 10.1201/9781003348351-7

always be handled by men working in the human resources department by utilizing their rational thinking but not by machine and its AI. If there is a human resources department in an organization, then the personnel needs to be motivated, satisfied, and stress-free and should make the employees motivated and improve their performance. We need to build a very strong organization culture, and as we know, an organization's culture cannot be built using a machine but by men. In the literature review section, we have discussed about the stress prevailing in an organization and the culture of an organization and their effect on employee performance and hence retention. Hence, before linking AI and human resources, we should always consider these points and those aspects for which we require the human resources; perhaps, new ideas can be generated regarding how AI can help human resources in getting things done quickly and effectively too.

7.1.1 What Is Human Resources Management?

HRM is a distinguished operation that is to be performed by all the executives and personnel. HRM is a special segment or specialization of management, and it has its distinguished functions such as manpower planning to compensation. The main aim of HRM is that everyone should give their best for the achievement of the goal and its HRM, which leads to drastic changes such as industrial policy.

One of the very significant roles of HRM is trade union movement, wherein the human resource personnel acts as a linking pin between the employer and the employee.

As time progresses, the upcoming era concentrates on technical updating as well as making human resource more skillful. HRM considers humans as the most valuable resource to make HR policies.

Considering this point, it can be said that now that the traditional concept of personnel management is suitably replaced with HRM.

The main functions of HRM are

- Manpower planning
- Hiring and placement
- Development and career growth
- Evaluation of the contribution of employees
- Motivating and retaining
- Stability in tenure and fringe benefits
- Making the place legal
- Linking the relationship between the employer and the employee

7.1.2 What Is Artificial Intelligence?

Tecuci (2012) described that AI is rapidly invading the whole world through the Internet, and it will show its effect not only on organizations or the business world but also on our daily life. AI was introduced in 1956 (Stuart & Norvig, 2016). In its initial stages AI was treated as a manmade machine with the ability to perceive things, including cognitive ability. AI is a machine that can speed up the tasks of the organization, but it is true that we cannot think of an organization without human resources, and if there will be human resources, then there will be some aspects that cannot be ignored such as STRESS. Stress is a big problem nowadays in any organization, and this cannot be solved by any machine unless and until the whole organization is replaced by a machine and there is no men. In the next segment, we have reviewed the literature related to stress in an organization.

Next is organization culture, which is closely linked to an organization and when we believe that all components prevail in the organization and are equally important, such as men, machine, material, and money. It is then important to maintain the culture, which is not the task of a machine, and this can be executed only by men.

7.1.2.1   Literature Review

Various published articles have been reviewed from 2013 to 2021 to understand the effect of AI on human resources working in the organization and have reported that the introduction of AI has brought drastic changes in today's era, and organizations have to be very careful in fixing the ratio of men and machine because fixing the ratio is the key to get rid-off the problem arising out of the introduction.

According to Danysz et al. (2019) and Scherer (2015), the main task or aim of introducing AI was to execute the tactical tasks using a machine.

Nowadays, AI is also called as "*human intelligence emulation*" or "*mind machine*". Carrel (2019) reported that, for example, Amazon has launched a unique kind of watch or wrist band that can track all the moves of the person wearing it. According to Oliveira (2018) and Delfanti and Frey (2020), AI is gradually improving the overall efficiency of a human. Tracking of every move of the person sets a benchmark regarding the sensitivity of AI to the environment and its reactivity (Bryndin, 2019; Carrel, 2019; Paschen et al., 2020).

Various examples have indicated that operational tasks can be expedited using AI but cognitive tasks and analytical tasks are required to be done correctly only by human resources personnel (Soni et al., 2019).

There are many things that cannot be solved by AI, an aspect that is really problematic but cannot be solved without Human resource and its rational and analytical power. As we discussed that only machine is not enough to run an organization, human resource is a vital part of the organization (e.g., for decision-making and analytical things), and human resources personnel can resolve stress, as stress will have an impact on the organization and its functioning.

1. RG Ratnawat and Dr PC Jha (2014) conducted a study on the impact of job-related stress on employee performance. The objective of the study was to determine occupational stress inducers and their impact on employee performance. Occupational stress inducers were categorized into job-specific factors, role-related factors, career factors, organizational factors, relationship factors, and miscellaneous factors. These authors have proposed a model to establish the relationship among these factors and job performance.

2. Prakash B Kundaragi and Dr AM Kadakol (2015) conducted a study on the effect of work stress of employees. Their study reveals the effect of stress on employees. They concluded that when stress is managed properly, it benefits in a productive and constructive manner. However, when the organization is in the form of distress, it affects the performance and the positive attitude of an employee. Time, pressure, and role ambiguity also reduce employee performance.

3. MDVS Mendis and WAS Weerakkody (2017) conducted research on "The impact of work-life balance on employee performance with reference to the telecommunication industry'. Based on the research, they have recommended that a better work-life balance will enhance the performance of an employee. Training programs should be conducted to highlight the importance of work-life balance. Training programs such as time management and personal effectiveness, effective workload management, personal and professional development training courses can be used to impart training. Stress management can help the organization in improving the performance of an employee.

4. A study on the impact of job stress on employee performance was undertaken by Sharmilee Bala Murali, Abdul Basit, Zubair Hassan (2017). The authors have analyzed the impact of job stress on the performance of employees in an organization.

5. Mathangi Vijayan (2018) conducted research on the impact of job stress on employees' performance. Workload was found to be the main reason for stress according to the study, and it affected the performance of an employee. Management must initiate measures such as counseling, incentives, and meditations to mitigate stress factors in an organization.

6. Samuel Ajayi (2018) conducted a study on the effect of stress on employee performance and job satisfaction in the Nigerian banking industry. The study analyzed the impact of job-related stress on employee performance and job satisfaction. Stress factors such as lack of administrative support, excessive work load, customers' problematic relations, and work-life balance were examined during the study. It was found that these factors negatively affected the performance of an employee. The study recommended that the employer should take measures to minimize stress.

7. Anu Jossy Joy and Dr GS Gireesh Kumar (2018) conducted a study on the impact of job stress on employee performance. The study was conducted to evaluate parameters that cause job stress among software professionals in Kerala. The study highlighted that job stress was found to be inversely related to employee performance. The study also found out that role ambiguity, safety, and workload played a role in deciding job stress.

8. Dr Chandra Sekhar Patro and Dr K Sudesh Kumar (2019) carried out a study on the effect of workplace stress management strategies on employees' efficiency. The purpose of the study was to find the relationship between work stress and employee efficiency in private enterprises. According to the study, stress management strategies tend to influence the performance of employees. Stress management training, yoga, meditation, and seminar on job burnouts were found to be useful in handling stress.

9. Mrs Vijayalakshmi Urs K and Dr PSV Balaji Rao (2019) conducted a study on turnover intentions among employees working in software industry. They have carried out a study to find the reasons for turnover intentions among IT employees. The main factors responsible for turnover intentions are work-life balance, salary and other benefits, training, growth & development, culture, and process. These issues are required to be studied in detail with reference to IT employees for further research.

10. Haque AU and Oino I (2019) conducted a study on "Managerial challenges for software houses related to work, worker, and workplace. Excessive control, long hours, pressure, and distraction were the main reasons for stress for an employee and stress also caused depression, other health issues, making them lose concentration and develop frustration.

11. Dhruba Lal Pandey conducted research on "work stress and employee performance" (2020). The purpose of the study was to identify the problems in reference to bankers and analyze the factors for stress among bank staff. Work overload was found to be the main reason behind the stress. The other factors causing stress were job security, poor communication, and type of work.

12. Cross Ogohi Daniel (2020) conducted a study on the effect of job stress on employees' performance. The study highlighted that negative factors had a negative effect on employee performance. The study also showed that employees thought about leaving the job due to stress. The study recommended that measures should be instituted to help employees to minimize the stress.

13. Yoko Kachi (2020) conducted a study on occupational stress and the risk of turnover. The study was conducted in a financial service company. The study concluded that occupation stress increased the risk of actual turnover.

14. Dedi Iskamto (2021) performed research on stress and its impact on employee performance. Quantitative methods were used to find the effect of job stress on employee performance. Working condition, role, interpersonal factors, career development, and organizational structure were considered as variables for work stress, whereas work result, job knowledge, initiative, mental agility, attitude, discipline, and attendance were considered as work performance variables. The study also reported that work stress affects the performance of an employee.

15. Effects of stress on employees' productivity in service industries were assessed by Dr CK Gomathy, RA Aparrajit, J Vishnu, S Vishal Rangaprasad (2022). The purpose of the study was to find the reasons for stress and ways to overcome it. The authors found out that work load and work-life balance were the main reasons for the stress and occurrence of anxiety due to stress. To overcome the stress, organizations must provide appropriate training and administration support to their employees.

In addition to stress, there are many more components of the organization that cannot be maintained or executed only by a machine, and in such cases, we need the full involvement of human resources to maintain the **culture of the organization.**

7.1.3 CONCEPT OF ORGANIZATION CULTURE

The culture of an organization comprises an organization's vision, concepts, thinking, and principles that tie it as a whole and is an organization's impression of the management, internal culture of working, interpersonal relationships with the external environment, and vision. It is based on the attitude of the employees of the organization as a whole and their beliefs and norms that have been set after gaining long experiences and are considered legal, which is called organization culture. Organization culture depends on

- The ways of working in the workplace, employer-employee relationships, and the wider community.
- The way of involvement and authority to be given to employees for decision making, innovation, and self-presentation.
- How is the delegation of authority according to the designation and
- Extent of commitment of employees toward the goal set by the organization.
  It affects the organization's productivity and performance and provides guidelines on customer care and service, product quality and safety, attendance and punctuality, and concern for the environment. "Organizational culture is unique for every organization and one of the hardest things to change." For example
  - When working in the mental health field, the company's organization culture is one of the caring and compassion aspects at all times.
  - Each company's organization culture stems from the vision of their own leaders.
  - The organization culture brings all the employees on a common platform.
  - The work culture unites the employees who are otherwise from different backgrounds.
  - Organizational culture clears the roles and responsibilities of each member. It is important for implementing the policies.
  - Culture promotes a healthy relationship among the employees.
  - It is the culture of the organizations that extracts the best out of each team member.

7.1.4 Defining Organization Culture

Therefore, how do we define organization culture?

7.1.5 Characteristics of Organization Culture

The **six characteristics of organization culture** are

- **Creativity** (risk orientation)–There are two types of companies: one that takes risk and adds new unique features to its companies and products, and the other that continues working with the same culture, without any change and risk.
- **Accuracy in work** (precision orientation)–In this context, there are two types of culture: one in which the organization can give stress on promptness and clarity of the work of its employees, and the other that gives low stress on these matters.
- **Result orientation** (achievement orientation)–Organizations give high importance to the outcome or objective achieved but not on by which way it is achieved;

these organizations are more culture oriented whereas those organizations who instruct their employees how to achieve outcome, they give more importance to the outcome, not to the culture characteristic.

- **Employee orientation** (fairness orientation)–Companies that place a high value on this characteristic of organization culture give more importance that any decision taken by them affects up to what limit to their employees; for these types of organization, respect and dignity of their employees play a vital role.
- **Coordination** (collaboration orientation)–Organizations that believe in teamwork, instead of individuality of employees, adhere more to this type of culture, and they build very healthy relationships at all levels in the organization. **Aggressiveness** (competitive orientation)–This characteristic of organization culture dictates whether group members are expected to be assertive or easygoing when dealing with companies they compete with in the marketplace. Companies with an aggressive culture place a high value on competitiveness and outperforming the competition at all costs.
- **Stability** (rule orientation)–A company whose culture places a high value on stability is rule-oriented, predictable, and bureaucratic in nature. These types of companies typically provide consistent and predictable levels of output and operate best under nonchanging market conditions.

7.1.6 ORGANIZATION CULTURE

We do not act in the same way at a rock concert as you would while watching a symphony orchestra. Even though there are no written guidelines that describe the perfect way to act at a rock concert and a symphony orchestra.

Based on the types of events, the event crowd will try to make it very clear to you that your gesture or posture will not match to the extent of suitability.

We do not dress in the same manner to attend a golf tournament as you do to be in a football game. Even though both are sports activities, there are some unstamped rules that describe what is considered the best way to dress for each type of event, and again audience will send you signals as to whether you fit to the particular event or not.

Always there is no need for any written set rules for all communities, but the crowd or, we can say, the people related to that event will let you know that whether you are following the trend, customs, and traditions or they will let you know whether or not you are appropriate for a particular event in the context of dress or etiquettes.

7.1.7 DEFINITION OF CULTURE

Culture of every organization makes the organization unique from others, as one person varies from another. The distinguished features of any organization are termed as its culture. In groups of people who work together, organization culture is an invisible but powerful force that influences the behavior of the members of that group. Therefore, how do we define organization culture?

Organization culture is a process of common thinking, principles, and attitude that tells how members or teams in an organization behave in organizations. These common thinking and principles impose strong impact on the employees of the organization and let them know how to behave. Each organization adopts unique culture that acts as policies or norms or protocol for setting their behavior in the organization.

7.1.8 Seven Unique Features of Organization Culture

- **A purpose-driven company culture**–In an organization with a purpose-driven company culture, employees are keen on achieving their goals; they concentrate on immediate- and long-term goals, and for this, they shift their resources and manpower toward the achievement of the goals, resulting into strong, sustainable culture.
- **Effective communication patterns**–This includes three main features–clarity, courtesy, and proactively.
  Clarity is a very important element for communication when anything is communicated in an effective way and it is all very easy for both leaders and subordinates to work upon, as a leader can express his expectations clearly and subordinates can express their problems or keep their point of view without creating any chaos.
  Courtesy means a very important aspect in communication because when information is transmitted with dignity and respect, there is full chance of clear feedback that results to cooperation in a relationship.
  Proactively is very beneficial in communication in which discussion is based on the present situation instead of the past situation because past discussion leads to blame-game but proactively concentrates on at-the-spot situation.

- **A culture of feedback**–Adopting feedback culture is great because it helps in knowing the point of internal and external persons that how we are accomplishing your task.
- **Embracing diversity**–Organizations that include diversity have more tolerance power, as they make certain common culture that can suit everyone in the organization who came from different places and cultures. This type of organization evaluates how cultural differences affect people at work and up to what extent the organization has to interact without discrimination or perception distortion.
- **Teamwork**–Teamwork focuses on the team rather than on the individual. It is a misconception that the work of a team depends on the personalities of the team members, but the real factor is that the team works efficiently when the target is conveyed properly and when the target is clearer than group cohesiveness increases and teamwork becomes easier.
- **Engagement and loyalty**–Employee engagement is a very challenging and discussive matter in the current scenario. The main issue is that, nowadays, employees tend to be fully engaged, but they need to understand what the engagement is really like. In the 1990s, William Kahn, profess or of organization behavior at Boston University, introduced the term "engagement" based on his

observation that people have a choice as to how much of themselves they are willing to invest in their jobs. Kahn discovered that employees were far more emotionally and physically engaged when they experienced the following condition: the conclusion is that "Employee engagement cannot be brought; it should be earned."

- **Growth and development**–Growth-oriented organizations motivate their employees for growth, and they also give opportunities in terms of innovation and development as one individual or as a team. They regard growth as a vital element or determinant in employee engagement. There are different parameters of growth.

Position-based growth–This subset of people who are hardworking wants to upgrade their position and have desire to get promoted, and if they do not find such kind of opportunity, they leave their present job.

Professional growth–These professionals seek the opportunities to improve their skills; their desire is to achieve progressive professional growth, and they get this growth from their workplace.

Financial growth–Financial upgradation and growth play an important role in the case of employee engagement, as it indicates the value of the company as well as the individual professional; none of the individual likes to work on dry promotion if they feel the lack of financial growth leads to disengagement and employee turnover.

Employees perform best when the environment is growth oriented, which is an essential characteristic of successful company cultures.

7.1.9 Types of Organization Culture

The culture of the company is not at all a traditional concept, but it is the most challenging and dynamic concept. Each organization has their own and unique culture difference is of being their logical. Organization culture can be of two kinds: strong and weak. Employees adopt their organization's culture up to the extent of being strong and weak.

Strong organization culture: According to Madu, a strong culture can be called strong only when values and beliefs are kept very strongly and are shared in very wide range, and the culture requires to be unique and added with specific investment and should be unlikely to change. More universal the meaning is shared among the organization's members, the stronger the culture. Cultures where employees' goals are aligned to the organization's goals are often thought of as successful cultures.

Weak organization culture: In the weak culture, values and beliefs are not strongly and widely shared and every individual in the organization works on their own personal principles.

7.1.10 Weak Culture

A weak culture of an organization could be a loosely knit one. Sometimes, it may push an individual thought's and contributions, and in a company that needs to grow through innovation, it could be a valuable asset, sometimes not. According to Deal and Kenndy (1982), a weak culture of organization could be a loosely joined one. Rules are imposed strictly on the employees that may create diversity between the person's personal objectives and organization goals.

7.1.11 Dimensions of Organization Culture

In the year 1980, one study was conducted by Hofstede, and in this study, he gathered data from IBM from approximately more than 50 countries, and from this study, he generated four dimensions of organization culture:

- Power distance
- Individualism
- Uncertainty
- Masculinity

After some years, the study was taken ahead with Bond by Hofstede, and by their combined efforts, they added the fifth dimension, that is, short-term v/s long-term orientation, and their study was conducted on scholars of 23 countries using a questionnaire.

Even though Hofstede has worked very keenly, there is certain criticism by the researchers.

Shortcomings of Hofstede's instrument for measuring organization culture– The first and foremost criticism of Hofstede's was based on data from one company, which was not sufficient enough to obtain valid information regarding the culture of the entire country.

The finding of one company cannot be implemented on the overall culture to determine culture dimensions (Graves, 1986; Olie, 1995).

Udai Pareek's OCTOPACE Dimensions–In this study, we will be using Udai Pareek's OCTAPACE. Udai Pareek specifically measures organization ethos in eight values:

Openness, Confrontation, Trust, Authenticity, Proaction, Autonomy, Collaboration, and Experimentation.

The most important aspect of organization culture is the values it practices. Eight values may be examined to develop the profile of an organization culture, called OCTAPACE (Openness, Confrontation, Trust, Authenticity, Proactively, Autonomy, Collaboration, and Experimenting).

- **Openness**–the comparative openness in the system should influence the design of HRS. Organizations can be classified in continuum from completely open to completely close. No organizations may be on the two extremes of the continuum. However, they will tend to be toward one or the other end. The degree of openness of the organization will be an important factor in determining the nature of various dimensions of HRD being designed, as well as the way in which these dimensions should be introduced. Organizations that are fairly open may start with several confronting designs of HRS.

- **Confrontation**–This term is used in relationship with the problem putting the front rather than the back to escape the problems. A better term would be confrontation exploration that implies facing a problem and working jointly with other concerned people to find a solution. If an organization encourages people to recognize a problem, then bring it to the people concerned and explore with them to search possible ways of dealing with it.
- **Trust**–Introducing the HRD in an organization trust in another factor that should be considered along with openness. If the level of trust is low, then the various dimensions of HRS are likely to be seen with suspicion; therefore, the credibility of the system may go down. In such a case, the system, if introduced, may become a vital aspect and cease to perform the main functions for which it was meant.
- **Authenticity**–This aspect is the value underlying trust. It is the willingness of a person to acknowledge the feelings the person has, and accept them as well as others who relate to the individual as persons. Authenticity is reflected in the narrowest gap between the stated vales and the actual behavior. This value is important for the development of a culture of mutuality.
- **Proactive**–can be contrasted with the term "react." In the latter, the action is in response to an act from some source, while in the former, the action is taken independently of the act from another source. Being proactive means anticipating issues in advance to take advantage of this undertaking conflict or responding to needs of the future and, in fact, creating the future.
- **Autonomy**–nothing but willingness to use power without fear and helping others to do the same. It multiplies power in the system, and the basis is collaboration.
- **Collaboration**–involves working together, with both people's strengths for a common cause. Instead of solving problems by themselves, individuals share their concerns with one another and prepare strategies and work out action plans and implement them together.
- **Experimenting**–as a value emphasizes the importance given to innovating and trying out new ways of dealing with problems in the organization.

7.1.12   Positive Organization Culture

Flamholtz and Randle (2011)–described that other than a strong culture, efforts should be made to create positive culture, to improve the organization's condition and profitability.

According to Childress (2013)–to develop a harmonious relationship among employees and to build a healthy relationship among superiors and subordinates, all of which can lead to a positive culture.

Inabinett and Ballaro (2014)–described that after many studies, they found that there is a positive correlation between positivity in culture and its success.

Andish et al. (2016)–Positive culture helps in building trust among members of any organization. According to them, owners of Google and Apple also advocated for adopting positive culture in the organization.

According to Simoneaux and Stroud (2017)–Members as well as stakeholders of any organization get attracted and attached by a positive organization culture.

7.1.13 WORK CULTURE: DIMENSIONS AND VARIOUS STUDIES

Four basic dimensions or conceptual domains appear to be common in most questionnaires.

First, "people orientation" reflecting perceived support, cooperation, mutual respect, and consideration between organizational members is prevalent. This orientation refers, for instance, to the group culture quadrant of the competing values model. Second, the dimension of "innovation," indicating general openness to change and propensity to experiment and take risks, is also apparent. In Reynolds's instrument, risk and innovation are opposed to safety and stability. Third, "control" is another significant component. It focuses on the level of work formalization, the existence and implementation of rules and procedures, and the importance of the hierarchy. This construct is similar in tone to the "bureaucratic" dimension prevalent in some instruments (e.g., in the organizational culture index, competing values model, and Reynolds' instrument).

Finally, "results/outcome orientation" is another core dimension that measures the level of productivity or performance expected inside an organization.

According to Ginevičius and Vaitkūnaitė, the multidimensional nature of organization culture should be investigated in terms of involvement, collaboration, transmission of information, learning and care about clients, strategic direction, reward and incentive system, system of control, communication, coordination, and integration. Pryce reported on the profile of organization culture in hotels. She identified 28 dimensions of organization culture and suggested that the organization culture of hotels overall could be described as one placing the greatest emphasis on the importance of job, rituals, customer orientation, training, role ambiguity, values, team spirit, and being a valued member.

Pareek defines the concept of ethos as the underlying spirit of character or group and is the root of culture. He defines organizational ethos as eight dimensions relevant to institution building. These eight cultural dimensions are also called as OCTAPACE. In addition to being an acronym for the eight dimensions, OCTAPACE symbolizes "octa" or eight and "pace" or steps to create functional ethos. The eight dimensions of OCTAPACE culture are Openness, Confrontation, Trust, Authenticity, Proactive, Autonomy, Collaboration, and Experimentation.

Building a culture that is ingrained in the OCTAPACE values will help in creating an organization that is agile, responsive, and alive to changes. Mehn Hee Yoon suggested several managerial implications on the basis of his empirical findings. He stated that the employee perception of work culture not only influences organizational variables such as work effort and job satisfaction but also affects service evaluation by customers. He concludes that it is necessary to explicitly design and establish various organizational policies such as employee empowerment, detailed service codes, service performance reward/award, and employee education/training to develop a system that will facilitate a service-oriented environment and supportive management.

Jafari and Rezaei, in their research to define the dimensions and components of effective organization culture, extracted nine dimensions and 42 components as its constituents. A model was designed that included five basic elements of philosophy and aims, theoretical basics, conceptual framework (scientific culture, innovation/ entrepreneurship culture, quality-oriented culture, knowledge-oriented culture, programming culture, answering culture, collaboration/contribution culture, life-time learning culture, and networking culture), executive stages and assessment, engineering. Gillespie and Consulting emphasize in their study that organization culture relates significantly and positively to employee and customer satisfaction. By extension, diagnosing and changing an organization's culture may thus be a viable way to improve employee and customer satisfaction.

7.1.14 ARTIFICIAL INTELLIGENCE IN HUMAN RESOURCE MANAGEMENT

AI technologies give an important chance to make more effective human resource operations, such as self-motivation Exchange of views, placements, talent acquiring and management, payroll, performance appraisal, and execution of rules and regulations. In this era, only any organization can just not rely upon human resources, and AI's importance and its role are reaching new heights. AI has an important effect on how we run our business. Human resources executives believe that merging AI into human resources administration functions will uplift and excel the overall organization. This will enhance the capabilities, competitive intelligence will save the time, budget and will uplift the Information system of organization. According to Nilsson (2005), a machine will be called as human–level AI when it reaches the level of performing all tasks of human resources.

Employees and AI are interlinked to yield an enhancing amount of HR data in the market, and the use of machine analyses offers knowledge into how to work. The well-being of any organization depends on the proper combination of men, machine, material, and money. When combined properly, this combination enhances the performance of an organization and reduces the cost. AI will help to efficiently automate many back-office functions for reliable human resources transactions and service delivery. The launch of machine in HRM and in placement can be called as "HR Revolution," as AI changes the recruitment industry by replacing routine tasks that have been conducted by human recruiters (Upadhyay & Khandelwal, 2018).

Introducing AI is not so easy, as it has various obstacles that retard the process. One of the very important barriers are financial barrier.

- **Skill gap**: it can be expensive and difficult to find properly educated or skilled people.
- **Confidentiality**: confidential human resources data must be accessed securely and available only to the authorized person.
- **Procurement**: as with other innovative technologies, AI requires deep learning and regular review and updates.
- **Connectivity:** data availability is limited, due to the human resource trend toward SAAS (Software as a Service).
- **Feasibility**: many products and services are feasible based on proof-of-concept only. However, the cost of using AI can be justified for the following human resource functions:
- Optimum utilization of HR professionals' tasks instead of wasting them on administrative tasks

- Reducing the burden of shared service centers and help desks by performing human resource transactions and providing answers for routine queries
- Recruiting and retention
- Measuring return on investments
- Reducing bias in human resource decision-making

If organizations wish to remain competitive in today's global economy, then they will need to look at ways to incorporate conversational AI for human resource transactions in their decision-making process. Organizations should rely on AI to perform administrative duties so that human resource departments may become more efficient. Human resource professionals will be able to focus more on strategic planning on an organizational level. AI processes data more quickly than the average human. It is also able to cast a wider net, bringing attention to people who employers might not have considered or who may not even be looking for work. Having more qualified candidates from the beginning shortens the process, enabling managers to dedicate more time to analyzing human resource data and improving strategic planning.

7.1.14.1 Significance of the Study

This chapter attempts to determine the techniques or strategies to find out the middle pathways to bring out the balance between AI and human resource. Undoubtedly, machine cannot replace humans fully; it can only be a support system for speeding up the work of any organizations (error-free work) but the main talent of human resource as analyst or director can never be undertaken by machines. The second part of the chapter emphasized on the strategies to build a perfect structure of the organization in context with AI and skillful workforce to be perfect enough to work with hand-in-hand with machines. Thus, an organization can compete the today's era of AI in technology as well as with skillful workforce who can cope-up with the machine era, and this can only be achieved when there is proper talent management and there should a good talent reservoir. The third section will suggest the middle pathways to bring out the balance between AI and HRM.

7.2 METHODOLOGY

The research will be conducted in the form of review research:

The first part will be "exploratory research" to build upon conceptual base, followed by "descriptive research."

Year wise–cited articles-

7.3 RESEARCH DESIGN

a) **Data Collection**
   i) **Secondary data:** Scopus online database from 2007 to 2021. (books, journals, articles, and research papers)
b) **Sampling Design:**
   i) **Sample Unit:** Scopus online database.

      ii) **Sample Size:** Research papers–629, published articles-342, Year-wise cited articles-90

      iii) **Sampling Method:** Stratified random sampling.

      iv) **Sample Groups:** Students

  c) **Statistical Design:** Review method based on papers, articles arranged in chronological order, and conclusion drawn out of that

Literature was considered from the Scopus online database from January 2007 to December 05, 2021. To extract full information, the researcher incorporated steps to obtain the right information to draw results, discussion, and food for future research. Reviews, book chapters, editorials, and the information shown in Table 7.1 and Table 7.2.

After going through the abstracts, the researcher reviewed intensively and considered only the related material, thus removing the other articles. Again, the research was limited to business studies and record-keeping and sociology by using keywords or titles through search query (TITLE-ABS-KEY ("artificial intelligence") AND TITLE-ABS-KEY ("human resource management")) AND (LIMIT-TO

TABLE 7.1
Subject-Wise Distribution of Papers

Subject Area	Number of Papers
Human resource management	123
Engineering	101
Principles and practices of Management	13
Business, Management and Accounting	50
Decision sciences	78
Social sciences	56
Economics, Econometrics and Finance	43
Talent management	39
Communication skills	23
Environmental science	**19**
Earth and Planetary Sciences	15
Energy	14
Materials science	12
Chemical engineering	8
Health professions	8
Agricultural and Biological Sciences	6
Arts and Humanities	6
Psychology	6
Multidisciplinary	3
Biochemistry, Genetics, and Molecular Biology	2
Chemistry	2
Neuroscience	2
Total	629

Source: Scopus online database

TABLE 7.2
Article Publication Platform

Subject Area	Number of Papers
Conference paper	223
Article	102
Book chapter	6
Conference review	3
Review	5
Book	2
Editorial	1
Total	342

Source: Scopus online database

TABLE 7.3
Year-Wise Cited Articles

Year	No. of Articles
2020	1^2
2019	11
2018	6
2017	4
2016	2
2015	5
2014	1
2013	I
2012	0
2011	39
2010	2
2009	0
2008	3
2007	1
Total	90

Source: Scopus database

(SUBJAREA, "BUSI")); here the researcher obtained many documents and extracted the summary and topic of the research as a project after the intense analysis; the researcher found that only few were relevant. So, the research accepts these as models, research, etc., and the description is shown in Table 7.3 and Table 7.4.

As the final step, the researcher used selected papers for analysis, and based on that, the present study answered the research question through the results and discussion.

TABLE 7.4
Article Publication Platform

Platforms	No. of Articles
Conference paper	54
Article	33
Book chapter	2
Conference review	2
Review	2
Total	93

Source: Scopus database

RESULTS AND DISCUSSION

Data analysis revealed that AI has its importance in various fields and departments of the organization such as HRM, talent management, human resource planning, compensation management, accounting, recruitment and selection, and training but simultaneously for rational thinking and decision–making, for which both men and machine are required. Introduction of AI causes change, and to cope up with this change and make human resources aware and convinced for introducing machine, the Kurt Lewin model of change is required to be introduced so that men and machine can work hand-in-hand simultaneously to enhance the productivity and achieve the goal.

LIMITATION AND FUTURE RESEARCH DIRECTION

Every study has a limitation, and the present study discussed nine functional areas of human resources. The study can be extended by more of the segment and also a comparative study is to be done to analyze the difference between the rational decision making and the cognitive capacity of machine with men.

REFERENCES

Abdeldayem, M.M., & Aldulaimi, S.H. (2020). Trends and opportunities of artificial intelligence in human resource management: Aspirations for the public sector in Bahrain. *International Journal of Scientific and Technology Research, 9*(1), 3867–3871.

Ahmed, O. (2020). Artificial intelligence in human resources. *International Journal of Research and Analytical Reviews, 5*(4), 971–978.

Anderson, J., Rainie, L., & Luchsinger, A. (2018). Artificial intelligence and the future of humans. Pew Research Center.

Ben-Ari, D., Frish, Y., Lazovski, A., Eldan, U., & Greenbaum, D. (2017). *Danger, will robinson?* Artificial intelligence in the practice of law: Analysis and proof of concept experiment. *RichmondJournal of Law& Technology, 23*(2), 2–55.

Berhil, S., Benlahmar, H., & Labani, N. (2020). A review paper on artificial intelligence at the service of human resources management. *Indonesian Journal of Electrical Engineering and Computer Science, 18*(1), 32–40.

Bhardwaj, G., Singh, S.V., & Kumar, V. (2020). An empirical study of artificial intelligence and its impact on human resource functions. In *2020 International Conference on Computation, Automation and Knowledge Management (ICCAKM)* (pp. 47–51). IEEE.

Bryndin, E. (2019). Robots with artificial intelligence and spectroscopic sight in the hi-tech labor market. *International Journal of Systems Science and Applied Mathematics, 4*(3), 31–37.

Bryndin, E. (2020). Formation of technological cognitive reason with artificial intelligence in virtual space. *Britain International of Exact Sciences (BIoEx) Journal, 2*(2), 450–461.

Caldwell, R. (2003). The changing roles of personnel managers: Old ambiguities, new uncertainties. *Journal of Management Studies, 40*(4), 983–1004.

Caldwell, R. (2008). HR business partner competency models: Re-contextualising effectiveness. *Human Resource Management Journal,* 18(3), 275–294.

Carrel, A. (2019). Legal intelligence through artificial intelligence requires emotional intelligence: A new competency model for the 21st century legal professional. *Georgia State University Law Review* 35(4), 1153–1183.

Carter, D. (2018). How real is the impact of artificial intelligence? The business information survey 2018. *Business Information Review, 35*(3), 99–115.

Chapuis, R. (2018). Les impacts de l'intelligence artificielle sur l'emploi: comment favoriser la complémentarité avec l'humain et faire émerger de nouveaux types de métiers?, *Annales des Mines, 1,* 38–43.

Danysz, K., Cicirello, S., Mingle, E., Assuncao, B., Tetarenko, N., Mockute, R., & Desai, S. (2019). Artificial intelligence and the future of the drug safety professional. *Drug safety, 42*(4), 491–497.

De Mauro, A., Greco, M., Grimaldi, M., & Ritala, P. (2018). Human resources for Big Data professions: A systematic classification of job roles and required skill sets. *Information Processing & Management, 54*(5), 807–817.

De Stefano, V. (2019). Negotiating the algorithm: Automation, artificial intelligence, and labor protection. *Comparative Labour Law & Policy Journal, 41*(1), 15–46.

Delfanti, A., & Frey, B. (2020). Humanly extended automation or the future of work seen through amazon patents. *Science, Technology, & Human Values, 46*(3), 1–28.

Dhanpat, N., Buthelezi, Z.P., Joe, M.R., Maphela, T.V., & Shongwe, N. (2020). Industry 4.0: The role of human resource professionals. *SA Journal of Human Resource Management, 18,* 1–11.

8 Leveraging Artificial Intelligence for Talent Management

Sowmya G.
Symbiosis Centre for Management Studies, Nagpur,
Constituent of Symbiosis International University, Pune
Maharashtra, India

Aruna Polisetty
Symbiosis Centre for Management Studies, Nagpur
Constituent of Symbiosis International University, Pune
Maharashtra, India

Ganesh Dash
College or Administrative and Financial services
Saudi Electronic University, Riyadh, Saudi Arabia

8.1 INTRODUCTION

Talent management is increasingly gaining recognition and developing as a matured human resource (HR) intervention by both researchers and HR practitioners. Talent management, which has, so far, remained as a miniscule idea of academic interest, has many conflicting definitions and criticisms (Lewis & Heckman, 2006). While it has been criticized for rebinding of the core HR initiatives, the lack of sound empirical evidence in this discipline has a lamenting gap. Talent management in many countries is remaining highly dysfunctional, leading to ultimate failure in people management, especially during uncertainties (Cappelli & Keller, 2014). In general, talent management involves anticipating the human capital requirement of the organization through well-defined strategies and practices. It involves a systematic approach wherein the employee talent can be identified, deployed, nurtured, developed, and retained for the benefit of the organization (Collings et al., 2015). As the workplace is facing radical shifts in the way people were managed, traditional models of talent management will not be effective. A reengineered talent management framework that encompassed the varied needs

DOI: 10.1201/9781003348351-8

of employees, work lace diversity, and environmental uncertainties must be developed and implemented (Schiemann, 2014). The modern talent management framework requires a talent-on-demand framework that stays equivocally with the just-in-time manufacturing. The most innovative dimensions to talent management involve integrating the principles of supply chain and operation management in the talent management practices. Integrating talent management with other managerial functions typically answers two questions—whether to make or buy talent in the organization and how the core talent can be retained in the organization. Even though companies have succeeded in attracting and developing talent, the failure to retain the talent will drain the organizational resource and can even benefit the competitors (Bethke et al., 2011). Inventing talent management for the twenty-first century requires heavy investment in technology integration and allied technological products (O'Neal & Gebauer, 2006). One of the most feasible and effective technological innovations in the field of talent management is artificial intelligence (AI). The use of high-powered technology leads to talent analytics, which becomes a core element of strategic HR management. The presence of SHRM itself will attract and create a talent pool that optimizes the employee job performance in the short run and organizational performance in the long run (Ashton & Morton, 2005). Technology-based talent management involves a blend of social media, analytics, robotics, big data, AI, and other software applications. Even though both technology and talent management are visible in companies as fragmented pieces, the impact of technology in creating a better talent management framework remains as an under-researched area (Dries et al., 2013; Thunnissen, 2016; Garrow & Hirsh, 2008; Sonnenberg et al., 2014). Even though technological integrations have benefitted talent management, the negative implications should not be neglected (Swailes, 2013). The increased adoption of technology outpaces face-to-face interactions in the recruitment process, which proves fatal in many organizations. As Albert Einstein rightly pointed out, "human spirit must prevail over technology," every aspect of innovation in technology should move toward sustainable talent management in organizations.

Sustainable talent management involves strategies, practices, and interventions to attract, develop, and retain organizational talents, capabilities, and competitive advantage for the present and uncertain future scenarios (Saleh & Atan, 2021). A dynamic and sustainable talent ecosystem answers how effectively the existing talent management systems is contributing to organizational effectiveness without compromising on the future needs. The concept of talent sustainability is complex and interrelated; hence, it cannot be confined as the sole responsibility of HR management (Ogbazghi, 2017). Talent sustainability is perceived as the mutual responsibility of everyone involved in the organization—not just the leaders, but also the employees. The board of directors must act as talent overseers who ensured the overall organizational effectiveness through talent sustainability (Mohapatra & Sahu, 2018). The CEO and senior leaders act as talent orchestrators who are responsible for aligning organizational resources with talent management objectives and laid down the strategies to achieve it. The line managers act as talent management influencers who are responsible for effective succession planning in companies. Every HR leader act as a talent accelerator who paves the way for talent identification to talent development (Necula & Strîmbei, 2019). The employees constitute the core talent who become the central focus of talent sustainability, which has to be managed effectively for meeting the present and future organizational needs. This chapter has been organized around the contours of sustainable talent management through technological lens by way of AI. The researchers discuss the potential challenges in building a sustainable talent management architecture and address the core benefits of AI in talent management. Accordingly, the researcher's strategy is to highlight the pitfalls in technological integration in talent management and march toward a sustainable talent management culture.

8.2 CHALLENGES IN GLOBAL TALENT MANAGEMENT AND STRATEGIC OPPORTUNITIES FOR TALENT SUSTAINABILITY

In today's workforce, characterized by rapidly moving, volatile, and uncertain work environment, there are many challenges encountered by global talent management. Talent management challenges at the global level are considered relevant and are embedded in every HR practice, which strategically have to answer the situations of assigning the right person to the right job at the right time in the right role (Schuler et al., 2011). The global challenges are discussed here in line with the concept of "Porters Diamond," which discussed four key attributes for the competitiveness of a nation including strategy, structure, rivalry, demand conditions, supply networks, and factor endowments. The factor endowment refers to the qualitative and quantitative abilities of the country in developing its workforce capacities to meet the global workforce challenges. The expansion of workers' mobility and dramatically expansion of economies across countries has resulted in four major global challenges for talent (Tarique & Schuler, 2010). Studies on global talent management challenges have conceptualized these on the basis of an evolving and dynamic business environment (Collings, 2014). The researchers discuss four major talent management challenges here that are to be addressed by building a talent sustainability framework.

8.2.1 GLOBALIZATION AND ALLIED CHALLENGES

The processes of integrating the world market together have created numerous talent management issues globally. The challenges due to globalization cover four major dimensions, namely the issues of wage differentials, intense competition, changing customer needs, and diverse individual aspects. As the international market is evolving, there is a high degree of wage differentials that affects the rewards and recognition component in the talent framework. Also the intense competition amplified by increased labor mobility adds to more retention headache to the global HR managers (Minbaeva & Collings, 2013). The drastic changes in the customers' needs and expectations call for more talented employees and rich expertise. Also, the individual needs in the employees are heterogeneous and require thoughtful interventions to align them with the organizational objectives. The traditional talent management systems will not work effectively in the changing trends of globalization. This necessitates more effective people-oriented talent structure that can tap into global competitive advantage.

8.2.2 CHANGING DEMOGRAPHICS

The composition of the world population is witnessing rapid pacing changes that require customized talent management practices. Many developed countries' economies face the challenges of aging population, whereas the developing economies have to cope up with the changing need of millennial employees (Anlesinya et al., 2019). The contribution of women employees is increasingly counted for organizational growth. With new methods of working such as telecommuting, virtual office, and alternative working pattern, the organizations have to strategically plan and execute talent management interventions that suit the need of all minority groups in the organization (Farndale et al., 2010).

8.2.3 DEMAND FOR MORE COMPETENCIES AND MOTIVATION

The dramatic changes in the nature of work, emergence of new job, and new job roles required increased skills and competencies in the labor market. The needs for effective technical competencies are manifold in the global market. Another crucial challenge in global talent management is the managerial efficiency to attract and retain motivated employees (Sidani & Ariss, 2014). Self-motivated employees have high focus and energy and work with high productivity. According to report of Mckinsey (2009), 29% of the global workforce is considered highly motivated, and a vast majority of 62% are considered moderately motivated. The organizations have to design and develop talent management interventions in such a way that it attracts the best competencies of the labor market and keep them motivated (Collings & Isichei, 2018).

8.2.4 SUPPLY OF HIGH-QUALITY WORKERS

The fourth major challenge in global talent management is the availability of the talented workforce for the requirements of the organization. The issues of talent shortages should be effectively tackled with. The organization should reach out to cross-countries labor market to attract the required talent in the organization (Stahl et al., 2012). Attracting talent during deficiencies also shoots up the cost to the companies. When times change, there will be excess of competencies in the market that should be also taken care of by the organization.

The global talent management challenges require a robust mechanism that takes care of the present organizational needs without compromising on the future growth of the companies (Garavan, 2012; Skuza et al., 2013; Morris et al., 2016). Hence, building a talent sustainability framework is of strategic imperative for the companies. In the following sub-section, the researchers discuss some of the viable solutions for meeting the global challenges and achieving talent sustainability.

8.2.5 Building a Talent Sustainability Framework

The talent sustainability framework has been operationalized based on the existing literature and lamenting gap in talent management, organizational practices, and need for addressing talent sustainability. This framework is a descriptive model for addressing the needs of talent sustainability by balancing talent strategies and elements of organizational culture. There are eight pillars for sustainable talent management that are embedded and intertwined with the organizational practices for the benefit of each other. A sustainable talent management strategy articulates effective ways of identifying, deploying, developing, and retaining employee capabilities for tangible organizational outcomes. Metrics have become an indisputable component in talent sustainability. They provide instant feedback about the effectiveness of various talent management practices and measure the outcomes of talent management.

The executive commitment and engagement form the first important pillar of talent sustainability. The organization should have effective managerial support and involvement in the talent development process. One of the primary responsibilities of the board is to ensure and promote 100% employee engagements. Every employee and

FIGURE 8.1   Talent sustainability framework.

the respective talent and skill should be fully engaged by the organization for effective outcomes. The organizational commitment in engaging the employee talent should be visible and must be communicated to the employees properly. The employee engagement should be participatory and reviewed periodically. The second important element in talent sustainability is critical talent identification, development, and employee succession. Talent identification poses pertinent challenge to the organizations—who should be identified as talent? Who should not be labeled as talent? There are many philosophies that support this dilemma. To a great extent, employee identification and labeling have to be inclusive and should consider the talent of the entire employee alike. Equality in the talent management process also improves the relational and transactional affinity of employees toward the organizations. The managerial intervention of talent development also gains an important role in the talent development approaches. The talent development interventions have to customize and should cater to the diverse needs of the employees. Employee succession faces leap backward in the talent management process. However, succession planning should be performed effectively, and the development of a right successor is a necessary aspect in talent pipeline development. The third important element in ensuring sustainable talent management is promoting rooms for continuous learning and development. Initiatives such as mentoring and coaching should be aligned with continuous learning. One of the most important aspects in a modern organization is the provision for informal learning. The younger generations are no longer interested in the formal methods of learning and require innovating learning techniques. The fourth important element in the talent sustainability development in competency development and deployment in companies. The focal point of talent development initiatives must be the development of employee unique competencies. The employee's talent also acts as a core element in creating sustainable competency for the companies, as each employee talent is unique and cannot be imitated or copied by the competitor. The challenges in work force diversity should be considered while developing the competencies of the employees. Another important aspect in the talent sustainability is sourcing and recruiting proper talent in the organizations. The source from where the talent has to recruit must be answered specifically and strategically. The recruitment should happen based on realistic job previews where the needs of the organizations and individuals are agreed upon. To meet the challenges of future organizations and upcoming uncertainties, organizations should recruit from diverse talent pools with rich expertise and skills. The sixth important element in talent sustainability is the reward and recognition process in organizations. It has to be realized that the mere presence of extrinsic rewards will not motivate or attract the talent anymore. The neglected role of intrinsic rewards in the organizations should be understood and implemented in the employee recognition process. Talented employees should be rewarded properly and recognized on an egalitarian basis. Any loopholes and biases in the reward and recognition process will have heinous negative impact in the talent management process and will negatively impact the retention processes. The seventh important element in talent sustainability is performance management. Performance management or appraisal in organizations should be re-engineered and must be based on metrics. Data-informed decisions should be considered while evaluating the performance of the employees to avoid personal judgments and biases. The final, yet the most important, component in talent sustainability is knowledge management. Knowledge erosion in organizations is unavoidable because of massive resignations and employee mobility, but how can the organizations ensure that employee knowledge can be transferred and does not get eroded? Organizations must adopt strategic plans to enable effective knowledge transfer from one employee to another. Both formal and informal mechanisms should be in place for effective knowledge transfer.

8.3 THREE TS: TECHNOLOGY, TALENT INTELLIGENCE, AND TALENT ANALYTICS

The landscape of talent management in getting transformed at an increasing pace. Talent management is no more considered as a replacement for HR interventions; instead, it is considered as a form of strategic HR management for making the HR operations more effective, employee friendly, and sustainable. As a research area, this discipline is explored more qualitatively and quantitatively using multi-level studies, complex methodologies, and sophisticated modeling. Talent sustainability is also receiving wide attention as a subset of the talent management framework (Sivathanu & Pillai, 2019). Talent sustainability involves adopting those practices and making an intervention in talent identification, deployment, development, and retention of employees that meet both the present and future organizational needs without compromising on employee sentiments, skills, and organizational growth (Benitez et al., 2015). Every spectrum of the organization is increasing, being converged with the techniques of technology; talent management is also no exception. Organizations are competitively harnessing their employee talent pool and organizational resources using various innovative technologies for better decision making. However, the values of talent sustainability and ethics have limited and questioned the scope of such technologies (Salau et al., 2018). The adoption of disruptive technologies is becoming prominent in talent management practices. The use of technologies is a major source of strategic competitive advantage to face the challenges of global talent management. In this section, the researcher briefs on three important Ts in current talent management trends—technology, talent intelligence, and talent analytics (Alias et al., 2014).

Technology in talent management is helping the organization to meet the global needs of talent. The Chief Human Resource Officers (CHROs) are seamlessly integrating technology into various aspects of talent management for tackling various business problems. The latest technologies such as predictive analytics and data science have been receiving more attention in the talent management environment. Organizations are building a talent management ecosystem incorporating advanced tools, technologies, and software programs that assist in real-time business decision making, which are rationally informed by the data (Wiblen et al., 2012). Technology adoption in talent management also has countless benefits. It digitizes the whole process of talent management and aligns the talent management essentials with the strategic and future needs of the organization. It aids in timely and precise decision making with careful crunching of mass data. Technology assists in effective talent pipeline development with a wider coverage of the global labor market. It also helps reduce unnecessary costs in employee hiring and recruitment. Technology ensures effective networking, collaboration, and employee engagement, facilitating optimum talent mobilization and deployment. Technologies such as predictive analytics forecast the future and business strategies can be realigned accordingly. It effectively integrates compensation packages with the performance of the employees, which is essential for HR value creation. The following points detail the potential application of technology in talent management (Frank & Taylor, 2004; Wassell & Bouchard, 2020).

8.3.1 TALENT ATTRACTION (RECRUITMENT AND ONBOARDING)

The seamless integration of technology in talent management leads to effective and errorless recruitment in companies. The fallacies of unconscious biases in face-to face recruitment can be completely avoided in tech-based hiring strategies. Technology eases the process of conducting a series of tests in the selection process. The hiring decision supported by proper employee data is more critical for organizational success. Advanced technologies help the recruiters in forming such informed decisions from the potential talent pool (González et al., 2019). Sometimes, when the employee mobility is increasing, the chances of labor shortages for a particular skill pose a major challenge in talent management. Technological integration makes talent attraction possible from a wider net of talent pool. Once the hiring decision is made, another important aspect is onboarding. Technology makes the document verification process simple and leak-proof. Using technology in the talent recruitment process makes it simple and easy for HR managers (Salau et al., 2018).

- **Learning and collaboration**: Learning and collaboration form an integral part of sustainable talent development of employees. Various dimensions such as mobile learning, social learning, and personal learning can be effectively achieved with technology. Technology builds an effective learning ecosystem wherein the learning of employees is self-paced and development oriented. An employee-friendly learning management system is essential to track and motivate the employee for continuous learning (McCauley & Wakefield, 2006). Effective technologies also help group cohesiveness and better collaboration. Technology-powered networking is more effective in making decisions and communication (Mihalcea, 2017).
- **Work culture and compensation management**: Another important use of technology is in shaping a contemporary work culture and rational compensation management (Barkhuizen, 2014). The reward and recognition strategies of the organization should be based on metrics for better employee satisfaction (Shaemi et al., 2011). The data science and data analytics help in forming better decisions about employee compensation and reward system. Technology assists in creating an innovative and creative work culture also. The traditional aspects of doing the work are outpaced, and it incentivizes employee innovations and creativity (Alias et al., 2016).

- **Skill development**: The primary benefit of technology in talent management is its visible outcomes on the skill development of employees. Employee skill forms the core component of individual talent. Technology-aided support systems help the organization to up skill their employees for future successions and leadership development (Hughes, 2018; Boudreau, 2013). Technology makes workers' effort more efficient; it offers ample opportunities for continuous learning, provides instant feedback about their performance, and assists in better career development. However, the role of intensive training during such technological transformation cannot be dismissed.
- **Talent access and mobility**: Another possible area for technological integration is ensuring talent access and mobility. Technology helps in combining multiple data outputs and additional outputs for managing better talent access and providing mobility (Collings, 2014; Collings et al., 2015). In the global labor market, the development of an individual employee is not just confined to the boundaries of an organization. Technology will reduce the employee growth boundary and allow the employee to be highly mobile and efficient.
- **Development of an agile workforce**: Technology is an essential ingredient for the development of an agile workforce. The use of high-end solutions of AI, machine learning, robotics, and data analytics will sharpen the employee's agility and improves their overall organizational performance. An agile workforce is a major requirement in the future. Technology helps in supplementing a digital mindset—well connected, open, and transparent—that ensures the agile and holistic growth of the employees.

The next major important "T" in talent management is talent intelligence. Organizations and practitioners are familiar with human intelligence, emotional intelligence, and, nowadays, AI. Nevertheless, the concept of talent intelligence is at infancy in the talent management framework. Talent intelligence includes the strategies of an organization in efficiently utilizing technology to build the talent management architecture for the benefit of organizational competitive advantage (Gergaud et al., 2012). Talent intelligence addresses how technology and organizational resources can be utilized to make talent management as a distinctive competitive edge of companies. A good talent intelligence platform will inform the company about the availability of different skills in the labor market and ways by which it can be attracted and retained in the companies (Gareth, 2013). Talent intelligence can be gained through third-party market studies; exit interviews of relieving employees; existing employees; industrial forums; and online resources such as competitor social media sites, salary aggregate sites, and website analytics (Faqihi & Miah, 2022). Organizations are also increasingly using AI to gain information through third-party software. The information from talent intelligence helps companies to make data-driven decisions about the talent pool. This further simplifies the recruiting efforts and results in efficient talent management. To align talent intelligence with organizational objectives and outcomes, companies should have proper accessibility to employee data such as previous experience, ambitions, career plans, and succession plans. It should be understood that the data collection process is not an isolated task, but it must be compiled during ongoing talent management practices (Pluchino et al.,

2018). The success of any talent intelligence platform depends on the right choice of talent tools and assessment techniques. Companies can adopt a unified data model for talent intelligence that allows the HR managers and employees to use and access the talent data during HR processes. The data collected during hiring, onboarding, performance reviews, and employee development plans should become the input data for the talent intelligence platform simultaneously. A single unified talent intelligence platform is the most desired from in the talent management process. The process of well-developed talent intelligence makes the whole process of talent management more holistic, the result of which can be tangibly mapped to business outcomes.

The final important T in the talent management framework is talent analytics. Also known in other semantics such as HR analytics, human capital analytics, people analytics, and workforce analytics are becoming increasingly important in shaping talent culture in companies. Talent analytics involves using an analytical platform to derive insights about the talent pool and employee skills to create a better understanding of the unique competencies of the employees for managing them effectively for organizational needs (Davenport et al., 2010). Some of the prominent tools for using talent analytics include R programming, Python, Tableau, SPSS, and MS-Excel. The fundamental practices using talent analytics include dashboard of employee metrics, reporting infrastructure, employee surveys, and analytics and modeling of employee data. In spite of the prominence of talent analytics, Indian companies have a fragmented and inconsistent approach toward talent analytics because of the paucity of resources and required analytical skills in the organizations (Nocker & Sena, 2019). The availability of clean data also affects the infancy-level acceptance of talent analytics in companies. The critical success factors for the implementation of talent analytics include advanced analytical skills, knowledge of industrial-organizational psychology, and health organizational IT support (N'Cho,2017). A typical talent analytics has to be the centralized function of HR, which is imperative of HR practices. A centralized talent analytics helps in better contextualization of data and for the development of a digital and analytical mindset in the organization (Fink & Sturman, 2017). The three core components of a matured talent analytics function include advanced analytics, organizational research, and reporting of data and infrastructure. The process of data structure and reporting includes the accessibility to clean,proper employee data (Burdon & Harpur, 2014). Availability of accurate data forms the basic approach for talent analytics without which the body of statistics will be meaningless. Using advanced analytics includes the use of complex statistical analysis and sophisticated modeling for making data-driven decisions (Fink, 2017; Minbaeva & Vardi, 2018; Levenson, 2021). The use of advanced data analytics helps in predictive analytics. Organizational research involves systematic approaches for studying and understanding HR components beyond a single company. It helps to answer futuristic challenges and uncertainties in the workforce.

8.4   ENABLING ARTIFICIAL INTELLIGENCE IN TALENT MANAGEMENT

Enabling AI in talent management, that is, from acquisition to performance appraisal, benefits organizational costs and increases the productivity also.

8.4.1 Artificial Intelligence Tools for Candidate Sourcing

Several AI tools such as Entelo, Hiretual, and Arya are available and used in talent acquisition. Sourcing the right employee from appropriate sources is a critical success factor in organizational recruitment. To get the desired result, AI tools help firms to use technology. The aforementioned tools are AI tools specially developed to allow recruiters to find prospective employee candidature with the required skill set. Entelo collects candidates' information from various prominent social media platforms. The recruiters may identify from the data based on gender, age, and experience requirements. Reputed companies such as Lyft and PayPal use Entelo to hire skilled employees. Hiretual is another tool used by companies such as IBM and Intel to source candidates from more than 30 platforms. These platforms convert the job titles and job descriptions as smart Boolean strings which increases recruitment efficiency. The AI tool Arya is used by companies such as Kimco services, Headway Workforce Solutions, Personify, and many others. This tool uses AI and behavioral recognition patterns to analyze profiles to provide a perfect candidate.

8.4.2 Candidate Screening Using AI Tools

Once the potential candidates for jobs are identified, the next tedious task is employee profile screening. Organizations are increasingly using AI-based tools for job resume parsing, which makes the screening process less redundant and highly effective. The widely used AI tools for employee screening is listed below:

Pomato: This platform uses AI to screen the proper candidate from voluminous applications. The technology designed using AI will help visualize the most suitable candidate for the role using Resume Analyzer and Job Matching Engine technology. This can do nearly five lakh computations in determining the right candidate for the right position. After this, the talent acquisition team will design the interview process based on the available job descriptions.

CVVIZ: This platform considers AI and cloud services as complementary to each other. This application uses the machine learning algorithm to screen the right candidate from the talent pool within a short span of time. Integrating the machine learning algorithm will help screen the resumes contextually and based on the recruiters' methodology to recruit the appropriate candidate. The AI tools understand the organizational requirement and expectations from the candidate. Hence, these technologies help match the right opportunities with the right candidates based on various parameters. CVVIZ's significant clients include Alstom, Societe Generale, Headsnminds, and Iglobus.

8.4.3 Candidate Assessment Using Artificial Intelligence Tools

AI tools are extensively used in providing immediate results for analyzing the candidates using AI-driven technologies; it saves the recruiters' time.

Mya: Mya is an ideal chatbot based on natural language processing and machine learning algorithms. This platform simulates real human conversations using

AI-based tools. During the conversation, Mya conducts candidate screening and helps the recruiters to understand why the shortlisted candidates are suitable. Presently, Mya renders its services to many organizations including Fortune 500 companies and many of the largest global staffing firms. Apart from Mya, there are AI-based platforms such as Harver and Talview. Harver offers a customized assessment of the candidature of an individual. It provides the capabilities of the individual's aptitude and fitness to the particular job roles, which the talent acquisition team can use for proper employee assessment.

8.4.4 Artificial Intelligence Reshaping Talent Acquisition Process

AI-based processes are bringing dramatic changes in the way talent acquisitions were designed in organizations. This process synthesizes voluminous sets of candidates' data and suggests to the team the pros and cons of an individual. In the current talent acquisition process, the applications of AI is mostly witnessed in employee assessment; however, the potential applications are much broader. Below are potential applications of AI in talent acquisition.

- Talent acquisition using chatbot
  Chatbots are already used for recruitment purposes, which help spot candidates' skill sets and drive them to the funnel. Chatbots are used by many organizations to answer the candidates' questions during the application procedure.
- Finding highly qualified talent
  When an organization's employee intake is enormous, it will be a daunting task for the companies to go through all the resumes of candidates; it is time-consuming. AI tools can find suitable employee resumes from multiple sources and filter them based on the firm's requirements and the candidate's requirements to get the best fit.

8.5 EFFECT OF ARTIFICIAL INTELLIGENCE IN SUSTAINABLE TALENT MANAGEMENT

Earlier, in organizations, decision making regarding recruitment was a time-consuming process and involved multiple hierarchies. Human intelligence is increasingly getting replaced by AI or machine intelligence, which is quick in decision making. The benefits of AI in talent management are considered as a swinging pendulum (Claus, 2019). The greater the rush in the organization toward adopting AI, the pendulum will swing back. One of the critical success factors for adopting AI is leak-proof organizational preparedness. AI machines work based on complex algorithms, which poses several challenges in the HR management domain (Visvizi, 2022). Even though AI is revolutionizing the talent management model, the core limitations of the machine in being sensitive, having an inclusive understanding, and becoming emotional to the employee needs cannot be dismissed of (Al Aina & Atan, 2020). In the present period of transformation, the positive impacts of AI in talent management, in general, and talent sustainability, in particular, need to be emphasized (Stopochkin et al., 2022). Any technology without proper human intervention will have fatal impacts on the mankind; hence, discussions around the impact of AI in talent management in parallel also address human concerns in it. AI applications in talent management have also raised countless criticisms regarding ethics and fairness in decision making. Hence, it is important to understand how the benefits of AI can be harnessed and pitfalls can be controlled for (Gardas et al., 2019). AI is acclaimed to have a direct link with employee creativity and employee innovative behavior. With machine interference, the organizations have creative flairs in managing their workforce, which fosters employee innovations. Another visible impact of AI-based talent management is on transformation-based leadership. The traditional forms of leadership will not work in an environment characterized by less human interference and more machine intelligence (Devins & Gold, 2014). The leadership in the organization should be modified and transformed in such a way that the core challenges of employee resistance to such innovative technologies can be minimized. Unpacking the black box of AI will help improve HR processes such as employee hiring, employee development, and organizational development. The decision-making ability of AI-powered talent management is widely appreciated for its core components of enhancement, improvement, automation, discovery, and detection. However, there is strong organizational resistance about the use of AI in talent management, which has to be tackled by educating and reassuring the candidates about the significant role of AI in the future workplace. With more protected and ethical boundaries of AI, it can be solidified for best practices in data analytics using high standards. AI-powered interviews are an efficient tool for talent hiring and supplement HR processes in cognitive ability tests, psychometric tests, and other hiring decisions (Jyoti & Rani, 2014).

AI also has negative impacts on talent sustainability. The integral part of AI, such as machine learning and natural language processing, are not silver bullets that can be easily applied by anyone. These interventions require huge investment in research and development to serve mankind sustainably. With AI, the chances of biases are more in talent decision making. A biased input to the system will create a wrong talent decision with adverse impacts. AI applications are more complex and are less transparent in nature. The way in which they work adds to more load of HR managers, which results in compromising the basic ethics of talent management. Moreover, this technology lacks transparency in the way sensitive employee talent can be managed. AI also requires a voluminous amount of data, which are inaccessible to many organizations. Additionally, repurposing the existing processes into AI-based talent management is subjected to many errors. Using AI in HR is a balancing act wherein organizations should focus on doing the right things rather than focusing on the shiny technologies. To make talent management more fair, accurate and defensible organizations require a partner to implement AI-based talent management. This technological partner will smoothen the ways of organizational resistance, calms down the ambiguities of AI, and ensure error-free transitions.

8.5.1 Responsible Talent Management Model

The need for ethical talent management to ensure sustainability in HR management is increasingly becoming important. This necessitates a responsible talent management model that answers the requirements of the organization by protecting the stakeholder's values and organizational justice. The construct of responsible talent management has been defined earlier (Anlesinya & Amponsah-Tawiah, 2020):

TM practices and strategies that emphasize an organization's responsibility to manage the talent of the employees by adopting an inclusive framework where the contribution of every single person is recognized and valued. The responsible talent management framework stresses on fair and equitable management of employee weaknesses and opportunities. The responsible talent management model was propounded to make ethical and sustainable changes in talent management. The responsible talent management is rooted in three major principles—employee inclusivity, corporate social responsibility, and equal opportunities to all the employees—which were widely neglected in talent management literature–. The practice of employee inclusivity has many implications in the organization. It boosts employee morale, creates better employee morale, makes a positive relational and transactional contract among employees, and improves the retention of top talent in organizations (Swailes, 2020). The argument for inclusivity outrightly rejects the idea of ABC management in the talent framework—A refers to star performers, B refers to moderate performers, and C refers to below-average performers. Exclusive talent approaches have so far recognized the need for only the star talent, whiles it outrightly rejects the miniscule contribution of every other employee in the organization. The exclusive talent approaches make the talent management dysfunctional and act as a double-edged sword. The practice of inclusivity is most needed in the present working environment, where each employee represents a unique skill set and source of competitive advantage. Another major dimension that explains the responsible talent management is the element of corporate social responsibility (Kaliannan et al., 2016). A responsible talent management is expected to deliver societal demands such as honesty, transparency, and integrating ethics in building the talent management architecture. Talent management initiatives should deliver and fulfill the social responsibility of the HR department toward all stakeholders. The responsible talent management integrates the principles of the stakeholder theory in fulfilling the responsibilities. The talent managers and the organization are indebted to all the employees they have onboard and should strategically plan their inclusive development (Khalil et al., 2017). The idea of inclusivity itself is an act of corporate social responsibility in the companies. Apart from the extrinsic rewards, the organizations should recognize the needs of the intrinsic rewards also. Another important principle in which the responsible talent management is operationalized is based on ensuring equal and fair developmental opportunities to the employees (Bhatia & Baruah, 2020). Notably, the previously discussed aspects of inclusivity and corporate social responsibility equivocally become part of equal opportunities and fairness. The process of talent management right from the identification of talent-to-talent retention should offer equal opportunities to the talent pool in the organization. Thus, responsible talent management is an effective way through which organizations can discharge their

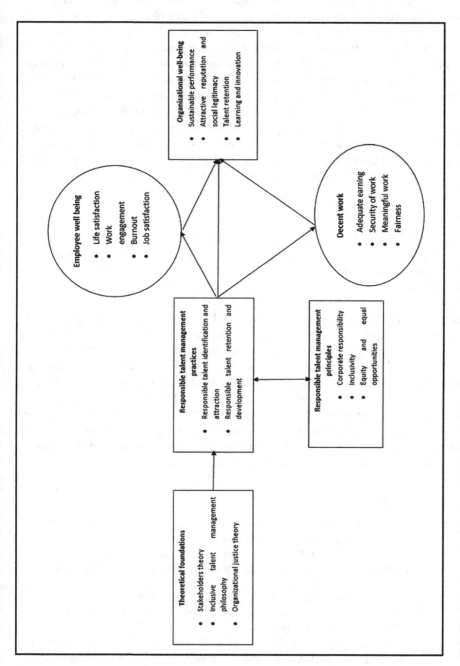

FIGURE 8.2 Conceptual framework for responsible talent management (Anlesinya & Amponsah, 2020).

responsibility to all stakeholders such employees, management, and society. In responsible talent management, the economic cost incurred in the talent management process ensures equal opportunities and fairness to the employees and allows them to grow boundaryless. All the employees are equally allowed to recognize and develop their potential by simultaneously contributing to the organizational talent pool (Iles & Preece, 2010). The responsible talent management strives to achieve a balance between the need of the employees, organizational objectives, and the HR ideas about talent management. Moreover, responsible talent management can be considered as a hybrid talent management model with twin goals of stakeholder satisfaction and minimizing the economic cost of talent management for reaping maximum benefits. The responsible talent management is lauded for its employee-centric approaches that recognize the organizational contribution of each employee in the organizational development process, however, meager their contribution may be.

8.6 CONCLUSION

This chapter discusses the potential of technological integration in talent management sustainability. The study addresses the three Ts of talent management—technology, talent intelligence, and talent analytics. The use of AI and organizational prepared-ness for the same has been discussed in the study. The study also highlights the importance of building talent sustainability in the organization, which not only takes the present needs of the present organizational needs but also ensures employee's sustainable competitive advantage in the future also. AI is considered an important disruptive technology in talent management; however, the long-term effectiveness of this technology depends on the organizational preparedness, employee training, and other organizational factors. The rush toward AI as a fancy technology will have futile implications in the organization. Even though AI-based talent management is gaining a prominent momentum, the importance of human inference should not be dismissed. More quantitative and qualitative research that explores the contextual factors in AI-related interoperability and talent management sustainability is essential for better convergence to a technology-based talent management.

REFERENCES

1. Lewis, R. E., & Heckman, R. J. (2006). Talent management: A critical review. *Human resource management review*, *16*(2), 139–154.
2. Cappelli, P., & Keller, J. R. (2014). Talent management: Conceptual approaches and practical challenges. *Annu. Rev. Organ. Psychol. Organ. Behav.*, *1*(1), 305–331.
3. Collings, D. G., Scullion, H., & Vaiman, V. (2015). Talent management: Progress and prospects. *Human Resource Management Review*, *25*(3), 233–235.
4. Schiemann, W. A. (2014). From talent management to talent optimization. *Journal of World Business*, *49*(2), 281–288.
5. Bethke-Langenegger, P., Mahler, P., & Staffelbach, B. (2011). Effectiveness of talent management strategies. *European Journal of International Management*, *5*(5), 524–539.
6. O'Neal, S., & Gebauer, J. (2006). Talent management in the 21st century: Attracting, retaining and engaging employees of choice. *The Journal of Total Rewards*, *15*(1), 6.

7. Ashton, C., & Morton, L. (2005). Managing talent for competitive advantage: Taking a systemic approach to talent management. *Strategic HR review, 4*(5), 28–31.
8. Swailes, S. (2013). The ethics of talent management. *Business Ethics: A European Review, 22*(1), 32–46.
9. Dries, N. (2013). The psychology of talent management: A review and research agenda. *Human Resource Management Review, 23*(4), 272–285.
10. Thunnissen, M. (2016), "Talent management: For what, how and how well? An empirical exploration of talent management in practice ", *Employee Relations*, 38 (1), 57–72.
11. Garrow, V., & Hirsh, W. (2008). Talent management: Issues of focus and fit. *Public Personnel Management, 37*(4), 389–402.
12. Sonnenberg, M., van Zijderveld, V., & Brinks, M. (2014). The role of talent-perception incongruence in effective talent management. *Journal of World Business, 49*(2), 272–280.
13. Saleh, R., & Atan, T. (2021). The Involvement of Sustainable Talent Management Practices on Employee's Job Satisfaction: Mediating Effect of Organizational Culture. *Sustainability, 13*(23), 13320.
14. Ogbazghi, R. (2017). Talent management as a new form of sustainable human resources management. *Latgale National Economy Research, 1*(9), 95–108.
15. Mohapatra, M., & Sahu, P. (2018). Building a sustainable talent acquisition model in a dynamic business environment. *International Journal of Human Capital and Information Technology Professionals (IJHCITP), 9*(3), 42–52.
16. Necula, S. C., & Strîmbei, C. (2019). People analytics of semantic web human resource résumés for sustainable talent acquisition. *Sustainability, 11*(13), 3520.
17. Schuler, R. S., Jackson, S. E., & Tarique, I. (2011). Global talent management and global talent challenges: Strategic opportunities for IHRM. *Journal of world business, 46*(4), 506–516.
18. Tarique, I., & Schuler, R. S. (2010). Global talent management: Literature review, integrative framework, and suggestions for further research. *Journal of world business, 45*(2), 122–133.
19. Collings, D. G. (2014). Integrating global mobility and global talent management: Exploring the challenges and strategic opportunities. *Journal of World Business, 49*(2), 253–261.
20. Minbaeva, D., & Collings, D. G. (2013). Seven myths of global talent management. *The International Journal of Human Resource Management, 24*(9), 1762–1776.
21. Anlesinya, A., Dartey-Baah, K., & Amponsah-Tawiah, K. (2019). A review of empirical research on global talent management. *FIIB Business Review, 8*(2), 147–160.
22. Farndale, E., Scullion, H., & Sparrow, P. (2010). The role of the corporate HR function in global talent management. *Journal of world business, 45*(2), 161–168.
23. Sidani, Y., & Al Ariss, A. (2014). Institutional and corporate drivers of global talent management: Evidence from the Arab Gulf region. *Journal of World Business, 49*(2), 215–224.
24. Collings, D. G., & Isichei, M. (2018). The shifting boundaries of global staffing: Integrating global talent management, alternative forms of international assignments and non-employees into the discussion. *The International Journal of Human Resource Management, 29*(1), 165–187.
25. Stahl, G., Björkman, I., Farndale, E., Morris, S. S., Paauwe, J., Stiles, P., ... & Wright, P. (2012). Six principles of effective global talent management. *Sloan Management Review, 53*(2), 25–42.

26. Garavan, T. N. (2012). Global talent management in science-based firms: an exploratory investigation of the pharmaceutical industry during the global downturn. *The international journal of human resource management, 23*(12), 2428–2449.

27. Skuza, A., Scullion, H., & McDonnell, A. (2013). An analysis of the talent management challenges in a post-communist country: the case of Poland. *The International Journal of Human Resource Management, 24*(3), 453–470.

28. Morris, S., Snell, S., & Björkman, I. (2016). An architectural framework for global talent management. *Journal of International Business Studies, 47*(6), 723–747.

29. Sivathanu, B., & Pillai, R. (2019). Leveraging technology for talent management: Foresight for organizational performance. *International Journal of Sociotechnology and Knowledge Development (IJSKD), 11*(2), 16–30.

30. Benitez-Amado, J., Llorens-Montes, F. J., & Fernandez-Perez, V. (2015). IT impact on talent management and operational environmental sustainability. *Information Technology and Management, 16*(3), 207–220.

31. Salau, O., Osibanjo, A., Adeniji, A., Oludayo, O., Falola, H., Igbinoba, E., & Ogueyungbo, O. (2018). Data regarding talent management practices and innovation performance of academic staff in a technology-driven private university. *Data in Brief, 19*, 1040–1045.

32. Alias, N. E., Noor, N., & Hassan, R. (2014). Examining the mediating effect of employee engagement on the relationship between talent management practices and employee retention in the Information and Technology (IT) organizations in Malaysia. *Journal of Human Resources Management and Labor Studies, 2*(2), 227–242.

33. Wiblen, S., Dery, K., & Grant, D. (2012). Do you see what I see? The role of technology in talent identification. *Asia pacific journal of human resources, 50*(4), 421–438.

34. Frank, F. D., & Taylor, C. R. (2004). Talent management: Trends that will shape the future. *Human Resource Planning, 27*(1).

35. Wassell, S., & Bouchard, M. (2020). Rebooting strategic human resource management: integrating technology to drive talent management. *International Journal of Human Resources Development and Management, 20*(2), 93–113.

36. González-Masip, J., Martín-de Castro, G., & Hernández, A. (2019). Inter-organisational knowledge spillovers: attracting talent in science and technology parks and corporate social responsibility practices. *Journal of Knowledge Management, 23*(5), 975–997.

37. Salau, O., Osibanjo, A., Adeniji, A., Oludayo, O., Falola, H., Igbinoba, E., & Ogueyungbo, O. (2018). Data regarding talent management practices and innovation performance of academic staff in a technology-driven private university. *Data in Brief, 19*, 1040–1045.

38. McCauley, C., & Wakefield, M. (2006). Talent management in the 21st century: Help your company find, develop, and keep its strongest workers. *The Journal for Quality and Participation, 29*(4), 4.

39. Mihalcea, A. (2017). Employer branding and talent management in the digital age. *Management Dynamics in the Knowledge Economy, 5*(2), 289–306.

40. Barkhuizen, N. (2014). Exploring the importance of rewards as a talent management tool for Generation Y employees. *Mediterranean Journal of Social Sciences, 5*(27 P2), 1100.

41. Shaemi, A., Allameh, S. M., & Bajgerani, M. A. (2011). Impact of talent management strategies on employees' emotional intelligence in Isfahan Municipality (Iran). *Interdisciplinary Journal of Contemporary Research in Business, 3*(6), 229–241.

42. Alias, N. E., Nor, N. M., & Hassan, R. (2016). The relationships between talent management practices, employee engagement, and employee retention in the information and technology (IT) organizations in Selangor. In *Proceedings of the 1st AAGBS*

International Conference on Business Management 2014 (AiCoBM 2014) (pp. 101–115).

43. Hughes, C. (2018). The role of HRD in using diversity intelligence to enhance leadership skill development and talent management strategy. *Advances in Developing Human Resources, 20*(3), 259–262.

44. Boudreau, J. W. (2013). Appreciating and 'retooling'diversity in talent management conceptual models: A commentary on "The psychology of talent management: A review and research agenda". *human Resource management Review, 23*(4), 286–289.

45. Collings, D. G. (2014). Integrating global mobility and global talent management: Exploring the challenges and strategic opportunities. *Journal of World Business, 49*(2), 253–261.

46. Collings, D. G., Scullion, H., & Vaiman, V. (2015). Talent management: Progress and prospects. *Human Resource Management Review, 25*(3), 233–235.

47. Gergaud, O., Ginsburgh, V., & Livat, F. (2012). Success of celebrities: talent, intelligence or beauty?. *Economics Bulletin, 32*(4), 3120–3127.

48. Gareth Bell, I. (2013). How Talent Intelligent is Your Organization? an Interview with Nik Kinley and Shlomo Ben-Hur, Authors of Talent Intelligence: What You Need to Know to Identify and Measure Talent. *Development and Learning in Organizations, 28*(1), 29–31.

49. Faqihi, A., & Miah, S. J. (2022). Designing an AI-Driven Talent Intelligence Solution: Exploring Big Data to extend the TOE Framework. *arXiv preprint arXiv:2207.12052.*

50. Pluchino, A., Biondo, A. E., & Rapisarda, A. (2018). Talent versus luck: The role of randomness in success and failure. *Advances in Complex systems, 21*(03n04), 1850014.

51. Davenport, T. H., Harris, J., & Shapiro, J. (2010). Competing on talent analytics. *Harvard business review, 88*(10), 52–58.

52. Nocker, M., & Sena, V. (2019). Big data and human resources management: The rise of talent analytics. *Social Sciences, 8*(10), 273.

53. N'Cho, J. (2017). Contribution of talent analytics in change management within project management organizations The case of the French aerospace sector. *Procedia Computer Science, 121*, 625–629.

54. Fink, A. A., & Sturman, M. C. (2017). HR metrics and talent analytics. *The Oxford handbook of talent management*, 375–390.

55. Burdon, M., & Harpur, P. (2014). Re-conceptualising privacy and discrimination in an age of talent analytics. *University of New South Wales Law Journal, 37*(2), 679–712.

56. Fink, A. A. (2017). Getting results with talent analytics. *People & Strategy, 40*(3), 36–41.

57. Minbaeva, D., & Vardi, S. (2018). Global talent analytics. In *Global talent management* (pp. 179–199). Routledge.

58. McCauley, C., Smith, R., & Campbell, M. (2007). CCL's Talent Sustainability Framework. Greensboro, NC: Center for Creative Leadership.

59. Levenson, A. (2021). Talent Analytics. *The Routledge Companion to Talent Management*, 501–521.

60. Claus, L. (2019). HR disruption—Time already to reinvent talent management. *BRQ Business Research Quarterly, 22*(3), 207–215.

61. Visvizi, A. (2022). Sustainability in International Business: Talent Management, Market Entry Strategies, Competitiveness. *Sustainability, 14*(16), 10191.

62. Al Aina, R., & Atan, T. (2020). The impact of implementing talent management practices on sustainable organizational performance. *Sustainability, 12*(20), 8372.

63. Stopochkin, A., Sytnik, I., Wielki, J., & Karaś, E. (2022). Transformation of the Concept of Talent Management in the Era of the Fourth Industrial Revolution as the Basis for Sustainable Development. *Sustainability*, *14*(14), 8727.

64. Gardas, B. B., Mangla, S. K., Raut, R. D., Narkhede, B., & Luthra, S. (2019). Green talent management to unlock sustainability in the oil and gas sector. *Journal of Cleaner Production*, *229*, 850–862.

65. Devins, D., & Gold, J. (2014). Re-conceptualising talent management and development within the context of the low paid. *Human Resource Development International*, *17*(5), 514–528.

66. Jyoti, J., & Rani, R. (2014). Exploring talent management practices: antecedents and consequences. *International Journal of Management Concepts and Philosophy*, *8*(4), 220–248.

67. Anlesinya, A. and Amponsah-Tawiah, K. (2020), "Towards a responsible talent management model", *European Journal of Training and Development*, 44 (2/3), 279–303.

68. Swailes, S. (2020), "Responsible talent management: towards guiding principles", *Journal of Organizational Effectiveness: People and Performance*, 7 (2), 221–236.

69. Kaliannan, M., Abraham, M., & Ponnusamy, V. (2016). Effective talent management in Malaysian SMES: A proposed framework. *The Journal of Developing Areas*, *50*(5), 393–401.

70. Khalil, M., Elsaay, H., & Othman, A. (2017). Talent management: a novel approach for developing innovative solutions towards heritage communities' development. *ArchNet-IJAR: International Journal of Architectural Research*, *11*(3), 132–145.

71. Bhatia, R., & Baruah, P. (2020). Exclusive talent management and its consequences: a review of literature. *Asian journal of business ethics*, *9*(2), 193–209.

72. Iles, P., Chuai, X., & Preece, D. (2010). Talent management and HRM in multinational companies in Beijing: Definitions, differences and drivers. *Journal of world Business*, *45*(2), 179–189.

9 Transformation of Human Resources

Future of Workforce Analytics

Aruna Polisetty
SCMS, Nagpur, Symbiosis International University
Pune, India

T. Sowdamini
Gitam School of Business, Gitam University,
Visakhapatnam, India

R. Seetha Lakshmi
VIT AP School of Business (VSB), VIT AP University,
Amaravati, India

Vidya Sagar Athota
University of Notre Dame, Sydney, Australia

9.1 INTRODUCTION

The use of information technology (IT) has impacted human resources (HR) procedures and methods. Everyone is worried about edifice-smart organizations under the current system. We have actually seen changes in the workplace. Physical employment is disappearing, brain-based jobs are increasing, labor-based units have emerged from skill-based businesses, and knowledge-based industries are predicted to occur in the future. In this highly competitive environment, where everyone interacts through technology and innovation is transforming the world into a global village, artificial intelligence (AI) is assisting businesses in carrying out any tasks more successfully and effectively. With the mounting burden to include HR managers in the critical choices, the companies have understood the inference of utilizing novelties and technological advancement in their HR systems. Immediate changes in business environments require quick reactions. The associations invest money in R&D to bring some new innovations to compete in the market. AI is the technology that enables quick evaluation of data by people who do not possess exceptional skills in data analysis. Similar to how AI is a novel idea in IT, AI-based workforce analytics ensures a variety of services, from employee exit to talent acquisition.

DOI: 10.1201/9781003348351-9

9.2 APPLICATIONS OR ROLE OF AI IN HRM

To drive optimization and efficiency in business, humans always utilize technology. Taking it to the next level, AI will now change how humans are going to work together with technology (Oracle Corporation, 2019). Before we discuss the role of AI in HRM, let us know the fundamentals of AI. There are three categories of AI: machine learning (ML), deep learning (DL), and artificial neural networks (ANN). The former refers to decisions made by the machine by interpreting the behavioral patterns. DL uses algorithms to build predictive models, where the models are then compared with available data and take necessary corrections accordingly. ANN is far superior to its predecessors, which develops self-consciousness within the system, such as "DATA" in "Star Trek New Generation" (Sowdamini, 2022).

As we all know, HRM consists of multiple functions ranging from talent acquisition to exit of an employee. In these functional areas, the implementation of AI should be in a phased manner. Even though the functions have an independent AI, they are part of the network, providing an overall understanding of HR. HRM has multiple functions, but organizations may not employ all of them.

So, let us see the applications of AI in some of the most common HR functions.

9.2.1 WORKFORCE PLANNING

1. Workforce planning is all about extracting data from different departments, namely, finance, operations, and HR, analyzing it and drawing to a conclusion on the staffing requirement. Workforce analytics collates the data, improves workforce planning, and helps management to make informed decisions. This methodology assesses how employee performance and other applicable variables influence the business as a whole.

2. Multiple organizations are using workforce analytics solutions, and the necessity for innovative HR cases for labor management is increasing. Key performance indicators utilized in workforce analytics enhance and pursue workforce execution in areas such as hiring (Holliday, 2020). By blending skills across markets and managerial specialties, guided by employment requirements and equipped with up-to-date data analytics and reporting tools, HR can plan the workforce more efficiently.

3. The technology evolved in recent years, as well as the research it creates now, is used further beyond than hiring new employees and altering departmental requirements to consider whether such modifications affect a positive return on investment (Wallask, 2017).

4. Businesses must ensure that the appropriate personnel is in the proper positions at the correct times. Accordingly, HR executives must hire personnel who fit the company's culture.

9.2.2 TALENT ACQUISITION AND RECRUITMENT

1. Talent acquisition is vital for any organization's growth. The hiring process has been modernized by inducing AI into the process. Gone are those

days when it would take days to screen and shortlist the candidates from the resumes received. It is the era of AI that processes data volumes in an instant. The mundane of HR has been reduced, and the AI will pick up the right candidate from the database based on the job requirements (Seetha Lakshmi, R., Sowdamini, T., Biswas, 2020).

2. AI has not only shortened the screening process but aided HR executives in posting jobs by creating more targeted job adverts. Even though work from home (WFM) is not new, the pandemic has necessitated WFM. In such times, AI is a great help in assessing the candidates' skills, personalities, and competencies (DAWSON, 2020).

3. It is clear that AI is becoming more prevalent in the talent acquisition area, especially for businesses that prioritize employee quality, workforce diversity, and recruiters' effectiveness. AI and advanced ML have slashed the cost and time associated with hiring and candidate screening in only a few years (Jennings, 2021).

9.2.3 EMPLOYEE ENGAGEMENT

1. Employee engagement is the positive mindset of each employee toward the business and the organization's value. Employee engagement is one factor that significantly impacts company operations (Sari et al., 2020).

2. The current workforce constitutes people from four generations, and employee engagement tends to change accordingly. According to a study performed by Dell, generation Z embraces technological changes and tends to show close attention to their job roles (SivaSubramanian, 2022).

3. According to the research conducted by Gallup (State of the Global Workplace: 2022 Report), 87% of millennials opine that career growth and professional development are significant to them. AI has an exceptional ability to offer directed and personalized suggestions in terms of learning and development. AI may also be useful for assessing employees' motivation and using the results to determine the best team composition. All recruiters are currently focused on increasing employee engagement (Fatemi, 2019).

9.2.4 LEARNING AND DEVELOPMENT PROGRAMS

1. Companies commonly employ traditional employee engagement such as "two-way communication," "learning development," and "recognition programs"

2. Most companies have similar learning modules but not all employees are alike. Employees tend to learn based on their needs and interests, which are sometimes ignored in traditional learning and development methods (ETHR World, 2021).

3. It is vital to introduce AI into learning and development, as it can take care of the preferences and requirements of the learners. Like digital assistants, namely, SIRI, Alexa, or Cortana, the AI will learn and evolve, enabling people

to accomplish personal and organizational goals, lessen impediments in accessing learning and development, and enhance efficiency and productivity (Donovan, 2021).

4. According to research by Deloitte (HR and business perspectives of Future of Work), millennials rank those companies that provide learning development.

5. Gamification is one of the AI tools that have become popular in recent years. Some influential organizations such as Walmart use gamification to train their employees. Gamification is similar to game-based learning; however, the former will increase the learner's curiosity. Through gamification, learning becomes more accessible and creates enthusiasm in those who typically are not that inclined to learn (Anuj Kumar et al., 2021).

9.2.5 PERFORMANCE APPRAISAL

1. Similar to learning development, performance management will also vary from person to person. However, performance management can be generalized based on the industry. Before implementing, the administration should be aware of some aversion toward AI-based performance appraisal systems. At the same time, some will welcome this change with open hands (Schneider, 2021).

2. Data collection plays a vital role in any process. In performance management, it is even more critical to have accurate data to understand the person and evaluate their performance without bias. In AI-based PA models, data are collected automatically and continuously. AI will then compare the data collected with the historical information and other resources available within

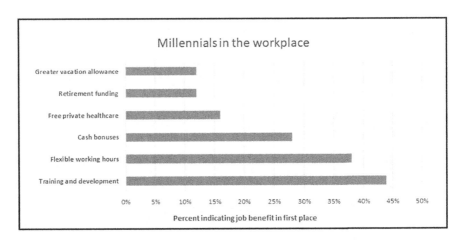

FIGURE 9.1   Millennials in the workplace.

Source: "https://virtualspeech.com/blog/ai-ml-learning development#:~:text=AI%20 can%20dramatically%20shorten%20the,and%20modules%20for%20the%20 employee"

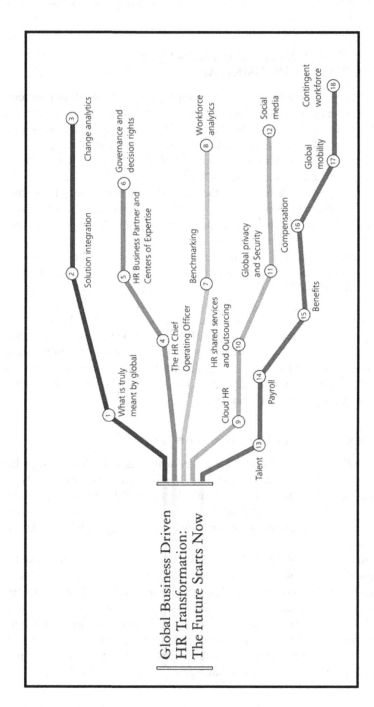

FIGURE 9.2 HR transformation.

Source: https://www2.deloitte.com/content/dam/Deloitte/de/Documents/human-capital/global-business-driven-hr–transformat ion.pdf

the company. So that 360-degree appraisal can be performed (Business World, 2020; Profit co, 2022).

9.3 TRANSFORMATION OF TRADITIONAL HR TO CONTEMPORARY HR USING AI

Desperate time needs desperate measures. In changing times, HR needs to transform to meet the need of the hour and to be future-ready. If we roll more than 60 years back, the word HR would be a new word for many people, as HR is known as personnel management. Personnel management merely used to take care of job interviews, payroll, and people issues. Its precedence is more on clerical tasks related to employees' coordination, welfare, and convenience. HRM does not just build strategies for the good of the company while disregarding the demands and objectives of the staff. Processes and practices are created to match people's needs and the organization's goals. HRM works by keeping the organization's concerns and employees' interests in mind and striking a balance between them (Gibson, n.d.).

Nowadays, the main aspect of HR is often a website instead of an individual. Most companies now cater global ingress to HR provisions, vide web tools and technology, considerably changing HRM practice. These changes often result from cutting costs and expanding or improving services. Current research reveals entities that effectively embrace refined HR technology applications overtake those that do not.

The phrase "e-HR" illustrates the makeover of HR facility dispensing by expending web-based technology. Executing e-HR necessitates structural modification in how HR mavens foresee their jobs. Now HR professionals must master not only customary HR methodology and proficiency but also be able to smear that understanding through technology (Johnson & Gueutal, 2017).

9.3.1 RELATIONSHIP BETWEEN HUMANS AND THE DIGITAL

By 2025, it is anticipated that the HRM industry would have a $30 billion global impact. People can use traditional HR processes with much more simplicity and efficiency thanks to technological advancements and the availability of tools such as predictive analytics and AI. There is also an opposite side. The unbridled debate about AI, and ML is pressing entities to shell out money on technology with lack of knowledge on how to use it seamlessly.

According to the KPMG's report, 50% of HR leaders feel unrehearsed to take the benefits of technology. The biggest challenge the companies face is the lack of skills and capabilities to understand the technology and adapt to the swift stride of alteration. The utmost way to endure this digital makeover is by employing accomplished employees and upskilling them periodically so they can work in a digitally thought-provoking environment (Rao, 2019). Prominent HR organizations are the ones which by this time have been explored the technologies by employing experienced personnel and tiling the way for a better combination of digital and individuals.

9.3.2 BENEFITS, LIMITATIONS, AND CHALLENGES IN IMPLEMENTING THE AI IN HRM

AI has embraced a variety of possibilities in a wide range of industries, and the recruiting sector has also benefitted from all the advantages AI provides. Moreover, 56% of HR corporations are already employing AI for talent acquisition, according to the report "2021 Hiring Trends–Automation and Artificial Intelligence." It is forecasted that, by 2023, 77% of HR organizations will benefit from AI in their recruitment processes. The future of AI in recruitment looks encouraging, as the tools offered by AI make the hiring process much simpler for recruiters. It saves time that can be used more efficiently strategically (Delaney, 2021) (Merin, 2021) (Pavlou, 2022).

HR is growing into a more technology-based department because companies need to

- Simplify administrative tasks and HR procedures.
- Lessen HR processing and compliance expenses.
- Contend more commendably for global forte.
- Develop service and entree to data for managers and employees.
- Make available real-time system for the measurement of decision-makers to identify the tendencies and administer the workers more commendably.
- Facilitate HR to transmute so that it can engage in a more tactical role in the business
- The most apparent benefits of AI in the office are allied to computerizing essential functions. Systems use data to imitate human understanding and evaluate, making the job less tense and more competent.
- From reviewing CVs to arranging interviews to responding to probable applicants' questions, AI can curtail the period spent scrutinizing information and doing regular enrollment responsibilities. It can also eradicate prejudices and aid in finding the right candidate.
- Because AI tech is accessible 24/7 and can eradicate human mistakes from regular activities, it can generate a healthier HR experience for managers and employees.
- New employees' onboarding experience significantly impacts their job satisfaction and retention rates.
- AI can create tailormade training programs for a better learning experience.

9.4 TRANSFORMATION OF TRADITIONAL HR TO CONTEMPORARY HR WITH AI

The famous saying goes as follows: "the only constant changes," as evidenced in HRM. It is meant to be a powerhouse of the organization. Traditional HR merely emphasized rules and policies on the essential functions of HR, such as workforce planning, recruitment, compensation, and the like. The image of HR is transformed into portals rather than an individual. In the digital era, organizations dramatically change the mode of delivery of HR services into web–based technology. AI assumes a significant role in transforming traditional HR into contemporary HR.

It focuses on the system that aids in strategic decision-making. It revolutionizes the employee experience by streamlining the HR functions, including talent management, operations, training, and development. The organizations integrate AI platforms into the HR functions to enhance employee productivity, speed, accuracy, and personalization. AI supports employees by automating tasks and not replacing them. The chatbots simulate a person-to-person conversation and is available 24/7. It also offers an immediate response. With the new technology, disruption is inevitable. The potential of AI combines human and digital capabilities, thus enabling HR to play a strategic role and supporting positive changes across the HR functions. The business integrates AI, as it is more proactive, looks at the bigger picture, and is more futuristic.

9.4.1 BENEFITS, LIMITATIONS, AND CHALLENGES IN IMPLEMENTING THE AI IN HRM

Implementing AI brings rampant growth to the HR ecosystem. In the event of digitalization, AI looks like a promising tool for enhancing the performance of HRM functions and actively changing the workplace. The benefits are as follows:

9.4.1.1 Streamline in Process

AI helps reduce manual work and streamline the process of HR functions. The first phase of the HR function is recruitment. AI is used as an integrated tool for screening applicants at this phase. AI enables the screening process in a short duration. It narrows down the applicant list by capturing the relevant skill set. Second, screening software considers the qualification of a candidate and thus eliminates unconscious bias. Third, AI aids in performing the background checks of a qualified candidate. The fourth recruitment chatbot or conversational agent uses AI in talent acquisition. It helps the recruiter collect information on the candidate's resume, asking screening questions about the candidate's knowledge, experience, and skills and ranking them. Thus, AI enables the recruiter to save time and streamline the process.

9.4.1.2 Reduce Bias in Recruitment

AI screens the candidate with a larger quantity of data and assesses the data points on skills, qualifications, and traits. Combining these data points, AI uses an algorithm to predict the right candidate, thus reducing unconscious bias objectively. The superiority of AI is achieved by testing and validating the results of identifying a potential candidate's profile. AI can be programmed to ignore the basic demographic information based on gender and age to reduce unconscious bias in human decision-making. AI is also trained to find the bias already in the recruitment process.

9.4.1.3 Improving the Onboarding Process

Organizations use AI in the onboarding process for the success of the business. The onboarding process for a new employee significantly impacts performance and retention rates. AI plays a vital role in the onboarding process by reducing time and saving the cost of an organization. AI simplifies the document verification process. AI virtual assistant provides HR support to the new employees to answer queries from any device 24 hours a day. It increases the employee's access to obtain information on compliance and clarification.

9.4.1.4 Improves the Quality of Hiring

The application of AI in human capital helps automate the process faster. The human touch can never be replaced by technology; however, AI helps improve the process. AI ensures the quality of hiring, which is a significant component from sourcing to succession for an organization. AI can be effectively applied to achieve quality recruitment goals.

9.4.2 LIMITATIONS

AI improves the productivity and performance of an organization. However, it cannot replace the human touch. There are pitfalls in using AI.

9.4.2.1 High Cost

AI is an umbrella term widely used to mimic human intelligence and decision-making. Development and implementation costs stem from optimization, data integration, security, and control efforts. This requires frequent updates and an efficiently built-in data system. Therefore, it requires a high cost to meet the demands of the required updation.

9.4.2.2 Job Insecurity

Automating clerical work may build a stress level resulting in job insecurity. The usage of chatbots and robots replaces humans for work efficiency. Although it creates an opportunity, it replaces the human for achieving the high competence level. Furthermore, the application of AI into the system demands effective communication and transparency. They play an essential role in understanding the importance of AI. Employees who are unaware of the technology and its benefits are negatively impacted.

9.4.2.3 Risk

Using AI with cognitive computing lends risk management. It involves risk issues that include unlikely or unambiguous events.

9.4.3 CHALLENGES

Although implementing AI optimizes the benefits in HRM, bottlenecks still exist in the system. There is almost a debate on how the decisions are based on AI-driven results. It is a challenging situation where employees do not accept the decisions. The AI-based performance appraisal system gives a skewed result. Furthermore, it is difficult to gauge the data and measure the performance appraisal metrics for an individual working in a team (Budhwar et al., 2022). AI has its challenges in implementation.

9.4.3.1 Requires a Large Dataset

AI is built on a large volume of data. Implementing AI in HRM requires a large dataset, programming, and framework. It needs to be accessed frequently to deliver benefits to the HR system. The evaluation of AI is performed based on security and privacy issues.

9.4.3.2 Human Bias

The screening is performed based on the inputs given by humans. There is a possibility of human error in missing input data. This impact is unnoticed. Furthermore, if any pattern is followed, this may be favorable to one candidate and unfavorable to the other.

9.4.3.3 Lacks Human Touch

The surface level of a candidate can be screened with the help of AI. The skills, competencies, and knowledge of a person can be screened using AI. However, more profound analysis of family, morality, and values cannot be performed using AI. Hence, AI lacks a human touch.

9.4.3.4 High Costs and Less Availability of Infrastructure

Computing infrastructure is seldom available. Furthermore, training and development are required for the operation of AI. There is a rapid development of cloud storage with a limited capacity. As there is limited availability, adapting the infrastructure at a low cost poses a significant challenge.

9.4.3.5 Paucity of Talent in AI

It is a well-known fact that a meagre percentage of AI professionals exists in India. The shortage of talents imposes a more significant challenge in adopting AI technology (Hossin et al., 2021).

9.5 POLICY RECOMMENDATIONS

Policies are recommended for enhancing the acceptance of AI in India. The initiatives play a significant role in promoting AI technology across various sectors of the industry.

9.5.1 CONSTRUCTING A MARKETPLACE

Like each product, AI has its value chain. It includes data capturing to develop a solution. The process involved in this value chain is not easy to follow. IT poses a serious threat to new entrants in the market. Furthermore, the investment in this technology poses a more significant challenge. Therefore, to create a conducive AI ecosystem, the marketplace for its stakeholders should manifest the required resources for adopting AI technology. It should develop a platform for easy data availability for creating a value chain.

9.5.2 CREATING AWARENESS OF THE CONTRIBUTION OF AI

The stakeholders should be given awareness of the contribution of AI technology and its application to help the workforce. Information relating to the application facilities of AI must be made available to the stakeholders. The wide range of sharing knowledge based on AI across the stakeholders will help solve AI-related issues. Creating awareness of AI technology will increase the talents in the economy and thus reduce the shortage of AI professionals.

9.5.3 COLLABORATION

A collaborative approach plays a vital role in promoting the widespread use of AI technology. The collaboration might be with a different set of partnerships. The collaboration with different industries, venture capitalists, or trade bodies will enhance the quality of research on AI applications.

9.5.4 AN AID FOR START-UP

The start-up ecosystem in the Indian economy is considered one of the sources of growth. By establishing an incubation unit for AI technology, the start-ups or the budding players in the market eventually use this platform as a hub to boost their activities and thus contribute to society. Launching a particular drive by the government to fund start-ups to adopt and apply AI technology would significantly support and enhance the field of AI.

9.5.5 SECURITY AND PRIVACY ISSUES

A data protection law enhances the progress of AI. With growing complexities of the business, establishing protection from vulnerabilities will provide security for the end-users (Chatterjee, 2020).

9.6 CONCLUSION

In the event of digitalization, AI looks like a promising tool for increasing the performance of HRM functions and actively changing the workplace. In the years to come, we can expect even better and more optimized tools and functions of HR. The effect of AI on HRM is now outspreading to use cases and problems hitherto unexplored. AI offers to facilitate hands to human resources of every potential business application in their work, such as health, finance, research, banking, computing, marketing, management. AI helps achieve balanced results and the ability to improve further; however, AI is already contributing significantly to the HR industry. It has made substantial strides in easing the recruitment process to yield the best results with little effort. There are multiple AI applications, one among which is the applicant tracking system (ATS), a software application that fully utilizes AI to maneuver its operations. With such advanced solutions, it is revolutionizing how the HR industry hires and recruits; thus, implementing AI produces extensive progress in the HR ecosystem. The goal of AI-based HRM is to individually link businesses with both current and potential employees. The use of AI technology in India should be supported by numerous policies, which are advised for this to be accomplished on a wide scale by HR departments. However, the initiatives have a big impact on spreading AI technology throughout various industries.

REFERENCES

Anuj Kumar, Sowdamini, T., Manocha, S., & Pujari, P. (2021). Gamification as a Sustainable Tool for HR Managers. *Acta Universitatis Bohemiae Meridionalis*, *24*(2), 1–14. https://doi.org/10.32725/acta.2021.003

Budhwar, P., Malik, A., Silva, M. T. T. De, & Thevisuthan, P. (2022). Artificial intelligence–challenges and opportunities for international HRM: a review and research agenda. *The International Journal of Human Resource Management*, *33*(6), 1065–1097. https://doi.org/10.1080/09585192.2022.2035161

Business World. (2020). *Will AI-Based Appraisal System Help?* Business World. www.businessworld.in/article/Will-AI-Based-Appraisal-System-Help-/06-03-2020-185671/

Chatterjee, S. (2020). AI strategy of India: policy framework, adoption challenges and actions for government. *Transforming Government: People, Process and Policy*, *14*(5), 757–775. https://doi.org/10.1108/TG-05-2019- 0031

DAWSON, J. (2020). *The Rise of AI in Talent Acquisition*. Ideal. https://ideal.com/the-rise-of-ai-in-talent- acquisition/#:~:text=AI enables recruiters and hiring,talent acquisition and retention significantly.

Delaney, J. (2021). *2021 Hiring Trends–Automation and Artificial Intelligence*. LinkedIn. www.linkedin.com/pulse/2021-hiring-trends-automation-artificial-jessica-delaney/

Donovan, M. (2021). *'Black Mirror' or better? The role of AI in the future of learning and development*. CLO Media. www.chieflearningofficer.com/2021/03/19/black-mirror-or-better-the-role-of-ai-in-the-future-of-learning- and-development/

ETHR World. (2021, April). Importance of Artificial Intelligence in Learning & Development. *Economic Times*. https://hr.economictimes.indiatimes.com/news/workplace-4-0/learning-and-development/importance-of-artificial-intelligence-in-learning-development/82288174

Fatemi, F. (2019). *How AI Can Drive Employee Engagement*. Forbes. www.forbes.com/sites/falonfatemi/2019/07/05/how-ai-can-drive-employee-engagement/?sh=543469364275

Gibson, J. (n.d.). *Traditional vs. Contemporary HR*. Retrieved September 4, 2022, from https://empowerhr.com/traditional-vs-contemporary-hr/

Holliday, M. (2020). *What is Workforce Management? The Complete Guide*. Oracle. www.netsuite.com/portal/resource/articles/human-resources/workforce-management.shtml

Hossin, S., Arije Ulfy, M., Ali, I., Karim, W., & Karim, M. W. (2021). Challenges in Adopting Artificial Intelligence (AI) in HRM Practices: A study on Bangladesh Perspective. *International Fellowship Journal of Interdisciplinary Research*, *1*(1), 66–73. https://doi.org/10.5281/zenodo.4480245

Jennings, M. (2021). *Smart HR: How AI is Transforming Talent Acquisition*. Techopedia. www.techopedia.com/smart-hr-how-ai-is-transforming-talent-acquisition/2/34667

Johnson, R. D., & Gueutal, H. G. (2017). The Use of E-HR and HRIS in Organizations Transforming HR Through Technology. *The SHRM Foundation*, 48. www.shrm.org/foundation.

Merin. (2021). *Benefits & Challenges of Using AI in Recruitment*. Hrshelf.Com. https://hrsh elf.com/ai-in-recruitment/

Oracle corporation. (2019). *AI in Human Resources: The time is now*.

Pavlou, C. (2022). *AI in HR: The good, the bad, and the ugly*. Efront Learning. www.efrontl earning.com/blog/2022/05/ai-in-hr.html

Profit co. (2022). *Use of Artificial Intelligence in Performance Reviews*. Profit.Co. www.pro fit.co/blog/performance-management/use-of-artificial-intelligence-in-performance-reviews/#:~:text=As a part of the,surveys or even self–evaluations.

Rao, P. (2019). *The future is now: The changing role of HR*. Economic Times. https://econom ictimes.indiatimes.com/small-biz/hr-leadership/leadership/the-future-is-now-the-chang ing-role-of- hr/articleshow/68229542.cms?from=mdr

Sari, R. E., Min, S., Purwoko, H., Furinto, A., & Tamara, D. (2020). Artificial Intelligence for a Better Employee Engagement. *International Research Journal of Business Studies*, *13*(2), 173–188. https://doi.org/https://doi.org/10.21632/irjbs

Schneider, I. (2021). *Limitations of HR performance appraisals using AI* (Issue February) [HULT International Business School]. https://doi.org/10.13140/RG.2.2.17122.25286

Seetha Lakshmi, R., Sowdamini, T., Biswas, A. K. (2020). The Rise of Artificial Intelligence In Talent Acquisition. In *Perspectives on Business Management & Economics* (Vol. 3, pp. 161–164).

SivaSubramanian, R. (2022, February 22). Machine learning and Artificial Intelligence: A futuristic approach to employee engagement. *The Times of India*. https://times ofindia.indiatimes.com/blogs/voices/machine-learning-and-artificial-intelligence-a-futuristic-approach-to-employee-engagement/

Sowdamini, T. (2022). Is AI the Magic Wand for a Sustainable Future? In *Artificial Intelligence and Digital Diversity Inclusiveness in Corporate Restructuring*. https://doi.org/https:// doi.org/10.52305/DPEM1704

Wallask, S. (2017). *workforce analytics*. TechTarget. www.techtarget.com/searchhrsoftware/ definition/workforce-analytics

10 Fraud Detection with Machine Learning and Artificial Intelligence

Seema Garg
Amity University, Noida, Uttar Pradesh, India

Ritu Sharma
Torrens University, Adelaide, Australia

10.1 INTRODUCTION

Fraud occurs in all spheres of life. Frauds are increasing each day in various businesses, agencies run by government; the finance and other related sector, other frauds related to credit card is a growing and has become a major threat. A high reliance on the Internet has led to the increase in credit card fraud transactions; nonetheless, both online transactions and physical transactions frauds have increased. Despite the usage of data mining techniques, there are certain hurdles that the results are not very precise in identifying various frauds. The discovery of these losses is the only method to reduce them and employing effective algorithms, which is a promising method, of the fraud how to lower credit card fraud. With the development of big data and artificial intelligence, there are more opportunities than ever to identify fraud using cutting-edge machine learning models. As Internet usage has increased continuously, the finance department issues credit cards to customers. Using credit card, one can borrow funds that can be used for any of the purposes by the company.

In credit card frauds, fraudsters can carry out any illegal transactions by stealing the PIN or account-related information of the credit card without taking the original physical card. The card, such as a credit card or a debit card, may be used in the fraud event that is performed. In this instance, the card itself serves as a source of fraud in the transaction. Gaining products without paying money or obtaining an unlawful fund may be the motivation behind the crime. Fraudsters often choose to target credit cards. The rationale is that a lot of money can be made quickly without incurring many risks, and even a crime may not be discovered for several weeks. Given how frequently people use the Internet, there may be many opportunities for fraudsters to use credit cards fraudulently. The majority of fraud cases that are now active are on e-commerce websites.

Researchers, programmers, and managers of AI-based systems specific for identifying financial fraud can learn from the study's conclusions. The investigation is

DOI: 10.1201/9781003348351-10

among the earliest comprehensive analyses of the technical possibilities and political ramifications of employing artificial intelligence (AI) technologies to identify financial crime. Many of the findings are applicable to other systems even though the study examines a particular task and set of technological parameters. For instance, the study points out a variety of technological difficulties with widespread applicability, such as large amounts of data, high rates of false positives, shifting profiles, adaptable opponents, and similarities between honest and dishonest behavior.

10.2 MACHINE LEARNING

Machine learning is a branch of AI technology that is used around everywhere in the environment. By creating computer programs in software development that can automatically access data and complete tasks through future predictions, this innovative technology aids computer systems in learning from experience and improving. An approach of machine learning is a field in which computers learn concepts from data as well as predict and classify the input as an output value using statistical analysis. The value of input data is predicted by supervised learning, which is categorized using the assigned label. By contrast, unsupervised learning—which is frequently referred to as a clustering process—is carried out when the data are not labeled.

"Deep learning" is a branch of machine learning that uses artificial neural networks for predictive analysis. More data entering a machine help the algorithms train the computer, thereby enhancing the results produced. Alexa on the Amazon Echo will go to the station that person has played most frequently when they ask her to play their favorite music station. Moreover, by directing Alexa to skip songs, increase or decrease the volume, and many other conceivable instructions, one can personalize his listening experience. Machine learning and rapid advances in AI make these tasks possible and feasible. Machines utilize reinforcement learning to determine the best possibility that needs to be considered and to take the appropriate actions to improve the reward.

10.3 ARTIFICIAL INTELLIGENCE

AI is the intelligence of perceiving and inferring information that machines display and may be programmed to mimic human behavior or thought processes. AI refers to the use of particular types of inquiry to carry out tasks with a broad range, from driving a car to fraud detection. AI refers to the use of machines that behave like humans, primarily computers. AI involves the use of machines to carry out activities such as speech recognition, learning, and problem-solving. If given enough information, machines are capable of doing human-like actions. Consequently, knowledge engineering is crucial to AI. To perform knowledge engineering, the relationship between objects and properties is established. AI is a combination of machine learning techniques and deep learning.

Thus far, fraud has been detected using rule-based calculations, which are frequently complicated but easy to circumvent. These tactics run the risk of overlooking a lot of fraud-related actions or leading to extravagant measures of fictitious benefits, where customers' cards are denied because of misidentified and suspicious behaviors. Traditional models are almost wholly uncompromising, which is problematic in a situation where fraudsters are constantly looking for new ways to evade detection.

Organizations and educational foundations had to temporarily conduct their operations remotely because of the spread of COVID-19 and the implementation of lockdown. This oddity caused an unstoppable flood in the acceptance of advancements for routine tasks. As a result, the country experienced increased efforts and instances of electronic blackmail. Between March 2020 and 2021, compared with the previous year, the incidence of fraud activities increased by more than 28% after the flare-up began in March 2020.

10.4   FRAUDS

Fraud refers to cheating with intention for unethical and unauthorized gains and benefits at the cost of victims. It can be categorized broadly as internal fraud, occupational fraud, or employee dishonesty. It includes banks frauds, credit card and debit card frauds, healthcare frauds, bankruptcy frauds, consumer frauds, securities frauds, and other types of fraud. Fraud is defined as "the crime of acquiring money by deceiving people; hence, it can have a devastating impact on a business, resulting in financial loss. Fraudster will defraud the victim when individuals trade the products online and through services."

10.4.1   Types of Fraud

Fraud occurs in all spheres of life. This spread of continuous increase in e-banking, which includes online transactions through various payment options, for example, credit/debit cards, Google Pay, Paytm. Fraudulent activities and frauds related to them have also increased and spread in the market. Every lock has its key, and similarly, fraudsters or criminals have solutions to escape. They are very skilled or smart in finding escapes from it. With the development of big data and AI, there are opportunities to identify fraud using cutting-edge machine learning models. Different types of frauds in this study include credit card frauds, telecommunication frauds, computer intrusions, bankruptcy fraud, theft fraud/counterfeit fraud, application fraud, and behavioral fraud (Khyati 2012). Figure 10.1 shows the types of different frauds.

1. **Credit Card Fraud**:
   This type of fraud is categorized in two major categories:
   a) **Online and Offline fraud**
      Online fraud can be perpetrated through phone, web, shopping, or even while the cardholder is not present.
      Offline fraud can occur when a stolen physical card is used at a call center or another location.
   b) **Theft/Counterfeit Fraud**
      The use of a card that is not your own constitutes theft fraud. Similarly, remote use of a credit card leads to counterfeit fraud because only the card's data are required, as described by Khyati Chaudhary (2012).

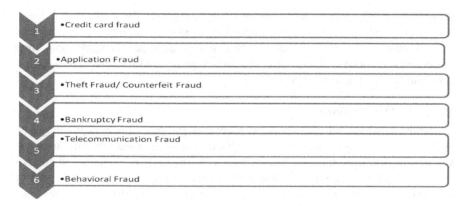

1	•Credit card fraud
2	•Application Fraud
3	•Theft Fraud/ Counterfeit Fraud
4	•Bankruptcy Fraud
5	•Telecommunication Fraud
6	•Behavioral Fraud

FIGURE 10.1 Types of frauds.

2. **Telecommunication Fraud**: The victims of telecommunication fraud include customers, enterprises, and communication service providers.
3. **Financial Fraud**: Financial fraud includes fake check's frauds and credit and debit frauds. Another fraud is bankruptcy fraud, which is one of the most complicated types of fraud to predict, as described by Phua et al. (2006).
4. **Consumer Fraud**: Consumer fraud includes merchant fraud and cheating of all types, for example, hacking of consumers' information and many more frauds such as healthcare frauds, security fraud.

10.4.2 Fraud Detection Methods for Credit Cards

A relevant study of various methods through extensive literature for fraud and fraud detection reported that to control and detect credit card fraud, various approaches are available, as described by S. Benson (2011) and Zareapoor (2012).

- Neural Network
- Hidden Markov Model Approach
- A Fusion Approach
- Genetic Algorithm
- Bayesian Network Approach
- Decision Tree
- Blast-Ssaha Hybridization

10.4.3 Machine Learning–Driven Fraud Detection

This section covers the methods for identifying false statements, estimating client risk, and forecasting future behavior. Various steps for this purpose are as follows:

10.4.3.1 Data Cleansing

The process of identifying, correcting, or deleting erroneous and damaged information from a dataset is known as data cleansing. The basic goal is to identify incomplete data, fill in missing values, and eliminate incorrigible data. Typically, this is due to human intervention, transmission, processing, or storage failures produce unclean data. Benefits of the data cleaning process include decreased computational costs associated with model training, improved dataset quality, and accelerated data exploration and feature engineering procedures.

10.4.3.2 Data Exploring

In machine learning, one of the major types of data analysis, namely exploratory data analysis, is used; it uses statistical and graphical techniques to analyze and summarize key information from the available dataset. The frequency of features and computation of their association to gain a comprehensive understanding of the pool of dataset is determined, and it identifies the most crucial characteristics for the machine learning model. It is a useful tool for removing elements from the model that do not add much information through the correlation matrix.

10.4.3.3 Privacy Preserving

Categorization and generalization can be utilized to anonymize data while protecting client privacy. Most client data and claim attributes are converted to a binary representation through classification. Other forms are created using both personal and generic data. Low-level information is replaced with high-level notions through generalization. Personal information about customers, for instance, will not be displayed for privacy reasons in layouts.

10.4.3.4 Model Building

Detection of fraud refers to a specific kind of fraud that has been discovered. A multiclass classification is necessary because there are numerous fraud techniques in use. Additionally, a logistic regression or regression issue can be used to derive or framing of a model, that is, model building for the prediction of future client claim amounts, depending on risks available for their level of risk.

Currently, banking and e-commerce sectors' top priorities are preventing, detecting, and eliminating fraud. Machine learning development services are one of the most promising ways to achieve them. E-mail spam has already been successfully identified using machine learning. It also provides millions of Internet shoppers with targeted product recommendations. Big data's accessibility enables machine learning to grow rapidly and improve greatly in a short period of time. Machine learning is now being used in the e-commerce and banking industries thanks to improvements in statistical modeling and steadily increasing processing capacity. These sectors have high expectations for machine learning–based effective fraud detection as a tool to combat cybercrime.

10.5   MACHINE LEARNING IN FRAUD DETECTION

Machine learning enables the design of algorithms that can distinguish between fraudulent and lawful transactions without revealing the names of the parties involved. A great use case for machine learning is fraud detection. The transactions are differentiated by machine learning techniques. Big data outperform humans in the detection and prevention of financial fraud.

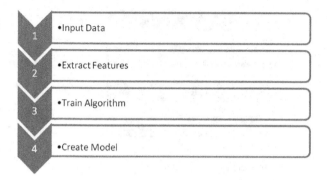

FIGURE 10.2   Procedure of fraud detection using machine learning.

Unlike humans, the models are more effective and efficient at spotting frauds. The idea that fraudulent transactions differ from authentic ones in several distinguishing ways is the cornerstone of machine learning for fraud detection. Machine learning is a group of AI algorithms used in fraud detection that have been trained using the historical data at hand and analyzed to identify risk rules. Machine learning algorithms look for trends in financial transactions and evaluate the trustworthiness of certain transactions. Machine learning fraud detection algorithms outperform humans by a wide margin. More swiftly than even the best team of analysts, they can process a large amount of data. Following that, the rules to restrict or permit specific user activity, including suspect logins, identity theft, or fraudulent transactions, will be put into place. Machine learning algorithms may identify patterns of typical behavior and learn from them. By looking into and analyzing several instances of fraud, machine learning algorithms can discover and pinpoint the patterns of fraud. As a result, the model can recognize suspect clients even in the absence of a chargeback. Machine learning works for fraud detection in this order.

10.5.1   MANAGEMENT OF LOAD

Machine learning is effective in managing the level of load on the system whether under load or overload. Online fraud involves false representation of the true facts and is becoming increasingly prevalent. Fraudsters use latest updated technology to stay one step ahead. As machine learning models are effective in analyzing massive volumes of data therefore they are used in fraud detection come to the rescue since they can quickly, efficiently and easily analyze massive volumes of data.

10.5.2   PERFORMANCE COMPARISON

Machine Learning outperforms it is all other conventional fraud detection methods. An expert system which is a part of AI is the most important for fraud detection. It is more efficient, more quick and more effective than other fraud detection methods. The amount of data being produced by any company can only be handled via machine learning. As ML algorithms analyze more data, they learn more and get better at learning. It works on large volume of data in order to identify fraud.

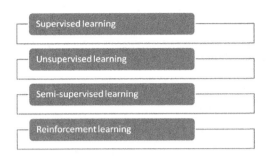

FIGURE 10.3   Various models for fraud detection.

10.5.3   Machine Learning Algorithms and Models for Fraud Detection

The following categories of machine learning algorithms exist. Figure 10.3 shows the algorithms and models

10.5.3.1   Supervised Learning

Supervised machine learning relies on input and output training data that are labeled. Its model is based on predictive data analysis. It has the ability to identify fraud that was part of the training set and not part of the historical dataset.

10.5.3.2   Semi-Supervised Learning

This method is an intermediate between supervised and unsupervised learning.

10.5.3.3   Unsupervised Learning

Unsupervised machine learning relies on unlabeled or raw data. It is used to identify unusual activity. Their models continuously process and examine fresh data; if required, they also remodel in accordance with the results. These methods are typically linked to deep learning in fraud detection.

10.5.3.4   Reinforcement Learning

It enables automated detection of optimum conduct in a certain setting. It frequently and continuously learns from its surroundings to develop answers or take actions that minimize threats, risks, and rewards.

10.6   BOTTOM OF FORM

Literature Review

Heta Naik and Prashasti Kanikar (2019) conducted research on several algorithms. Among the other classification algorithms, the Bayes theory is a prerequisite and required initially for this procedure. The linear regression algorithm and the logistic regression algorithm are comparable. For making predictions or anticipating values, linear regression is used.

Navanushu Khare and Saad Yunus (2018) discussed their findings using decision trees, random forests, and logistic regression. The dataset used was more dispersed and had lack of symmetry (asymmetry). To evaluate the performance, various criteria such as efficiency, accuracy, and precision were used. They came to the conclusion that the random forest algorithm was best, as it was most accurate among all algorithms in spotting fraud.

Priya and Saradha (2021) explained and raised a concern that all industries are at risk of digital fraud. They focused on identifying and preventing fraud occurrence. By automating routine tasks with the push of a button, digitization has transformed how we do daily business. On the flip side, it has created dangers from malicious users who may abuse the lack of safeguards in digital apps to pose as legitimate users, carry out pricey transactions on their behalf, and incur losses in money. Organizations must pay attention, as it affects the value of their brand. Organizations have used a variety of techniques, including deploying sophisticated algorithms to look for trends in fraud and to detect fraudulent activity in real time. The application of AI and machine learning will have a positive impact on automated learning and fraud pattern identification.

As described by El Hajjami et al. (2021), credit card use is becoming increasingly democratized and widespread, which inescapably increases the number of fraudulent transactions. In most cases, the problem of anomaly detection includes fraud detection. Current methods and strategies in this area are always searching for the most effective ways to spot anomalies. These strategies are put to test when dealing with a vast and expanding volume of data, which results in a significant number of undetected abnormalities. The development and application of scalable systems capable of continually consuming and processing enormous volumes of data are necessary for real-time fraud detection. New views in the field of anomaly detection (fraud detection) are made possible by recent improvements in data analytics processing, storage, and open-source solutions.

There are many productive uses of machine learning. It is used as a classifier that will study email messages and identify and discriminate spam from nonspam texts, which requires systems that use historical sales data to forecast customer purchasing fraud detection and behavior. The use of machine learning includes association analysis through supervised and unsupervised learning. However, in this study, we will focus on learning and reinforcement learning regarding algorithms for classifying the strengths and weaknesses of supervised learning. Building a clear understanding is the aim of supervised learning. It is a model of the predictor feature–based distribution of class labels.

10.7 MACHINE LEARNING IN FRAUD DETECTION

Businesses are currently developing AI and machine learning–oriented fraud detection solutions for many solutions. Many sectors may protect their financial information with contemporary fraud prevention systems that are machine learning powered. For FinTech, security, banking, and various other fields, some fraud detection methods are already existing. The fraud analyst team is not replaced by machine learning, but it does enable them to spend less time on manual reviews and data analysis. Machine learning is a group of AI algorithms that have been taught using your previous data to advise risk criteria in fraud detection. Data analysis and predictive analytics are handled by machine learning, which enables businesses to expand and thrive without having to worry about fraud. Data analysis and predictive analytics are handled by machine learning, which enables businesses to expand and thrive without having to worry about fraud. According to Capgemini, their machine learning fraud detection technology can increase accuracy by 90% while reducing fraud investigation time by 70%. Machine learning fraud protection solutions from a different vendor can identify 95% of all fraud cases.

10.8   CHARACTERISTICS AND CHALLENGES

In the same research, we discover that the following traits and difficulties are common to online fraud detection:

- Given that the time between a consumer making a payment and the payment being transferred to its destination account is typically quite brief, fraud detection must be done in real-time. A fraud detection notice should be generated as soon as possible to prevent immediate money loss. This calls for highly effective fraud detection for massive and unbalanced data.
- Fraud behavior is dynamic; as information technology develops on a daily basis, fraudsters constantly improve the methods they use to gain access despite online banking security.
- There are many different types of customer behavior patterns; in this situation, fraudsters frequently imitate actual customer behavior. Additionally, they frequently alter their behavior to keep up with developments in fraud detection. All these make it challenging to define fraud and even more challenging to separate it from sincere action.
- Customers access the same online banking system, as it is fixed, which makes it possible to characterize typical genuine behavior sequences and spot red flags in online banking fraud. The aforementioned traits make fraud detection particularly difficult, which is why numerous machine learning algorithms have been created to address this issue.

10.9   CONCLUSION

It is imperative that quick and effective solutions be developed for fraud detection, risk assessment, and data management that can maintain an ideal balance between the protection of client personal information, loss prevention, and phone alert detection. Currently, there are systems in use for monitoring fraud risk for credit cards. The primary responsibility of financial institutions such as banks is the coordination to increase the default degree of risk control for customers using a scientific method. There are numerous ways to find credit card frauds. One of the available algorithms, or several algorithms combined, is applied to bank credit cards for detecting fraud and likelihood of transactions including fraud. Moreover, a number of antifraud tricks are advised to be used to lower risks and avoid banks from suffering significant losses. Data science is useful to stop and control various kinds of fraud. Machine learning is used, as it can currently assist businesses in preventing fraudulent activities. Machine learning employs modern fraud detection technologies. Big data analytics and machine learning have the ability to enhance fraud detection in every business.

REFERENCES

1. Baker, N. (2005). Fraud and artificial intelligence: new machine-learning technology may help businesses detect suspicious activity and mitigate the risk of fraudulent transactions. *Internal Auditor*, *62*(1), 29–32.
2. El Hajjami, S., Malki, J., Berrada, M., Mostafa, H., & Bouju, A. (2021, January). Machine learning system for fraud detection. a methodological approach for a development platform. In *International Conference on Digital Technologies and Applications* (pp. 99–110). Springer, Cham.
3. G. J. Priya and S. Saradha, "Fraud Detection and Prevention Using Machine Learning Algorithms: A Review," *2021 7th International Conference on Electrical Energy Systems (ICEES)*, 2021, pp. 564–568, doi: 10.1109/ICEES51510.2021.9383631.
4. Jain, V., Agrawal, M., & Kumar, A. (2020, June). Performance analysis of machine learning algorithms in credit cards fraud detection. In *2020 8th International Conference on Reliability, Infocom Technologies and Optimization (Trends and Future Directions)(ICRITO)* (pp. 86–88). IEEE.
5. Khyati Chaudhary, Jyoti Yadav, Bhawna Mallick, "A review of Fraud Detection Techniques: Credit Card", International Journal of Computer Applications (0975–8887) Volume 45–No.1, May 2012
6. Linda Delamaire (UK), Hussein Abdou (UK), John Pointon (UK), "Credit card fraud and detection techniques: a review", Banks and Bank Systems, Volume 4, Issue 2, 2009 [8] S. Benson Edwin Raj, A. Annie Portia, "
7. Masoumeh Zareapoor, Seeja. K.R, and M. Afshar. Alam (2012), "Analysis of Credit Card Fraud Detection Techniques: based on Certain Design Criteria", International Journal of Computer Applications (0975–8887) Volume 52–No.3, August 2012
8. McCorduck, P., Minsky, M., Selfridge, O. G., & Simon, H. A. (1977, August). History of artificial intelligence. In *IJCAI* (pp. 951–954).
9. Muhammad, I., & Yan, Z. (2015). SUPERVISED MACHINE LEARNING APPROACHES: A SURVEY. *ICTACT Journal on Soft Computing*, *5*(3).
10. Prasad, R., & Rohokale, V. (2020). Artificial intelligence and machine learning in cyber security. In *Cyber Security: The Lifeline of Information and Communication Technology* (pp. 231–247). Springer, Cham.
11. S. Benson Edwin Raj, A. Annie Portia (2011), "Analysis on Credit Card Fraud Detection Methods", International Conference on Computer, Communication and Electrical Technology–ICCCET2011, 18th & 19th March, 2011
12. Tripathi, K. K., & Pavaskar, M. A. (2012). Survey on credit card fraud detection methods. *International Journal of Emerging Technology and Advanced Engineering*, *2*(11), 721–726.
13. Raghavan, P., & El Gayar, N. (2019, December). Fraud detection using machine learning and deep learning. In *2019 international conference on computational intelligence and knowledge economy (ICCIKE)* (pp. 334–339). IEEE.

11 Performance of Artificial Intelligence in Fraud Detection

Saurabh Tiwari
School of Business,
University of Petroleum & Energy Studies, Dehradun,
Uttarakhand, India

Rajeev Srivastava
IMS Unison University, Dehradun, Uttarakhand, India

11.1 INTRODUCTION

In the past few years, a accumulating data have been produced by different sources such as social media platforms, Internet of Things, and transactional data, giving birth to a new type of data, known as "big data." Big data help tools and techniques such as artificial intelligence (AI), machine learning (ML), and deep learning to improve processes, better decision-making, predict futures, and many other perspectives. AI has the potential to greatly boost business efficiency while freeing up more work for people. When AI reduces time-consumption or dangerous activities, individual workers focus on responsibilities that they are additionally trained for, such as those that require imagination and responsiveness. Work that people find more enjoyable could make them happier and more satisfied with their jobs. The input energy for AI algorithms is data. As more data are collected, every second person's day privacy is at stake. If organizations and governments chose to base their judgments on what they discover about you, as China does with their social credit system, it might result in social tyranny. On the one hand, it helps businesses to become digital. On the other hand, it gives birth to a new problem, known as "fraud." Nowadays, various digital payment platforms are available that help people with cashless payments, but simultaneously, the number of fraud cases keeps increasing daily. Through improved internal security and more efficient business processes, businesses have benefited from using AI to detect fraud (Choi and Lee, 2018; Ryman-Tubb and d'Avila Garcez, 2010). AI has accordingly developed into an important instrument for decreasing financial offences because

DOI: 10.1201/9781003348351-11

of its enhanced efficiency. A huge number of transactions may be examined using AI to detect fraud tendencies, which can subsequently be used for present fraud identification (Bao et al., 2022; Ryman-Tubb et al., 2018). When fraud is suspected, transactions may be flagged for further investigation, transactions may be rejected outright, or the likelihood of fraud may be rated using AI models. This permits examiners to emphasize their efforts on fraud cases with the best chance of success. The AI model can also provide flagged transaction's cause codes. These reasons help accelerate the examination by pointing out where the examiner should look for flaws. Technology plays an important role in handling this problem to a great extent (Tiwari & Srivastava 2022). Many researchers have contributed through their studies to understand the way AI, ML, and deep learning help in fraud detection. These studies are contributed to different sectors such as banking, healthcare, energy, e-commerce, and many more. Over the coming years, AI will probably change the banking sector. Banks are increasingly used to process and analyze credit applications and look through huge amounts of data. Consequently, fraud is reduced and resource-intensive, repetitive processes, and client operations can be automated without sacrificing quality. Several factors contribute to this relative lack of implementation. In actuality, not every fraud scheme lends itself to the AI intervention similarly. Consider the environment of credit card fraud as a good place to test ML algorithms. Large datasets are needed for training, backtesting, and validation of ML algorithms because of the volume of credit card transactions (Hand et al., 2008). Labeling historical data to train classification algorithms is simplified because a fraudulent activity is fairly clearly defined. The historical datasets include many features such as transaction characteristics, cardholder details, or transaction history, which could be incorporated into models. Contrarily, catching people engaging in money laundering can be harder. For instance, it might be quite difficult to determine whether a certain behavior fits the legal description of money laundering. They could require a number of individuals pretending beyond the boundaries of the business. Financial organizations may be less willing to disclose data given the sensitivity of the information at stake (even in the quasi-anonymized format). Obviously, preventing credit card fraud using ML techniques has progressed more than addressing money laundering activities. Since the 1950s, when credit and debit cards were made widely available for ordinary purchases, fraud trajectories have grown over time and are now well-known within the sector (Tiwari, 2020; Tiwari, 2022). Criminal tactics have only recently undergone a rapid change (Mann, 2006), which may partially account for the absence of the research rationale. Up to the 1970s, all businesses were conducted using studies that were actually published (Evans & Schmalensee, 2005). The technique may be automated with the advent of the magnetic stripe, which could be used to store cardholder data that terminals could automatically read (Svigals, 2012). At this stage, early research concentrated on the straightforward automation of identifying fraud and developing new procedures utilizing rules (Parker, 1976). The first significant work in this field was not published until 1994 (Ghosh & Reilly, 1994). Few studies are conducted to resolve credit card fraud exposure, which is one of the measurable problems nowadays. Many of the latest techniques such as ML, blockchain, AI, and deep learning multistage models are utilized to resolve that problem (Lacruz et al., 2021; Kapadiya et al., 2022; Zioviris et al., 2022). Few studies are focused on understanding fraud detection in credit cards. Studies were conducted to determine how research on AI and ML influences credit card fraud detection (Nick et al., 2018) utilizing a deep learning multiplex prototype (Zioviris et al., 2022). Sadly, the public views payment card fraud as a relatively minimal offense, the consequences of which are lessened by the card issuer reimbursing any individual fraud; the effect on the fraud sufferer is therefore lessened. There are two common misconceptions about payment fraud: (1) that it only affects banks, large corporations, and the government; and (2) that it is typically carried out by "bedroom hackers" (Castle, 2008). It has been established, however, that organized crime organizations and criminal businesses employ credit card fraud to fund their operations, which include terrorism, drug trafficking, and weapon sales (Financial-Fraud-Action-UK, 2014). Individuals committing fraud have a human cost because these criminals engage in violent and murderous behavior (Everett, 2003; Jacobson, 2010). Digitalization assists in identifying the pattern of energy consumption in the energy sector, and future needs are also predicted. However, many fraud detections were identified as discussed in the study, an Energy-Fraud Detection (Calamaro et al., 2021). Detection of healthcare insurance fraud is performed using blockchain and AI (Kapadiya et al., 2022). Identity theft is detected when opening an e-banking account (Desrousseaux et al., 2019). How research on AI and ML affects the detection of payment card fraud (Nick et al., 2018; Navaneethakrishnan & Viswanath, 2022). The current and future effects of digital technologies and AI are on law enforcement, policing, and the practice of law (Nissan, 2017). Decision trees are used to analyze uncertain data in the banking system to detect fraud (Khare et al., 2020). Identity theft is a risk when opening an e-banking account (Desrousseaux et al., 2019). AI techniques are used in instant payment for real-time clean fraud detection (Said et al., 2021).

Researchers contribute many studies to understand the way AI is used in fraud detection across various sectors. Therefore, a comprehensive evaluation that uses the most credible Web of Science (WoS) database and does not negotiate on both excellence or capacity is required. The current chapter also presents an existing account of AI and fraud detection that will aid in advancing future scholarly investigations in this field. A recent study supported the research question with this objective:

RQ1.   *What is the present status of expertise and insight of fraud detection using artificial intelligence?*

RQ2.   *What have been the most prolific authors, influential journals, most impactful journals, significant themes, sources, nations, and affiliations in artificial intelligence and fraud detection publications over the past 20 years?*

Performance analysis was performed on the documents contributed in this field extracted from the WoS database. This research was divided into five sections. The first section of this chapter provides a broad outline of the subject and the leading study issues we developed established on the literature analysis. In the second section, we trace our procedures for locating available literature using the WoS database. In the third section, we discussed our study outcomes and conclusions regarding the most productive authors, influential journals, essential themes, and cluster analysis. The fourth section presents the conclusion based on the findings. In the final section, we present the study's shortcomings and possible future research objectives.

11.2 METHODS

Using bibliometric analysis, it is possible to investigate patterns in a research field's relationships with the fields, journals, authors, institutions, keywords, and articles that are involved (Tiwari et al., 2022a; Bahuguna et al., 2022; Chawla & Goyal, 2022; Kruggel et al., 2020; Mas-Tur et al., 2020). Science mapping analysis applications are made to texts taken from the Scopus database during 2002-2022. The Bibliometrix package for the R programming language was applied to perform bibliometric assessment. Bibliometrix suite is an instrument for quantitative bibliometrics and scientometrics investigation. WoS was used to import bibliographic data into this package.

Additionally, both bibliometric analysis and the creation of various networks are possible with this package. Science mapping analysis was performed by utilizing the functions of the Bibliometrix package through the Shiny user interface, Biblioshiny. Research themes in the literature on AI and fraud detection wee found using science mappings and performance analyses, which examine the efficiency and influence of the keywords "artificial intelligence" and "fraud detection" in publications (Bao et al., 2022; Ryman-Tubb et al., 2018; Dubey et al., 2012). The first section briefly summarizes the research fields for AI and fraud detection. In the event of the research area being identified under more than one discipline, it can be considered as multidisciplinary or even interdisciplinary research. The relevance of the publication outlets was then monitored using journal citation analysis. The occurrence of the journals mentioned in other studies was examined using journal co-citation assessment to recognize research subjects. Monitoring the authors' research output was the goal of the author citation analysis (Culnan, 1986). Finding commonalities between their research was the goal of the author's co-citation assessment. When two or more writers are jointly referenced in another work, there is a co-citation connection. Therefore, co-citation assessment makes it feasible to distinguish research themes that grab the authors' attention.

Additionally, it facilitates the development of links among leading researchers in the area (Rosetto et al., 2018). Institutional citation assessment was applied to follow a university's study output built on the volume of citations the articles on AI and fraud detection received. The connections between research institutions have been assessed. This study focuses on how fraud detection and AI have hidden capabilities. Utilizing keyword co-occurrence assessment is a different technique for locating research groups. This methodology seeks to determine how frequently particular keywords are used in conjunction. Using document citation analysis, the citations produced by journal papers and book chapters were tracked to ascertain their perceived usefulness.

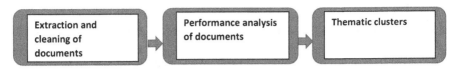

FIGURE 11.1   Steps of performance analysis.

Researchers used article co-citation assessment to recognize recurring groups. When two or more AI and fraud detection articles (also referred articles) are together cited by another article, a co-citation association exists.

11.2.1   SEARCH CRITERIA (KEYWORDS)

Performance evaluation is performed to understand the contribution of different research constituents in the area of fraud detection using AI. This analysis is performed in three steps. In Step 1, the documents are extracted from the WoS database using the search keyword "artificial intelligence" and "fraud detection." Then, the extracted documents are manually screened, and the papers not related to the field are filtered. Finally, 308 documents were used in this study. In Step 2, performance analysis was performed on these documents using the Biblioshiny App developed in R language. The analysis reveals the contribution of different research constituents contributed in this field. This part presents the details of the most productive, influential, and impactful authors, sources, countries, and documents that contributed to this field. In the final step, that is, Step 3, the VOSviewer tool was used to identify the relevant thematic clusters of this field along with the discussion.

11.3   ANALYSIS AND RESULTS

11.3.1   DATA SYNTHESIS AND ANNUAL SCIENTIFIC PRODUCTION

The dataset used in this analysis is defined in detailed in this section, along with the patterns in publishing in the last two decades. The study assesses the documents published in the WoS database from 2002 to mid-2022. A total of 308 articles have been printed in the past 20 years, focusing on how AI helps in fraud detection. More than 1000 authors contributed to this field. The details of the data are shown in Table 11.1.

TABLE 11.1
Synthesis of Data

Details	Results
Duration of publication	2002-2022
Total documents	308
Authors' keywords (DE)	865
Authors	1026

The annual growth rate of publication was 17.46%. This is because the concept of big data and AI developed more in the previous few years, due to which the number of publications continuously increased from 2017 onwards.

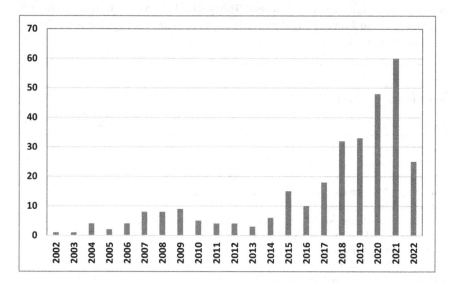

FIGURE 11.2   Annual scientific production.

Source: Authors' own elaboration.

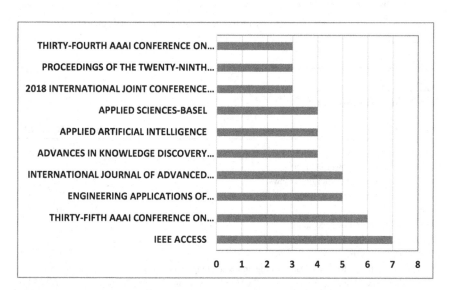

FIGURE 11.3   Most contributed journals.

Source: Authors' own elaboration.

11.3.2   Most Productive, Influential, and Impactful Sources

This section presents the details of sources with the maximum number of articles (most productive), the maximum number of citations (most influential), and the maximum h-index (most impactful). The details of the most productive sources are provided in Figure 11.3. IEEE Access, Thirty-Third AAAI Conference on Artificial Intelligence, and Engineering Applications of Artificial Intelligence were the most productive sources.

TABLE 11.2
Most Impactful Sources

Source	h_index	TC	NP
IEEE Access	4	48	7
Engineering Applications of Artificial Intelligence	4	139	5
Advances in Knowledge Discovery and Data Mining, Proceedings	2	57	4
Proceedings of the 29th International Joint Conference on AI	2	15	3
34th AAAI Conference on AI	2	34	3
2019 IEEE Second International Conference on AI and Knowledge Engineering	2	5	2
Advances in Knowledge Discovery and Data Mining	2	30	2
Artificial Intelligence Review	2	38	2
Proceedings of the 12th International Conference on Agents and AI	2	5	2
IEEE Transactions on Knowledge and Data Engineering	2	8	2
Renewable & Sustainable Energy Reviews	2	144	2
23rd AAAI Conference on AI	2	40	2

Source: Authors' own elaboration.

This table shows the most impactful sources with h-index, total citation, and net publications.

TABLE 11.3
Most Influential Sources

Source	h_index	TC	NP
SIGMOD Record	1	261	1
IEEE Transactions on Power Delivery	1	213	1
Renewable & Sustainable Energy Reviews	2	144	2
Engineering Applications of Artificial Intelligence	4	139	5
Entropy	1	94	1
IEEE Transactions on Power Systems	1	74	1
International Journal of Health Geographics	1	69	1
Proceedings of the IEEE	1	67	1
Wiley Interdisciplinary Reviews-Data Mining and Knowledge Discovery	1	66	1
Advances in Knowledge Discovery and Data Mining, Proceedings	2	57	4

Source: Authors' own elaboration.

This table shows the most influential sources with h-index, total citation, and net publications.

Two sources, namely IEEE Access and Engineering Applications of Artificial Intelligence, were the most impactful sources, with an h-index equal to 4.

From the top cited perspective, SIGMOD Record having a total citation of 261, followed by IEEE Transactions on Power Delivery (TC= 213), and Renewable & Sustainable Energy Reviews (TC=144), were sourced with maximum citations.

It is interesting to know that the two sources were among the top three most productive and impactful sources.

11.3.3 Most Influential and Impactful Authors

The details of the most influential and impactful authors are listed in Table 11.4 and Table 11.5. Cetintemel U, Stonebraker M, and Zdonik S were the authors with the maximum number of citations. Sadaoui S was the author with a maximum h-index, equal to 3.

11.3.3.1 Most Relevant Institutions

This section describes the details of the most contributing universities/institutes and the corresponding author's country. According to the details shown in Table 11.6, the University Chinese Academy of Science, the University of Porto, and the University of Technology Sydney are the most productive universities/institutes.

From the corresponding country perspective, China has the maximum contribution in terms of multi-country production (MCP) and single-country production (SCP). However, the United States (US) and India also contributed extensively. The details of the most contributing corresponding author's country are shown in Figure 11.4.

TABLE 11.4
Most Influential Authors

Author	h_index	TC	NP
Cetintemel U	1	261	1
Stonebraker M	1	261	1
Zdonik S	1	261	1
Ahmed SK	1	213	1
Mohamad M	1	213	1
Nagi J	1	213	1
Tiong SK	1	213	1
Yap KS	1	213	1
Martin-Bautista MJ	2	147	2
Ruiz Md	2	147	2
Gomez-Romero J	1	139	1
Molina-Solana M	1	139	1
Ros M	1	139	1

Source: Authors' own elaboration.

This table shows the most influential authors with h-index, total citation, and net publications.

TABLE 11.5
Most Impactful Authors

Author	h_index	TC	NP
Sadaoui S	3	24	7
Khoshgoftaar TM	2	37	4
Zhang CQ	2	23	4
Gama J	2	69	3
Gade K	2	34	3
Kenthapadi K	2	34	3
Mithal V	2	34	3
Taly A	2	34	3
Anderka M	2	22	3
Klerx T	2	22	3

Source: Authors' own elaboration.

This table depicts the most impactful authors with h-index, total citation, and net publications.

TABLE 11.6
Most Relevant Affiliations

Affiliations	Articles
University Chinese Academy of Science	11
University Porto	10
University Technology Sydney	9
University Regina	7
Shanghai Jiao Tong University	6
Babes Bolyai University	5
Dong A University	5
George Mason University	5
Institute Comp Technology	5
Shandong University	5

Source: Authors' own elaboration.

The table shows the most relevant affiliation with the name of the institutes and the number of articles published by the institute affiliation.

Corresponding Author's Country

From a citation point of view, the US (n=504), China (n=347), and Malaysia (n= 251) are the most influential countries. Malaysia was the country with the maximum average article citations (n = 62.57). The details of the most influential countries are shown in Table 11.7.

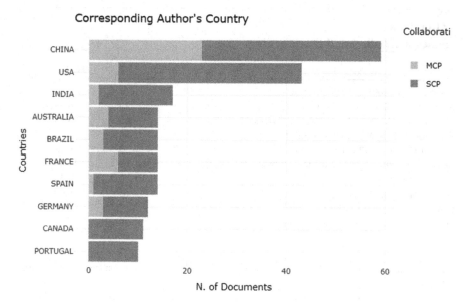

FIGURE 11.4 Corresponding authors with MCP and SCP details.

Source: Authors' own elaboration.

TABLE 11.7
Highest Influential Countries

Country	TC	Average Paper Citations
United States	504	11.72
China	347	5.88
Malaysia	251	62.75
Spain	209	14.92
Brazil	134	9.57
United Kingdom	124	17.71
Germany	109	9.08
Poland	98	24.50
India	93	5.47
Portugal	87	8.70

Source: Authors' own elaboration.

This table depicts the highest influential countries with total citation and average paper citation.

Most Global Cited Documents

Many authors and journals contributed to research on AI utility in fraud detection. Table 11.8 lists the papers that have received the most number of citations. The top three articles that received more than 100 citations are "Stonebraker M, 2005,

TABLE 11.8
Highest Globally Cited Documents

Article	TC	TC/Year
Stonebraker M, 2005, SIGMOD Record	261	14.50
Nagi J, 2010, IEEE T Power Deliver	213	16.38
Molina-Solana M, 2017, Renewable and Sustainable Energy Reviews	139	23.16
Berezinski P, 2015, Entropy-Switzerland	94	11.75
Ramos CCO, 2011, IEEE T Power Systems	74	6.16
Boulos MNK, 2018, International Journal Health Geography	69	13.80
Ruff L, 2021, P IEEE	67	33.50
Oliveira M, 2012, Wires Data Mining Knowledge	66	6.00
Ren JT, 2008, Lecture Notes AI	52	3.46
Sundarkumar GG, 2015, Engineering Applications AI	49	6.12

Source: Authors' own elaboration.

This table depicts the highest global cited documents with total citation per document and total citation per year.

Sigmod Record," "Nagi J, 2010, IEEE T Power Deliver," and "Molina-Solana M, 2017, Renew Sustainable Energy Reviews."

Most Frequent Words

This section describes the keywords that are more frequently used in publications in this field. The frequent use of keywords such as classification, neural network, outlier detection, prediction, support vector machines, and anomaly detection suggests that these are the techniques more frequently utilized in the research field of fraud detection using AI. The details of these frequently used keywords are shown in Table 11.9.

The word cloud of these frequently used keywords is shown in Figure 11.5. The bigger the size of the keywords, the more frequently they are used in publications. The more frequently used keyword, "model," indicates that different models have been developed and tested to understand fraud detection in various sectors using AI techniques. Other keywords such as "SMOTE" describe the ML technique useful in case of an imbalanced dataset. In the real world, many of the datasets are imbalanced.

The frequency of usage of these keywords changes year by year. To understand the trend of usage of these keywords, trend analysis is performed as shown in Figure 11.6. The trend shows that keyword classification has continuously increased from 2005 onward. However, from 2015 onward, there is a huge increase in the usage of this keyword. The usage of other keywords such as "model," "fraud detection," "SMOTE," and "system" also increased from 2014 onward. Additionally, usage of the keyword "neural network" increased from 2016 onward.

Co-authorship

Furthermore, co-authorship analysis was performed to identify the thematic cluster based on the concept that the authors identified more frequently with other authors of

TABLE 11.9
Most Relevant Keywords

Words	Occurrences
Classification	21
Model	17
Fraud detection	15
System	10
Neural networks	9
Networks	7
Smote	7
Algorithms	6
Artificial intelligence	6
Models	5
Network	5
Risk	5
Selection	5
Support	5
Algorithm	4
Fraud	4
Outlier detection	4
Prediction	4
Support vector machines	4
Anomaly detection	3

Source: Authors' own elaboration.

This table shows the most relevant keywords used in articles with the keywords and the number of its occurrences.

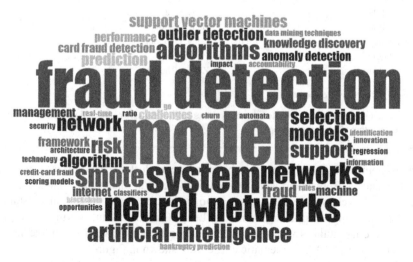

FIGURE 11.5   Word cloud of relevant keywords.

Source: Authors' own elaboration.

Word Growth

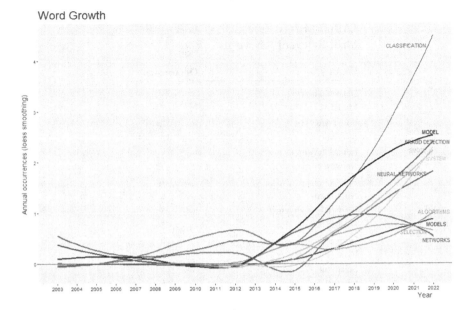

FIGURE 11.6   Trend of keyword growth during the last 20 years.

Source: Authors' own elaboration.

TABLE 11.10
Cluster Network

Author's Name	Cluster	Links	Total Link Strength	Author's Name	Cluster	Links	Total Link Strength
Bohlscheid, Hans	1	5	10	Jiang, Jing	2	4	8
Cao, Longbing	1	5	10	Jiang, Xinxin	2	4	8
Wu, Shanshan	1	5	10	Long, Guodong	2	4	8
Zhang, Huaifeng	1	5	10	Pan, Shirui	2	4	8
Zhao, Yanchang	1	5	10	Zhang, Chengqi	2	9	18

Source: Authors' own elaboration.

This table depicts the cluster in a network which shows a set of densely connected nodes that is sparsely connected to other clusters in the graph.

---

similar themes. Hence, they need to be in the same cluster. Two clusters were identified: cluster 1, Bohlscheid, Hans; Cao, Longbing; Wu, Shanshan; Zhang, Haifeng; and Zhao, Yancheng are the authors who conducted more collaborative studies; in cluster 2, Jiang, Jing; Jiang, Xin Xin; Long, Guodong; Pan, Shirui; and Zhang, Chengqi are the authors who conducted more collaborative studies. The details are shown in Table 11.10. The thematic clusters are shown in Figure 11.7.

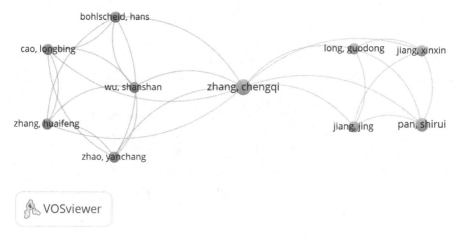

FIGURE 11.7 The co-authorship network.

Source: Using Biblioshiny.

Thematic Clusters

Furthermore, co-word analysis was performed to identify the thematic cluster based on the concept that the keywords identified more frequently with other keywords are of similar themes; hence, they need to be in the same cluster. The clustering algorithm was used to identify these clusters. A total of four clusters were identified. These clusters are shown in Figure 11.8. In Cluster 1, the keywords are shown in red color; in Cluster 2, the keywords are shown in green color; in Cluster 3, the keywords are shown in blue color font; and in Cluster 4, the keywords are shown in yellow color font. The details of all these clusters along with link strength and the number of appearances are shown in Table 11.11.

In Cluster 1, the keyword "classification" was the maximum link strength (n=65) and showed the maximum occurrence (n=28). This indicates that supervised learning technique classification is more utilized to detect fraud in different sectors. The use of the keywords "credit card fraud detection," "finance," and "big data" suggests that more research focused on identifying fraud detection in financial institutions using big data.

In Cluster 2, the usage of the keywords "data mining," "decision tree," "neural networks," "supervised learning," and "support vector machines" suggests the latest techniques used to identify fraud detection across various sectors. In this cluster, the neural network was the keyword with the maximum linkages with other keywords. The keyword "data mining" was the second frequently used one based on the number of linkages and the first frequently used with reference to the number of occurrences.

Cluster 3, comprises the keywords "anomaly detection," "deep learning," and "outlier detection," which describes the latest techniques used in fraud detection. In this cluster, anomaly detection is the keyword with the maximum linkages and occurrences.

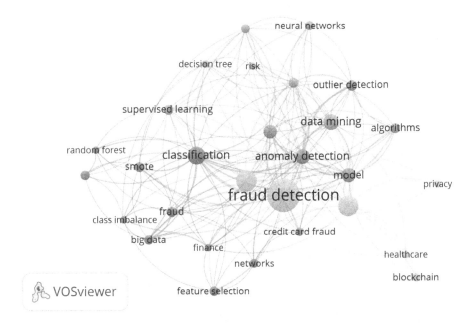

FIGURE 11.8   Thematic clusters identified from the keywords.

Source: Using Biblioshiny.

In Cluster 4, the focus is more on the keywords "AI," "ML," "block chain," and "healthcare," which discusses the latest techniques used to resolve fraud detection in the healthcare sector. In this cluster, ML was the keyword with the maximum linkages and occurrences.

11.4   CONCLUSION

Researchers have contributed many studies to understand AI utility in fraud detection across various sectors. However, no study has focused on the contribution of various research constituents in this field. Hence, performance analysis was performed on the documents pertaining to this field that were extracted from the WoS database. Overall, 308 documents were extracted from the WoS database. The Biblioshiny App developed in R language and VOSviewer were utilized to identify the thematic clusters. The study included documents published in the WoS database from 2002 to mid-2022. The annual growth rate of publication was 17.46%. The concept of big data and AI developed more in the previous few years because of which the number of publications continuously increased from 2017 onwards. IEEE Access, Thirty-Third AAAI Conference on AI, and Engineering Applications of Artificial Intelligence were the most productive source. IEEE Access and Engineering Applications of Artificial Intelligence were the most impactful sources. SIGMOD Record, IEEE Transactions on Power Delivery, and Renewable and Sustainable Energy Reviews were sourced with the maximum number of citations. Two sources, namely IEEE Access and

TABLE 11.11
Thematic Clusters Details

Keyword	Cluster	Total Link Strength	Occurrences	Keyword	Cluster	Total Link Strength	Occurrences
Big data	1	25	8	Data mining	2	34	22
Class imbalance	1	15	5	Decision tree	2	20	5
Classification	1	65	28	Neural networks	2	64	16
Credit card fraud detection	1	11	8	Risk	2	11	5
Feature selection	1	10	8	Supervised learning	2	20	9
Finance	1	19	5	Support vector machine	2	24	7
Fraud	1	15	9				
Networks	1	8	7				
Random forest	1	11	5				
Smote	1	23	9				

Keyword	Cluster	Total Link Strength	Occurrences	Keyword	Cluster	Total Link Strength	Occurrences
Algorithms	3	25	9	Artificial intelligence	4	56	36
Anomaly detection	3	58	18	Block chain	4	6	7
Credit card fraud	3	16	6	Healthcare	4	8	5
Deep learning	3	34	16	Machine learning	4	92	38
Model	3	39	17	Privacy	4	9	5
Outlier detection	3	28	10				

Source: Authors' own elaboration.

Thematic clusters analyze the distribution-based clustering analysis grouped data into objects of the same distribution. This method is the most widely used statistical analysis method.

Engineering Applications of Artificial Intelligence, were among the top three most productive and impactful sources. Cetintemel U, Stonebraker M, and Zdonik S were authors with the maximum number of citations. Sadaoui S was the author with a maximum h-index. University Chinese Academy of Science, the University Porto, and the University Technology Sydney are the most productive universities/institutes. From the corresponding author's country perspective, China has the maximum contribution in terms of MCP and SCP. The US and India also contributed a lot. From a citation point of view, the US, China, and Malaysia are the most influential countries. Malaysia was the country with the maximum average article citations. The top three articles that received more than 100 citations are "Stonebraker M, 2005, Sigmod Record," "Nagi J, 2010, IEEE T Power Deliver," and "Molina-Solana M, 2017, Renew Sustainable Energy Reviews."

The frequent use of the keywords "classification," "neural network," "outlier detection," "prediction," "support vector machines," and "anomaly detection" suggests that these techniques are utilized more in the research field of fraud detection using AI. The trend shows that keyword classification has continuously increased from 2005 onward. However, from 2015 onward, there is a huge increase in the usage of this keyword. The usage of other keywords such as "model," "fraud detection," "SMOTE," and "system" also increased from 2014 onward. The usage of the keyword "neural network" increased from 2016 onward. Co-authorship analysis was accomplished to distinguish the thematic cluster. Two clusters were identified. In Cluster 1, Bohlscheid, Hans; Cao, Longbing; Wu, Shanshan; Zhang, Huaifeng; and Zhao, Yanchang were the authors contributing more collaborative studies. In Cluster 2, Jiang, Jing; Jiang, Xin Xin; Long, Guodong; Pan, Shirui; and Zhang, Chengqi are the authors conducting more collaborative studies.

During the identification of thematic clusters, a total of four clusters were identified. In Cluster 1, the keyword "classification" had the maximum link strength (n= 65) and the maximum occurrences (n=28). This indicates that supervised learning technique classification is utilized more to detect fraud in different sectors. Use of the keywords "credit card fraud detection," "finance," and "big data" suggests that more research focuses on identifying fraud detection in financial institutions using big data. In Cluster 2, the usage of the keywords "data mining," "decision tree," "neural networks," "supervised learning," and "support vector machines" describes the latest techniques used to identify fraud detection across various sectors. In this cluster, neural networks were the keyword with maximum linkages with other keywords. The keyword "data mining" was the second most commonly used one based on the number of linkages and the first most commonly used one with regard to the number of occurrences. Cluster 3 comprises the keywords "anomaly detection," "deep learning," and "outlier detection," which describes the latest techniques used in fraud detection. In this cluster, anomaly detection is the keyword with maximum linkages and occurrences. In Cluster 4, the focus is more on the keywords "AI," "ML," "blockchain," and "healthcare," which discuss the latest techniques used to resolve fraud detection in the healthcare sector. ML was the keyword in this cluster with maximum linkages and occurrences.

11.5   LIMITATION AND FUTURE DIRECTION

This study presents the important aspects of the research constituents contributing to fraud detection using AI in the research field. Additionally, AI could identify pertinent themes in this area. To build more potent and flexible learning models, we think it would be advantageous for future investigations to merge the proficiency from the accounting and ML fields. We believe that researchers interested in these issues should pay special attention to the following interdisciplinary challenges. However, like every research has some constraints and scope for imminent direction, this research also has some shortcomings. First, the study intentionally covered the documents published in the WoS database to cover only the research papers published in impact factor sources. Nevertheless, including and evaluating the documents from other databases such as Scopus and Google Scholar may give some other direction. Second, the study focuses on identifying the most contributing research constituents. Future studies may be conducted to determine the factors responsible for fraud, specifically for digital platforms. Finally, a promising and expanding area of research involves using ML to spot anomalies, mistakes, and fraud.

REFERENCES

Aamir, J., Ali, S. M., Boulos, M. N. K., Anjum, N., & Ishaq, M. (2018). Enablers and inhibitors: a review of the situation regarding mHealth adoption in low-and middle-income countries. *Health policy and technology*, 7(1), 88–97.

Adewumi, A. O., & Akinyelu, A. A. (2017). A survey of machine-learning and nature-inspired based credit card fraud detection techniques. *International Journal of System Assurance Engineering and Management*, 8(2), 937–953.

Ait Said, M., & Hajami, A. (2021, December). AI Methods Used for Real-Time Clean Fraud Detection in Instant Payment. In *International Conference on Soft Computing and Pattern Recognition* (pp. 249–257). Springer, Cham.

Aleskerov, E., Freisleben, B., & Rao, B. (1997, March). Cardwatch: A neural network based database mining system for credit card fraud detection. In *Proceedings of the IEEE/IAFE 1997 computational intelligence for financial engineering (CIFEr)* (pp. 220–226). IEEE.

Akhilomen, J. (2013, July). Data mining application for cyber credit-card fraud detection system. In *Industrial Conference on Data Mining* (pp. 218–228). Springer, Berlin, Heidelberg.

Bahuguna, P.C., Srivastava, R. and Tiwari, S. (2022), "Two-decade journey of green human resource management research: a bibliometric analysis", *Benchmarking: An International Journal*, https://doi.org/10.1108/BIJ-10-2021-0619

Bao, Y., Hilary, G., & Ke, B. (2022). Artificial intelligence and fraud detection. In *Innovative technology at the interface of finance and operations* (pp. 223–247). Springer, Cham.

Bereziński, P., Jasiul, B., & Szpyrka, M. (2015). An entropy-based network anomaly detection method. *Entropy*, 17(4), 2367–2408.

Calamaro, N., Beck, Y., Ben Melech, R., & Shmilovitz, D. (2021). An Energy-Fraud Detection-System Capable of Distinguishing Frauds from Other Energy Flow Anomalies in an Urban Environment. *Sustainability*, 13(19), 10696.

Castle, A. (2008). Drawing conclusions about financial fraud: crime development and international co-operative strategies in China and the West. In *Transnational Financial Crime Program, The International* Centre for Criminal Law Reform & Criminal Justice Policy.

Chawla, R.N. and Goyal, P. (2022), "Emerging trends in digital transformation: a bibliometric analysis", *Benchmarking: An International Journal*, 29(4), 1069–1112.

Chaquet-Ulldemolins, J., Gimeno-Blanes, F. J., Moral-Rubio, S., Muñoz-Romero, S., & Rojo-Álvarez, J. L. (2022). On the Black-Box Challenge for Fraud Detection Using Machine Learning (I): Linear Models and Informative Feature Selection. *Applied Sciences*, 12(7), 3328.

Choi, D., & Lee, K. (2018). An artificial intelligence approach to financial fraud detection under IoT environment: A survey and implementation. *Security and Communication Networks*, 2018.

Culnan, M. J. (1986). The intellectual development of management information systems, 1972–1982: A co-citation analysis. *Management science*, 32(2), 156–172.

Deecke, L., Ruff, L., Vandermeulen, R. A., & Bilen, H. (2021, July). Transfer-based semantic anomaly detection. In *International Conference on Machine Learning* (pp. 2546–2558). PMLR

Desrousseaux, R., Bernard, G., & Mariage, J. J. (2019, September). Identify Theft Detection on e-Banking Account Opening. In *IJCCI* (pp. 556–563).

Dhieb, N., Ghazzai, H., Besbes, H., & Massoud, Y. (2020). A secure ai-driven architecture for automated insurance systems: Fraud detection and risk measurement. *IEEE Access*, 8, 58546–58558.

Dubey, R., Singh, T., & Tiwari, S. (2012). Supply chain innovation is a key to superior firm performance an insight from indian cement manufacturing. *International Journal of Innovation Science*. 4(4), 217–230.

Everett, C. (2003). Credit card fraud funds terrorism. *Computer Fraud & Security*, *2003*(5), 1

Evans, D.S., Schmalensee, R., 2005. More than money. In: Paying with Plastic. The MIT Press, pp. 72–73. (Ch. 3).

Ferreira, M. P., Santos, J. C., de Almeida, M. I. R., & Reis, N. R. (2014). Mergers & acquisitions research: A bibliometric study of top strategy and international business journals, 1980–2010. *Journal of Business Research*, 67(12), 2550–2558.

Financial-Fraud-Action-UK, 2014. Fraud the Facts 2014. The UK Cards Association, London, UK.

Ghosh, S., & Reilly, D. L. (1994, January). Credit card fraud detection with a neural-network. In *System Sciences, 1994. Proceedings of the Twenty-Seventh Hawaii International Conference on* (Vol. 3, pp. 621–630). IEEE.

Hand, D. J., Whitrow, C., Adams, N. M., Juszczak, P., & Weston, D. (2008). Performance criteria for plastic card fraud detection tools. *Journal of the Operational Research Society*, *59*(7), 956–962.

Hasheminejad, S. M. H., & Reisjafari, Z. (2017). ATM management prediction using Artificial Intelligence techniques: A survey. *Intelligent Decision Technologies*, *11*(3), 375–398.

Jacobson, M. (2010). Terrorist financing and the Internet. *Studies in Conflict & Terrorism*, *33*(4), 353–363.

Jawale, S., & Sawarkar, S. D. (2020, December). Interpretable Sentiment Analysis based on Deep Learning: An overview. In *2020 IEEE Pune Section International Conference (PuneCon)* (pp. 65–70). IEEE.

Kamel Boulos, M. N., Wilson, J. T., & Clauson, K. A. (2018). Geospatial blockchain: promises, challenges, and scenarios in health and healthcare. *International Journal of Health Geographics*, *17*(1), 1–10.

Kang, Q., Li, H., Cheng, Y., & Kraus, S. (2021). Entrepreneurial ecosystems: analysing the status quo. *Knowledge Management Research & Practice*, 19(1), 8–20.

Kapadiya, K., Patel, U., Gupta, R., Alshehri, M. D., Tanwar, S., Sharma, G., & Bokoro, P. N. (2022). Blockchain and AI-Empowered Healthcare Insurance Fraud Detection: an Analysis, Architecture, and Future Prospects. *IEEE Access*, *10*, 79606–79627.

Karypis, G. (2022, February). Graph Neural Network Research at AWS AI. In *Proceedings of the Fifteenth ACM International Conference on Web Search and Data Mining* (pp. 4–4).

Khare, N., & Viswanathan, P. (2020). Decision tree-based fraud detection mechanism by analyzing uncertain data in banking system. In *Emerging research in data engineering systems and computer communications* (pp. 79–90). Springer, Singapore.

Kruggel, A., Tiberius, V., & Fabro, M. (2020). Corporate citizenship: Structuring the research field. *Sustainability*, 12(13), 5289.

Lacruz, F., & Saniie, J. (2021, May). Applications of Machine Learning in Fintech Credit Card Fraud Detection. In *2021 IEEE International Conference on Electro Information Technology (EIT)* (pp. 1–6). IEEE.

Lebichot, B., Verhelst, T., Le Borgne, Y. A., He-Guelton, L., Oblé, F., & Bontempi, G. (2021). Transfer learning strategies for credit card fraud detection. *IEEE access*, *9*, 114754–114766.

Li, J. (2022). E-Commerce Fraud Detection Model by Computer Artificial Intelligence Data Mining. *Computational Intelligence and Neuroscience, 2022.*

Luther, L., Tiberius, V., & Brem, A. (2020). User Experience (UX) in business, management, and psychology: A bibliometric mapping of the current state of research. *Multimodal Technologies and Interaction,* 4(2), 18.

Mann, R.J.(2006). The introduction of the payment card. In: Charging ahead: The growth and regulation of payment card markets. Cambridge University Press. (Ch. 7).

Mas-Tur, A., Kraus, S., Brandtner, M., Ewert, R., & Kürsten, W. (2020). Advances in management research: a bibliometric overview of the Review of Managerial Science. *Review of Managerial Science,* 14(5), 933–958.

Merediz-Solà, I., & Bariviera, A. F. (2019). A bibliometric analysis of bitcoin scientific production. *Research in International Business and Finance,* 50, 294–305.

Mitra, S., & JV, K. R. (2021, October). Experiments on Fraud Detection use case with QML and TDA Mapper. In *2021 IEEE International Conference on Quantum Computing and Engineering (QCE)* (pp. 471–472). IEEE.

Molina-Solana, M., Ros, M., Ruiz, M. D., Gómez-Romero, J., & Martín-Bautista, M. J. (2017). Data science for building energy management: A review. *Renewable and Sustainable Energy Reviews, 70,* 598–609.

Navaneethakrishnan, P., & Viswanath, R. (2022). Fraud Detection On Credit Cards Using Artificial Intelligence Methods. *Elementary Education Online, 19*(2), 2086–2086.

Nissan, E. (2017). Digital technologies and artificial intelligence's present and foreseeable impact on lawyering, judging, policing and law enforcement. *Ai & Society, 32*(3), 441–464.

Oliveira, M., & Gama, J. (2012). An overview of social network analysis. *Wiley Interdisciplinary Reviews: Data Mining and Knowledge Discovery, 2*(2), 99–115.

Parker, D. B. (1976, June). Computer abuse perpetrators and vulnerabilities of computer systems. In *Proceedings of the June 7–10, 1976, national computer conference and exposition* (pp. 65–73).

Ramos, C. C. O., de Souza, A. N., Falcao, A. X., & Papa, J. P. (2011). New insights on non-technical losses characterization through evolutionary-based feature selection. *IEEE Transactions on Power Delivery, 27*(1), 140–146.

Ren, J., Zhou, T., & Zhang, Y. C. (2008). Information filtering via self-consistent refinement. *EPL (Europhysics Letters), 82*(5), 58007.

Rossetto, D. E., Bernardes, R. C., Borini, F. M., & Gattaz, C. C. (2018). Structure and evolution of innovation research in the last 60 years: Review and future trends in the field of business through the citations and co-citations analysis. *Scientometrics, 115*(3), 1329–1363.

Roy, D., Srivastava, R., Jat, M., & Karaca, M. S. (2022). A complete overview of analytics techniques: descriptive, predictive, and prescriptive. *Decision intelligence analytics and the implementation of strategic business management,* 15–30.

Roy, D., & Srivastava, R. (2021). The Impact of AI on World Economy. In *Artificial Intelligence and Global Society* (pp. 25–29). Chapman and Hall/CRC.

Ryman-Tubb, N. F., Krause, P., & Garn, W. (2018). How Artificial Intelligence and machine learning research impacts payment card fraud detection: A survey and industry benchmark. *Engineering Applications of Artificial Intelligence, 76,* 130–157

Ryman-Tubb, N. F., & Garcez, A. D. A. (2010, July). Soar—sparse oracle-based adaptive rule extraction: knowledge extraction from large-scale datasets to detect credit card fraud. In *The 2010 International Joint Conference on Neural Networks (IJCNN)* (pp. 1–9). IEEE.

Silva, J. T. M., Ablanedo-Rosas, J. H., & Rossetto, D. E. (2019). A longitudinal literature network review of contributions made to the academy over the past 55 years of the IJPR. *International Journal of Production Research*, 57(15-16), 4627–4653.

Stonebraker, M., Çetintemel, U., & Zdonik, S. (2005). The 8 requirements of real-time stream processing. *ACM Sigmod Record*, *34*(4), 42–47.

Srivastava, R., & Bahuguna, P. C. (2022). A Bibliographic Analysis of E-Waste Recycling Research. In *Redefining Global Economic Thinking for the Welfare of Society* (pp. 162–177). IGI Global.

Srivastava, R., & Sharma, M. (2022). Critical Analysis of Covid-19 Vaccination Status in India and Future Direction for Policy Makers. In *Advancement, Opportunities, and Practices in Telehealth Technology*. IGI Global.

Srivastava, R., & Saxena, S. (2022). The Current State of Business Intelligence Research: A Bibliographic Analysis. In *Business Intelligence and Human Resource Management* (pp. 145–160). Productivity Press.

Sundarkumar, G. G., & Ravi, V. (2015). A novel hybrid undersampling method for mining unbalanced datasets in banking and insurance. *Engineering Applications of Artificial Intelligence*, *37*, 368–377.

Svigals, J. (2012). The long life and imminent death of the mag-stripe card. *IEEE Spectrum*, *49*(6), 72–76.

Tian, Y., & Liu, G. (2020, October). MANE: Model-agnostic non-linear explanations for deep learning model. In *2020 IEEE World Congress on Services (SERVICES)* (pp. 33–36). IEEE.

Tiwari, S. (2020). Supply chain integration and Industry 4.0: a systematic literature review. *Benchmarking: An International Journal*. 28(3) 2020, 990–1030

Tiwari, S. (2022). Supply Chain Innovation in the Era of Industry 4.0. In *Handbook of Research on Supply Chain Resiliency, Efficiency, and Visibility in the Post-Pandemic Era* (pp. 40–60). IGI Global.

Tiwari, S. (2015). Framework for adopting sustainability in the supply chain. *International Journal of Automation and Logistics*, *1*(3), 256–272.

Tiwari, S., & Srivastava, R. (2022). Cyber Security Trend Analysis: An Indian Perspective. In *Cross-Industry Applications of Cyber Security Frameworks* (pp. 1–14). IGI Global.

Tiwari, S., Dubey, R., & Tripathi, N. (2011). The journey of lean. *Indian Journal of Commerce and Management Studies*, *2*(2), 200–210.

Tiwari, S., Bahuguna, P. C., & Srivastava, R. (2022a). Smart manufacturing and sustainability: a bibliometric analysis. *Benchmarking: An International Journal*, https://doi.org/10.1108/BIJ-04-2022-0238

Tiwari, S., Bahuguna, P. C., & Walker, J. (2022b). Industry 5.0: A Macroperspective Approach. In *Handbook of Research on Innovative Management Using AI in Industry 5.0* (pp. 59–73). IGI Global.

Zioviris, G., Kolomvatsos, K., & Stamoulis, G. (2022). Credit card fraud detection using a deep learning multistage model. *The Journal of Supercomputing*, 1–26.

12 Sustainable Education and Differently Abled Students

Abrar Saqib
Amity University Kolkata, Kadampuku, India

Rita Karmakar
Amity University Kolkata, Kadampuku, India

12.1 INTRODUCTION

Education is an intangible resource that empowers, liberates, and frees an individual's mindset and perceptions. Most societies, nations, and continents prioritize education because if a country's citizens receive good education, then crime rates will go down and, consequently, economic prosperity, philanthropic attitudes, and harmony among the people will be developed. The advent of postmodern technology in the 21st century has contributed to a drastic change in the design and infrastructure of education, which has led many thinkers, educators, decision-makers, and ministers to carefully think about the pros and cons of artificial intelligence (AI)–supported education. The blend of technology with education has raised many heated questions, discussions, and debates among communities and groups. The target of the discussions is to assess the goals and aims of technology use in education systems and to design a well-organized model so that the beneficial outcomes of education and knowledge can be enjoyed by all.

During uncertain times in the COVID-19 pandemic, everyone was increasingly dependent on technology and online forums. After the World Health Organization declared COVID-19 to be a pandemic, the entire education system was forced to shift from offline to online. According to reports published by the United Nations Educational, Scientific and Cultural Organization, after China, India has the world's second-largest school system.

There was a collapse in the structure of the educational institutions in India because of the pandemic, and the Ministry of Human Resource Development set regulations on continuing education online. Educational channels such as Swayam Prabha and online educational content platforms such as National Digital Libraries of India and ePathshala were used intensively during the pandemic. The online platform has served unparallel benefits to students globally to continue their education, and online content served as a learning resource for everyone.

A differently abled child can acquire knowledge and wisdom just like any average developing child. Every child is born with a unique talent and skill set that sets them apart from others. Educators and decision makers must try to implement systems that can amplify the potential of all children.

Unlike normal and healthy students, differently abled students are a vulnerable population, and they experience certain barriers to education. There is increasing importance to creating an education system that is more inclusive, resulting in bridging the gap between normal and differently abled students. According to Maskey (2020), AI-assisted Learning (AIAL) can create an adaptive environment and enhance our natural styles of learning through machine intelligence. Models such as universal design in learning and sharable content object reference model (SCORM) have been designed to make education environments more diverse and inclusive. The universal design in learning is defined by Nelson (2014) as a framework that can assist educators and teachers in designing learning activities that are open to all students irrespective of their race, gender, nationality, disability, and place of residence. The SCORM, as mentioned by Olivier and Liber (2003), is now becoming the de jure standard for transferring content to students; this is more useful for students who have certain physical disability because mobility is often challenging to them.

Some learning disabilities such as dyslexia are not often visible to instructors; hence, it is better if the resources taught are shared by the instructors beforehand so that such student can refer to the resources whenever necessary because, on the computer, they can use the text to speech software application to comprehend the content shared (Gierdowski & Galanek, 2020).

Latest devices such as iPads and tablets are widely used by the general student population, but they have a more vital role to play in the academic lives of differently abled students. For example, students with fine motor impairment can use the dictation feature of iPads and tablets to take notes dictated in the classroom instead of having difficulty in writing down notes.

Different countries are now trying to overcome the conventional mindsets of education environments and recreate a setting that can adhere to children's needs and demands. This chapter provides an overview of the rapidly changing scenario of education systems and the technical assistance that is required for the education of differently abled students.

12.2   IMPACT OF COVID-19 ON EDUCATION

Distance education through technological devices was the only way to study during the pandemic (McBrien, Cheng, & Jones, 2009), as locomotion was not an option in the first place. Cojocariu et al. (2014) mentioned the emergence of online learning, computer-aided learning, blended learning, web-based learning, and AIAL has been steadily increasing. However, in India, the scenario was rather bleak for children in government schools; survey reports by Vyas (2022) suggest that, because of poverty in many households, children belonging to needy families could not receive any educational materials during the lockdown. More than 80% of students in many Indian states (Bihar, Chhattisgarh, Jharkhand, Odisha, and Uttar Pradesh) were academically lagging due to COVID-19.

Online teaching and learning are no more an option in today's world but a necessity that encompasses our education environments and settings. The National Education Policy (NEP 2020) in India re-examined the purpose of education and is trying to bring significant changes to the education system. According to the agendas laid down by the National Education Policy, digital learning, computational thinking, and computational learning are the three key areas among students. One of the targets of World Bank (2021) is to incorporate digital technology to improve the literacy and numeracy skills of the students.

For approximately two decades, computers have been used in education, and its invasion in contemporary lives started mainly from the 2000s. Keeping in mind the diverse aims and applications of the use of AI in our lives and how it can be implemented for the benefit of mankind, the following objectives have been considered:

i) The first objective of this study is to understand the strategies to be adopted in order to sustain after the reopening of educational institutions after COVID-19.

ii) The second objective is to determine the impact of AI on education and its sustainability in the long run.

iii) The third objective of the study is to find out technological strategies to be adopted for differently abled students to make an inclusive educational environment.

12.3 METHODOLOGY

The research methodology used in this research is the literature review method. A literature review is a comprehensive summary of previous and existing research on a specific topic of interest (Coffta, 2010). This study includes verified facts, knowledge, and information from scholarly articles, books journals, websites, and other online authentic sources. The type of data included in this study is mainly a secondary data source. Research findings from various disciplines such as AI, machine learning, psychology, and education have been included in this chapter keeping in mind the holistic approach to the topic.

12.4 DISCUSSION

12.4.1 STRATEGIES TO BE ADOPTED TO SUSTAIN EDUCATION AFTER THE REOPENING OF EDUCATIONAL INSTITUTIONS AFTER COVID-19

It is not surprising that, during the COVID-19 pandemic, we have used online mode of communication such as mobile and computer applications including Gmail, G-meet, Google Forms, Calendars, G-Drive, Google Hangouts, Google Jamboard and Drawings, Google Classroom, and Open Board Software (not a product of Google but helps in recording meetings in the form of files); all these applications were heavily used as an alternative to offline classroom environments (Basilaia & Kvavadze, 2020). Furthermore, apps such as Zoom meets, Microsoft teams, and WhatsApp group video calls were also used for teacher and learner interaction. Laurillard (2004) proposed a concise definition of e-learning, which is *"e-learning describes the interaction in which students use different types of ICTs in their learning process."*

After the reopening of educational institutions, many colleges and schools had a new process of education known as the hybrid education model. In this model, students were seen attending offline classes on some days and online classes on some days. Thus, as Doering (2006) put forth, the hybrid learning model refers to the amalgamation of offline (face-to-face) and online teaching.

Algahtani (2011) has distinguished e-learning into two types:

i) Computer-based learning: it includes information and communication technology (ICT) and comprises hardware and software. One part of ICT is computer-managed instruction, where the reacquiring and storing information is mainly obtained using computers. The other part of it is computer-assisted learning system (CALS) where the learner uses the computer as an interactive tool for the exploration of knowledge and concepts. Interactive software applications of the computer act as a supporting tool.

ii) Internet-based e-learning: According to Almosa (2001), Internet-based e-learning is one step ahead of computer-based e-learning, where e-contents are available with proper links and sources that can be accessed easily (e.g., e-mail services) and references that can be accessed at any time or place.

The paramount development around multimedia, information technologies, and ICT has led to newer and updated teaching techniques that challenge the traditional process and environment of teaching (Wang, 2007). Educational institutions have now recognized that e-learning can transform future generations for good (Henry, 2001). The use of digital technologies has made it possible for everyone (teachers and learners) to access free sources of knowledge and information. Nonprofit organizations, philanthropists, and private firms are investing in online open platforms for educational resources and courses of various disciplines.

The emergence in massive open online courses (MOOCs) has an added advantage for students and learners worldwide for education and research. The United States in the year 2011 took this initiative to make educational resources available for students, and the Massachusetts Institute of Technology designed this online platform. Following that, several Edtech companies emerged to develop online materials and courses for students. Online courses designed by many government organizations as well as foreign organizations are now available as resources for younger students. Indian websites such as ePathshala, Swayam, National Programme on Technology Enhanced Learning, and BYJU'S Learning App and foreign learning apps such as Udemy, Coursera, Duolingo. Through e-learning, the objective of knowledge transfer from educators to students can be easily accomplished within a short period (Khan, 2005).

Technological devices have made education more learner-centric in nature than teacher-centric. As mentioned by Alsalem (2004), the e-learning environment encourages the learner to depend on the individual's ability rather than the teacher's. This signifies that instructors are not the only solitary source of guidance and information in educational settings. e-learning has made it possible for us to continue education even in adverse situations. For example, in February 2011, Christchurch was shaken by a 6.3-magnitude earthquake, which led to the collapse of the University of

Canterbury; online learning helped the university to restart its mission of imparting education (Todorova and Bjorn–Andersen, 2001). Technology can provide us with new solutions to promote virtual communication and thereby adaptive solutions in critical times to cope up and increasing sustainability in the long run. This leads to many system changes within organizations, as they are looking for new technology for interaction and work (Mark & Semaan, 2008).

12.4.2 IMPACT OF ARTIFICIAL INTELLIGENCE ON EDUCATION FOR ITS SUSTAINABILITY IN THE LONG RUN

The field of AI has undeniable applications in the field of education, wherein it mainly addresses the long-term nature of the question: How can computer systems facilitate learning and enable the measurement of learning progress? (Lesgold et al., 1988). In the case of the computer-based educational system, the student does not always receive individualized attention that a student would receive from a human tutor (Bloom, 1984). For computers to provide such individualized and personalized attention, the field of intelligent tutoring systems (ITSs) is prompted. ITSs offer flexibility with regard to the presentation of materials and is well suited for idiosyncratic student needs. ITSs are highly beneficial for the student's performance and motivation. Students who have used Smithtown (an ITS for economics) performed as good as students taking a normal economics course; instead, the students who used ITS required lesser time to complete the course (Shute, Glaser, and Raghaven., 1989). ITS aims to use AI and simulatede human learning so that the computer can be a tutor, however, giving the learner enough autonomy to pace their own learning and understanding. This principle of ITS is based on Vygotsky's scaffolding, also called instructional scaffolding, a style of teaching that produces quick learners. In instructional scaffolding, the learner works in close relation with their teachers or parents to attain their goals of learning.

12.4.3 ROLE OF EDUCATIONAL DATA MINING AND NEURAL NETWORKS IN ARTIFICIAL INTELLIGENCE EDUCATION

A multitude of AI-driven educational applications already exists in our schools and universities, which goes without saying. Many researchers are now merging AI Education (AIEd) and educational data mining (EDM) techniques are used to monitor the learning behaviors of students online. EDM is a branch of AI that deals with the development and use of methods to analyze and interpret data that might give an insight into the patterns and relations of human and computer interactions. In the case of education, data mining will deal with the data obtained from universities, colleges, schools, and institutions.

AI research is now trying to augment AIEd by navigating novel physiological user interfaces such as natural language processing, speech recognition, gesture recognition, and eye tracking. Recently developed ITSs are using self-learning algorithms, machine learning techniques, and neural networks to make appropriate decisions. In AI, neural networks refer to the interconnected sets of data, which helps one to understand the neural circuitry of the human brain. This raises the question whether machine or advanced AI technologies will ever be able to mimic the complex human brain functions.

12.4.4 ROLE OF INTELLIGENT TUTORING SYSTEMS IN AIED

As described by Woolf (1992), there are four models of ITS: the student model, the pedagogical module, the domain knowledge module, and the communication module. Each of them is briefly described below:

i) The student model
    The primary aim of the student model is to gather and dispense the required information for the pedagogical module of a system; all the information and facts that are gathered should be used by the tutor. This stores the necessary information specific to each learner's requirements. At a base level, such a model helps to track how well a learner is performing on the material being handed out.

ii) The pedagogical module
    The pedagogical objective of the module is to provide teachers training in teaching literacy skills and critical thinking using learning technologies. The module is based on the concept that learning occurs both inside and outside the classroom and that students learn best when they are motivated and have opportunities to apply their knowledge and understanding. The pedagogy of the module consists of a series of activities designed to introduce learners to various aspects of reading comprehension, writing, and mathematics. A particular feature of the module is its use of digital tools, which allow learners to interact with text, take notes, create presentations, and write reports. These tools are integrated throughout each activity.

iii) Domain knowledge
    Domain knowledge is the knowledge gained about a particular subject area. In education, domain knowledge refers to the understanding of concepts, principles, theories, and skills related to specific disciplines, subjects, programs, and courses, which are learned by learners over time. As students progress through their respective educational careers, they encounter various challenges that require them to apply what they have been taught. To aid them in problem solving, teachers use instructional techniques to communicate. Instructional techniques including lecture notes, videos, and interactive lessons are used. Many times, these methods fail because of the lack of proper communication of the domain content and its relevance to the problem at hand. An effective way to overcome this limitation is to develop a domain-aware ITS.

iv) Communications module
    Interactions with the learner include screen layouts and dialogue layouts that are controlled and monitored using this final module. How should the materials be presented using this model so that the student can retain the

knowledge from them is still being explored by AI developers and scientists; nonetheless, there have been certain promising studies in this area too.

It is generally expected that ITS can execute the following functions with ease and efficiency:

i)   Understanding the cognitive processes of the learner and providing them with materials using which they can process better.
ii) Control a question-and-answer interaction with its audience.

Model-based adaptive systems can also be adaptable for learners, as they have justification for each decision, thereby making the system explicit and more understandable by humans. For example, the iTalk2Learn system (www.italk2learn.com/) is designed to help students with mathematics; this app uses a model-based adaptive system to understand the mental needs and requirements of the students and then provide feedback based on the responses the app receives.

12.4.5   PARADIGMS IN AIED

The emergence of e-learning in the 1980s was due to advances in computing and coding, information technologies, and extensive use of the Internet. AI hugely contributed to the ongoing and developmental stages of e-education, and there are three paradigms in AI education as mentioned in an article published by Ouyang and Jiao (2021), which are as follows:

- (Paradigm 1) AI directed (where the learner is the recipient)
  Paradigm 1 is characterized by AI that represents the source of knowledge and guides the learning processes, while the learner (student) acts as a recipient of AI services to walk through the specific learning pathways. The psychological theoretical underpinning of paradigm 1 is behaviorism, which emphasizes the view of learning as a reinforcement, leading to the learner's correct response to the stimulus presented by the AI (Skinner, 1953). For example, ITSs (also called CALS), which are software applications that help people learn by providing them with needful content.
  The process of knowledge acquisition nowadays is through programmed instructions that introduce new concepts to the learner and offer them immediate feedback about incorrect responses and maximize the positive reinforcement (Greeno et al., 1996; Schommer, 1990) to reach the learning goal. AI systems act as the teacher to make logical presentations of subject knowledge, require the learner's overt responses, and present immediate knowledge of correctness (Burton et al., 2004). Paradigm 1 is the least learner-centered paradigm.
- (Paradigm 2) AI supported (where the learner is a collaborator)
  In this paradigm, dialogue-based tutoring systems (DBTs) are used to create a learning experience that is driven by the natural language dialogue of students'

natural language responses (Graesser et al. 2011). DBT conversations can be described as Socratic in approach because the tutor guides the student through concepts using dialogue moves, which can include questions, hints, and other prompts.

In paradigm 2 of AI-supported learning, the learner is a collaborator and a partner, thls makes the AI system a supporting tool, where the learner is a collaborator with the system to focus on the individual and personal learning journey. This paradigm is based on the cognitive and social constructivism view of learning, which emphasizes the process of learning when a learner (student) interacts with people, information, and technology to construct their own knowledge in socially situated contexts (Bandura, 1986; Liu & Matthews, 2005; Vygotsky, 1978). Thus, in paradigm 2, the AI system and the learner's mutual interactions are optimized, resulting in personalized learning. Overall, compared with paradigm 1, paradigm 2 is more of a learner-centered human learning where a harmonious collaboration between the learner with human intelligence and the computer with AI system is established.

- (Paradigm 3) AI-powered learning (where the learner is the leader)

In paradigm 3, the learner is the leader who holds the core of AIEd (Bandura, 2006) and views AI as a tool to augment and enhance human intelligence (Law, 2019). Here a perspective from the complexity theory is seen, which views education as a complex adaptive system (Mason, 2008), where a synergetic collaboration between multiple entities (e.g., the learner, the instructor, information, and technology) in the system is essential to ensure the learner's augmented intelligence. Human-AI collaboration (Hwang et al., 2021), and human-centered AI in education (Yang et al., 2021) are aiming to approach AI from a human perspective by considering human conditions, expectations, and contexts. Paradigm 3 is viewed as the developmental trend of AIEd, with the goal of applying AI in education, to augment human intelligence, capability, and potential (Gartner, 2019; Law, 2019; Tegmark, 2017). The amalgamation of human intelligence and computer systems gives rise to a cooperative system, which integrates advanced AI algorithms and human decision-making.

12.4.6 TECHNOLOGICAL STRATEGIES TO BE ADOPTED FOR SPECIALLY ABLED STUDENTS TO MAKE A MORE INCLUSIVE EDUCATIONAL SYSTEM

The inclusion of learners with special needs has been a concern for many years. Governments, institutions, and policymakers are now more sensitive to creating a nurturing environment for differently abled students (Holt, 2004). The Disability Discrimination Act of 1992 in Australia has made educational institutions more aware of the inclusion of students with disability, and many schools have made it a point to prioritize differently abled students (Forbes, 2007). Differently abled students are those who are unable to learn or act at par with other children of their age. In other words, these children need some special attention or care as they have certain needs that are different from those of other children of their age group. Differently abled students may have certain developmental problems, neurodevelopmental problems, lower mental abilities (having below average IQ levels), and physical impairments (visual impairments, bodily impairments, hearing impairments). These children are often excluded from social gatherings and social activities; that is why it is even more important to create and design education environments that are more inclusive of these neglected students of every society. There are many challenges that these student face in their academic career throughout their lives, and AI as a tool can help overcome these problems.

12.4.7 SOLUTIONS THAT TECHNOLOGY CAN PROVIDE FOR DIFFERENTLY ABLED STUDENTS

Some students with learning disabilities may face a difficult time reading advanced texts. It might be difficult for them to comprehend harder texts or struggle with the range of vocabularies provided within texts. Scientists and researchers are trying to mold AI in a way that can make these harder texts into simpler ones and understandable contexts. This would be helpful for these students, as they will be able to understand the texts and gain knowledge just like any other ordinary student. Psychologist Carol Dweck of Stanford University states that "growth mindsets" can be taught to students and children. Learners with growth mindsets can face challenges and would work hard to achieve recognition in an area.

Through AI-designed learning games, education content can be made engaging for specially abled students. Special educators and teachers often find it difficult to hold the attention of differently abled students; hence, attractive educative content in the form of games and play can be presented to these children for holding their attention. For example, if a specially abled child is learning to spell, then a computer game can be used in a fun way to make the child learn the spelling.

AI also has prospects for people who are differently abled if we consider the techno-optimistic approach (Winston and Edelbach, 2011), as AI tools can learn algorithms to understand images, sound, and even language, and they can adapt to the needs of disabled persons. For example, Microsoft has designed a virtual assistant called Cortana, which is implemented on Windows. It helps blind or visually impaired users to navigate and use their computers simply by using their voice, tone, and pitch. It is similar to Siri or Alexa.

People with speech impediments can benefit from AI technology thanks to machine learning. Apps such as VoiceItt can recognize and easily understand the speech of people with brain injury and Parkinson's disease. VoiceItt normalizes speech to create an output of audio or text so that people with speech impediments can communicate with others.

Transcription AI apps such as Ava, Rogervoice, and TapSOS are used to transcribe the conversation within seconds, it is helpful for people with hearing impairment, as they do not have to rely on just lip reading. The inclusion of AI in the education of a child with intellectual disability/developmental disability could ameliorate the educational, adaptive, and social skill gaps that occur as a direct result of persistent health problems (Kharbat, Alshawabkeh & Woolsey, 2020).

Ghafghazi et al (2021), in their paper, "AI-Augmented Behavior Analysis for Children with Developmental Disabilities: Building Toward Precision Treatment" focus on how AI can be used in clinical practices and to help children with autism spectrum disorder in learning and education. Artificial reality/virtual reality platforms are being found beneficial for improving soft skills, behaviors, and emotional skills (Shahin et.al, 2018).

12.5 FUTURE PROSPECTS OF THE STUDY

Our understanding of the rapidly changing scenario in the education sector has led to some prospects that are given below:

1. Currently, there exist high socio-economic differences between nations and within a nation. The gap or difference between those who achieve the most out of education and others who receive returns out of education still exists. A child who would get good exposure and environmental support will do well in education, whereas a child lacking education funds and support will have a poorer academic record. If AI and online learning can take over the education system, then it will be easier for children irrespective of their religion, ability (abled and differently abled), socioeconomic, and cultural backgrounds (Conroy & Rothstein, 2013). We can think of an educational system that irradicates inequality in the field of education and creates a more inclusive education environment settings for future generations.

2. Education will suit the needs and demands of the learner more than ever before. The increasing use of e-learning and AIEd allows self-pacing learning environments, for instance, the asynchronous way of online mode of education permits each student to proceed with the study of the syllabus in their own way. Thus, increasing the number of students decreases stress satisfaction and reduces academic stress (Codone, 2001; Amer, 2007; Urdan and Weggen, 2000; Klein and Ware, 2003). On the latest learning websites, one can pause videos, reflect on them more, and then play back the video again for better understanding.

3. AIEd can influence and facilitate students and Ph.D. scholars to a greater extent. Online tools for statistical data and complex statistical applications have made it easier to understand demographics and gain inferences about a population. Online surveys, online forms, and feedback portals have made communication and interaction easier than ever before. Manual data calculations are prone to certain technical and calculation errors, but computer codes and statistical software have made it easier to obtain accurate data.

4. AIEd has given opportunities for the differently abled population to continue their education and made learning easier for them in many ways. AI-assisted apps can also control the wheelchairs of many disabled students, which has made their locomotion easy.

5. The connection and networks in the world have now become way easier than it was before. The transfer of knowledge and information from one country to another country can influence the systems of other countries. For example, as previously mentioned in the paper, MOOCs initially started in the United States, but their strategies have reached throughout the world thanks to the

worldwide web. Similarly, in the future, if one country can design a good online education model for students, then other countries can also adapt their strategies for progression.

6. We all know that the world is now more polluted than ever before. The reduction in greenery and increase in pollutants has led to far-reaching consequences of global warming and higher temperatures. Previously, in the education sector, the requirement for paper textbooks was of crucial importance; even now, as we read this paper, thousands of trees are being cut to produce paper and other goods. Because of technology and AIEd, we can reduce the number of trees being cut and contribute a little to a sustainable eco-friendly environment. PDFs, e-books, articles, and websites are available in the online mode, leading to a reduction in the costs of buying books and cutting down trees for paper.

12.6   STUDY LIMITATIONS

This paper elucidates the impact AI has on the educational system and the lives of differently abled students. However, there are certain limitations that can be pointed out in this study:

1. Globally, because of the emergence of online education and dependence on Internet content, there is a high chance that learners may not be able to make proper decisions for themselves, which is one downfall of the learner-centered approach. Because of the overload of information available online, we often end up making incorrect decisions, as the information available may not be authentic and reliable. For this, we need prior expertise in a certain area to judge whether the information is authentic or not or seek assistance from a knowledgeable person in that area who can guide us according to our needs.

2. Until 2021, the global digital education has increased up to 5% (Docebo, 2016) initiated by private sectors, whereas in most of the cases, the government sectors are still struggling to implement AI in education. In this context, globally, the public–private collaborative initiatives are required to accelerate AI development in education and research.

3. Making an education system entirely inclusive may be a utopian concept. No matter how much we try, there will be outliers existing in the societies. We will have genius students who excel on average students in academic performance, and we would have students with low mental abilities (extremely low IQs). Both these groups have different abilities and capacities, and special schools are available for the differently abled students so that we can cater to their needs specifically. It might not always be possible to include students with severe mental/physical conditions in regular classroom environments.

4. Techers are the key people in an educational system. Teachers must be given adequate training to acquire and update competencies to use AI-based technologies to improve pedagogy (Luckin et al., 2016). In addition to this, some

repetitive and routine activities can be better accomplished using AI-enabled technologies and thereby providing opportunities to teachers to invest more energy to innovate, create, and develop unique styles of management.

5. There still exists a high amount of inequality in terms of wealth among people in societies. Poorer people may not prioritize the importance of education in the first place; they may send their sons and daughters to work to earn money rather than pursue education and be independent. Even if financially weak, households try to encourage their children to pursue higher education, but there still exists a problem of funding for education.

6. We must consider that governments of many countries may not have the infrastructure and wealth to invest in advanced AIEd for future generations. Many counties may find it difficult to gather equipment such as good Internet connections, scientists for research, machines, and computers necessary to build a sound online learning education system.

7. AIEd may not be suitable for primary school children because they will need proper guidance for their academic understanding. A child needs support from teachers, parents, and other members for their development. AIEd is mostly suited for students who are mature and self-learners. That is why it is mostly recommended in higher education systems rather than primary school education. This is because, in high school and college education, autonomy is more encouraged, whereas the primary education system is more structured.

12.7 CONCLUSION

We are at a stage and time where our undeniable dependence on technology has led us to think in newer ways and perspectives. From this chapter, we can conclude that the future of online education is prominent, and high use of sophisticated AI will be introduced in the future to facilitate flexible education. Human–AI collaboration (Hwang et al., 2021) and human-centered AI in education (Yang et al., 2021) are aiming to approach AI from a human perspective by considering human conditions, expectations, and contexts.

The teacher–learner interaction will be AI-assisted as both learn and grow using technological aids. Differently abled students will find it easier to deal with education with AI-assisted applications. For example, students with fine motor impairment can use the dictation feature of iPads and tablets to take notes dictated in the classroom instead of having difficulty writing down notes. If a student has reading problems, then the student can just use the text-to-speech AI tool to listen to the text rather than read through the texts. Thus, AI can be used to design inclusive classroom settings that create a space for differently abled students and normal students.

Despite the advantages that AI provides, there are certain drawbacks that we might face while implementing it. Tech giants such as the United States, China, Korea, and Australia have already proposed AI strategies, but developing countries lack the infrastructural requirements needed to develop technologically sophisticated systems. It might not always be possible to include children with severe disabilities to attend normal schools, as they would need specially trained teachers who are available to provide services in special schools. Globally, education systems need to be actively reframed with the help of AI-enabled strategies in such a way so that it can ensure the continuous growth and development of learners and teachers.

REFERENCES

1. Algahtani, A. (2011). *Evaluating the effectiveness of the e-learning experience in some universities in Saudi Arabia from male students' perceptions* (Doctoral dissertation, Durham University).

2. Almosa, A. (2002). *Use of Computer in Education, (2nd ed)*, Riyadh: Future Education Library.

3. Alsalem, A. (2004). *Educational Technology and E-learning*, Riyadh: Alroshd publication.

4. Amer, T. (2007). E-learning and Education. *Cairo: Dar Alshehab publication.*

5. Bandura, A. (2006). Toward a psychology of human agency. *Perspectives on psychological science*, *1*(2), 164–180.

6. Bandura, A. (1986). Social foundations of thought and action. Englewood Cliffs, NJ, 1986(23–28).

7. Basilaia, G., & Kvavadze, D. (2020). Transition to online education in schools during a SARS-CoV-2 coronavirus (COVID-19) pandemic in Georgia. *Pedagogical Research*, *5*(4).

8. Bloom, B. S. (1984). The 2 sigma problem: The search for methods of group instruction as effective as one-to-one tutoring. *Educational researcher*, *13*(6), 4–16.

9. Burton, J. K., Moore, D. M. M., & Magliaro, S. G. (2004). Behaviorism and Instructional Technology.

10. Coffta, M. (2010). Literature Review. Bloomsburg University of Pennsylvania. Retrieved September 8, 2022, from https://guides.library.bloomu.edu/litreview#:~:text =A%20literature%20review%20is%20a%20comprehensive%20summary%20 of,summarize%2C%20objectively%20evaluate%20and%20clarify%20this%20 previous%20research.

11. Codone, S. (2001, November). Measuring Quality in the Production of Web-based Training: Instrucional Design, Process Control, and User Satisfaction. In *Interservice/ Industry Training, Simulation and Education Conference, Orlando, FL* .

12. Cojocariu V.-M., Lazar I., Nedeff V., Lazar G. (2014). SWOT analysis of e-learning educational services from the perspective of their beneficiaries. *Procedia-Social and Behavioral Sciences*, 116, 1999–2003.

13. Docebo (2016). Elearning market trends and forecast 2017–2021. Toronto: Canada.

14. Doering, A. (2006). Adventure learning: Transformative hybrid online education. *Distance Education*, *27*(2), 197–215.

15. Forbes, F. (2007). Towards inclusion: an Australian perspective. *Support for learning*, *22*(2), 66–71.

16. Gartner *Hype cycle for emerging technologies, 2019* Gartner (2019, August) www.gart ner.com/en/documents/3956015/hype-cycle-for-emerging- technologies-2019

17. Gierdowski, D., & Galanek, J. (2020, June). *ECAR Study of the Technology Needs of Students with Disabilities, 2020*. EDUCAUSE. Retrieved September 8, 2022, from www.educause.edu/ecar/research-publications/ecar-study-of-the-technology-needs-of-students-with-disabilities/2020/teaching-with-technology#MobileDevicesintheCla ssroom

18. Graesser, A. C., McNamara, D. S., & Kulikowich, J. M. (2011). Coh-Metrix: Providing multilevel analyses of text characteristics. *Educational researcher*, 40(5), 223–234.
19. Greeno, J. G., Collins, A. M., & Resnick, L. B. (1996). Cognition and learning. *Handbook of educational psychology*, 77, 15–46.
20. Henry, P. (2001). E-learning technology, content and services [Review of *E-learning technology, content and services*]. *Education + Training*, 43, 249–255. emerald insight. https://doi.org/10.1108/EUM0000000005485
21. Ghafghazi, S., Carnett, A., Neely, L., Das, A., & Rad, P. (2021). AI-Augmented Behavior Analysis for Children With Developmental Disabilities: Building Toward Precision Treatment. *IEEE Systems, Man, and Cybernetics Magazine*, 7(4), 4–12.
22. Holt, L. (2004). Children with mind–body differences: performing disability in primary school classrooms. *Children's Geographies*, 2(2), 219–236.
23. Hwang, G. J., & Tu, Y. F. (2021). Roles and research trends of artificial intelligence in mathematics education: A bibliometric mapping analysis and systematic review. *Mathematics*, 9(6), 584.
24. Khan, B. H. (Ed.). (2005). Managing e-learning: Design, delivery, implementation, and evaluation. IGI Global.
25. Klein, D., & Ware, M. (2003). E-learning: New opportunities in continuing professional development. *Learned publishing*, 16(1), 34–46.
26. Kharbat, F. F., Alshawabkeh, A., & Woolsey, M. L. (2020). Identifying gaps in using artificial intelligence to support students with intellectual disabilities from education and health perspectives. *Aslib Journal of Information Management*.
27. Laurillard, D. (2004). E-learning in higher education. Changing higher education. The *Journal of Interactive Online Learning*, 2(3), 7.
28. Law, N. W. Y. (2019). Human development and augmented intelligence. In The 20th international conference on artificial intelligence in education (AIED 2019). Springer.
29. Lesgold, A., Rubinson, H., Feltovich, P., Glaser, R., Klopfer, D., & Wang, Y. (1988). Expertise in a complex skill: Diagnosing x-ray pictures.
30. Luckin, R., Holmes, W., Griffiths, M. & Forcier, L.B. (2016). Intelligence Unleashed: an argument for AI in Education. London: Pearson.
31. Vygotsky, L. (1978). Interaction between learning and development. *Readings on the development of children*, 23(3), 34–41.
32. Liu, C. H., & Matthews, R. (2005). Vygotsky's Philosophy: Constructivism and Its Criticisms Examined. *International education journal*, 6(3), 386–399.
33. *UDL framework An introduction to UDL and its value in an Aotearoa New Zealand context.* (n.d.). Inclusive Education. Retrieved September 8, 2022, from https://inclusive.tki.org.nz/guides/universal-design-for-learning/udl-framework/
34. Urdan, T. A., & Weggen, C. C. (2000). Corporate elearning: Exploring a new frontier.
35. Mark, G., & Semaan, B. (2008, November). Resilience in collaboration: Technology as a resource for new patterns of action. In *Proceedings of the 2008 ACM conference on Computer supported cooperative work* (pp. 137–146).
36. Maskey, S. (2020, July 8). *AI-Assisted Learning And Its Impact On Education. Forbes*. Retrieved September 8, 2022, from www.forbes.com/sites/forbestechcouncil/2020/07/08/ai-assisted-learning-and-its-impact-on-education/?sh=e81609f781c9
37. Mason, M. (2008). Complexity theory and the philosophy of education. *Educational philosophy and theory*, 40(1), 4–18.
38. McBrien, J. L., Cheng, R., & Jones, P. (2009). Virtual spaces: Employing a synchronous online classroom to facilitate student engagement in online learning. *International review of research in open and distributed learning*, 10(3).

39. National Education Policy 2020, Ministry of Human Resource Development, Government of India

40. Nelson, L. L. (2014). Design and Deliver: Planning and Teaching Using Universal Design for Learning. Baltimore: Paul H. Brookes Publishing.

41. Ouyang, F., & Jiao, P. (2021). Artificial intelligence in education: The three paradigms. *Computers and Education: Artificial Intelligence*, *2*, 100020.

42. Olivier, B., & Liber, O. (2003). Learning content interoperability standards. Reusing online resources: a sustainable approach to e-learning, 146–155.

43. Sahin, N. T., Abdus-Sabur, R., Keshav, N. U., Liu, R., Salisbury, J. P., & Vahabzadeh, A. (2018, September). Case study of a digital augmented reality intervention for autism in school classrooms: Associated with improved social communication, cognition, and motivation via educator and parent assessment. In *Frontiers in education* (Vol. 3, p. 57). Frontiers Media SA.

44. Shute, V., Glaser, R., & Raghavan, K. (1988). *Inference and Discovery in an Exploratory Laboratory*. PITTSBURGH UNIV PA LEARNING RESEARCH AND DEVELOPMENT CENTER.

45. Schommer, M. (1990). Effects of beliefs about the nature of knowledge on comprehension. *Journal of educational psychology*, *82*(3), 498.

46. Skinner, B. F. (1953). Some contributions of an experimental analysis of behavior to psychology as a whole. *American Psychologist*, *8*(2), 69.

47. Tegmark, M. (2017). *Life 3.0: Being human in the age of artificial intelligence*. Vintage.

48. Todorova, N., & Bjorn-Andersen, N. (2011). University learning in times of crisis: The role of IT. *Accounting Education*, *20*(6), 597–599.

49. Vyas, A. (2020, September). *Status Report–Government and private schools during COVID-19* [Review of *Status Report–Government and private schools during COVID–19*]. Oxfam India. www.oxfamindia.org/sites/default/files/2020-09/Status%20report%20Government%20and%20private%20schools%20during%20COVID%20-%2019.pdf

50. Wang, L. (2007). *Sociocultural learning theories and information literacy teaching activities in higher education*. Reference & User Services Quarterly, 149–158.

51. Winston, M. E., & Edelbach, R. D. (2011). Society, Ethics, and Technology, Update Edition.

52. Woolf, B. 1992. AI in Education. Encyclopedia of Artificial Intelligence, Shapiro, S., ed., John Wiley & Sons, Inc., New York, pp. 434–444.

53. Yang, S. J., Ogata, H., Matsui, T., & Chen, N. S. (2021). Human-centered artificial intelligence in education: Seeing the invisible through the visible. *Computers and Education: Artificial Intelligence*, *2*, 100008.

13 Artificial Intelligence for Sustainable Agricultural Practices

Sangeeta Chaudhary
School of Commerce and Business Management,
Geeta University
Panipat, India

Preeti Dahiya
DMS, Panipat Institute of Engineering & Technology
Panipat, Samalkha, India

Prerna Dawar
School of Commerce and Business Management,
Geeta University
Panipat, India

Annu Dahiya
Geeta University
Panipat, India

13.1 INTRODUCTION

In the past decades, agriculture has seen many technological transformations. Agriculture is the pillar of developing countries such as India. In developing countries, farmers use traditional agriculture systems [1]. Traditional agriculture systems are time-consuming and are not appropriate for dealing with the new challenges emerging in farming. As several sectors in the world have started adopting artificial intelligence (AI), the agriculture industry should also implement new technologies for improving productivity and yield [2-3]. AI is helpful in crop management and optimization of irrigation operations in agriculture. AI-based agriculture systems can reduce production cost. Researchers have focused on various kinds of AI-based techniques to monitor information regarding crop management. In agriculture, sensors and robots are used to achieve the desired smart agriculture [4-5]. Autonomous tractors and agriculture drones have transformed the agriculture sector into a new business model.

DOI: 10.1201/9781003348351-13

AI has attracted several researchers for exploring this area because of the application of its technological advancement in a wide range of sectors. Agriculture is also an important sector where AI is utilized. Earlier, agriculture was seen as an area that requires extensive hard work, persistent efforts, and perseverance despite the low income and uncomfortable lifestyle [6-8]. As mentioned in the above sentence, people who depend on agriculture receive very less profit or face loss many times because of bad weather conditions and lack of resources to cope with uncertainties [9-11]. Despite all these problems, they are forced to adopt agriculture as an occupation for several reasons. This creates financial problems for the person whose main source of income is agriculture [12]. When this situation becomes worse, it leads to the suicide of farmers, which is a very unfortunate reality in India. Despite other occupations, agriculture remains an important sector, and ignorance or absence of this sector will create several problems [13-15]. AI can play a significant role in fixing these problems by reducing the time required for these activities and decreasing the hard work near to null [16]. A good agricultural yield can be expected with AI application, such as uniform plantation and proper growth of crops [17]. This will add value to the lifestyle of the farmers. This technology also assists farmers to choose some secondary path for income that is favorable for maintaining their financial status and reduces the chances of a worse situation that results in the suicide of farmers [18-19].

Technology has caused dramatic transformation in various industries and sectors [20-21]. The field of agriculture is the least modernized and digitalized. The evolution of AI has a great impact on our daily life, forming and rebuilding our perceptions, and it can also modify the environment in which we are living [22-24]. This technology provides an opportunity for employment in numerous sectors that were earlier confined to a few industrial sectors. AI has emerged through a combination of various disciplines such as computer science, biology, linguistics, psychology, mathematics, and engineering [25-27]. Researchers have focused on the use of Internet of Things (IoT) and AI in botanical farming, for example, an automated system, that should be implemented for the identification of leaves and give a brief overview of automation currently implemented in the agriculture sector [29-30].

The basic idea behind AI application is to develop an automated system that works like the human brain [31]. This is a learning machine that replicates the human learning style such as how the human brain thinks, decision-making activity, and problem-solving process. These are the criteria for developing intelligent software and systems [32-33]. These machines are equipped with some data and trained in a manner that can produce the desired output [34-35]. AI is a scientific discipline that deals with making machines intelligent, and the concept used for it is machine learning [36]. Robots have been used in several activities such as ploughing, picking, and packing of props, and these robots are developed with the help of robotics [37]. AI also contributes to the diagnostic analysis of satellites for weather predictions that lead to deciding crop sustainability. Weather prediction in advance helps farmers to a great extent in selecting the type of crop and in deciding ploughing, sowing, and irrigation time of crops [38]. Driverless tractor is another important AI technique that can have a greater contribution in this field. Just like other fields, farmers' Alexa can converse with farmers like chatbots to figure out the solution to a wide range of possible problems. Spraying techniques developed through AI, such as aerial spraying with drones, can produce the desired result five times faster than that by traditional spraying techniques [39].

Agri-E-calculator is another smart application of AI in the field of farming that helps farmers to select suitable and affordable crops [40]. It calculates its cost, time, and selling price. Several useful applications are available in the market, but the main problems are the cost of these applications and the difficulty in using them [41-42].

Globally, a remarkable growth is being indicated by the investment trends in smart agriculture systems using AI and machine learning by 2025. It is expected that AI-based technologies will be helpful in providing real-time data for improving agricultural productivity and diminishing input costs [43]. By 2030, the global market for AI is anticipated to reach at 8,379.5 million USD. The adoption of IoT in the agriculture sector and the installation of data generation through sensors and aerial photographs are driving market expansion. In the global perspective, AI technology must support a variety of regionally appropriate methods that not only draw on the indigenous knowledge system but also foster innovation along the entire value chain [44-45].

This chapter is divided into five parts. The first part provides an introduction to AI and the role of various AI techniques used in agriculture. The second part consists of a theoretical framework to provide insights into the model applied in the study to know the perception of farmers. Furthermore, the third part presents questionnaire development, data collection, and hypothesis development. Subsequently, in the fourth part, results are displayed, and a discussion is included to draw the implications of the study. Finally, in the fifth part, conclusions are drawn.

13.2   THEORETICAL FRAMEWORK

Based on the aim of the study, a conceptual framework for the acceptance of AI by farmers is centered upon the technology acceptance model (TAM) [46]. It includes a strategic approach for data-driven decision-making techniques [46-47]. This model suggests that technology plays a crucial role in decision-making, and it includes attitude toward using (AT), perceived usefulness (PU), perceived behavior control (PBC), perceived social norms (PSN), and perceived ease of use (PEU). The present study focused on the perception of farmers for the implementation of AI systems in agriculture for sustainable development.

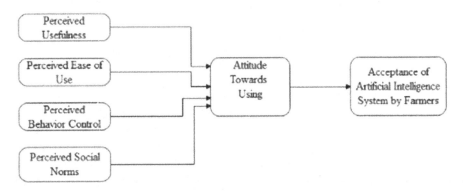

FIGURE 13.1   Technology Acceptance Model (TAM).

Source: TAM model [47].

TABLE 13.1
Definition of Variables

Variables	Definition
Perceived usefulness	The degree to which a farmer perceives that using an artificial intelligence–based system in agriculture would improve job performance [47,48]
Perceived ease of use	The extent to which a farmer perceives that the use of an artificial intelligence–based system in agriculture would make the purpose easy [47, 48]
Perceived behavior control	The extent to which a farmer perceives that the use of an artificial intelligence–based system in agriculture as simple or difficult [50]
Perceived social norms	The extent to which a farmer perceives the use of an artificial intelligence–based system in agriculture based on normative pressure [50, 51]
Attitude toward using	The extent to which a farmer perceives the use of an artificial intelligence-based system in agriculture as positive or negative [48]

The flexibility of TAM has provided extensions based on research objectives and characteristics of the technology. In this study, the following variables are used for analyzing the perception and opinion of farmers toward AI applications in Indian agriculture for farmers' 4.0 approach [48-49]. In this model, perceived behavior control and social norms are also added to analyze the perception of farmers toward the acceptance of AI tools [50]. Table 13.1 shows the descriptions of these variables in the context of AI.

13.3 METHODS

13.3.1 QUESTIONNAIRE DEVELOPMENT

The questionnaire is structured in two sections. The objective of the study and the respondents' demographic profile were both presented in the first part. The second section included 17 items to measure the opinion of farmers concerning the acceptance and implementation of AI in Indian agriculture. An initial screening of the questionnaire was carried out based on five determinants: PU, PEU, PSN, PBC, and AT. The five-point Likert Scale was used to measure these determinants, varying from strongly disagree to strongly agree: 1 signifies strongly disagree, 2 signifies disagree, 3 signifies neutral, 4 signifies agree, and 5 signifies strongly agree. Appendix A presents all items of the questionnaire.

13.3.2 HYPOTHESIS DEVELOPMENT

H1:The perception of farmers differs significantly based on the knowledge of computers regarding the implementation of AI for sustainability in agriculture.

H1a:Farmers "do not know computers" perceived that the implementation of AI positively impacts sustainability in agriculture

H1a:Farmers "with low knowledge" of computers perceived that the implementation of AI positively impacts sustainability in agriculture

H1a:Farmers with "moderate knowledge of computers" perceived that the implementation of AI positively impacts sustainability in agriculture

H1a:Farmers with "high knowledge of computers" perceived that the implementation of AI positively impacts sustainability of agriculture

H2: The perception of farmers differs significantly based on their experience in agricultural activities regarding the implementation of AI for sustainability in agriculture.

H2a:Farmers having experience of less than 5 years in agricultural activities perceived that the implementation of AI positively impacts sustainability in agriculture

H2b:Farmers having experience of 5-10 years in agricultural activities perceived that the implementation of AI positively impacts sustainability in agriculture

H2c:Farmers having experience of 10-20 years in agricultural activities perceived that the implementation of AI positively impacts sustainability in agriculture
H2d:Farmers having experience of more than 20 years in agricultural activities perceived that the implementation of AI positively impacts sustainability in agriculture

13.3.3 DATA COLLECTION

This study is based on the collection of data from farmers for scientific research, which is quite challenging because the target population of this study was farmers who have experience in agricultural activities. In this study, data were collected from six administrative divisions of Haryana: Ambala, Faridabad, Gurugram, Hisar, Rohtak, and Karnal. As an initial sample, 139 farmers were chosen, and data were collected using convenience sampling. Among the 139 samples, 134 were valid and complete and hence used for further analysis. Data were collected from mid-February 2022 to the end of May 2022.

13.4 RESULTS

13.4.1 PROFILING OF RESPONDENTS

IBM Statistical Package for Social Science (SPSS) was used to examine the data. To proceed with the analysis, internal consistency and reliability of the scale were measured through the application of Cronbach's alpha. The value of Cronbach's alpha was 0.69, which indicated significance [52] to perform the statistical analysis. Table 13.2 depicts the basic information of the respondents. The responses were collected from male farmers, and the maximum number of respondents was from the age group of 31–40 years. A moderate level of education and moderate frequency of computer usage were reported by the respondents. Moreover, 21% of the participants had more than 20 years of experience in the agriculture field. With regard to administrative divisions, most participants were from Karnal and Ambala divisions.

TABLE 13.2
Profiling of Respondents

Particulars	Demographics	Frequency	Percentage
Age	21–30 years	29	21.5
	31–40 years	36	26.7
	41–50 years	34	25.4
	Above 50 years	35	25.9
Education	No education	27	20.0
	Higher and Secondary	23	17.8
	Graduation	44	32.6
	Post-graduation	40	29.6
Knowledge of computer	Never Used	19	14.1
	Low	43	31.9
	Moderate	50	37.8
	High	22	16.3
Experience in agricultural activities	Less than 5 years	24	17.8
	5–10 years	41	30.4
	10–20 years	40	30.4
	More than 20 years	29	21.5
Administrative division	Ambala	25	18.7
	Faridabad	19	14.1
	Gurugram	22	16.4
	Hisar	18	13.4
	Rohtak	24	17.9
	Karnal	26	19.4

Source:　Primary Data

13.4.2 RELIABILITY AND VALIDITY

Reliability represents the consistency of the measure, that is, a test should generate the same results when repetition is performed [53]. Validly refers to the accuracy of the construct that it wants to measure. Internal consistency of the scale was measured through composite reliability, average variance extracted, and Cronbach's alpha [54]. As shown in Table 13.3, the Cronbach's alpha was greater than 0.7; hence, the model was found to be reliable, as it fulfilled the condition of internal consistency [55]. As suggested by Hair et al. [56], convergent validity is confirmed through factor loading and average variance extracted (AVE)greater than 0.5. Furthermore, the composite reliability of the construct was found significant for all factors (greater than 0.7), hence fulfilling the condition of reliability [57].

As indicated in Table 13.3, except for perceived behavior control, the mean score of all the factors was greater than the midpoint of the scale, as items were measured on a five-point Likert scale [55]. This result suggests that farmers have a positive attitude toward the implementation of AI in the Indian agriculture system. Moreover, the standard deviation of all items ranged from 0.976 to 1.787, showing that the value around the mean has a moderate range.

TABLE 13.3
Construct Reliability and Validity

Factors	Items	Mean	SD	Variance	AVE	CR	CA
Perceived usefulness	4	3.744	0.909	0.827	0.651	0.876	0.821
Perceived ease of use	5	3.937	1.787	0.619	0.777	0.933	0.647
Perceived social norms	2	3.426	0.976	0.953	0.673	0.792	0.820
Perceived behavior control	3	2.785	1.143	1.308	0.711	0.886	0.847
Attitude toward using	3	3.906	1.495	0.631	0.732	0.854	0.750

Source: Primary Data

TABLE 13.4
Perception of Farmers Based on Computer Knowledge

Factors	Never Used		Low		Moderate		High		F	Sig. (p-Value)	Hypothesis
	Mean	SD	Mean	SD	Mean	SD	Mean	SD			
Perceived usefulness	3.764	0.760	3.106	0.731	3.534	1.135	3.683	0.742	2.174	0.045	H1a*
Perceived ease of use	3.950	0.672	3.913	0.895	3.873	0.878	3.981	0.342	0.438	0.226	H1b
Perceived social norms	3.528	0.977	3.058	1.191	3.637	0.735	3.545	0.872	3.133	0.028	H1c*
Perceived behavior control	2.148	0.777	2.891	1.192	2.719	1.152	3.288	1.085	3.652	0.014	H1d*
Attitude toward using	3.704	1.041	4.116	0.577	4.000	0.593	3.409	1.103	4.889	0.003	H1e*

Source: Primary Data

*   Significant at 5% level
*   SD stands for standard deviation

13.4.3   ANALYSIS OF HYPOTHESIS

For analyzing the perception of the farmers based on computer knowledge and experience in agricultural activities, one-way analysis of variance (ANOVA) has been applied at a 5% level of significance [58]. This function measures the significant difference in the perception of farmers among different variables. The mean and standard deviation of all variables was calculated. Table 13.4 shows data on the perception of farmers based on computer knowledge. Except for perceived behavior control, the mean values of all variables were greater than the midpoint of the scale.

TABLE 13.5
Perception of Farmers Based on Experience in Agricultural Activities

Factors	Less than 5 years		5–10 years		10–20 years		More Than 20 Years		F	Sig. (p-value)	Hypothesis
	Mean	SD	Mean	SD	Mean	SD	Mean	SD			
Perceived usefulness	3.771	0.837	3.348	1.143	3.919	0.789	4.026	0.532	4.302	0.006	H2a*
Perceived ease of use	4.031	0.760	4.134	0.581	3.963	0.794	3.552	0.953	3.463	0.018	H2b*
Perceived social norms	3.063	1.106	3.512	0.965	3.613	0.873	3.328	0.984	1.823	0.046	H2c*
Perceived behavior control	2.569	1.047	3.220	1.139	2.542	1.161	2.713	1.094	3.019	0.032	H2d*
Attitude toward using	3.694	0.856	3.772	0.858	3.992	0.832	4.126	0.507	1.887	0.035	H2e*

Source: Primary Data

* Significant at 5% level
* SD stands for standard deviation

This confirmed that AI has a positive impact on farmers. The results depicted that except H1b, all the hypotheses (H1a, H1c, H1d, and H1e) were confirmed at a 5% level of significance [59]. This postulated that the perception of farmers differs significantly based on computer knowledge regarding the implementation of AI for sustainability in agriculture.

Furthermore, Table 13.5 presents information on the perception of farmers based on their experience in agricultural activities. To detect significant differences in the perception of farmers among different variables, one-way ANOVA was applied at a 5% level of significance. All the hypotheses (H2a, H2b, H2c, H2d, and H2e) were confirmed at a 5% level of significance. This result suggested that the perception of farmers differs significantly based on their experience in agricultural activities regarding the implementation of AI for sustainability in agriculture.

13.5 DISCUSSION

Survey results indicated that AI-based solutions to various farming problems can enable farmers to gain maximum benefits with the given resources in the form of greater yield per hectare; these solutions are useful in other sectors such as making life easy with high-tech machinery in education, hospitals, and governance [60–61]. The results confirmed the positive perception of farmers toward the implementation of an AI-based system for sustainable development in agriculture. As far as social norms are considered, farmers' intention to use AI-based systems is positive [62].

As shown in this study, the main aim of AI application is the easiness of work and the increase in output. In other words, it is associated with smart work. AI application in the agricultural sector is expected to decrease cost and facilitate easy processing. Some problems in agriculture are tackled by AI within a short time and very quickly [63]. AI can contribute to various agricultural techniques such as introducing indoor farming and improving harvesting quality for improving the production rate of crops. AI detects the target weeds, potential diseases in plants, need for pest control, and similar events. It also enables farmers to analyze farm-related data that provide valuable information for further decision-making. AI helps tackle labor challenges to a great extent. In the global context, it is evident that the agricultural sector has stronger chances for digital transformation, supported by the use of AI-based tools. For promoting sustainable development worldwide, appropriate AI algorithms should be applied in an effective manner.

13.6   CONCLUSION

This chapter suggests that farmers should use AI-based devices for better production. It is well-known that this occupation requires intensive efforts but brings low returns; therefore, farmers face a shortage of workforce concerning completing time-bound activities of the process. Farmers can actively use AI technology for faster harvesting of crops and completing work very quickly in a large area. Agriculture robots with the aid of Blue River Technology are used to control weeds. An enormous amount of crops need to be produced in order to reduce the hunger index worldwide [64]. Many kinds of automation are being carried out in farming, yet there are challenges that have not been overcome thus far. If smart and self-automated systems are used in farming, then the scenario can be changed to a great extent. The high costs of AI-based techniques are a big hindrance for farmers in developing countries. Furthermore, as for machinery, high maintenance costs and breakdown create issues for farmers. Therefore, there is a need for change in the agricultural ecosystem owing to many global developments to enhance the overall sustainability of food and agricultural systems.

Author's contribution
Each author made substantial contributions. At every stage, the results and their implications were discussed by all the authors.

Availability of information and resources
The main article includes all pertinent information and data.

ANNEXURE A

Concept	Question	Theory	Measurement
	Perceived usefulness [46]		
	To what extent do you agree that artificial intelligence		
(PU1)	… will enable me to accomplish farming tasks more quickly	[46]	5-point Likert scale
(PU2)	… will improve the Indian agricultural productivity	[46]	5-point Likert scale
(PU3)	… will give me greater control over the agricultural processes	[46]	5-point Likert scale
(PU4)	… is not suitable for every kind of agricultural process	[46]	5-point Likert scale
	Perceived ease of use [46]		
	To what extent do you agree that artificial intelligence		
(PEU1)	… can not be used without proper help and training	[47]	5-point Likert scale
(PEU2)	… will enables me to provide accurate information	[46]	5-point Likert scale
(PEU3)	… will provides more flexibility in the agriculture process	[46]	5-point Likert scale
(PEU4)	… will not be comprehensible in Indian agriculture	[46]	5-point Likert scale
(PEU5)	… learning will easy to use for me	[46]	5-point Likert scale
	Perceived social norms [50] [51]		
	To what extent do you agree that		
(PSN1)	Policy makers should support artificial intelligence in agriculture	[50-51]	5-point Likert scale
(PSN2)	Use of artificial intelligence will fulfil the expectations of farming	[50-51]	5-point Likert scale
	Perceived behavior control [50]		
	To what extent do you agree that		
(PBC1)	It will be not easy to use AI-based agriculture system	[50]	5-point Likert scale
(PBC2)	I have not enough knowledge to use AI-based agriculture system	[50]	5-point Likert scale
(PBC3)	I have not resources and control over using AI-based agriculture system	[50]	5-point Likert scale
	Attitude toward using [65-66]		
	To what extent do you agree that use of artificial intelligence		
(AT1)	… is a good tool for innovations in agriculture	[65-66]	5-point Likert scale
(AT2)	… will be appropriate for sustainable agriculture	[65-66]	5-point Likert scale
(AT3)	---on regular basis will be valuable in Indian agriculture	[65-66]	5-point Likert scale

REFERENCES

[1] F. Caffaro, M.M. Cremasco, M. Roccato, and E. Cavallo, "Drivers of farmers' intention to adopt technological innovations in Italy: The role of information sources, perceived usefulness, and perceived ease of use," *J. Rural. Stud.*, vol 76, pp. 264–71, 2020.

[2] E. Cavallo, E. Ferrari, L. Bollani, and M. Coccia, "Attitudes and behaviour of adopters of technological innovations in agricultural tractors: A case study in Italian agricultural system," *Agric. Syst.*, vol.130, pp. 44–54, 2014.

[3] C.H. Lin, W.C. Wang, C.Y. Liu, P.N. Pan, and H.R. Pan, "Research into the E-learning model of agriculture technology companies: Analysis by deep learning," *Agronomy*, vol. 9, pp. 83, 2019.

[4] D.I. Mercurio, and A.A. Hernandez, "Understanding user acceptance of information system for sweet potato variety and disease classification: An empirical examination with an extended technology acceptance model," In Proceedings of 16th IEEE International Colloquium on Signal Processing & Its Applications (CSPA), Langkawi, Malaysia, 28–29 February 2020; pp. 272–77.

[5] F. Abdullah, and R. Ward, "Developing a general extended technology acceptance model for E-Learning (GETAMEL) by analysing commonly used external factors," *Comput. Hum. Behav*, vol. 56, pp. 238–56, 2016.

[6] S.A. Wheeler, "What influences agricultural professionals' views towards organic agriculture," *Ecol. Econ.*, vol. 65, pp. 145–54, 2008.

[7] J. Sneddon, G. Soutar, and T. Mazzarol, "Modelling the faddish, fashionable and efficient diffusion of agricultural technologies: A case study of the diffusion of wool testing technology in Australia," *Technol. Forecast. Soc. Chang.*, vol. 78, pp. 468–80, 2011.

[8] R. Cullen, S.L. Forbes, and R. Grout, "Non-adoption of environmental innovations in wine growing," *N. Z. J. Crop Hortic. Sci.*, vol. 41, pp. 41–48, 2013.

[9] W. Sroka, M. Dudek, T. Wojewodzic, and K. Król, "Generational changes in agriculture: the influence of farm characteristics and socio-economic Factors," *Agriculture*, vol. 9, pp. 264, 2019.

[10] L.A. Jimenez, L.C. Cepeda García, M.G. Violante, F. Marcolin, and E. Vezzetti, "Commonly used external tam variables in e-learning, agriculture and virtual reality Applications," *Future Internet*, vol.13, issue 7, 2021.

[11] Y.C. Lee, "An empirical investigation into factors influencing the adoption of an e-learning system," *Online Inf. Rev.*, vol.30, pp. 517–41, 2006.

[12] G. Arvind, V.G. Athira, H. Haripriya, R.A. Rani, and S. Aravind, "Automated irrigation with advanced seed germination and pest control," IEEE Technological Innovations in ICT for Agriculture and Rural Development (TIAR) April 2017, pp. 64–67.

[13] J. Gutiérrez, J.F. Villa-Medina, A. Nieto-Garibay, and M.A. Porta-Gándara, "Automated irrigation system using a wireless sensor network and GPRS module," IEEE transactions on instrumentation and measurement, vol. 63, issue 1, pp. 166–76, Aug. 2013.

[14] K.S. Krishnan, K. Jerusha, P. Tanwar, and S. Singhal, "Self-automated agriculture system using IoT," *Intern. Jour. of Recent Techno. and Engin.*, 2020.

[15] M.S. Farooq, S. Riaz, A. Abid, K. Abid, and M.A. Naeem, "A survey on the role of IOT in agriculture for the implementation of smart farming," IEEE Access, vol. 7, pp. 156237-71, Oct. 2019.

[16] Y. Kim, R.G. Evans, and W.M. Iversen, "Remote sensing and control of an irrigation system using a distributed wireless sensor network," *IEEE trans. on instrum. and measurement*, vol. 57, issue 7, pp. 1379–87, May 2008.

[17] A. Walter, R. Finger, R. Huber, and N. Buchmann, "Smart farming is key to developing sustainable agriculture," Proceedings of the National Academy of Sciences, June 13, 2017, vol. 114, issue 24, pp. 6148–50.

[18] Q. Wang, A. Terzis, and A. Szalay, "A novel soil measuring wireless sensor network," IEEE Instrumentation & Measurement Technology Conference Proceedings May 3, 2010, pp. 412–15.

[19] B.S. Shruthi, K.B. Manasa, and R. Lakshmi, "Survey on Challenges and Future Scope of IOT in Healthcare and Agriculture," *Int. J. Comput. Sci. Mob. Comput*, vol. 8, issue 1, pp. 21–6, 2019.

[20] L. Nóbrega, P. Gonçalves, P. Pedreiras, and J. Pereira, "An IoT-based solution for intelligent farming," *Sensors*, vol.19, issue 3, pp. 603, Jan. 2019.

[21] P.P. Jayaraman, A. Yavari, D. Georgakopoulos, A. Morshed, and A. Zaslavsky, "Internet of things platform for smart farming: Experiences and lessons learnt," *Sensors*, vol. 16, issue 11, pp. 1884, Nov. 2016.

[22] T. Dalhaus, and R. Finger, "Can gridded precipitation data and phenological observations reduce basis risk of weather index–based insurance," *Weather, Climate, and Society*, vol. 8, issue 4, pp. 409–19, Oct. 2016.

[23] K. Jha, A. Doshi, P. Patel, and M. Shah, "A comprehensive review on automation in agriculture using artificial intelligence," *Artificial Intelligence in Agriculture*, vol.2, pp.1–2, June 2019.

[24] V. Kakani, V.H. Nguyen, B.P. Kumar, H. Kim, and V.R. Pasupuleti, "A critical review on computer vision and artificial intelligence in food industry," *Journal of Agri. and Food Res.*, vol.1, issue 2, pp. 100033, Dec. 2020.

[25] V. J. Das, S. Sharma, and A. Kaushik, "Views of Irish farmers on smart farming technologies: An observational study," *Agri Engineering*, vol. 1, issue, pp. 164–87, Apr. 2019.

[26] F.J. Dessart, J. Barreiro-Hurlé, and R. Bavel, "Behavioural factors affecting the adoption of sustainable farming practices: a policy-oriented review," *European Review of Agricultural Economics*, July 2019.

[27] T. Kutter, S. Tiemann, R. Siebert, and S. Fountas, "The role of communication and co-operation in the adoption of precision farming," *Preci. Agricul*, vol. 12, issue 1, pp. 2–17, Feb. 2011.

[28] J. Lowenberg-DeBoer, I.Y. Huang, V. Grigoriadis, and S. Blackmore, "Economics of robots and automation in field crop production," *Preci.Agricul.*, vol. 21, issue 2, pp. 278–99, Apr. 2020.

[29] A. Chlingaryan, S. Sukkarieh, and B. Whelan, "Machine learning approaches for crop yield prediction and nitrogen status estimation in precision agriculture: A review," *Computers and electronics in agriculture*, vol.15, 61–69, Aug. 2018.

[30] T.B. Long, V. Blok, and I. Coninx, "Barriers to the adoption and diffusion of technological innovations for climate-smart agriculture in Europe: evidence from the Netherlands, France, Switzerland and Italy," *Journal of cleaner production*, vol. 112, pp. 9–21, Jan. 2016.

[31] M. Michels, V. Bonke, and O. Musshoff, "Understanding the adoption of smartphone apps in crop protection," *Preci. Agricul.*, vol.21, issue 6, pp. 1209–26, Dec. 2020.

[32] M. Michels, W. Fecke, J.H. Feil, O. Musshoff, J. Pigisch, and S. Krone, "Smartphone adoption and use in agriculture: empirical evidence from Germany," *Preci. Agricul*, vol. 21, issue 2, pp. 403–25, Apr. 2020.

[33] F.D. Davis, "A Technology Acceptance Model for Empirically Testing New End-User Information Systems: Theory and Results," Ph.D. Thesis, Massachusetts Institute of Technology, Cambridge, MA, USA, Dec. 1985.

[34] J. Pfeiffer, A. Gabriel, and M. Gandorfer, "Understanding the public attitudinal acceptance of digital farming technologies: a nationwide survey in Germany," *Agricul. and Human Value*, vol. 38, issue 1, pp. 107–28, Feb. 2021.

[35] V. Partel, S.C. Kakarla, and Y. Ampatzidis, "Development and evaluation of a low-cost and smart technology for precision weed management utilizing artificial intelligence," *Comp. and elect in agri*culture, vol.157, pp. 339–50, Feb. 2019.

[36] M. Paustian, and L. Theuvsen, "Adoption of precision agriculture technologies by German crop farmers," *Preci. Agricul*, vol. 18, issue 5, pp. 701–16, Oct. 2017.

[37] M. Michels, W. Fecke, J.H. Feil, O. Musshoff, J. Pigisch, and S. Krone, "Smartphone adoption and use in agriculture: empirical evidence from Germany," *Preci. Agricul.*, vol. 21, issue 2, pp. 403–25, Apr. 2020.

[38] H.S. Pathak, P. Brown, and T. Best, "A systematic literature review of the factors affecting the precision agriculture adoption process," *Preci. Agricul.*, vol. 20, issue 6, pp. 1292–316, Dec. 2019.

[39] E. Pierpaoli, G. Carli, E. Pignatti, and M. Canavari, "Drivers of precision agriculture technologies adoption: a literature review," *Proc. Techno.*, vol. 8, pp. 61–9, Jan. 2013.

[40] S.H.W Chuah, P.A. Rauschnabel, N. Krey, B. Nguyen, T. Ramayah, and S. Lade, "Wearable technologies: The role of usefulness and visibility in smartwatch adoption," *Comput. Hum. Behav.*, vol. 65, pp. 276–84, 2016

[41] K.H. Coble, A. K. Mishra, S. Ferrell, and T. Griffin, "Big data in agriculture: A challenge for the future," *Applied Economic. Persp. and Policy*, vol. 40, issue 1, pp. 79–96, Mar. 2018.

[42] R. Rezaei, L. Safa, and M.M. Ganjkhanloo, "Understanding farmers' ecological con- servation behavior regarding the use of integrated pest management-an application of the technology acceptance model," *Glob. Ecol. Conserv.*, vol. 22, pp. e00941, 2020.

[43] FAO, "Thinking about the future of food safety–A foresight report," Rome, 2022, Available: https://doi.org/10.4060/cb8667en.

[44] UN Food Systems Summit, "Secretary-General's Chair Summary and Statement of Action on the UN Food Systems Summit," 23 September 2021, Available: www. un.org/en/food-systems-summit/news/making-foodsystems-work-people-planet- and-prosperity.

[45] T. Talaviya, D. Shah, N. Patel, H. Yagnik, and M. Shah, "Implementation of artificial intelligence in agriculture for optimisation of irrigation and application of pesticides and herbicides," *Artificial Intelligence in Agriculture*, vol 4, pp.58–73, 2020 Available: https://doi.org/10.1016/j.aiia.2020.04.002. [Accessed February 3, 2022].

[46] F.D. Davis, "Perceived usefulness, perceived ease of use, and user acceptance of information technology," *MIS Q*, vol. 13, pp. 319–40, 1989.

[47] F.D. Davis, "User acceptance of information technology: system characteristics, user perceptions and behavioral impacts," *International journal of man-machine studies*, vol.38, issue 3, pp. 475–87. March, 1993.

[48] V. Venkatesh, M.G. Morris, and G.B. Davis, and F.D. Davis, "User acceptance of information technology: Toward a unified view," *MIS Q.*, vol. 27, pp. 425–78, 2003.

[49] C.H. Lin, W.C. Wang, C.Y. Liu, P.N. Pan, and H.R. Pan, "Research into the E-learning model of agriculture technology companies: Analysis by deep learning," *Agronomy*, vol. 9, pp. 83, 2019.

[50] I. Ajzen, "The theory of planned behavior," *Organ. Behav. Hum. Decis. Process,* vol.50, pp. 179–211, 1991

[51] F.J. Dessart, J. Barreiro-Hurlé, and R. van Bavel, "Behavioural factors affecting the adoption of sustainable farming practices: a policy-oriented review," *European Review of Agricultural Economics*, Jul. 2019.

[52] N. Malhotra, D. Nunan, and D. Birks, *Marketing research: An applied approach*, 5th ed., Pearson; 2017.

[53] E.G. Carmines, and R.A. Zeller, *Reliability and Validity Assessment*; New York: Sage Publications, 1979.

[54] J.F. Hair, W.C. Black, B.J. Babin, R.E. Anderson, and Tatham, R.L, *Multivariate Data Analysis*, 5th ed., Upper Saddle River: Prentice Hall, 1998.

[55] J.C. Nunnally, *Psychometric Theory*, 2nd ed., New York: Sage Publications, 1978.

[56] D. Gefen, D. Straub, and M.C. Boudreau, "Structural equation modeling and regression: Guidelines for research practice," *Commun. Assoc. Inf. Syst.*, vol. 4, issue 7, 2000.

[57] C. Fornell, and D.F. Larcker, "Evaluating structural equation models with unobservable variables and measurement error," *Jour. Mark. Res.*, vol. 18, pp. 39–50, 1981.

[58] J. Palant, *SPSS Survival Manual: A Step by Step Guide to Data Analysis Using IBM Spss.* 2013.

[59] P.M. Bentler, and D.G. Bonett, "Significance tests and goodness of fit in the analysis of covariance structures," *Psychol. Bull.*, vol. 88, pp. 588, 1980.

[60] N. Vidanapathirana, K. Hirimburegama, W. Hirimburegama, and S. Nelka, "Exploring farmers' acceptance of e-learning using Technology Acceptance Model-case study in Sri Lanka," In Proceedings of the EDULEARN15 Conference, Barcelona, Spain, July 6-8, 2015.

[61] I.A. Castiblanco Jimenez, L.C. Cepeda García, F. Marcolin, M.G. Violante, and E. Vezzetti, "Validation of a TAM Extension in Agriculture: Exploring the Determinants of Acceptance of an e-Learning Platform," *Applied Sciences.*, vol. 11, issue 10, pp. 4672, Jan. 2021.

[62] W. Sroka, M. Dudek, T. Wojewodzic, and K. Król, "Generational Changes in Agriculture: The Influence of Farm Characteristics and Socio-Economic Factors," *Agriculture*, vol. 9, pp. 264, 2019.

[63] S. Mohr, and R. Kühl, "Acceptance of artificial intelligence in German agriculture: an application of the technology acceptance model and the theory of planned behavior," *Preci. Agriculture*, vol. 22, issue 6, pp.1816–44, Dec. 2021.

[64] P. Tangwannawit, and K. Saengkrajang, "Technology Acceptance Model to evaluate the adoption of the internet of things for planting maize," *Life Sciences And Environment Journal*, vol. 22, issue 2, pp. 262–73, Nov. 2021.

[65] C.T. Chang, J. Hajiyev, and C.R. Su, "Examining the students' behavioral intention to use e-learning in Azerbaijan: The general extended technology acceptance model for e-learning approach," *Comput. Education*, vol. 111, pp. 128–43, 2017.

[66] C. Kamrath, S. Rajendran, N. Nenguwo, V. Afari-Sefa, and S. Broring, "Adoption behavior of market traders: an analysis based on Technology Acceptance Model and Theory of Planned Behavior," *International Food and Agribusiness Management Review*, vol. 21, issue 1030-2018-3337, pp.771–90, 2018.

14 Impact of Artificial Intelligence in Personalized Banking Service

Gargi Sharma
TAPMI School of Business,
Manipal University Jaipur
Jaipur, Rajasthan, India

Umesh Solanki
TAPMI School of Business,
Manipal University Jaipur
Jaipur, Rajasthan, India

Vikas Solanki
Chitkara University Institute of Engineering
and Technology, Chitkara University
Punjab, India

Mohammed Rashad Baker
Software Department, College of Computer Science
and Information Technology
University of Kirkuk, Kirkuk, Iraq

14.1 INTRODUCTION

Artificial intelligence (AI) is **any technology** that lets computers recreate human behaviors such as **decision-making, problem-solving, and language use**. AI machines can **"learn" and improve their performance by processing large amounts of data to gain insights and make predictions**. AI is being used to provide personalized customer experiences and deliver more tailored products and services. At the organizational level, AI implementation is providing edge in reducing costs and improving efficiency by optimizing operations and automating processes.

AI has been used in financial services for decades, but it has only recently become sophisticated and user-friendly to be applied to banking services in a mass-market way. AI is already used in banks to improve **customer service, accelerate customer**

DOI: 10.1201/9781003348351-14

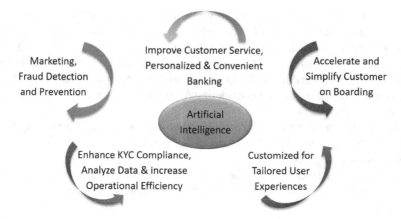

FIGURE 14.1   AI application in banking services: a game-changer.

onboarding, and enhance KYC compliance for compliance officers. AI is also used for **fraud detection and prevention and** can be customized for tailored user experiences.

The application of AI technology in financial services can be deemed a **game-changer**. It transforms the way banks deliver their services to customers and makes banking more personalized and convenient than ever before. AI can be used in many ways to provide a better experience. Banks can use it to create more tailored products, simplify the onboarding process, improve customer service, and enhance compliance. AI is also a powerful tool for marketing, enabling banks to better understand their customers and thereby provide more personalized offers and services. AI can also be used to analyze data and increase operational efficiency. For example, it can help banks to analyze customer data to optimize branch staffing.

14.2   LITERATURE REVIEW

AI and machine learning (ML) enabled robots, and medical services can help both healthcare professionals and doctors to treat patients without coming in direct contact to them and share the loads. AI and deep learning can help in detecting and analyzing stress-level patterns and mental health during pandemics (Solanki, Solanki, Baliyan, Kukreja, Lamba & Sahoo, 2021).

Healthcare professionals can be protected and supported in surveillance, thermal scanning, epidemiology, patient diagnosis, research, and vaccine evolution and can fight with the COVID-19 outbreak or other similar pandemics through the application of AI- and ML-enabled mechanization (Solanki, Solanki, Baliyan, Kukreja, Lamba & Sahoo, 2021).

AI is very powerful technology that have proven abilities in various fields such as healthcare, stock market, agriculture, robotics, finance, and image processing (Lamba et.al, 2021, Solanki et. al., 2021).

The banking industry has already implemented AI in various areas such as automated data management, QR code transactions, chatbots, fraud detection, authentication, personal finance management solutions, and commercial advice. Bankers are considering cost-effectiveness as a very prominent feature of AI for implementation at the organizational level. Banks are targeting mainly individual and SME consumers. Bank managers are not considering AI as a risky avenue for implementation (Oztrurk & Kula, 2021).

The type of customization is the decisive point in producing positive effects, higher tendencies to stay with the website, and higher perceived costs than the absence of customization (Fung, 2008).

Personalized services allow the customer to manage the bunch of financial decisions on a single point. It is the key to retain the customer for the bank (Prasanna, 2020).

Personalized services will help the customer to have access to preferred banking. It facilitates time consumption and is cost-effective. The customers will be more connected to the bank (Jha, 2019).

The present study concludes that customer satisfaction and perception is positively influenced by banking service quality. More research is required to measure customer satisfaction (Wafaa & Abderrezzak, 2014).

Advanced speech recognition uses ML and AI techniques such as deep learning and neural networks. To process audio and voice signals for speech, these systems use grammar, structure, syntax, and signal composition. ML systems become more knowledgeable with each use, making them suitable for subtleties including accents (Hassan, Nasret, Baker, & Mahmood, 2021).

The banking sector is facing competition from both banking and nonbanking sectors. Services provided by technology are changing the scenario of banks. AI is the key to implement technology in many services to retain the customer at a personal level (Satheesh and Nagaraj, 2021).

In rural areas, younger and middle-aged individuals aged up to 40 years use AI in banking services. Beyond the age of 40 years, people are facing issues in using AI-based services. There is a need to analyze the gap between bankers' knowledge and customer understanding of AI application in bank sectors (D'Cunha, Babu & Almeida, 2022).

Customer satisfaction is impacted by service personalization, and it has impact on e-loyalty in the Internet banking sector in Hong Kong (Tong, Wong & Lui, 2012).

AI is the future of new ways of banking and financial services. The implementation of AI is dependent on the skill set and training provided to humans and machines. AI can be implemented through a new business model in the banking industry. AI and blockchain are having immense scope in the future in the financial industry (Suresh & Rani, 2020).

The present study concludes that AI can influence the banking sector in many aspects such as core banking, operational performance, and customer support. AI can be used to create a new banking model that is cost-effective, technically sound, and more customers oriented. The future of AI is penetrating all areas related to banking and analytics (Kaur, Sahdev, Sharma & Siddiqui, 2020).

The main components of any industry are quality and data. The implementation of technology such as AI in these components will increase efficiency in the industry (Smith & Nobanee, 2020).

Financial frauds are the main concern of any financial institution and banks. Fraudulent activities are increasing day by day and are caried out using different methods. Identification of these frauds is the key to stop them at the initial level. ML methods have more efficiency in fraud detection given that the process performed should be selected on the basis of input data and verification of algorithms (Choi & Lee, 2018).

The customers are well aware of AI use in the provided services in banking and require more customized, innovative support from AI. AI is more commonly used in the field of KYC/AML, security aspects, and chatbots. The perception of consumers in reference to AI applications in banking and financial services is the main aspect to customize banking services. AI is extending its benefits to customers in marketing, risk mitigation, and compliance. The banking sector is inclining toward the use of AI in many aspects to sustain in the competitive arena. How a machine algorithm can replace the real-time decision-making capabilities of human resource effectively is hidden in the future (Geetha, 2021).

AI is already implemented in some areas of the banking arena, but credit risk calculation, credit rating, better decision making, efficiency, bond rating, and image recognition can be the future scope. AI is the solution and can be a proved a full-fledged or semi-fledged performer as compared to human resources (Veerla Veeranjaneyulu, 2021).

ML models can rapidly detect any deviations from normal user behavior and transactional patterns. ML algorithms can reduce the risk of fraud and enable more secure transactions by identifying anomalies, including fast growth in transactional amount or geographical change (Baker, Mahmood, & Shaker, 2022).

AI adoption is still not highly favored by the financial industry. AI adoption depends on many factors. The impact of AI is also related to the way of implementation and ability to use it by the organization and its employees (Kruse, Wunderlich & Beck, 2019).

AI is effective in cutting cost, minimizing risk, and providing personalized services (Ashta & Herrmann, 2021).

The present research suggests that AI adoption is in nuisance stage in the financial industry because of some constraints such as complex algorithm, non-availability of infrastructure, and decreasing level of clarity and skill set. Banks are using chatbots and other techniques of AI to create innovative customer services (R & Ravi, 2018).

Risk assessment in agriculture exposure can be carried out through speech emotion identification of the customer. A model related to this based on bidirectional long short-term memory (Bi-LSTM) networks and convolutional neural networks (CNNs) is developed, i.e., speech emotion recognition model. The proposed model's applicability can be verified in different areas of banking such as credit card fraud recognition and customer loss of banks (Zhao & Yao, 2022).

AI is facing many obstacles in its implementation, among which explaining ability is one of the obstacles. Decision-making is related more to exposition and exactness in the finance industry. Multi-criteria decision-making principles are the one that can be implemented to analyze the processes in financial decision-making (Cerneviciene & Kabašinskas, 2022).

The sustainable finance area is still limited; there is more scope according to countries. Quantitative data include the area of improvement. Therefore, an analysis of quantitative data can provide better insights about sustainable finance (Kumar, Sharma, Rao, Lim & Mangla, 2021).

14.3   STUDY OBJECTIVES

1) To study the preferences of personalized services in banking.
2) To determine the preferences of implementation of machines and AI in personalized banking services.
3) To study the preferences of customers about the applications of AI.
4) To identify factors affecting AI implementation in personalized services.

14.4   METHODOLOGY

This study is empirical in nature, and data are collected from primary sources. The convenience sampling technique was used for collecting primary data. The first primary source was bank customers. For the sampled survey, structured questionnaires were circulated in the districts of Rajasthan. The sample size for the study was 550 bank customers from public, private, and other bank sectors.

The second primary source was bankers, and 108 bankers were surveyed from different types of banks. Visualization tools were used to show the data analysis.

14.5   DATA ANALYSIS AND INTERPRETATION

In this study, we have explored the need and preferences of personalized services by customers and bankers in different areas. AI implementation in personalized banking

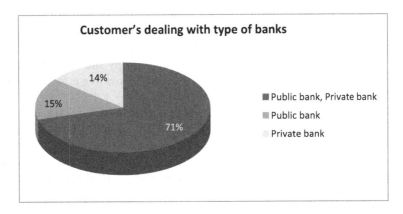

FIGURE 14.2   Customers' dealing with type of banks.

services, their applications and impact, and factors affecting that implementation have also been analyzed.

14.5.1 CUSTOMERS' VIEW

Overall, 71% of the respondent customers were availing the facility at both public and private sector banks; 15% were availing the services of only public sector banks. Customers were more inclined toward public sector banks because of the reliability, better services, and wider presence. Some of the main reasons to choose private sector banks are upgraded technology and online services.

TABLE 14.1
Responses for the Preferred Mode of Bank Services

Preferred Mode of Bank Services	Responses
Through Internet banking, mobile banking application, machine/technology, or AI	340
Through branch/banker	43
Through Internet banking or mobile banking application	37
Through branch/banker, Internet banking, or mobile banking application	30
Through branch/banker, Internet banking, mobile banking application, machine/ technology, or AI	25
Through branch/banker or Internet banking	18
Through Internet banking	16
Through branch/banker or mobile banking application	10
Through Internet banking, mobile banking application, or AI	7
Mobile banking application or machine/technology	6
Through branch/banker, Internet banking, or AI	6
Through branch/banker, Internet banking, or mobile banking application	6
Through Internet banking, mobile banking application, or machine/technology	6

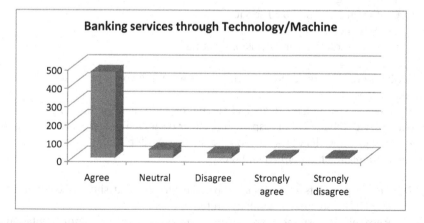

FIGURE 14.3   Banking using AI technology.

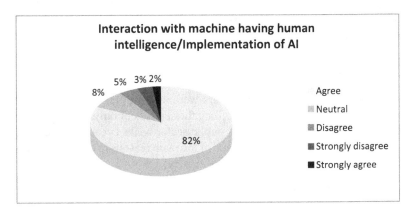

FIGURE 14.4   AI interaction for banking services.

The services that are availed from public sector banks are saving accounts, current accounts, and loans, whereas the services availed from private sector banks are credit card and loans. Almost all the customers are satisfied with the services provided by both public and private sector banks.

A total of 340 (61%) of 550 respondents preferred all modes of banking, but overall, the trends are inclined toward online banking, mobile application, and AI-based banking. Some services that are still transacted through bank branches are transactions related to cash and other documents; otherwise, all the other mediums facilitate easy transactions of customers.

More than 85% of the respondents agreed to take the services through machines/technology.

Moreover, 82% of the respondents were comfortable in interacting with machines in place of bankers for the services. The contributing factors toward the interaction were as follows:

- Time saving
- Customized/personalized services
- Convenience
- Real-time solutions and decision-making

Furthermore, 88% of respondent customers were in favor of personalized services for themselves.

Moreover, 55% of respondents had agreed for AI implementation in personalized banking services, but 23% of respondents either disagreed or were neutral about the same. As they either had lack of awareness about AI implementation or up to what extent the implementation of AI could occur.

7) The respondents were aware about the services that should be provided to them as personalized, and they preferred them.
8) Respondent customers are referring many areas for AI implementation in personalized banking services. They require quick and prompt personalized

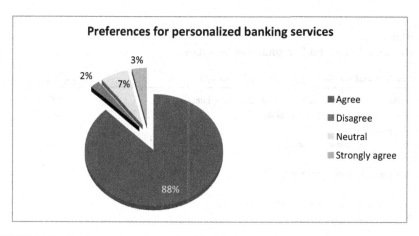

FIGURE 14.5   Preferences to personalized banking.

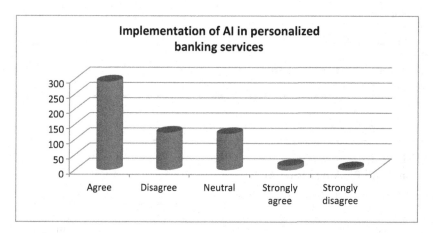

FIGURE 14.6   AI implementation in personalized banking.

banking services such as complaint resolution and loan doorstep banking. Most of the respondents of the age group of 20-40 years are aware and want to use AI-based services.

According to a study, the relation has reflected that the young age group prefers the technical and more advanced AI implementation in banking services (D'Cunha, Babu & Almeida, 2022).

TABLE 14.2
Customers' Preferred Personalized Services

Type of Personalized Services Customers Preferred	Responses
Net banking, loan documentation, mobile app, complaints	100
Loan documentation, investments, DSB	80
Interest rates	78
Net banking, mobile banking application	66
Mobile application	62
Net banking, loan documentation	44
Loan, DSB	31
Investment opportunities, credit card opening	15
Credit card, offers	8
Investment, loan, net banking	7
Complaint resolution, business transaction application	6
Investment	6
Investment planning	6
KYC	6
Loan, complaint resolution	6
Online	6
Senior citizen services, loan, investment	6
Loans and investments	3

TABLE 14.3
Personalized Banking Using AI

Type of Personalized Banking Services Using AI	Responses
Complaints	132
Loan processing	91
Investment	66
Complaints, loan processing	58
Complaints, cash transaction, DSB	56
Account history, compliant solve	46
Cash deposit	32
KYC, loan settlement	22
Cash deposit and withdrawal, document submission after retirement	15
Cash deposit, loan processing	11
Cash deposit, complaints	6
Cash withdrawal	6
Great user experience in the application	6
Complaint resolution quickly	3

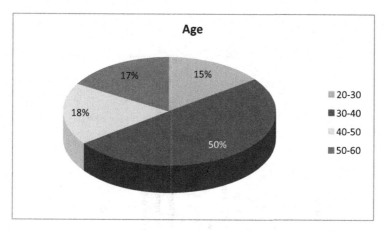

FIGURE 14.7 Respondent Bankers' Age.

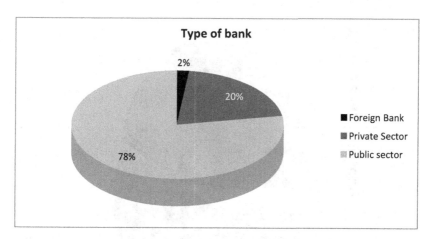

FIGURE 14.8 Type of bank.

14.5.2 BANKERS' VIEW

Fifty percent of the respondents belonged to the age group of 30-40 years. More than 90% of the total respondents were in favor of the implementation of personalized services for customers apart from the age group they belong to.

Seventy-eight percent of the respondent bankers were from public banks. The remaining respondents were from private and foreign banks.

More than 85% of the respondent bankers were in favor of AI implementation in back-end services of public sectors, private sectors, and other categories of banks.

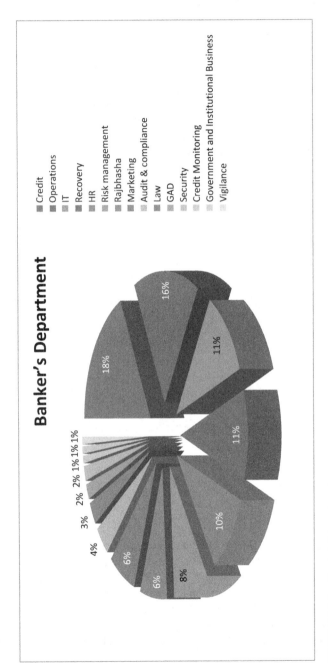

FIGURE 14.9 Bankers' department.

TABLE 14.4
Preferred Personalized Services

Department-Wise Preferred Personalized Services	Responses
Complaints	21
Account Types, Documentation, KYC, Updating of Documents	18
Investments such as PPF, Sukanya, Gold Bond, NPS, Demat, Mutual Fund categorically	15
Loan products and related facility such as interest rate, charges, paying calculation, documentation category, and interest rate	15
Institutional account, business wise, farmer services, and dairy services	11
Credit cards	9
Category-wise OTS scheme, government OTS scheme, for the deceased	5
Checkpoints for categorical customer risk	5
None	4
Category-wise compliance processes	2
Hindi niyamavali	1
IT supports	1
Updating leaves	1

TABLE 14.5
Preferred Personalized Services Using AI

Department-Wise Preferred Personalized Services Using AI	Responses
Alarm checkpoints for risk/fraud detection, complaints, and assistance	49
Account opening, inoperative account, initial account opening, and complaint registration and solution	18
Not applicable/sure	15
Document verification and risk management process	6
Due pay intention	4
IT support, branch, and customer end ready solutions	4
Digital service	2
Checkpoints in loan documentation	2
Hindi app for awareness and niymavali	2
Clerical work	1
Customer preferences, customer requirements at a specific place	1
Customer recognition at the bank door, alarm	1
Guarding	1
Legal opinion about a customer according to account transaction	1
Pattern of loan payments	1

Forty-nine percent of the respondent bankers of public sectors, private sectors, and other categories of banks were not in the favor of AI implementation in personalized banking services.

More than 85% of respondent bankers were not in favor of providing all types of services to customers using AI in place of bank employee/DSA/BC/customer care representative.

Eighteen percent of banker respondents were from the credit card department; 16% belonged to the operation department; 11% each from IT, human resources, and recovery department; and the remaining from the different deartments contributed to the survey.

All IT-related bankers were in favor of personalized services and back-end services using AI.

Most bankers were reluctant to AI implementation in all types of banking services for the following reasons:

- Data loss
- Absence of human involvement
- Increase in unemployment
- Risky
- More chances of fraud
- Less reliable
- Policy issue
- Heavy investment

Among the aforementioned reasons, operation and credit departments emphasized on data loss, no human involvement, fraud, and risks whereas IT bankers were concerned more about investments and policy. Hindi, law, and audit departments were concerned about data loss and risks involved with AI implementation. However, unanimously, all bankers of different departments were more concerned about unemployment and absence of human involvement.

4) Almost all respondent bankers preferred different types of personalized services according to their departments.

Bankers were interested in AI implementation in personalized services as a cost-effective avenue, which is in line with the results of a study conducted in Turkey (Oztrurk & Kula, 2021).

Fourteen percent of the respondent bankers have denied any applicability of AI in their departments at the customers' end. However, the remaining 86% were in favor of AI implementation at some levels up to some extent to cover the services of their departments. Bankers were more concerned about the risk or fraud involved in the different processes of banking services.

According to the study, fraudulent transactions are the main area of concern in financial institutions (Choi & Lee, 2018).

14.6 SUMMARY AND CONCLUSION

The outcome of the research shows that both customers and bankers are inclined toward personalized services according to the category. The implementation of technology is demanded at every aspect of banking. Although AI is in the nuisance stage in India as compared to that worldwide, customers and bankers still prefer some of the aspects of all the services through AI as well as personalized services. Time consumption and real-time complaint resolution are favoring contributing factors to implement AI from customers' viewpoint. AI is facing constraints in personalized services, as data privacy, risk, fraud, and unemployment are the main disturbing factors from bankers' viewpoint. Nevertheless, bankers are in favor of AI implementation at some levels up to some extent to cover services, especially in personalized services of their departments, as it will be cost-effective.

REFERENCES

[1] Ashta, A., & Herrmann, H. (2021). Artificial intelligence and fintech: An overview of opportunities and risks for banking, investments, and microfinance. *Strategic Change in May-June 2021, 211–222.*

[2] Baker, M. R., Mahmood, Z. N., & Shaker, E. H. (2022). Ensemble Learning with Supervised Machine Learning Models to Predict Credit Card Fraud Transactions. *Revue d'Intelligence Artificielle*, 36(4), 509–518. www.iieta.org/journals/ria/paper/10.18280/ria.360401

[3] Cerneviciene, J., & Kabašinskas, A. (2022). Review of multi-criteria decision-making methods in finance using explainable artificial intelligence.

[4] Choi, D., & Lee, K. (2018). An artificial intelligence approach to financial fraud detection under IoT environment: A survey and implementation. *Security and Communication Network, 1–15.*

[5] D'Cunha, A., Babu, J., & Almeida, S. M. (2022). Artificial intelligence in the banking sector: A common man's perspective. *International Journal Education and Teaching, 24(1(18), 54–58.*

[6] Fung, T. K. F. (2008). Banking with a personalized touch:Examining the impact of website customization on commitment. *Journal of Electronic Commerce Research, 9(4).*

[7] Geetha, A. (2021). A Study on artificial intelligence (AI) in banking and financial services. *International Journal of Creative Research Thoughts, 9(9).*

[8] Hassan, M. D., Nasret, A. N., Baker, M. R., & Mahmood, Z. S. (2021). Enhancement automatic speech recognition by deep neural networks. *Periodicals of Engineering and Natural Sciences (PEN)*, 9(4), 921–927.

[9] Jha, S. (2019). Preference of personalized banking services among generations: A study with reference to UT of Dadra and Nagar haveli. *International Journal of Science Technology and Management, 8(9), 1–6.*

[10] Kaur, N., Sahdev., S. L., Sharma, M., & Siddiqui, L. (2020). Banking 4.0:–The influence of artificial intelligence on the banking industry & how AI is changing the face of modern-day banks. *International Journal of Management, 11(6), 577–585.* https://doi.org/10.34218/IJM.11.62020.049

[11] Kruse, L., Wunderlich, N., & Beck, R. (2019). *Artificial intelligence for the financial services industry: What challenges organizations to succeed.*

[12] Kumar, S., Sharma, D., Rao, S., Lim, W. M., & Mangla, S. K. (2021). Past, present, and future of sustainable finance: Insights from big data analytics through machine learning of scholarly research. *Annals of Operations Research, 10(8).*

[13] Lamba, V., Hooda, S., Solanki, V., Ahuja, R., Ahuja, S., and Kaur, A. (2021). Comparative Analysis of Artificial Neural Networks for Predicting Nifty 50 value in The Indian Stock Market, *5th International Conference on Information Systems and Computer Networks (ISCON)*, pp. 1–5, doi: 10.1109/ISCON52037.2021.9702400.

[14] Öztürka, R., & Kula, V. (2021). A general profile of artificial intelligence adoption in banking sector: A survey of banks in Afyonkarahisar province of Turkey. *Journal of Corporate Governance, Insurance, and Risk Management, 8(2), 146–157.*

[15] Prasanna, S. S. M. (2020). A study on personalized banking services–A step towards rural development. *Global Journal for Research Analysis, 9(12), 69-71.*

[16] R, V., & Ravi, H. (2018). Application of artificial intelligence in investment banks. *Review of economics & business studies, 11(2), 131–136.*

[17] Satheesh, M. K., & Nagaraj, S. (2021). Applications of artificial intelligence on customer experience and service quality of the banking sector. *International Management Review, 17(1), 9–17.*

[18] Smith, A., & Nobanee, H. (2020). Artificial intelligence: In banking a mini review. *SSRN Electronic Journal.*

[19] Solanki, V., Solanki, U., Baliyan, A., Kukreja, V., Lamba, V., & Sahoo, B. K. (2021). Importance of Artificial Intelligence and Machine Learning in fighting with COVID-19 Epidemic. *5th International Conference on Information Systems and Computer Networks (ISCON),* pp. 1–8, doi: 10.1109/ISCON52037.2021.9702316.

[20] Solanki, V., Baliyan, A., Kukreja, V., & Siddiqui, K. M. (2021). Tomato Spotted Wilt Disease Severity Levels Detection: A Deep Learning Methodology. *8th International Conference on Signal Processing and Integrated Networks (SPIN),* pp. 361–366, doi: 10.1109/SPIN52536.2021.9566053.

[21] Suresh, A., & Rani, N. J. (2020). Role of artificial intelligence (AI) in the Indian banking scenario. *Journal of IT and Economic Development, 11(2), 1–11.*

[22] Tong, C., Wong, S. K., & Lui, K. P. (2012). The influences of service personalization, customer satisfaction and switching costs on E-loyalty. *International Journal of Economics and Finance, 4(3), 105–114.*

[23] Veerla, V. (2021). To study the impact of artificial intelligence as predictive model in banking sector: Novel approach. *International Journal of Innovative Research in Technology, 7(8).*

[24] Wafaa, H., & Abderrezzak, B. (2014). A study of the relationship between banking service quality and customer satisfaction in Algerian public banks. *International Journal of Science and Research, 3(1), 72–278.*

[25] Zhao, N., & Yao, F. (2022). Innovative mechanism of rural finance: Risk assessment methods and impact factors of agricultural loans based on personal emotion and artificial intelligence. *Journal of Environmental and Public Health, 1–9.*

15 E-Commerce and Trade

The Role of Artificial Intelligence

Shailee Thakur
Chandigarh Business School of Administration, Landran

Sukhmani Sandhu
Chandigarh Business School of Administration, Landran

Fekadu Yehuwalashet
Jigjiga University, Jigjiga, Ethiopia

15.1 INTRODUCTION

The actions and services involved in purchasing and selling products and services online are referred to as "e-commerce" (Holsapple & Singh, 2000; Kalakota & Whinston, 1997). As consumer demand for online services increases and chances to give them a competitive advantage arise, businesses are becoming increasingly involved in e-commerce. The integration of this e-business (IT) strategy with quickly advancing, extensively used, and extremely affordable information technology causes organizations to struggle. Consequently, businesses are compelled to continuously modify their business plans to satisfy shifting customer demands (Gielens & Steenkamp, 2019). Among these advancements, artificial intelligence (AI) is the most recent one. The ability of e-commerce to "accurately evaluate external data, learn from such data, and apply those insights to meet prescribed goals and obligations through flexible customization" is transforming the way that commerce is conduct. Depending on the context, AI can take the form of systems, tools, techniques, or algorithms. Big data can be used to target client demands through customized offers, giving businesses a competitive advantage. AI in e-commerce refers to the use of AI methodologies, systems, tools, or algorithms to speed up online transactions for buying and selling of goods and services. Research

DOI: 10.1201/9781003348351-15

on the use of AI in Internet business has been ongoing for the past 30 years. Nearly 4000 academic articles in various fields—both at the organizational and consumer levels—have been published on this subject. The findings of this study suggest that recommendation systems are the primary area of AI in e-commerce, with sentiment analysis, optimization, trust, and personalization as the primary research subjects. This study makes timely contributions to the discussion of the use of AI technology in corporate strategy. According to Gartner, during the past 4 years, there has been a 270% increase in the number of enterprises implementing AI. However, there are many misunderstandings about everything AI-related. In contrast to the popular belief, the area of AI has been studied for almost 70 years (the term AI first came into use in 1956). As expected, AI has altered extensively since 1956. For starters, only the largest businesses and academic institutions can afford AI. Small- to medium-sized businesses can now incorporate AI into their operations thanks to the inexpensive cost (versus many older technologies). Thus, technology has spread to almost all major industries on the planet, where it has been implemented in hundreds of different ways. Even the AI terms themselves have evolved. The phrase "artificial intelligence" has evolved to include several brand-new sub-fields. In a recent study conducted by Gartner, approximately 30 such AI subfields have been recognized as likely to become commonplace. Within this decade, it is anticipated that technologies such as chatbots, virtual assistants, speech recognition, machine learning, conversational user interfaces, natural language processing (NLP), and image recognition will significantly increase business value and provide an impressive return on investment (ROI). This decade (and especially 2022) will be crucial for AI and its related sectors because three key reasons are anticipated to cause a significant shift toward AI and smart automation: to decrease staff costs and reliance on human capital and to boost productivity with, accessibility to, and affordability of AI-based methods. Business productivity is anticipated to increase by up to 40% with AI technology, and individuals will be able to use their time more effectively. Apart from increasing productivity, AI is changing e-commerce in many other ways such as by enhancing customer service, addressing consumer requests, reducing costs, and obtaining a competitive edge. Despite the fact that there are thousands of AI applications, most of them fall into four categories that are currently crucial. Some e-commerce businesses have already reached their full potential, while others are further along in the process. However, each one is essential to the success of your e-commerce.

15.2 ARTIFICIAL INTELLIGENCE FOR PERSONALIZATION OR THE INTERNET

This kind of AI has traditionally been trained using data from Internet user behavior. Personalized product and service suggestions are made using AI in e-commerce, notably by well-known recommender systems from websites such as Amazon, Spotify, and Netflix. By offering a relevant and individualized context, personalization is essential for enhancing user experience.

15.3 ARTIFICIAL INTELLIGENCE: COGNITIVE OR PERCEPTUAL

Because of the widespread use of conversational agents in e-commerce, perceptual AI has gained extensive popularity. The e-commerce buying experience can become considerably more interactive and engaging with the help of perceptual AI. In this regard, a lot of websites now use chatbots to make it easier for users to navigate and extract the information they need. Additionally, perceptual and Internet-based AI can be merged to create conversational bots that promote products. An engaging and guided user experience with cognitive AI is more crucial than ever because of the post-pandemic flood of new consumers who might be inexperienced with your e-commerce interface.

15.4 ARTIFICIAL INTELLIGENCE: DECISION OR BUSINESS

AI-based automation, which is often utilized by business users as compared to end users, can be used to boost productivity, cut down expenses, and provide teams more time to focus on things that bring value such as managing complex circumstances and maintaining customer relations. AI in business can also help in the delivery of more consistent results by standardizing decision processes and optimizing decision outcomes. AI Business is essential to the survival of e-commerce, especially in light of the pandemic's disruption of demand and the decline in margins across numerous businesses.

15.5 AUTOMATED ARTIFICIAL INTELLIGENCE

The e-commerce sector will gain a lot from automated AI. Consumers can now browse, investigate, customize, and purchase goods and services online, although not all of them are instantly downloadable. Automated AI may be able to close the gap between offline and online commerce.

15.5.1 LITERATURE REVIEW

Both developing and developed nations are anticipated to significantly increase their demand for products and services from the e-commerce business. Today's retailers are concentrating on understanding consumer buying patterns; therefore, they are supporting the demand of the customer to shop at their convenience and ease. Online sales have increased dramatically because of changing customer behavior and the availability of trustworthy, affordable technologies for secure transactions. The demand for online commerce is also anticipated to increase globally because of reasons such as increasing mobile and smartphone adoption.

Future technical advancements including social commerce, driverless vehicles, 3D printing, and analytics will also have an impact on online enterprises. In the current environment, businesses are concentrating on investing in the data analytics sector to offer personalized customer experiences and, consequently, enhance insights into real-time consumer purchasing behavior. The companies investing in digital operations of their enterprises are anticipated to offer many advantages, some of which include greater brand awareness, a larger potential consumer base, and a few others. The success of e-commerce companies mostly depends on maximizing conversion rates, which raise prospective profits, overall income, and sales.

In the future, intelligent computers may supplement or replace some human abilities. AI refers to computer or programmed intelligence. It belongs to the field of computer science (Gidh, 2020). AI has become a popular field in computer science because of the numerous ways in which it has enhanced human existence. Over the past two decades, AI has significantly improved the efficiency of production and service activities. Expert systems, an ever-evolving technology, are a product of scientific study of AI. Application domains for AI significantly affect the field in several spheres of life, as specialized systems are increasingly deployed. Expert systems are frequently employed nowadays to address complex issues in various industries including engineering, business, medicine, and weather forecasting. A variety of diverse spheres of life are being significantly affected by applications of AI (Marda,2018). The productivity and performance of the fields that use AI technologies have increased. Robots are given the ability to think logically and conceptually thanks to AI. Over the past two decades, AI methods have significantly benefited many fields (Mittal and sharma,2021). AI is capable of gathering and analyzing large amounts of data to draw logical conclusions. This technique is additionally utilized in e-commerce to recognize trends based on browsing, order history, credit checks, account history, and other information (Kakkar,2017). According to Forrester, India is the country with the fastest e-commerce growth. AI would have a major impact on how e-commerce businesses attract and keep customers. AI growth in the e-commerce sector will provide an abundance of jobs in computer technology, AI, and engineering (Bandara et.al 2020). To better understand their customers and provide a better user experience, several e-commerce companies have begun to apply AI in a variety of ways (Gidh, 2020). A lot of new information science, computer learning, and engineering will be produced as a result of the AI revolution in the e-commerce industry. AI-driven e-commerce will generate jobs in the IT sector to develop and maintain the infrastructure and software that will power these AI calculations. In either instance, those with a restricted set of abilities who may soon face unemployment may be impacted by the introductionof AI and online business (K&K, 2020). To prevent payment default, additional risk control is required because of the increase in e-commerce orders. A customer has defaulted in payment if they do not pay a bill within 90 days of receiving it. The chance of a customer defaulting can be determined using credit score (Vanneshi, 2018). AI would undoubtedly alter how we function and live. Its adoption is referred to be the fourth industrial revolution because of its tremendous potential (Srivastva, 2018).

Applications of AI are dynamic social constructs that cannot and should not be evaluated only based on their accuracy and dependability. Like any significant technology advancement, there are benefits and challenges associated with it. On the one hand, numerous apps have been developed or are in the works that might significantly improve people's quality of life (Dhana Laxmi et al., 2020). However, the profits can be increased and dangers can be decreased by putting in place the necessary resources and procedures. Despite the fact that many other governments have developed their AI policies, India has not yet done so (Srivastva, 2018). A study examined the current policy landscape in India and drew a conclusion that the shortcomings of data-driven decision-making should be the main focus rather than a secondary one when developing AI policies (Marda, 2018). Practically, every aspect of modern life is being transformed by AI, including jobs, economics, connection, warfare, privacy, defense, and healthcare (Tyagi, 2016). Practically, every aspect of human existence is being transformed by AI, including jobs, economics, connection, warfare, privacy, defense, and healthcare. However, we are unsure of whether the long-term beneficial benefits of AI will still outweigh their short-term negative effects, and if not, what the repercussions will be. The long-term beneficial effects of AI may not always out-weigh the negative effects, and if that is the case, we are in serious trouble. As we look around us, we appear to embrace the changes that technology brings, whether they be smart homes, smart healthcare, Industry 4.0, or self-driving cars. On the con-trary, we were frequently seen protesting the government on various matters such as jobs, taxes, and privacy. With AI development, more robots or automated cars will be developed to replace human labor (Tyagi, 2016).

e-commerce company classification gives entrepreneurs and strategists a better understanding of both commercial and financial components of any given enterprise. The following are a few succinct descriptions of the various e-commerce business models based on the services they offer:

- Business-to-business (B2B): This e-commerce model comprises transactions between businesses, creating high-value and high-volume relationships.
- Business-to-consumer (B2C): This e-commerce model focuses on the interactions and exchanges between firms and their clients. This paradigm refers to online retail, as it is contrasted with traditional brick-and-mortar retail.
- Consumer-to-business (C2B): This e-commerce model enables customers to provide businesses with a variety of services or products. The model, which serves a larger firm, is quite similar to a single proprietorship.
- Consumer-to-consumer (C2C): This model includes all interactions between consumers about the exchange of products and services. Most of these transactions occur through a third party, which provides an online platform for the sales to be accepted (e-commerce).
- Public governance or administrative entities are referred to as "administra-tion" in business-to–administration (B2A) relationships. It covers interactions between organizations and the governmental administration. Along with this, the business model offers a variety of services in sectors including social security, finances, legal entities, employment paperwork, and a few others.
- Consumer-to-administration (C2A): This model includes interactions between the general public and public authorities. In this model, most transactions involve things like getting information on zoning regulations, paying taxes or fines, and a few other things.

B2C and B2B are the two most well-known types of business models among all those discussed above. The transaction is completely distinct from the other cat-egories because each addressee of the transaction has unique needs, wants, and business requirements.

Although models are anticipated to include the same goods or services, a wide range in the order of frequency, quantity, prices, product expectations, fulfillment strategies, and entrance hurdles is anticipated.

Features that are simple and convenient for consumers to use are one of the things supporting the expansion of the e-commerce sector. These features prove to be crucial for consumers because they can readily obtain a variety of product descriptions and information through a variety of consumer feedbacks and reviews, which aids them in furthering the success of their purchase. Consumers today place a greater focus on both simple payment processes and quick and secure product delivery. Numerous online apps provide clients with the option of at-the-door delivery, which positively influences their choices and preferences. Consequently, consumers can simply get the products through online channels and choose from a variety of models, which makes it even easier for them.

AI applications implemented in e-commerce:

A) Chatbots

Online company websites use chatbots to work on customer support administration. One way in which AI is used by humans is through chatbot SMS messages that inform users of their preferences.

B) Intelligent Visual Search

With the aid of visual search technology, customers may do online searches using any kind of image instead of words or a keyword. For those who do not know exactly what they are looking for or enter the wrong search words into the search bar, this approach is quite helpful.

C) Voice Search Technology

A voice command can be used with voice search technology to conduct an Internet, website, or application search. This function, which was made possible by improvements in speech recognition, originally emerged on smartphones and allowed the search bar to be removed. As indicated by the introduction of new technologies such as voice assistants (Alexa with Amazon Echo, Google Voice Search, Cortana, Siri...), voice search is currently becoming a more popular way to do Internet searches.

D) Assortment Intelligence Tool

Online retailers who use assortment intelligence track, examine, and compare their competitors' assortments to their own. This technique is effective thanks to a variety of intelligence technologies. You may learn about the breadth and depth of your competitors' variety across categories and brands using an excellent assortment intelligence tool such as Price Weave. It enables you to examine the selection using a variety of filters, including those for colors, variety, sizes, shapes, and other technical details. A store can have a thorough grasp of what items their rivals have, how well they perform, and whether they should add these products to their current catalog with the aid of an assortment intelligence tool.

Effective retail sales depend heavily on product selection. It affects how category managers; brand managers; and the teams in charge of merchandising,

planning, and logistics make decisions on a daily basis. The following goals are easier to attain with a solid selection mix:
- Lower the price of acquiring new customers (as well as retain existing customers).
- Increasing penetration through diverse consumer segmentation.
- Reduce the cost of planning and inventory control.

E) Artificial Intelligence Virtual Assistance

The AI-Powered Virtual Assistant extracts information and complex data from conversations to comprehend them and process them appropriately. RPA (robotic process automation) NLP, and machine learning.

F) Real-Time Product Targeting

Real-time product targeting is a subset of real-time personalization, as it concentrates on displaying product recommendations during the buying process rather than tailoring the site's or app's content and design to the individual customer. Selling things is the main goal rather than merely enhancing consumer experience. Most of the real-time product targeting solutions use email, mobile applications, and websites to offer customers particular products that, ideally, match what they are looking for.

G) Use of Augmented Reality

The phrase "augmented reality" (AR) refers to the real-time integration of digital information with the environment of the user (AR). Users of AR interact with the real environment.

This in comparison, virtual reality constructs a wholly constructed environment and adds produced perceptual data on top of it. By adopting AR, users can access additional information or alter the appearance of natural situations. AR, which successfully combines digital and three-dimensional (3D) elements with how humans perceive the physical environment, has a variety of benefits. AR has several applications, including entertainment and decision-making assistance. With the use of a gadget such as a smartphone or glasses, AR allows users to access visual components, audio, and other sensory data. The device has this information placed on top of it to produce a seamless experience in which the user's perspective of the outside world is changed by digital information. The information applied to the natural environment may hide or enhance some of it.

H) Artificial Intelligence Fake Review Detection

Customer surveys have become important for gauging online user trust. According to a recent investigation by Dimensional Research, 90% of respondents claimed that favorable online polls had an impact on their options for purchases. However, fake surveys can affect the results. Using AI to make purchasing decision, this problem can be solved. Amazon also makes use of AI to combat surveys of fake goods. Apple AI Framework ensures that only verified customer buy surveys are supported. It also provides a tendency to those studies that are rated as accommodating by several customers.

I) Customer-Centric Advertisement

Customer-centric marketing refers to a marketing approach that is focused on the desires and requirements of the consumer. It includes integrating common sense, intuition, and trustworthy facts regarding customer behavior while placing the needs of the client above all other factors.

J) Inventory Management

Inventory management systems with AI enhancements can identify demand trends and use this information to more precisely predict demand and optimize warehouse operations and strategies for replenishing. Based on real-time data, AI inventory management offers more precise and timely estimates.

K) Artificial Intelligence–Based Sales Process

AI is being used by businesses to boost lead volume, close rates, and sales performance overall so that technology can automate and improve a significant piece of the sales process. Sales people may focus on what matters and, consequently, which is closing the sale.

15.5.1.1 What Will E-Commerce Look Like in the Future with Artificial Intelligence?

With advances in AI, the e-commerce sector is constantly evolving. It now affects the way things are displayed and presented to clients by an online store. AI is enhancing the online shopping experience for both customers and businesses by providing a highly personalized purchasing experience with the aid of virtual buying assistants. e-Commerce businesses can use the technology's cutting-edge methodologies to analyze massive amounts of data and learn about customer behavior to interact, segment, and retarget their customers. Delivering a highly customized customer experience is crucial for an online business to succeed. Programs with AI may be able to identify and analyze customer data to forecast future shopper preferences and provide product recommendations based on those preferences. According to a report published by "Business Insider," by 2020, more than 85% of consumer contacts would be handled automatically. Given that automated systems can efficiently and quickly respond to emails, calls, and chats, these numbers appear to be accurate. Moreover, Tractica predicted that, by 2025, earnings of $59.8 billion will have been made through the direct and indirect use of AI software. However, more research needs to be conducted. According to some recent surveys, up to 85% of AI algorithms ultimately fail to achieve their objectives. There is little doubt that AI algorithms may be improved, and when new developments are integrated into existing AI solutions, this number should fall.

15.5.1.2 Artificial Intelligence in E-Commerce Companies: Advantages

Amazon has always acknowledged the benefits of technology connected to AI. The major online retailer uses AI to improve customer service, pick better products, and optimize logistics. According to a recent analysis from McKinsey & Company and the Retail Industry Leaders Association, each of the seven imperatives for rethinking retail in 2021 might be, in some way, made possible by AI-informed technology.

1) More Carefully Chosen Advertising and Marketing

According to the retailers surveyed, personalization was the top priority, although only 15% claimed to have fully implemented it across all channels.

Engaging in one-on-one conversations with clients can help differentiate our brand from that of our competitor. Advances in machine learning and AI have made the utilization of deep personalization methods possible. By analyzing vast amounts of information from past purchases and other contacts with customers, you can narrow down on what your customers genuinely want and communicate with them in a way that will connect.

2) Higher Rate of Consumer Retention

Sending clients individualized marketing and advertising communications helps increase retention. Omnichannel customization strategies have the potential to boost revenue and customer retention by 10%–15%, according to McKinsey's omnichannel personalization research. Building excellent customer data and insights is a key component of personalization, according to the study. This asset also adds value elsewhere in the value chain. According to our estimate, personalization will soon surpass conventional mass marketing in terms of ROI.

3) Continuous Automation

To accomplish a task with the least amount of human participation, automation is used. This might involve anything from scheduling emails using a CRM or marketing platform, automating tasks with Zapier, or employing cutting-edge technology to help with hiring.

However, some of the topics that are now being discussed the most frequently with regard to upcoming ecommerce trends are robotics and machine learning.

Automation of the monotonous tasks required to manage an online store can be established using AI tools. AI makes it feasible to automate a variety of tasks, including basic customer service, loyalty discounts, and product recommendations.

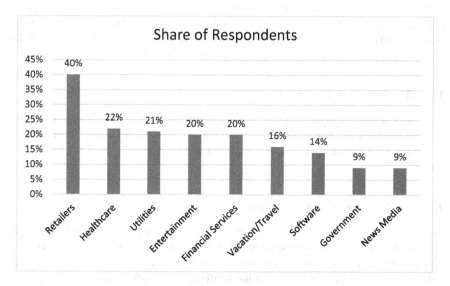

FIGURE 15.1   Share of consumers who have used chatbots to engage with companies in the US as of 2019 by industry.

4) Successful Sales Procedure
Using automation may Some of the subjects that are now being discussed
the most frequently in regard to upcoming ecommerce trends are robotics and
machine learning.

Automation of the monotonous tasks required to manage an online store
can be greatly helped by AI. AI makes it feasible to automate a variety of
tasks, including basic customer service, loyalty discounts, and product
recommendations.

15.5.1.3   Artificial Intelligence Use Cases in Online Shopping

You may be aware of many of the use cases for AI in ecommerce, but you may
not realize that the technology they are based on is actually connected to AI. The
following six technologies are the most typical ones:

- Individual product suggestions
- Optimizing the price.
- Improved clientele service.
- Client segmentation.
- Smart logistics.
- Forecasting of demand and sales.

15.5.2   INDIVIDUAL PRODUCT SUGGESTIONS

Data processing and collecting for online customer purchases are now easier than
before. AI is used to generate personalized product recommendations that are based
on past consumer behavior and lookalike customers. Websites that suggest things you
might like based on prior purchases employ machine learning to look at your buy history. To create a tailored experience, by implementing a marketing plan, optimizing of
pricing, and providing customer insights, retailers rely on machine learning to collect,
analyze, and apply data. In everyday e-commerce applications, machine learning will
eventually replace data scientists, gradually diminishing their importance.

15.5.3   OPTIMIZING THE PRICE

You can change the price of your product based on supply and demand using AI-
enabled dynamic pricing. With the right data, modern technologies can forecast when
and what to discount, dynamically calculating the minimum discount needed for
the sale.

15.5.4   IMPROVED CLIENTELE SERVICE

You can provide the appearance of offering higher touch customer service by using
chatbots and virtual assistants. Although these bots are not completely self-sufficient,
they can assist with simple tasks so that live support agents can focus on more challenging issues. Virtual agents are available around-the-clock; hence, you can quickly

address common questions and issues at any time without keeping your clients waiting.

15.5.5 CLIENT SEGMENTATION

Thanks to improved access to company and consumer data as well as increasing computer power, ecommerce businesses can now better understand their customers and identify new trends.

According to an insight from Accenture, "AI systems can evaluate very sophisticated and varied choices for customer engagement very quickly, and they can constantly improve their performance as new data becomes available." Marketers can set parameters and allow AI to optimize and learn in order to achieve precision.

15.5.6 SMART LOGISTICS

According to the study conducted by Emerging Tech Brew, machine learning's predictive capabilities "shine, helping to forecast transit durations, demand levels, and shipment delays." The core of smart logistics, also known as intelligent logistics, which strives to manage stocks and more precisely estimate demand, is the use of real-time data from sensors, RFID (radio frequency identification) tags, and other sources. Machine learning systems develop over time to deliver more accurate forecasts for various supply chain and logistics jobs.

15.5.7 FORECASTING OF DEMAND AND SALES

You should base your inventory planning, especially in the period during and following COVID-19, on both current and past data. You can accomplish that with the use of AI. According to a recent McKinsey analysis, investing in real-time customer analytics will remain crucial for tracking and responding to changes in consumer demand that may be used for targeted marketing or price optimization.

15.6 ARTIFICIAL INTELLIGENCE IN E-COMMERCE STATISTICS AND FACTS

Today, businesses such as Alibaba, Rakuten, eBay, and Amazon use AI for large data management, chatbots, product suggestions, and the identification of fraudulent reviews.

Let us now examine some intriguing information from a recent Ubisend report:

- One in five customers is receptive to making a chatbot purchase, and these customers are willing to part with up to £314.74.
- Chatbots are used by 40% of customers to search for bargains and offers.
- Google spent £400 million to purchase the AI company DeepMind.

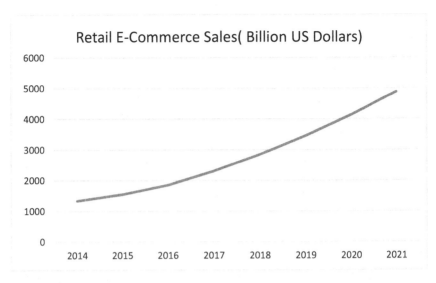

FIGURE 15.2   Retail e-commerce sales worldwide during 2014-2021 (in US billion dollars).

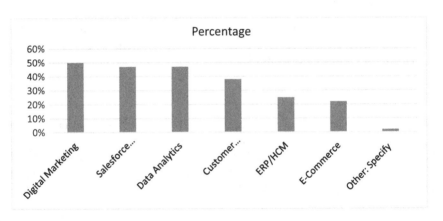

FIGURE 15.3   Some of the areas in software that are ripe for AI/ML investment.

Data mining, NLP, and machine learning are the three main components of AI. These components aid e-commerce companies in achieving better outcomes. The amazing aspect about AI is that robots are learning to help us and execute manual chores, and they are doing so really well, which frees us up to concentrate more at a strategic level of business. Now that we have the time we previously lacked, we can concentrate on generating more instead of performing the same chores repeatedly.

The technology behind image search is being developed by search engines. Not only that, but this new feature greatly advances clothing and fashion e-commerce! Examine medicine and retail sectors. This represents a hitherto unattainable chance for the expansion of smaller businesses. In this instance, it is less about the technology

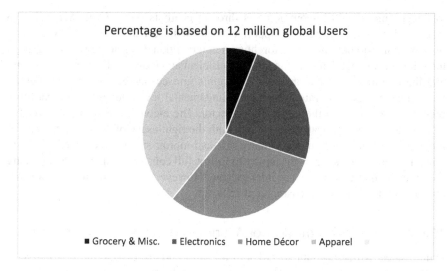

Percentage is based on 12 million global Users

■ Grocery & Misc.   ■ Electronics   ■ Home Décor   ■ Apparel

FIGURE 15.4   Consumers' use of visual search for retail categories.

and more about the ranks in search engines and online stores. For many years, the strongest indicators for search engines to find the appropriate image or content were metadata and tagging. Certainly, most of the time, it was done through handsearching. However, AI automates the categorization of images and the tagging of products, ensuring better alignment in search results based on improved attribute identification. When we consider that, photographs truly become data sources.

15.6.1   STATISTICS ON ARTIFICIAL INTELLIGENCE ADOPTION IN E-COMMERCE

The biggest industries based on AI in 2022 were FinTech, Online Media, and eCommerce (platforms such as YouTube). A recent study found that 84% of e-commerce organizations either actively integrate AI technology into their operations or consider it to be a key priority. Thus, the use of AI in e-commerce has considerably expanded over the past 5 years and will only keep increasing.

The adoption of conversational AI in e-commerce businesses is better understood by the following statistics: According to 86% of decision-makers (PwC), AI will be a "mainstream technology" by 2022. Voice recognition is crucial because 22% of users would rather speak to an AI voice assistant than type words (Pew Research). Another 26% of respondents claim that using other functions is made simpler through AI voice assistants. According to a 2021 poll conducted by the international consulting company PwC, 52% of decision-makers believe that integrating AI solutions has increased employee productivity (PwC). According to another study, 75% of IT leaders believe that using AI technology will improve security (Statista). A total of 23% of the businesses surveyed have already used AI chatbots, and another 31% expect to do so by 2021 (Salesforce). By 2025, it is anticipated that the global market for conversational AI would reach $13.9 billion. Enterprise Wire In uses more than 300,000 chatbots on Facebook Messenger. One of the most well-liked approaches to integrating AI with e-commerce is through chatbots (Hootsuite). According to Gartner, 15% of all customer support contacts will be handled by AI by the end of this year without the need for human intervention (Gartner). Many variables including new client demand, the need for efficient and individualized customer care, and the requirement for more precise insights into consumer patterns, are behind the increasing adoption rate. On a more fundamental level, however, compatibility propels AI adoption in the e-commerce sector. The e-commerce business model is well suited for the application of AI, and with the right usage of AI, e-commerce can move goods much more quickly than brick-and-mortar stores. One benefit of AI in e-commerce, for instance, is the ability to follow full consumer experience, including the products that consumers are interested in. However, brick-and-mortar stores are able to only track what the customer checks out.

15.6.2 Statistics on the Role of Artificial Intelligence in Online Sales

Online sales, which account for 18% of all sales and are expanding at a 1% year-on-year rate, have been steadily increasing for a long time. These sales and any company's overall bottom line will ultimately decide whether integrating AI technologies is worthwhile. In reality, the advancement of conversational AI has a positive impact on commerce sales across practically all industries. For instance, in the most recent state of AI report from McKinsey, 79% of survey respondents stated that integrating AI into marketing and sales has increased the firm's revenue.

Enterprises were able to produce at least 20% more revenue thanks to AI-based business methods, albeit the gain in revenue varies. e-Commerce companies can use AI in a variety of ways to increase sales. For instance, using AI into business message and moving away from conventional communication channels such as email can raise click-through rates by 13 times and quadruple open rates. Additionally, e-commerce businesses are spending money on AI to enhance suggestions, last-mile delivery optimization, and logistics. For instance, Amazon's AI-powered recommendation engine generates 35% of the business's annual sales through tailored recommendations. Big data analytics, which is also supported by AI, increased Amazon's profits by an average of 143% per year during 2016-2019 by optimizing prices as frequently as every 10 minutes based on a variety of external factors, such as average online price, availability of the product, and historical demand patterns. The bottom line, however, is not solely impacted by total sales. e-Commerce businesses are expanding profit margins and running more effectively by employing AI to save operating costs. One of the largest e-commerce platforms, Alibaba, for instance, has been investing in its smart logistics program and has been successful in reducing delivery faults by 40% while saving hundreds of millions of dollars on return logistics. When it comes to supply chain optimization, Amazon is not far behind either. Amazon has reduced shipping costs by more than half by optimizing delivery schedules and routes with the help of AI and big data analytics. Netflix is yet another fantastic example of how AI-driven cost reductions have prevented the company from losing $1 billion in revenue. This was accomplished through a personalized recommendations engine that used machine learning to increase its accuracy over time.

15.6.3 STATISTICS ON THE USE OF ARTIFICIAL INTELLIGENCE IN CUSTOMER SERVICE

Given current market trends and customer expectations, AI has been the most pervasive in customer service and will likely retain that status. In particular, the increased desire for quick satisfaction, personalization, and ease of use will make AI a key influence on how customers are treated in the coming decade. In reality, businesses want to allow AI virtual agents do an increasing number of customer care tasks, signaling that this trend toward increased automation has already started. According to IBM, it is feasible for conversational AI-powered AI virtual agents to respond to four of five customer service enquiries. More significantly, this change is a result of shifting customer expectations rather than just being implemented to cut labor expenses. Customers want responses to their questions in less than 10 minutes (often instantly). Consequently, e-commerce companies are turning to AI to offer customer support that is really quicker than human assistance. For instance, conversational AI-powered chatbots can resolve thousands of client inquiries quickly—5.4 minutes as opposed to the industry standard of 38 hours. AI chatbots are 30% less expensive than human customer support representatives, in addition to being more effective and always accessible. AI also plays a significant role in enhancing the shopping experience, going beyond its traditional use in resolving customer complaints. e-Commerce companies are using AI in a variety of ways, including more effective recommendations engine digital shopping assistants with websites and feature apps all in one place, more potent search engines with contextual AI, and so forth. For instance, voice assistants and visual search, the latter of which is the fastest-growing mobile search category, are two unmet client demands. Additionally, a current Gartner prediction indicates that the incorporation of voice and visual search options on websites and mobile devices will boost e-commerce revenue by 30%.

15.6.3.1 Statistics Using Artificial Intelligence in Marketing

AI will be used by e-commerce companies in 2022 to enhance their marketing efforts through big data analytics and business messaging. Almost all online merchants have access to crucial client data that can be used to enhance targeted advertising. However, despite having access to terabytes upon terabytes of data, most of the organizations are unable to exploit it. Big data analytics can help in this situation by employing AI to automate the analysis of enormous data volumes. Several large businesses are taking it a step further and utilizing machine learning to enhance their performance over time. The Luxury Escapes AI chatbot, which raised the company's response rate on retargeting efforts by 89%, is one example of how AI is being used for more successful marketing. Many other companies such as Lego, Subway, Esso, H&M, and Sephora, have engaged in comparable activities with equally amazing outcomes. Business messaging is also undergoing an industry-wide shift as a result of the enormous advancements AI is bringing to this particular business function. For starters, AI enables mass personalization for both huge merchants and small- to medium-sized e-commerce firms.

15.6.3.2   The Future of Artificial Intelligence in E-Commerce

Many firms, both e-commerce and non–e-commerce, have historically had reservations about the practicality of AI. Businesses simply did not see enough value in AI solutions, in addition to the cost. However, this has also altered, just like the cost. In the previous 3 years, there has been a significant change in consumer behavior and expectations. The younger generation, who currently makes up the bulk of online buyers, is one example. They are far less suspicious of conversational AI trends and even favor utilizing virtual agents over their human counterparts in many situations to save time. To better serve them, these younger generations also generate a lot more data that can be examined by AI. However, older generations place a higher importance on individualized corporate messaging and are gradually moving away from it. The e-commerce industry's next big thing is AI. Although AI solutions have been present for a while, new advancements in various technologies have made it simpler to integrate them in the e-commerce sector.

Increased consumer happiness, cheaper costs, and more effective procedures are just a few ways the e-commerce sector demonstrates its benefits. Furthermore, during 2020-2027, AI is predicted to grow at a rate of 33.2% annually.

You may use AI technology to build your business more successfully by giving your clients an AI-powered personalized search experience. This will boost their brand loyalty.

15.6.3.3   Research Methodology

For the purpose of writing this chapter, data from secondary source have been utilized (existing literature available) and some information is extracted from news such as various reports and studies mentioned in the book chapter.

15.7   CONCLUSION

AI and machine learning will ultimately introduce changes in the e-commerce sector, but they have already started having an impact now. Innovative solutions and improved consumer experiences are greatly aided by AI in the e-commerce sector. The most notable applications of AI in e-commerce include product suggestions, customized shopping experiences, virtual assistants, chatbots, and voice search. The advantages go beyond this. AI can be used to further boost the benefits of gathering insights from consumer data, collecting, and then dissecting it to customize online merchandising services to the likes and tastes of each customer. Today's e-commerce organizations use AI and data gathered from customers and businesses to more effectively estimate future results and modify their marketing strategies, enabling them to make educated decisions.

REFERENCES

Ayyapparajan, R., & Sabeena, S. (n.d.). *Impact of Artificial Intelligence in E-Commerce.*

Bala, S., Khalid, M.N., Kumar, H., Shukla, V.K. (2022). The Practical Enactment of Robotics and 8*7 Artificial Intelligence Technologies in E-Commerce. In: Tavares, J.M.R.S., Dutta, P., Dutta, S., Samanta, D. (eds) Cyber Intelligence and Information Retrieval. Lecture Notes in Networks and Systems, vol 291. Springer, Singapore. https://doi.org/10.1007/978-981-16-4284-5_40

Fonseka, K., Jaharadak, A.A. and Raman, M. (2022), "Impact of E-commerce adoption on business performance of SMEs in Sri Lanka; moderating role of artificial intelligence", *International Journal of Social Economics*, Vol. 49 No. 10, pp. 1518–1531. https://doi.org/10.1108/IJSE-12-2021-0752

Harvey, C., Moorman, C., & Toledo, M. (2018). *How Blockchain Will Change Marketing as We Know It.* Retrieved from https://ssrn.com/abstract=3257511 https://ssrn.com/abstract=3257511Electroniccopyavailableat:ht tps://ssrn.com/abstract=3257511

Jain, P., Vegesna, A., & Porwal, D. (2018). *Ontology based Chatbot (For E-commerce Website) Cite this paper Ontology based Chatbot (For E-commerce Website).*

Mahapatra, D., Patra, S., & Kumar Baral, S. (2022). *Unleashing the Potential of Artificial Intelligence (AI) in Customer Journey of Cognitive Marketing and Consciousness Intention in E-Commerce Websites.*

Mohdhar, A., Shaalan, K. (2021). The Future of E-Commerce Systems: 2030 and Beyond. In: Al-Emran, M., Shaalan, K. (eds) Recent Advances in Technology Acceptance Models and Theories. Studies in Systems, Decision and Control, vol 335. Springer, Cham. https://doi.org/10.1007/978-3-030-64987-6_18

Pal, R. (2022). *Applications of Artificial Intelligence in Company Management, E-Commerce, and Finance: A Review.* Retrieved from http://ijmer.in/pdf/e- Certificate%20of%20Publication-IJMER.pdf

Sazibur Rahman, M., Li, Y., Rahman Miraj, M., Islam, T., & BingYingAI, T. (2022). *Artificial Intelligence (AI) for Energizing the E-commerce "Artificial Intelligence (AI) for Energizing the E–commerce.".* Retrieved from www.researchgate.net/publication/359919374

Srivastava, A. (n.d.). *The Application & Impact of Artificial Intelligence (AI) on E-Commerce.* Retrieved from www.researchgate.net/publication/356635263

Sun, Z., Finnie, G., & Prasad, B. (2003). *Intelligent Techniques in E-Commerce on Scientific China View Project Driving Socioeconomic Development with Big Data: Theories, Technologies, and Applications View Project Intelligent Techniques for E-Commerce.* Retrieved from www.researchgate.net/publication/27827422

T. A. Malapane and N. K. Ndlovu, "The Adoption of Artificial Intelligence in the South African E–Commerce Space: A Systematic Review," 2022 Systems and Information Engineering Design Symposium (SIEDS), 2022, pp. 7–12, doi: 10.1109/SIEDS55548.2022.9799403.

Veysel, A. (2018). *Implications of Blockchain Technology on Marketing.* Retrieved from https://ssrn.com/abstract=3351196

16 Artificial Intelligence Tools for Reshaping E-Business and Trade

Princi Gupta
JECRC University Jaipur
Rajasthan, India

Nisha Singh
Swami Vivekanand Subharti University
Meerut, Delhi, India

16.1 INTRODUCTION

In the present world, artificial intelligence (AI) has an impact on everyone. Natural language processing (NLP), business applications (including advertising and manufacturing), and competitive analysis are only a few of the sectors that use AI. By using AI, huge problems are resolvable within nanoseconds. A strong product is produced, and the needs, requirements, and preferences of the target market are identified; the product is then sold to achieve customer base (Bawack, 2022). Every assignment is completed in accordance with customer requirements, as customers' satisfaction is always the main priority for producers. Every businessperson looks at consumer behavior for self-familiarize with the new product for the first time. Customers use a variety of methods, techniques, and technologies to use their product. E-commerce has a significant impact. because consumers can more readily purchase the product through an online payment thanks to e-commerce, marketers can easily acquire the product in their hands. AI enables e-commerce companies to successfully enter new markets; turn a profit; and quickly satisfy customer demands, wants, and wishes. Because AI incorporates human intellect to be used by machines and computer systems, businessmen employ AI with e-commerce together to increase sales. Our current age prioritizes time-saving electronic transactions, and AI offers ever-increasing convenience to consumers. AI facilitates the adoption of efficient and cost-effective processes for the production of high-quality goods. There are major economic threats to all nations worldwide (Gochhait, 2020). There is a lot of uncertainty globally. India's commerce and industry have suffered significantly. The COVID-19 outbreak has impacted both the nation's economy and daily life. With recent advancements in AI technologies, leading businesses from emerging markets have begun integrating AI to increase their profits and business. China and other developing nations are seeing

DOI: 10.1201/9781003348351-16

an increase in the use of AI as a means of increasing production. AI offers a techno-logical answer to the commercial obstacles and difficulties experienced by today's complicated business structures. It offers assistance and support to businesses in constructing robust data management platforms, smart business strategies, and cre-ative new business models (Yang, 2020). AI-based technologies have the potential to expand opportunities, open up new industries, and increase economic growth.

During the past 50 years, the global economy has undergone unprecedented levels of digitization, making it necessary for businesses to undergo a management and operations revolution to ensure durability and constancy. While cheap Internet connection has caused many negative economic effects, the retail sector has been mostly hit by these effects owing to a dramatic shift in consumer preferences in favor of convenience and dependability over all other factors when making purchases. In response, and primarily to maintain a competitive advantage in the market, the majority of retail firms have adopted the Internet retailing method (e-commerce) either substantially or gradually in tandem with offline concrete block shop sales.

AI is among the best potential future technologies for solving most urgent societal problems that is, religious, political, and economic issues, which is gaining appeal in the technological sector. AI is a sophisticated and intricate software program that handles tasks similar to what the human mind does. These professions include, among other things, the ability to make original decisions, interpret data, and recog-nize voice. Researchers and businesspeople alike are interested in AI because of its precision in achieving its goals and the underlying ideas (Panigrahi, 2021).

16.1.1 GLOBAL LEADERS: ARTIFICIAL INTELLIGENCE

It cannot be denied that AI growth is accelerating. Since 2010, the rate of AI develop-ment has been nearly 60% each year.

Figure 16.1 illustrates the top five nations for innovation in AI technology based on the volume of research papers released each year.

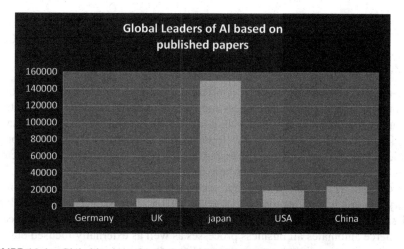

FIGURE 16.1 Global leaders of artificial intelligence (Haner, 2019).

The top-ranked nation on the list is China, which is renowned for its extensive manufacturing sector. According to the Times Higher Education website, China disseminated more than 41,000 papers on AI during 2011-2015, almost twice as many as those in the United States (US). The Chinese government firmly supports the choice of AI. A year ago, they stated their expectation to become "an important world focus of AI advancement" by 2030. Then, there are businesses such as Tencent, Baidu, and Alibaba. AI will be vital to the success of everything from online-based businesses to self-driving cars or web indexes (Haner, 2019).

Based on the aspect of papers distributed, the US ranks second among the leading countries that have implemented in AI. According to The Times Higher Education, the US published more than 25,500 articles on AI during 2011-2015. With more than 1000 businesses and US$10 billion in investment, the US is also among the top countries with the most AI organizations. As a result, the US is likely to become a superpower in this field. Additionally, there are numerous well-known AI businesses including Amazon, Google, Facebook, Microsoft, and IBM. The US publishes several papers and other resources and makes significant financial investments in AI (Mittal, 2021).

According to the Times Higher Education rankings, Japan stands third. It is not shocking that Japan publishes more than 11,700 papers and other resources related to AI each year. AI plays a critical role in the Japanese economy because of a declining labor force and an aging population. Indeed, Japan is able to automate and robotize more than half of all work tasks (Dhanalakshmi, 2020).

With more than 10,100 and 8000 research articles released each, the United Kingdom (UK) and Germany rank fourth and fifth, respectively. Germany and the UK both have intentions to become important centers for AI, similar to China. Germany is also experiencing a decline in the working population, much like Japan. It also has a great potential for computerization, with a percentage of 47.9%. It is a fertile field for AI thanks to its strong industry capacities, outstanding organizations, and excellent education (Murgai, 2018).

16.2   LITERATURE REVIEW: THEORETICAL BACKGROUND OF ELECTRONIC COMMERCE AND ARTIFICIAL INTELLIGENCE

16.2.1   Electronic Commerce

As e-commerce expands quickly, it offers convenience to consumers while also maximizing operational effectiveness and increasing service quality. The electronic commerce platform is constantly looking for innovative approaches to satisfy growing consumer needs. The development of AI tools has created new opportunities in the progress of electronic business, and its importance to the sector is going to be omnidirectional. Electronic trade (E-trade) is the management of any kind of commercial activity or data exchange through the Internet and contemporary communication technology (Wamba, 2020). Utilizing network technologies and smart gadgets as a business strategy is the foundation of e-commerce. e-Commerce automates all business processes as well as externally focused business processes such as digital transactions. Network advertising, transportation and operations, website design, the web, extranet, intranet, and databases are the fundamental technological pillars of e-commerce. The sciences of economics led to e-commerce., science, technology, and culture advancement. It is a technological and economic revolution. It is built on the Internet and supported by computer network technology, allowing strong comprehensive qualities such as trade software, telecommunications, and management systems to be tightly integrated. The growth of e-commerce transforms how businesses conduct their operations and how individuals shop and significantly advances the state of the world economy (Vanneschi, 2018).

16.2.2 ARTIFICIAL INTELLIGENCE: CONCEPTS AND ITS DEVELOPMENT

AI is the practice of incorporating and reproducing human intelligence in machines that have been trained to think and behave like people. Any device that displays human traits such as comprehension and problem-solving may also fall under this idea (Frankenfield, 2021). The engineering and science of AI is the development of intelligent devices, especially intelligent system software, according to John McCarthy, the founder of AI technology. AI is neither a novel idea nor a cutting-edge technology to researchers.

This idea is among the oldest ones, and there are still plenty of study opportunities (Lin, 2019). The development of AI may be traced back to 1943, when the first piece of work, known as AI in today's world, was finished by Warren McCulloch and Walter Pits. Following further advancement, John McCarthy, a computer scientist from the US, coined the phrase "artificial intelligence" in 1956 at the Dartmouth Conference, establishing AI as an academic discipline. Since then, AI has developed to an amazing degree. The current hot subjects are deep learning, big data, and data science. Companies such as Google, Facebook, IBM, and Amazon are also utilizing AI to create incredible products (Kumar & Trakru, 2020).

AI has been existing for a while; it may be discussed without respect and is currently expanding in line with new technological advancements in the commercial and business areas. Because of its comprehensive character, human ability to learn computational methods, and ability to change behavioral beliefs, it has recently been in high demand. AI is a multifaceted technology and equipment that can accept and understand from experience over time. It is incorporated in several ways such as execute, recognize, and sense (Bokovnya, 2020).

Generally, artificial intelligence can understand the nature of the business environment and the ability to resolve commercial and business-related issues. The intelligence of a person can be based on a variety of creative abilities, such as the ability to discover new things and to understand their purposes in the commercial world. This technology can also learn new skills and gain knowledge using AI techniques, and it possesses competitive ability for knowledge competition and uses that knowledge and experience for e-business analysis and solution. It has the ability to discover, create, innovate as well as its uniqueness, among others, in the commercial and business areas. It has the ability to appropriately, quickly, and reasonably deal with the complex environmental behaviors of an individual, which aids in better predictions of works and insights (Bandara, 2020).

The gestation phase, formation period, and development period are the general divisions in the historical evolution of AI. The rise and collapse of AI in the 1950s is known as the gestation period. Several noteworthy developments followed the first formulation of the AI concept, including the checkers program, universal issue solver, and LISP table processing language.

AI has fallen to the bottom because of its limited ability for reasoning and the failure of machine translation. Its significance characteristics are its ability toward problem-solving and downplay the value of information.

Formation: The introduction of expert systems sparked a fresh wave of AI from the late 50s to the 70s. AI has been put to use in expert systems such as the DENDRAL mass spectrometry system, the MYCIN illness diagnostic and treatment system, the PROSPECTIOR prospecting system, and the Hearsay-II speech interpretation system (Vanneschi, 2018).

Development Period: AI has advanced significantly since the 1980s, which was when the fifth-generation computer was constructed. The "fifth-generation computer development plan," or "knowledge information processing computer system kips," was launched in Japan in 1982 with the goal of making logical reasoning as quick as numerical processes. Despite the fact that this strategy ultimately failed, its invention spurred a wave of AI research.

16.3 EMERGING ARTIFICIAL INTELLIGENCE TECHNOLOGIES: RESHAPING E-BUSINESS

Figure 16.2 describes the continual evolution of existing technologies or new artificial technologies that are transforming e-business. AI incorporates several cutting-edge and emerging technologies. AI systems can be either based on a rule set or on data mining, machine learning, or deep learning techniques.

Data mining is the process of collecting both recent and old data to make predictions. The "knowledge discovery in databases" method, also known as knowledge discovery, includes an analysis stage called "data mining." With the unprocessed analysis step, several aspects of data and databases administration, considerations for

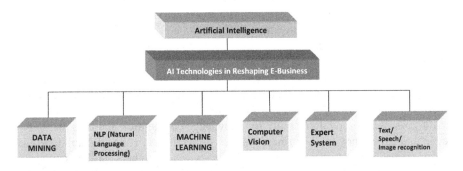

FIGURE 16.2   Emerging artificial intelligence technologies in reshaping e-business.

Source: Author.

models and inferences, data preprocessing, and interest measures, complex concerns, processing after identified structures, visualization, and digital update are all included (Srivastava, 2018).

The study of **NLP** focuses on how people interact with computers and how they comprehend spoken language. A branch of AI known as NLP enables machines to comprehend human speech and its syllable patterns. NLP market revenue has grown dramatically during the previous 5 years and is anticipated to keep growing as AI in e-commerce continues to expand.

NLP can be applied, for instance, to chatbots and voice-only tools. Additionally, NLP is a preferred tool for personalizing item descriptions and categorizing products (Tyagi, 2016).

Machine learning uses a variety of algorithms to use prior knowledge or examples given to solve a problem. Deep learning, a division of machine learning, primarily relates to e-commerce programs that are useful for identifying and monitoring customer behavior to give useful information for businesses. For instance, Alexa and other voice assistants from Amazon are powered by deep learning algorithms. Without being expressly coded, software systems may now predict outcomes more accurately thanks to machine learning. Machine learning aims to create algorithms that can forecast output data from input data utilizing analysis tools (Technology Target 2018a). Machine learning has an impact on businesses in many different ways (Srivastava, 2018). Saving money and enhancing customer experience are both beneficial uses of machine learning in business.

16.3.1 COMPUTER VISION

Computers and systems with computer vision capabilities can glean valuable information from images in films, pictures, and other digital visual inputs. The system has the ability to produce a customized offer based on the gathered data. Retailers can remain competitive and improve consumer happiness using this technology. For instance, using computer vision and augmented reality to create virtual showrooms works really well.

A computer-based expert system program uses breakthroughs in AI to emulate the decisions and actions either organization or a person with in-depth expertise and background in a certain sector. Additionally, in a considerable way, these systems have contributed to a number of endeavors, comprising customer services, social insurance, and financial benefit, transit, computer games, and broadcast communications, assembling, flight, and written correspondence (Anh, 2019).

16.3.2 SPEECH, TEXT, AND IMAGE RECOGNITION

Similar to human vision and thought, the ability to comprehend the images sent to it and identify distinct objects on them is the most crucial prerequisite for a machine with regard to image processing. One of the fields of AI with the most diverse applications is labeling, which is the procedure in question. Machines can understand spoken language from humans and other sources thanks to voice and speech recognition technology. This makes it possible for us to operate smart devices more swiftly and comfortably while also enabling sound recognition on those devices. In its simplest form, text interpretation involves extracting information from vast volumes of text-based data. This technique requires NLP, which enables the machine to comprehend and process manifestations of daily language. Without this, it is possible that computers may comprehend the meaning of each word, but NLP aids in the interpretation of words in context (Tyagi, 2016).

16.4 ARTIFICIAL INTELLIGENCE TRANSFORMING E–BUSINESS AND ECONOMIC SECTORS: ARTIFICIAL INTELLIGENCE METHODS AND FUNCTIONS

Heuristics, neural networks, support vector machines (SVMs), fuzzy logic, and other forms of AI are useful for decision support in management. It has mostly been used in process control and has a wide range of approaches that are helpful in forecasting; it also specializes in data mining and has, currently, a fundamental part in managing customer relationships in both business and marketing industries (Farooqi, 2019).

1. Artificial intelligence method using heuristics
2. Support vector machines
3. Computerized/artificial neural networks
4. Markov decision-making
5. Computer-aided/natural language processing
6. AI method using Fuzzy logic.

Table 16.1 illustrates new perspectives and innovative approaches to solving contemporary problems. AI techniques are essential for creating automated, intelligent, and smart systems that meet modern demands. AI technology is a way to effectively organize and apply knowledge while accelerating the speed at which a complicated program it contains is executed.

16.4.1 HEURISTICS ARTIFICIAL INTELLIGENCE METHOD

The word "heuristics" is defined "Involving or functioning as an aid to learning, discovery, or problem solving through experimental methods and particularly trial and error methods." In general, we can say that if issues arise, it is generally difficult to employ these procedures to find the precise and absolutely accurate potential solution. In "heuristics" approaches, we typically sought to use a workable approach to discover an answer. While it is not necessarily an ideal remedy, it is adequate in achieving the current objective in the commercial sector. Some of the components of the heuristic method, such as determining the issue, recognizing the issue, determining the answer to those issues, choosing a remedy for the issue, putting the problem's answer into practice, and assessing the issue's resolution, are crucial for understanding in the business and commercial sectors (Khan, 2021).

TABLE 16.1
Artificial Intelligence Tools/Methods and Their Applications Focused on the Economic Areas and E-Business

Artificial Intelligence Methods and Functions (Based on Electronic Business and Economy)	Techniques/Methods of Artificial Intelligence	Functions
	Heuristic Method	Identify the problem
		Understand the problem
		Identify the solution
		Select the solution
		Execute the solution
		Evaluate the solution
	Support Vector Machine	Stored data
		Recognition
	Artificial Neural network	Collect datasets
		Predict and solve business Problems
	Markov Decision Process	Predict models
		Countable state space
	Natural Language Processing	Classification
		Machine transformation
		Question answering
		Text generations
	Fuzzy Method	Machine learning techniques
		Mimic the logic of human thoughts
		Gives the complete guidance

Source: Mohammed, 2021

16.4.2 MACHINES THAT SUPPORT VECTORS

In essence, an SVM is a machine that understands the technique useful for classifying data and performing regression analysis (Iqbal, 2017). SVM is based on the supervised learning approach, which helps classify data into one of two groups: An SVM produces a sorting map having the maximum distance between the two points' margins and is helpful for categorizing text, classifying images, and recognizing handwriting, among other things. In addition to classifying objects, an SVM method should have the widest possible gaps between them on a graph (Micu, 2021). Applications of SVM include those that are necessary in the corporate world, such as text and hypertext classification. Additionally, it helps in image detection and classification, it is also capable of reading handwritten characters. It is helpful in biological sciences procedures, such as classifying proteins and amino acids.

For instance, the e-mail application uses the classification problem in the case of SVM to determine whether or not an e-mail is spam. To ascertain whether a given data point is connected to a specific class or not is the aim of these kinds of assignments. A class of fresh, unused sample of data after being trained on known-class data points can be determined using the classifier model (e.g., an e-mail collection that is classified as spam or not). SVM is a significant and potent solution for these kinds of issues that is now very useful in business and commerce sectors (Marda, 2018).

16.4.3 ARTIFICIAL NEURAL NETWORKS

By enabling us to use AI, neural networks changed business and daily life. It simulates how interconnected brain cells function, and it makes it possible for technologies such as smartphones and computers to train, learn, spot trends, forecast issues, and resolve issues in any industry (Igor, 2014). Artificial neural networks (ANNs) are useful in today's commercial sectors for identifying a variety of tasks and for categorization methods (Iqbal, 2019). When we feed a new image of a dog to ANN, it will answer with a numerical score showing how well the new image reflects the pattern before outputting the type of the dog. It has the capacity to store picture datasets, for example, various categories in pet breeds and images of trains in neural network methods. Additionally, neural networks for self-driving car recognition, categorization, text categorization, imagery reduction, securities exchange, and other intriguing applications are useful in the corporate and commercial areas.

16.4.4 MARKOV DECISION-MAKING

It is a stochastic control mechanism built on the mathematics developed in the late 19th and early 20th centuries by the Russian scientist Andrey Markov.

Modern game theory's Markov decision-making process and related Markov chains are built on the simpler mathematical work of a Russian scientist from a century ago. A Markov decision-making process examines a situation wherein a system transits from one group of states and advances with another in response to a decision-choice maker. As a model, a Markov chain depicts a series of events wherein the likelihood to a particular occurrence is reliant upon a previous level. Markov processes for decision-making frequently used in various complex sciences being developed by experts today, for instance, research models for business and commerce, robotics, and automation (Cui, 2021).

16.4.5 COMPUTER-AIDED NATURAL LANGUAGE PROCESSING

This technique fundamentally provides the AI approach credit for using a natural language such as English while corresponding using a corporate sector– and commercial sector–specific intelligent system. When creating an intelligent system to organize a robot's performance in accordance with our instructions, NLP is essential. It can also be useful when listening to a discussion based on a health expert system and making decisions from it (Singh, 2020).

Computers are often built for interpreting human language; thus, they must be modified in such a way that a computer can properly operate them. After all, converting text input to numbers is not a straightforward process. We need to extract patterns from a text document's structure, which is made of hundreds or thousands of words to extract the correct meaning from human language. Because of the difficulty of the work, we require a few strict guidelines that can be used to interpret spoken language in professional contexts. However, there are certain broad guidelines useful for deciphering the text characters, such as when the letter is used to indicate a plural item. As for the capabilities of a machine learning algorithm, it can be helpful in interpreting such manner; these broad rules work well together to extract the precise meaning from the text (Zhang, 2017).

16.4.6 Fuzzy Logic

In 1965, Al Zadeh coined the phrase "fuzzy logic." Fuzzy set and fuzzy logic theory was addressed by Cox and Von Altrock in relation to trading, with the goal of practicing this concept to create the capability of obtaining only a portion of a set's members to provide a live experience. Compared with a classical logic system, it is the most effective type of the logic system for real-time decision-making activities, as it makes the construction of intricate control systems simpler. Examples of fuzzy logic include washing machine, dishwasher, sports cars' cruise control, and cement industry's kiln control (Khrais, 2020).

16.5 EMERGING ARTIFICIAL INTELLIGENCE TRENDS: IMPLEMENTING AND PROMOTING E-BUSINESS AND TRADE

16.5.1 Chatbots

The best aspect of Internet purchasing is that e-commerce companies provide their clients with support and assistance around-the-clock through chatbots. Here is a description of a chatbot. "Chatbots are a category of software program that uses AI to have text- or voice-based online chat conversations with website visitors. These chatbots are direct users to a live human agent to offer more assistance. A few years ago, chatbots were created with the sole purpose of providing the consumer with some generic and expected responses (Soni, 2020). Chatbots may now provide potential consumers with answers and tailored support to their needs thanks to advancements in AI over time. These AI-powered chatbots are currently used on a wide range of e-commerce platforms including Amazon, Flipkart, Myntra, and others. AI is employed not only on e-commerce websites but also in well-known programs such as Facebook Messenger and other programs (Kar, 2016).

16.5.2 Management of Customer Relationships

You are in a world that has a vast history since the past if you still believe that the human resources department's responsibility is only to manage and maintain the customer relationship. To ensure that the potential clients are offered the best-in-class services in the modern world, a variety of information can be gathered and evaluated with the aid of AI. Only using AI, it is now feasible to transfer, use, and exchange large amounts of data with ease. The data are used to observe consumer buying trends, choices, and factors that influence their decision to buy to ensure proper and secure interaction. The CRM platform is a crucial component of the e-commerce sector, as it is the only way to thoroughly examine client buying patterns, among other factors, to make the finest and most profitable predictions for improved accuracy and outcomes (Kříž, 2017).

16.5.3 ACHIEVING SALES GOALS

Sales have the ability to change the course of history if they are trending in the right way, and this is beyond dispute. Additionally, e-commerce is a field entirely dependent on sales. This is the rationale underlying the usage of AI in this situation, as it can assist e-commerce businesses in gaining clarity and ensuring increased sales throughout the customer journey (Nadikattu, 2019). The "data scientists" and "data analytics" experts in AI claim that if one wants to make more sales pitches for more properties, AI may do so by producing superior insights and projections in the sales sector, including at the local and macro level patterns. All e-commerce businesses may make the most use of their resources and develop some solid pipeline ideas that will result in greater and more lucrative sales using the proper application of AI (Mohammad, 2020).

16.5.4 PRODUCT CONTENT MANAGEMENT

Every e-commerce business wants to give their customers the greatest possible experience, and AI can help them do so. Encompassing everything from product design to cataloging to ensuring that customers have the best experience. One may argue that the development of the effective and highest quality product content management in the e-commerce sector is made possible by AI (Sota, 2018).

16.5.5 CUSTOMER SERVICE

No matter how big or small an e-commerce company is, its consumers are its lifeblood and foundation. Therefore, it is crucial to make sure your consumers are receiving the best services and experience possible from you. AI is actually the best way that can help you do everything so that you can always have happy consumers; AI can help business in beginning the journey toward flawless and outstanding customer service. Regardless of the occasion or circumstance, AI enables one to learn about consumer satisfaction and how to respond to their demands and requirements. It is important to remember that excellent customer service results in increased profitable sales for a company. AI aids in the creation of such a harmonious environment where man and machine collaborate to increase revenue and sales (Kříž, 2017).

16.5.6 AUTOMATION

Most people mistakenly believe that the word "automation" means that robots would eventually replace humans in every task. Automation really benefits organizations by enabling them to discover about clients' desire irrespective of the time difference or other barrier. Sales people from various parts of the world may collaborate and connect with clients to provide the finest customer experience and achieve high sales with the aid of AI (Trappey, 2019).

16.5.7 ARTIFICIAL INTELLIGENCE IS EVERYWHERE

By the end of 2021, almost 90% of consumer interactions will be managed and dealt with or without the involvement of people, according to the creation of AI and its application to the e-commerce sector. Given the innovation and advancement that AI has brought to the e-commerce industry, it is safe to say that the company will experience a dramatic improvement unlike anything that has ever happened. e-Commerce platforms such as eBay, Flipkart, Amazon, and others are utilizing AI to grow their companies (Thiraviyam, 2018).

16.6 ARTIFICIAL INTELLIGENCE TECHNOLOGY: ITS APPLICATIONS IN ELECTRONIC BUSINESS AND TRADE

AI technology has steadily evolved into a potent instrument for accelerating sales growth and streamlining business processes, particularly in the area of electronic commerce. With its continued development, AI technology is fundamentally altering how people work and live (Varma, 2022). The following are the main ways that AI is now being used in the world of e-commerce:

16.6.1 ARTIFICIAL INTELLIGENCE ASSISTANT

Chatbot, a virtual assistant with AI, employs a system for automatic language recognition to automatically respond to customer inquiries and is part of the job. When carrying out basic voice and when chatting with customers on mobile and e-commerce platforms, machine learning techniques are utilized to personalize conversations. Customers can use chatbots to help them identify proper products, determine whether they are available, compare various products, and, in the end, help them make payments. If consumers have any complaints or inquiries, the chatbot can also help them contact the right customer service agents. Clients are able to converse with the robots through text, audio, and even photos. In March 2017, Alibaba unveiled Shop Xiaomi, an AI service robot and chatbot for Taobao sellers (Trappey, 2019).

16.6.2 ENGINE OF RECOMMENDATIONS

A complete recommendation engine based on machine learning technologies foundation is a recommendation engine. Evaluation and prediction of consumer behavior using machine learning and statistical programming uses the analysis of enormous data sets and the forecast for which AI algorithms enable the creation of all products that are most likely to attract customers. Using data from recent searches, the recommendation engine's machine learning algorithm can capture important information about the product that was searched for by potential customers. The recommender system then creates a useful option for the client based on the calculation results and puts them on a personal page, thereby benefiting clients in discovering the item fast (Varma, 2022). The dimensionality reduction technique is used to transform the AI recommendation system. The most significant shift due to an AI-based recommendation system is that it is now seen as the entire pattern of human-computer interaction rather than only a collection of recommendations. By adding the time dimension, it is possible to understand both user and system characteristics. Recommendation engines are frequently used by e-commerce businesses such as Amazon, AliExpress, Taobao, and JD.com to identify their valuable consumers.

16.6.3 ADVANCED SUPPLY CHAIN

The term "intelligent logistics" is used when information technology is employed to build equipment and control intelligent systems, and people will eventually be replaced by technical apparatus. Intelligent logistics may significantly increase service quality and operational efficiency when compared with traditional logistics. IBM first introduced the idea of intelligent logistics in 2009. AI usually has a noticeable direct effect on the logistics and back-end supply chain connections. Given the frequently shifting demand and the highly competitive markets, forecasting inventory is not an easy task. AI and machine leaning technologies, however, may identify crucial order cycle components and assess their effects on overstock and turnovers using models. The benefit of deep learning technologies is that they may learn more with time, improving the accuracy of inventory demand forecasting for firms (Khrais, 2020).

16.6.4 MAXIMUM PROFITS

Long-term continual pricing alteration is a good idea even for small inventory online stores and is a significant barrier in the current booming electronic businesses. The issue in automatically costing for a significant number of items has essentially been resolved through AI technology that handles vast information swiftly. The quality of the goods, the price of the logistics, and the degree of service will affect all the rankings. The ideal price is a challenge for businesses, and AI is well-suited to studying pricing issues in-depth. To address the issue of optimal pricing, AI technology uses very deep machine learning algorithms to assess trends in market and modify the business landscape.

16.7 ARTIFICIAL INTELLIGENCE IN E-BUSINESS: CASE STUDIES

16.7.1 AMAZON

The best known and popular AI product is Alexa that contributes to the operations and technologies and are vital to Amazon's targeted advertising program. With the use of AI, Amazon can forecast which products will be in high demand and offer tailored suggestions based on customer searches. Furthermore, 35% of total purchases are driven by Amazon's recommendation engine, claims Rejoiner (Rong, 2020).

16.7.2 JD.COM

Beijing-based Siasun Robot & Automation Co., Ltd, and JD.com collaborated to deploy robotics and automation technologies to enhance warehousing processes. The main goal is to increase the frequency and effective delivery of goods and warehouse storing filtering while decreasing expenses and raising income. By lowering physical labor and increasing efficiency, JD.com hopes to cut its workforce from approximately 120,000-80,000 over the course of 10 years. This will boost its profit margin.

16.7.3 ALIBABA

Tmall Genie and Ali Assistant are perhaps the first AI assistants that come to mind when thinking of Alibaba. In essence, Alibaba sought to strengthen its competitive edge by deploying AI. Overall, 89% of buyer enquiries, both written and spoken, are now processed by its customer support chatbot, which is quite effective. Additionally, Alibaba claims that AI algorithms support customer assistance, internal business processes, and smart product recommendations. Alibaba also uses AI to assist in determining the most effective delivery routes and is really effective. Furthermore, Alibaba asserts that the utilization of vehicles has decreased by 10% and travel distances have decreased by 30% because of smart logistics. It seems like Alibaba has made the perfect investment! (Chien, 2020)

16.7.4 EBAY

eBay views AI as a way to retain consumers and achieve an edge over competitors. Using NLP, the eBay Shopbot makes it simple for users to find the things they want. Customers can also use text, speech, or photographs from their phone to communicate with the bot. Currently, machine learning plays a key role in eBay's business strategy.

16.7.5 ASOS

ASOS, a fashion store, keeps spending money on speech recognition and AI to change consumer behavior. Additionally, it has already made a significant investment by incorporating a visual search option, the ASOS app can now compare users' images with relevant Internet retail sales using image recognition technology.

16.7.6 RAKUTEN

Rakuten, the biggest e-commerce platform in Japan, continuously invests in AI to enhance buyer behavior because it is essential for the success of the trade. Currently, they can accurately evaluate their 200 million goods and predict sales usingheir Rakuten Institute of Technology. Using real-time data, they can now segment customers more precisely. To increase customer satisfaction and sales productivity, image recognition technology is used in the Rakuten Fits Me app (Rong, 2020).

16.8 NEW ELECTRICITY IN E-BUSINESS: ARTIFICIAL INTELLIGENCE

16.8.1 CONSUMER-FOCUSED VISUAL SEARCH

Customers are frequently dissatisfied with their online shopping experiences because the results are frequently irrelevant. AI NLP helps enrich and contextualize Internet purchasers' search engine results to address this issue. Additionally, it enables visual product matching and product discovery. AI also makes it possible for customers to find related products and to have a better overall shopping experience. Consumers can now easily find comparable things through e-commerce stores by taking an image of your new sneakers from a pal or workout attire, uploading it, and then using AI. For instance, Amazon offers the possibility to click a product of your liking and Amazon would recognize it and present outcomes forare exactly what we are seeking (Nimbalkar, 2021).

16.8.2 IMPROVE SALES PROCESS AND RETARGET POTENTIAL CLIENTS

Conversica estimates that a minimum of 41% of marketing leads are unfollowed by the sales department, and it leads to interested prospective customers; those have been pre-qualified are simply left behind. Additionally, several workers are overburdened with customer data that are unmanageable and rarely used. At that point, AI is actually necessary. By customizing and overcoming issues and establishing a compelling sales pitch that is effective for consumers at the right moment on the suitable platform, AI may be able to accelerate the process of selling. These days, several AI technologies including Siri, Alexa, and others support NLP and voice input. As a result, a CRM system can respond to client inquiries, respond to their questions, and find fresh sales prospects. The North Face is a prime example of a significant online retailer. To comprehend their customers better, they use IBM's Watson AI solution. By posing questions like, "Where and when will you be utilizing your running clothes?" They can assist their users in finding the ideal clothing. Customers can respond orally or in writing. Then, using real-time client input, IBM's software evaluates hundreds of goods to identify the best matches. It also conducts additional research to learn about the local climate, among other things (Goldfarb, 2018).

16.8.3 HIGHER DEGREE OF CUSTOMIZATION

Many AI options are available right now, such as boomtrain. This organization examines various touch points such as mobile apps, websites, e-mails, to assist the enterprise in understanding the ways clients are behaving online. An AI engine is keeping an eye on all channels and devices to build a global customer view of all channels, not just one. Additionally, it aids online merchants in providing a cohesive client experience across all platforms. Sending pertinent messages at the appropriate time will be beneficial.

16.8.4 Chatbots and Virtual Helpers

User experience is now a priority in e-commerce. In the age of conversational commerce, using "chatbots" to drive the conversation is simply one method of applying AI. Chatbots can also automate order procedures; therefore, they can do even more than that. Additionally, they may collect important data, monitor behavior, and offer 24/7 customer service effectively and affordably. e-Commerce businesses can enhance conversion rates by using chatbots to customize the online experience for the user. Again, Alexa, which is Amazon's virtual assistant, is undoubtedly one of the more well-known examples. It has been incorporated into both Amazon's own products and goods made by other companies. Virtual assistants are anticipated to influence consumer purchasing decisions and offer a creative chance to e-commerce companies (Nguyenm, 2019).

16.8.5 Increase Customer Recommendations

With AI-powered businesses are better able to anticipate consumer demand and behavior and also provide relevant and helpful recommendations. A notable example is Starbucks, which utilizes AI to analyze all the data it has collected and produce more personalized solutions. The program considers user data, consumer trends, past purchases, third-party information, and relevant information.

16.8.6 Knowledgeable Actors

The new intelligent agent negotiating system is now a well-liked e-commerce tool. The three fundamental use cases are finding sellers and buyers enabling transactions, and offering infrastructure facilities.

16.8.7 Remove Fake Reviews

Unfortunately, bogus reviews started to affect e-commerce stores and online retailers. Additionally, 90% of respondents to dimensional research's survey claimed that favorable online reviews affect their purchasing choices. Additionally, 86% claimed that unfavorable online reviews had an impact on their purchasing choices. However, as we all are aware, some phony reviews have been posted by rival businesses and bots. Thus, how can AI handle this issue? Nowadays, a lot of e-businesses use AI to combat astroturfing by emphasizing reliable and beneficial evaluations. As an illustration, Amazon employs AI to battle inflated star ratings and fraudulent product reviews. Their AI emphasizes and boosts the importance and weight of verified consumer purchase feedback. Reviews that have been rated as useful by other users are also considered by AI (Nguyenm, 2019).

16.8.8 Automation

AI automation does not imply that humans will be replaced by machines. Many people now worry that, in the not-too-distant future, robots will accomplish everything.

Not really, no. Robots give merchants the chance to use technology and analytics to deliver precisely that what client desires, whenever they desire it. Automation became essential and a significant investment of their goals for e-commerce companies as businesses in the sector continued to develop and, with it, their consumer bases. Additionally, as we all know, when the electronic commerce industry expands, the amount of repetitive activities also increases. Anything from promoting new offerings on various platforms to setting up offers to providing discounts to devoted consumers can be taken over by robots (Goldfarb, 2018). According to Martechtoday, Alibaba has estimated that $15 billion will be spent on R&D in the next 3 years.

16.9 ELECTRONIC COMMERCE AND RELATED BUSINESS DOMAINS: ARTIFICIAL INTELLIGENCE APPLICATIONS

16.9.1 E-Commerce

An intelligent recommendation system for online stores offers customers the things they want based on user activity. The algorithm examines user behavior patterns including frequently viewed products, purchases, and considerations. The analyses are used to offer the most pertinent product recommendations.

Virtual dressing rooms Such an application uses a software program that simulates dressing rooms and allows customers to try on clothes online. AI technology allows the item to be overlaid on a live image of the customer, effectively serving like an improved shopping assistant (Agrawal, 2019).

16.9.2 Retailing

16.9.2.1 Planning the Supply Chain

AI systems are able to process and analyze colossal amounts of data, which helps retail companies identify logistical hiccups. According to IBM research, 40% of the organizations that took part in the survey use AI to address supply chain difficulties.

16.9.2.2 Customer Research:

AI makes it possible to conduct market research more cheaply and effectively. Choosing which follow-up questions to ask after analyzing open-ended survey responses (unstructured data) and locating survey respondents are activities that can currently be accomplished using machine learning algorithms (Nimbalkar, 2021).

16.9.2.3 Automation of Warehouse Operations

AI software that optimizes and automates activities can be used to power inventory processing. Amazon, a major player in online retail, has claimed that 40% more products have been stocked in its warehouses thanks to AI-powered computers. Intralogistics systems can learn from and be developed based on interactions with people in the factories where they are deployed, thanks to the work of companies such as Swisslog.

16.9.2.4 Tracking Customer Moods and Trends

AI-powered e-commerce technology that can track and identify particular consumer emotions can be advantageous for online retailers and patterns in maintaining more accurate product inventories.

16.9.2.5 The Very Group

In its machine-learning chatbot, The Very Group effectively integrated AI mood tracking technology. It recognizes the tone of customers' messages and modifies its responses accordingly. Over time, AI technology has surpassed all other customer assistance methods in the business.

16.9.3 MANUFACTURING

16.9.3.1 Manufacturing Process Control

Reducing costs and downtime by combining AI and production process control. According to Capgemini's market analysis, AI is used by 62% of European manufacturers (Cui, 2021).

16.9.3.2 Enhancement of Procedures by Automated Processes

AI innovations decrease menial, monotonous jobs that are present in manufacturing, but most critically, they also have the ability to foretell mishaps by studying vast amounts of data from sophisticated factory equipment. Businesses such as Canon are utilizing their expertise in factory automation driven using AI and providing consultancy services to other companies.

16.9.3.3 Apparatus Diagnosis

Software with AI is capable of carrying out equipment diagnosis without involving humans. Both on a big scale, as in production lines, and for specific cars, this is applicable. Many contemporary cars have AI systems that do engine and other auto-part diagnosis automatically built in. Hyundai's AI engine trouble diagnostics system is the most noteworthy example, which records interior automobile sounds and, using data processing, generates diagnosis with an accuracy rate of more than 90%.

16.9.4 MARKETING

16.9.4.1 Personalized Offers

By analyzing big datasets and identifying patterns in consumer behavior, AI solutions enable marketers to go beyond conventional customization efforts. The integration of personalized AI sales offers is made easier with the aid of these data results, which serve as reference points for decisions made at various phases of the creation of advertisements.

16.9.4.2 Order/Purchase Management

Until recently, order managers performed all of these tasks—checking SKU (stock keeping unit) availability and producing shipment labels—practically and manually.

Many AI-powered solutions available today can do this for you. Leading companies in the sector, such as Retalon, offer systems that handle stock control, retailing, and forecasting uses AI.

16.9.4.3 Automation of Advertising

Gathering data with first promotional activities and executing those again to a large targeted audience are typical steps in running ads. All of these can now be completed automatically thanks to AI software. For Google, Facebook, and Instagram ad campaigns, solutions such as Adext use machine learning algorithms that can automatically conduct tasks including audience segmentation, budget budgeting, and more (Agrawal, 2019).

16.9.4.4 Virtual Shopping Assistants/Virtual Chats

Additional AI technologies such as virtual shopping assistants and virtual chats help consumers make more efficient purchases and help organizations get the financial and risk management data they need.

16.9.5 PAYMENTS

Voice-activated payments are revolutionizing personal banking with 4.12 billion voice assistants are in use globally. It effectively cuts down on the time needed to complete financial tasks including logging in, activating cards, making transfers, and paying bills.

16.9.6 SUPPLY CHAIN

Efficiency has an impact on every industry, including manufacturing; retail; and the transportation, storage, and supply chain sectors. The expectation of consumers to receive their goods the same day has become the standard in many nations.

16.9.7 CYBERSECURITY

A significant increase in credit card transactions over a brief time period may indicate the use of fraud, although, unusually, many attempts to log in frequently indicates an online attack. Online stores can do threat analysis and stop financial cybercrime thanks to e-commerce machine learning technologies. AI also aids in preventing data theft and fraud (Aytekin et al., 2021).

16.10 CHALLENGES AND ISSUES: ARTIFICIAL INTELLIGENCE

16.10.1 FINDING USE CASES THAT ARE VALID

As more than 71% of B2B buyers are likely to switch brands if they do not receive a tailored experience, the customer experience is the main focus of the most common use cases for AI in B2B e-commerce. Computer vision, sentiment analytics, and product suggestions are some aspects that AI excels at handling.

Amazon made significant investments in its recommendation engine-powered by AI to comprehend clients at every touchpoint. For training and optimization purposes, Amazon Personalize assesses past purchases to provide better product recommendations.

NLP was utilized by the Home Depot AI division to create a model that translates user comments posted on the company's website. It enables other customers to quickly assess the benefits and drawbacks of each product without having to wade through many evaluations. More interaction and better conversion rates are the outcomes. By automatically assigning tags or directing them to the appropriate category, computer vision organizes photographs based on their content. This type of AI is used by digital commerce firms to improve customer search and decrease picture processing errors (Meltzer, 2018).

16.10.2 Sorting Out Data

The ability to extract insights from huge data is crucial for AI success, yet businesses still have problems with it. Some AI professionals (16%-21%) have reported issues with missing or incorrect data, according to an O'Reilly survey. The complexity of the method and the use case influence the amount of data. According to some estimations, an algorithm needs at least ten times as much data as there are examples for each model parameter. Data are not a primary resource. They need to be prepared and analyzed before being input into the algorithm.

16.10.3 Creating a Department for Artificial Intelligence

The data science team, which consists of data scientists, engineers, and BI (business intelligence) analysts, is necessary for AI. Machine learning engineers and AI architects who are in charge of the overall AI project collaborate with the data science team.

These AI experts are not only pricey but also difficult to locate. All skill and experience levels are affected by the talent shortage in the AI sector. Because of this, hiring is incredibly difficult (Hammoud, 2020).

16.10.4 Culture and Risk Management

As a young technology, everyone's conceptions of what AI is and what it can accomplish for a firm vary. All stakeholders can be included in your AI plan, and they can be involved in creating targets to prevent a mismatch of expectations.

There are also certain concerns associated with algorithms' changing nature. Can you ensure that AI technology is secure, private, and safe for both customers and staff to use? Machine learning bias, if ignored, may result in subpar customer service, decreased income, or even legal action (Hammoud, 2020).

16.11   E-BUSINESS AND TRADE: THE FUTURE OF ARTIFICIAL INTELLIGENCE

AI would have a brighter future in retail and e-commerce than was previously thought. The e-commerce industry is going to be significantly impacted by AI. AI in e-commerce makes sure that customers' experience in online shopping is easier, quicker, more personalized, more relaxed, and more seamless than ever. By 2030, AI will be worth more than 15 trillion dollars to the global economy. Therefore, investing in AI can have a huge positive impact on organizations. Store owners must uphold high consumer expectations to preserve competitiveness and enhance their e-commerce business in light of the intense rivalry among online retailer businesses. AI in e-commerce benefits players in the industry greatly. AI will undoubtedly transform the e-commerce industry and enhance how people find things online. The e-commerce boom may come to pass, but if you want your e-commerce site to succeed, you need more than simply a website or mobile app. You should make investments in cutting-edge technology such as machine learning and AI. A marketer's dream, AI in the e-commerce sector allows online businesses to evaluate thousands of client interactions each day and target offers to a single consumer.

16.12   DISCUSSION AND CONCLUSION

This chapter concludes that, although AI is becoming increasingly common in the e-commerce industry, it remains far from perfect. The contribution of this chapter offers global leaders of AI in electronic business and trade. e-Commerce companies are always better in satisfying consumer demand with the help of their AI tools. Additionally, they collaborate with other businesses to share their expertise in AI and develop more advanced products. AI in electronic business will affect consumer experience, transactions, customer loyalty, productivity, and a variety of other factors. Because of AI, buying and selling things online is changing. As AI includes a person's expertise to be used by the machines and frameworks, man-made intelligence and E-trade are combinedly used by the agent to intensify deals. Retailers, wholesalers, and agents use the E-trade business, and they are currently using different types of AI to explain their clients better and develop innovative methods for putting together high-quality products. Representatives use both AI and E-trade to improve the business environment. Recently, AI and E-trade have begun to work together. The online business has no physical presence with clients, and buyers' demands and wants occasionally vary. However, with the help of AI, creative new strategies to recognize buyers' purchasing behavior and according to buyers' requests were made. People possess fundamental knowledge, intuition, and flexibility that machines cannot match. These are obstacles that AI interpreters in online commerce would not have to overcome, according to human interpreters. Thanks to AI, the e-commerce sector has drastically changed how individuals sell, shop, and view products online. AI techniques are used by most of the corporate businesses in daily operations. AI advancements are altering people's daily lives and working environments, especially in the world of e-commerce. With advances in research and technology, the development of advanced AI technology has made it a powerful tool for driving revenue development and streamlining E-commerce processes. Fuzzy systems, ANNs, SVMs, and other AI techniques and methods are being used by both large corporations and small businesses to address challenges in a variety of business areas including choice, financial planning, forecasting, and risk evaluation.

This chapter further studies basic concepts and development of AI followed by the emerging AI technologies in reshaping e-business and trade. AI technologies include data mining, NLP, machine learning, computer vision, and expert system. This chapter covers AI methods with their functions in transforming e-business and economic sectors such as heuristics, SVM, and ANN. This chapter outlines the emerging role of AI with its opportunities with case studies of Amazon, Alexa, Alibaba, and eBay in boosting and benefiting the e-business and trade. This chapter describes the applications of AI in e-commerce and related commercial sectors. It also highlights the challenges and issues of AI as well as with future research directions.

REFERENCES

Agrawal, A., Gans, J., & Goldfarb, A. (2019). Economic policy for artificial intelligence. *Innovation policy and the economy, 19*(1), 139–159.

Anh, T. (2019). Artificial intelligence in e-commerce: Case Amazon.

Aytekin, P., Virlanuta, F. O., Guven, H., Stanciu, S., & Bolakca, I. (2021). Consumers' perception of risk towards artificial intelligence technologies used in trade: a scale development study. *Amfiteatru Economic, 23*(56), 65–86.

Bandara, R., Fernando, M., & Akter, S. (2020). Privacy concerns in E-commerce: A taxonomy and a future research agenda. *Electronic Markets, 30*(3), 629–647.

Bawack, R. E., Wamba, S. F., Carillo, K. D. A., & Akter, S. (2022). Artificial intelligence in E-Commerce: a bibliometric study and literature review. *Electronic Markets*, 1–42.

Bokovnya, A. Y., Begishev, I. R., Khisamova, Z. I., Narimanova, N. R., Sherbakova, L. M., & Minina, A. A. (2020). Legal approaches to artificial intelligence concept and essence definition. *Revista San Gregorio*, (41), 115–121.

Chien, C. F., Dauzère-Pérès, S., Huh, W. T., Jang, Y. J., & Morrison, J. R. (2020). Artificial intelligence in manufacturing and logistics systems: algorithms, applications, and case studies. *International Journal of Production Research, 58*(9), 2730–2731.

Cui, H., Xiao, L., & Zhang, X. (2021). Application of Mobile big data and artificial intelligence in the efficiency of E-commerce industry. *Mobile Information Systems, 2021*.

Dhanalakshmi, A., Hui, X., Roopini, R., & Supriya, R. (2020). Technological Advancements in E-Commerce and Customer Relationship Management. *International Journal of Engineering and Management Research (IJEMR), 10*(6), 9–20.

Farooqi, R., & Iqbal, N. (2019). Performance evaluation for competency of bank telemarketing prediction using data mining techniques. *International Journal of Recent Technology and Engineering, 8*(2), 5666–5674.

Frankenfield, J. (2021). Investopedia: 51% Attack. *Haettu, 15*, 2021.

Gochhait, S., Mazumdar, O., Chahal, S., Kanwat, P., Gupta, S., Sharma, R., & Sachan, R. (2020). Role of artificial intelligence (AI) in understanding the behavior pattern: a study on e-commerce. In *ICDSMLA 2019* (pp. 1600–1606). Springer, Singapore.

Goldfarb, A., & Trefler, D. (2018). Artificial intelligence and international trade. In *The economics of artificial intelligence: an agenda* (pp. 463–492). University of Chicago Press.

Hammoud, H. (2020). Trade Secrets and Artificial Intelligence: Opportunities & Challenges. *Available at SSRN 3759349.*

Haner, J., & Garcia, D. (2019). The artificial intelligence arms race: Trends and world leaders in autonomous weapons development. *Global Policy*, *10*(3), 331–337.

Igor, H., Bohuslava, J., Martin, J., & Martin, N. (2014). Application of neural networks in computer security. *Procedia Engineering*, *69*, 1209–1215.

Iqbal, N., & Islam, M. (2017). Machine learning for Dengue outbreak prediction: An outlook. *International Journal of Advanced Research in Computer Science*, *8*(1), 93–102.

Iqbal, N., & Islam, M. (2019). Machine learning for dengue outbreak prediction: A performance evaluation of different prominent classifiers. *Informatica*, *43*(3).

Kar, R., & Haldar, R. (2016). Applying chatbots to the internet of things: Opportunities and architectural elements. *arXiv preprint arXiv:1611.03799*.

Khan, M. A. (2021). Artificial intelligence in commerce and business to deal with COVID-19 pandemic. *Turkish Journal of Computer and Mathematics Education (TURCOMAT)*, *12*(13), 1748–1760.

Khrais, L. T. (2020). Role of artificial intelligence in shaping consumer demand in E-commerce. *Future Internet*, *12*(12), 226.

Kříž, J. (2017). Chatbot for laundry and dry cleaning service. *Masaryk University*.

Kumar, T., & Trakru, M. (2020). The colossal impact of artificial intelligence. E-commerce: statistics and facts. *Int. Res. J. Eng. Technol.(IRJET)*, *6*, 570–572.

Lin, J. (2019). Backtracking search based hyper-heuristic for the flexible job-shop scheduling problem with fuzzy processing time. *Engineering Applications of Artificial Intelligence*, *77*, 186–196.

Marda, V. (2018). Artificial intelligence policy in India: a framework for engaging the limits of data-driven decision-making. *Philosophical Transactions of the Royal Society A: Mathematical, Physical and Engineering Sciences*, *376*(2133), 20180087.

Meltzer, J. P. (2018). The impact of artificial intelligence on international trade. *Brookings Institution, Thursday, December*, *13*, 2016.

Micu, A., Micu, A. E., Geru, M., Căpăţînă, A., & Muntean, M. C. (2021). The impact of artificial intelligence use on the e-commerce in Romania. *Amfiteatru Economic*, *23*(56), 137–154.

Mittal, U., & Sharma, M. (2021). Artificial intelligence and its application in different areas of indian economy. *Int J Adv Res Sci Commun Technol*, *125*, 125–131.

Mohammad, S. M. (2021). Artificial intelligence in information technology. *Available at SSRN 3625444*.

Murgai, A. (2018). Transforming digital marketing with artificial intelligence. *International Journal of Latest Technology in Engineering, Management & Applied Science*, *7*(4), 259–262.

Nadikattu, R. R. (2019). New Ways in Artificial Intelligence. *International Journal of Computer Trends and Technology*.

Nguyen Gia, T., Nawaz, A., Peña Querata, J., Tenhunen, H., & Westerlund, T. (2019, November). Artificial Intelligence at the Edge in the Blockchain of Things. In *International Conference on Wireless Mobile Communication and Healthcare* (pp. 267–280). Springer, Cham.

Nimbalkar, A. A., & Berad, A. T. (2021). The Increasing Importance of Ai Applications In E-Commerce. *Vidyabharati International Interdisciplinary Research Journal*, *13*(1), 388–391.

Panigrahi, D., & Karuna, M. (2021). A Review on Leveraging Artificial Intelligence to Enhance Business Engagement in Ecommerce. *Journal homepage:* www. ijrpr. com *ISSN*, *2582*(7421), 2.

Rong, G., Mendez, A., Assi, E. B., Zhao, B., & Sawan, M. (2020). Artificial intelligence in healthcare: review and prediction case studies. *Engineering*, *6*(3), 291–301.

Singh, P., Singh, R., Singh, N., & Singh, M. K. (2020). A Distributed Artificial Intelligence: The Future of AI. In *Distributed Artificial Intelligence* (pp. 263–276). CRC Press.

Soni, V. D. (2020). Challenges and Solution for Artificial Intelligence in Cybersecurity of the USA. *Available at SSRN 3624487.*

Sota, S., Chaudhry, H., Chamaria, A., & Chauhan, A. (2018). Customer relationship management research from 2007 to 2016: An academic literature review. *Journal of Relationship Marketing, 17*(4), 277–291.

Srivastava, S. K. (2018). Artificial Intelligence: way forward for India. *JISTEM-Journal of Information Systems and Technology Management, 15.*

Thiraviyam, T. (2018). Artificial intelligence marketing.

Trappey, A. J., & Trappey, C. V. (2019). Global content management services for product providers and purchasers. *Computers in Industry, 53*(1), 39–58.

Tyagi, A. (2016). Artificial Intelligence: Boon or Bane?. *Available at SSRN 2836438.*

Vanneschi, L., Horn, D. M., Castelli, M., & Popovič, A. (2018). An artificial intelligence system for predicting customer default in e-commerce. *Expert Systems with Applications, 104*, 1–21.

Vanneschi, L., Horn, D. M., Castelli, M., & Popovič, A. (2018). An artificial intelligence system for predicting customer default in e-commerce. *Expert Systems with Applications, 104*, 1–21.

Varma, M. R. (2022). Artificial Intelligence and its Applications in Ecommerce. *New Perspectives on Commerce & Management, Volume-1*, 47.

Wamba-Taguimdje, S. L., Wamba, S. F., Kamdjoug, J. R. K., & Wanko, C. E. T. (2020). Influence of artificial intelligence (AI) on firm performance: the business value of AI-based transformation projects. *Business Process Management Journal, 26*(7), 1893–1924.

Yang, Y., Zhang, H., & Chen, X. (2020). Coronavirus pandemic and tourism: Dynamic stochastic general equilibrium modeling of infectious disease outbreak. *Annals of tourism research, 83*, 102913.

Zhang, X., Kim, J., Patzer, R. E., Pitts, S. R., Patzer, A., & Schrager, J. D. (2017). Prediction of emergency department hospital admission based on natural language processing and neural networks. *Methods of information in medicine, 56*(05), 377–389.

ADDITIONAL READING

Kouhihabibi, M. (2021). Feeling the Pulse of Trade in the Age of Corona: Artificial Intelligence and E-Commerce. *International Journal of Economic Behavior (IJEB), 11*(1), 23–35.

Kong, Y., Hou, Y., & Sun, S. (2020, July). The Adoption of Artificial Intelligence in the E-Commerce Trade of Healthcare Industry. In *International Conference on Digital Health and Medical Analytics* (pp. 75–88). Springer, Singapore.

Liu, H., & Liu, T. (2022). The Application of Artificial Intelligence Oriented to the Internet of Things Technology in the Complexity of Digital Crossborder Trade. *Wireless Communications and Mobile Computing, 2022.*

Irion, K., & Williams, J. (2020). Prospective policy study on artificial intelligence and EU Trade Policy. *Available at SSRN 3524254.*

KEY TERMS AND DEFINITIONS

1. **Machine Learning**–It is a subset of artificial intelligence that enables computer programs to forecast possibilities relatively accurately despite having been expressly taught to perform so.

2. **Computer Vision**–It is a branch of AI that makes it possible to retrieve useful data using image files, movies, and perhaps other visible sources.
3. **Natural Language Processing**–This software translates texts between languages.
4. **Artificial Neural Network**–This is a branch of artificial intelligence that is biologically motivated and is based on the mind.

17 Robotic Process Automation

The Emerging Technology

Divyesh Kumar
Department of Management Studies, T John College
Bangalore, India

Noor Afza
Department of Studies and Research in Business
Administration, Tumkur University
Tumakuru, India

17.1 CONCEPT OF ROBOTIC PROCESS AUTOMATION

Automation is neither a new concept nor a new phenomenon. Questions about its potential and effects have long accompanied its advances. According to US President Lyndon B. Johnson, who convened a national commission in 1966 to study the effects of technology on economy and employment, automation did not have to lead to job losses but instead quoted "can be the ally of our prosperity if we will just look ahead" (Technology and the American Economy, 1966). Parasuraman and Riley (1997) defined automation as, "the execution by a machine agent (usually a computer) of a function that was previously carried out by a human." Subsequently, Moray et al. (2000) describe automation in similar but more exhaustive manner that "automation is any sensing, detection, information processing, decision-making, or control action that could be performed by humans but is actually performed by a machine."

In the past, automation has not always been welcomed, and concerns about its implementation and its detrimental effects on employment have persisted. (Autor, 2015; Vagia et al., 2016).

Currently, the same situation prevails in the industry owing to significant advances in innovations and technological development such as robotic process automation, artificial intelligence (AI), machine learning (ML), and natural language processing (NLP).

In every walk of life of humans—personal and professional—the role of automation is significant. For all professionals—miners, welders, landscape gardeners,

DOI: 10.1201/9781003348351-17

fashion designers, commercial bankers, and even at the level of CEOs—automation plays a significant role in easing their jobs with more accuracy and minimum or zero errors. Every new change invites a change in the management strategy to address the resistance from different corners of the society about the risk of losing employment, difficulties in training and learning, and adjusting with new job descriptions. Gradually, technology has become a special edge to bring in phenomenal improvement in quality, performance, and delivery in the industry, and economy will attract all people to prefer automation technology in their firms.

At present, because of cut-throat competition, companies have been working in multi-dimensional ways, for example, on the one hand, they will increase product versions and new market segments entries and, on the other hand, they will reduce cost to maximize profitability. Since the 1990s, most of the companies were looking for cost reduction strategies such as labor arbitrage; hence, many tasks were moved to low-cost countries in continents such as Asia, Eastern Europe, and Latin America. Thus, the majority of the business firms worldwide have enjoyed the low-cost advantage. At present, business firms are looking for process standardization and system harmonization. Consequently, the RPA technology is very much in demand to automate the maximum possible business activities to take further benefits such as cost reduction, speed transactions, 100% accuracy with zero human errors, standardized performance, and transparency. In other words, business firms are badly in need of improving their cost-effectiveness and quality of their business transaction process. Herein, RPA suits their requirements.

Gejke (2018) has defined RPA as a technology involving the application of specific software and algorithms and a methodology to automate repetitive human tasks. An industrial answer to the enormous quantity of manual labor required to perform daily, weekly, or monthly tasks to support a wide range of high-volume business procedures is RPA (Aguirre & Rodriguez, 2017, Lacity & Willcocks, 2016).

RPA is a technical impersonation of a human worker with the objective of quickly and effectively automating structured tasks. It represents computer software designed to perform labor-intensive, repetitive activities. This implies that all repetitive and labor-intensive jobs can be automated, whereby one can accomplish the jobs with accuracy at minimal cost (Slaby 2012).

Mendling et al. (2018) had a panel discussion to determine the degree to emerging technologies such as machine learning, robotic process automation, and blockchain will make managing corporate processes more humane.

Aguirre and Rodriguez (2017) opined that RPA has emerged as a software-based solution to automate rule-based business processes that involve routine tasks, structured data, and deterministic outcomes. Furthermore, they observed that RPA enhances productivity, reduces cost, increases the speed of operations with minimal or zero errors. The results of their case study showed that productivity improvement was the main benefit of RPA and time reduction.

McKinsey & Company (Venkat Atluri et al., 2019) viewed RPA, one of the emerging and disruptive technologies, as anticipated to be wide-ranging and could have a $6.7 trillion economic impact by 2025. Of the technologies considered, such as 3D printing, cloud technology, and autonomous vehicles, the second-largest economic impact is projected to come from automation business, trailing only the growth of mobile Internet for smartphones and tablets (i.e., mobile data). Consequently, it is clear that RPA is expanding quickly and is anticipated to become one of the top technical platforms and to set new standards for effective business operations and performance. Hofmann et al. (2019) stated that RPA application is interesting to companies that pursue an operational excellence strategy, although RPA's use should not be limited to this strategy.

17.2 EVOLUTION OF ROBOTIC PROCESS AUTOMATION

RPA is also called a game-changing technology, as it has many strengths to bring in transformation in the industry to meet the global standards. The evolution of RPA can broadly be classified into three stages, which is as follows:

17.2.1 TECHNOLOGY

Screen scraping is defined as, "the process of collecting screen display data from one application and translating it so that another application can display it. Usually, this is to capture data from a legacy application to display it using a more modern user interface" (www.techopedia.com/). The screen scraping application must usually

a) record input from the screen and send it to the legacy system for processing.
b) provide the user with data from the program and properly display it on the user's screen.

17.2.1.1 Merits of Scraping
a) Fast prototyping, and
b) Easy to learn how to do.

17.2.1.2 Demerits of Scraping
a) If the code of the page is changed, then there will be problems with the scraping solution.
b) This runs slower than an application programming interface (API) call.
c) One cannot scrap easily, as most of the sites have policies against screen scraping.

Many firms seek more adaptive and versatile technologies as a result of the aforementioned drawbacks.

17.2.2 WORKFLOW AUTOMATION AND MANAGEMENT TOOLS

This technology has been present since 1920, but it is found to be used intensively since the 1990s. Workflow automation makes complicated business processes easier to manage operations. For instance, in the case of processing orders, capturing specific fields of interest, such as customer contact information (e.g., phone number, email address, and home address), invoice total amount, and details of ordered items; converting them; adding them to the company's database, and alerting the relevant employee to respond favorably and promptly. All online retail malls such as Amazon, Flipkart, and so on use automated tools. This software type reduces the need for human data entry and boosts order fulfilment rates; thus, its benefits include faster, more efficient, and more accurate operations.

17.2.3 Artificial Intelligence

The concept of AI is "concerned with the development of computers that can engage in human-like thought processes such as learning, reasoning, and self-correction." In other words, financial planning and fraud detection are two examples of the types of jobs that AI robots can now perform that were previously very dependent on people for their judgment and decision-making skills. The advantages of AI include enhanced accuracy and precision in jobs as well as the replacement of tiresome, time-consuming manual labor–oriented tasks, although it is somewhat expensive.

17.2.4 Robotic Process Automation: The Emerging Technology

Although RPA first became popular in the early 2000s, it is still a developing technology that relies on screen scraping, AI, and workflow automation. RPA takes these technologies to a new level and dramatically improves the way in which it advances their abilities. RPA enables users to create automation and manage workflows visually, without the need for coding, utilizing drag and drop functionalities. Additionally, in contrast to many web scraping tools, some of which do not involve human workers, RPA software employs optical character recognition technology to adapt to changing webpages. The evolution of RPA can again be classified into four stages depicted in Figure 17.1, and a brief description of the stages is provided as follows.

17.2.4.1   RPA 1.0 Assisted by RPA

The objective of this tool is to improve worker productivity, which was characterized by partial automation and nonscalable.

17.2.4.2   RPA 2.0 Unassisted by RPA

The objectives of this tool are end-to-end to automation and scalable virtual workers, and the important features are work orchestration (scheduling and/or queuing), centralized robot management, and robot performance analytics. The constraints of the technology are manual control and the management of robots, managing screen, and system changes.

17.2.4.3   RPA 3.0 Autonomous RPA

The objectives of this tool are end-to-end to automations and scalable and flexible virtual workforce. The main features are auto scaling, dynamic load balancing, context

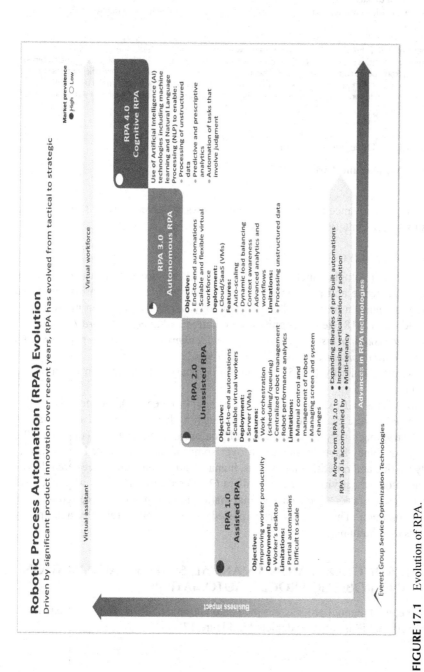

FIGURE 17.1 Evolution of RPA.

Source: https://www.everestgrp.com/2017-04-robotic-process-automation-rpa-evolution-market

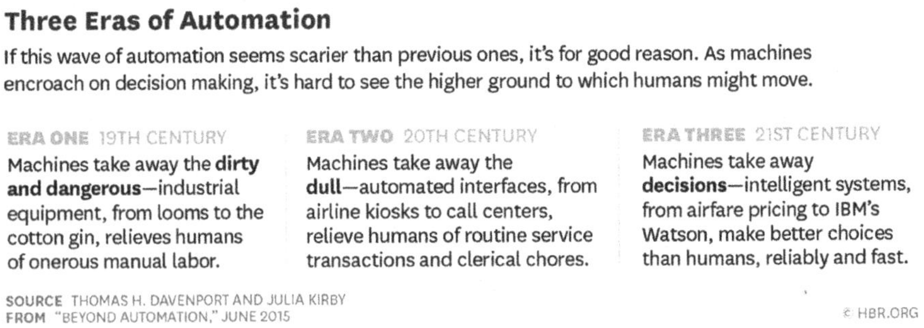

Three Eras of Automation

If this wave of automation seems scarier than previous ones, it's for good reason. As machines encroach on decision making, it's hard to see the higher ground to which humans might move.

ERA ONE 19TH CENTURY	ERA TWO 20TH CENTURY	ERA THREE 21ST CENTURY
Machines take away the **dirty and dangerous**—industrial equipment, from looms to the cotton gin, relieves humans of onerous manual labor.	Machines take away the **dull**—automated interfaces, from airline kiosks to call centers, relieve humans of routine service transactions and clerical chores.	Machines take away **decisions**—intelligent systems, from airfare pricing to IBM's Watson, make better choices than humans, reliably and fast.

SOURCE THOMAS H. DAVENPORT AND JULIA KIRBY
FROM "BEYOND AUTOMATION," JUNE 2015   © HBR.ORG

FIGURE 17.2   Three eras of automation.

Source: Davenport and Kirby (2015).

awareness, and advanced analytics and work flows. Unable to process unstructured data is its major limitation.

17.2.4.4   RPA 4.0 Cognitive RPA

It uses AI technologies including ML and NLP to process unstructured data, performs predictive and prescriptive analytics, and performs automation tasks that involve judgment. In other words, the technology works like a human mind. Lacity and Willcocks (2018) define cognitive automation as *"using software to automate or augment tasks that use inference-based algorithms to process unstructured and structured data to produce probabilistic outcomes."*

Davenport and Kirby (2015) reported three phases of automation as shown in Figure 17.2.

Figure 17.2 is self-explanatory. In the first era (19th century), the most dangerous and dirty jobs were executed by machines such as heavy cranes in the construction industry, machinery used in coal, and iron ore mining. In the second era (20th century), machines have further taken over some of the tasks called "dull tasks," namely routine and repetitive tasks; thus, human workers and employees are relieved such monotonous activities. In the third era (21st century), machines will take over decision-making tasks. This phase of automation is, in other words, called as intelligent automation. The systems are expected to make better, reliable, and speedy decisions than humans.

17.3   DISTINCTION AMONG MANUAL, SCRIPTED AUTOMATION, AND ROBOTIC PROCESS AUTOMATION

The concepts of manual process, scripted automation, and RPA are briefly explained, and the relevant illustration is depicted in Figure 17.3:

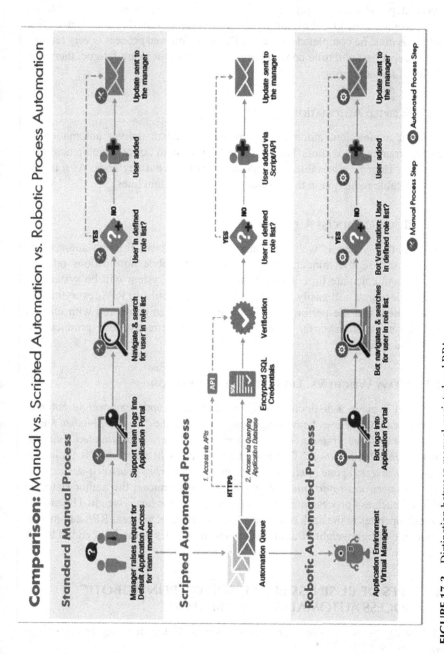

FIGURE 17.3 Distinction between manual, scripted and RPA.

Source: https://thelabconsulting.com/rpa-and-robotics-old

17.3.1 Manual Process

Manual process requires human to push a task (e.g., sending e-mails) through each and every step and know whom to send it to. Sending reminders is also done by humans. Keeping files in the digital or physical form kept in disparate places like this, all fields must be completed manually. The entire manual process is very tedious because of repetition and time consumption, and because of being fatigue, there is a possibility of human errors.

17.3.2 Scripted Automation

Under script automation, automation software is used to deliver automation in a managed framework without having to perform custom script development and maintenance. Hence, this enables automation scripts without any code. As a result, there is countable reduction in the development costs and timelines.

17.3.3 Robotic Process Automation

Under RPA, the system is well programmed to assign tasks through automation. The system can send reminders through mails and mobile notifications on specified dates and calculate time automatically. The filing system will be systematic and at one place and will easily be accessed. In other words, in RPA, everything is fully automated, and the performance through RPA, when compared with manual and scripted automation, is far better in terms of cost-effectiveness, productivity, accuracy, and speed.

17.3.4 Heavy Weight Vs. Light Weight Automation

Bygstad (2017) made a distinction between lightweight and heavyweight automation. The researcher defines heavyweight automation as the "*well-established knowledge regime of large systems, developing more and more sophisticated solutions through advanced integration.*" On the contrary, lightweight automation is applicable for "*new knowledge regime of mobile apps, sensors and bring-your-own-device, also called consumerization and Internet of Things.*" Furthermore, the author states an example of business process management automation for heavyweight IT automation, which operates in the back end of the IT infrastructure, whereas RPA automation is an example of lightweight IT automation, which operates in the front end of the IT infrastructure.

17.4 TYPES OF BUSINESS PROCESSES WHEREIN ROBOTIC PROCESS AUTOMATION CAN BE USED

The following are the business processes wherein RPA technology is applied, as shown in Figure 17.4:

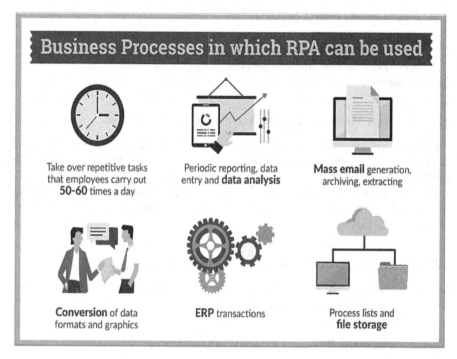

FIGURE 17.4   Where can RPA be applied.

Source: https://www.uipath.com/blog/the-robotic-process-automation

17.4.1   REPETITIVE TASKS THAT EMPLOYEES PERFORM 50–60 TIMES IN AN 8-HOUR WORKING DAY

This includes activities such as double data entry, regulatory reports, connecting legacy systems, information validation and audits, order processing, payroll processing, registration, onboarding, and claims processing.

17.4.2   REPORTING AND ANALYSIS

The process of arranging statistical tables in the required format and making data into informational summaries to monitor the performance of different areas (geographical regions such as districts and states), products (companies may have more than one product or service making and selling), and sales persons (companies are using the services of different sales persons) of a business. The analysis is the process of exploring data, analyzing the same, and making reports to dig out meaningful insights to take further steps to improve business performance. Data processing includes the following activities:

- It follows logical rules such as "if/then" rules
- It makes huge calculations

- It extracts data from documents
- It inputs data to forms
- It extracts and reformats the data into reports or dashboards
- It merges data from multiple sources
- It copies and pastes data.

17.4.3 MASS MAIL GENERATION, ARCHIVING, AND EXTRACTING

E-mail archiving is defined as the process of removing e-mails from your inbox and storing them in a location where access to those emails becomes further easy. This can be done either manually or through automation. The archived mails are arranged with reference to date, from, to, and key word; hence, it will be easy to retrieve the e-mail anytime for reference. The point of archiving is to give a central location to store mails for easy access.

17.4.4 CONVERSION OF DATA FORMATS AND GRAPHICS

Data conversion is defined as the conversion of computer data from one format to another. Data are encoded in many methods.

17.4.5 ENTERPRISE RESOURCE PLANNING TRANSACTIONS

Finishing a task becomes less complex and easier with zero mistakes. By combining RPA with Oracle Enterprise Resource Planning (ERP), the optimization process becomes faster and less labor-intensive. In other words, with RPA, the use of Oracle ERP becomes easier and faster.

17.4.6 PROCESS LISTS AND FILE STORAGE

The RPA technology processes lists and keeps the file storage safe, and whenever the files are needed, they can be easily accessed without any delay, as the files are arranged systematically based on the date, from whom the file is received and the purpose of the file.

17.5 CHARACTERISTICS AND STRENGTHS OF ROBOTIC PROCESS AUTOMATION

The following are the characteristics of RPA described briefly:

- RPA is a computer-coded software
- RPA imitates human interaction with applications
- RPA enables cross-functional application
- RPA plays like virtual workforce and is controlled by business operations
- RPA is agile and noninvasive and works with the IT infrastructure and governance also.

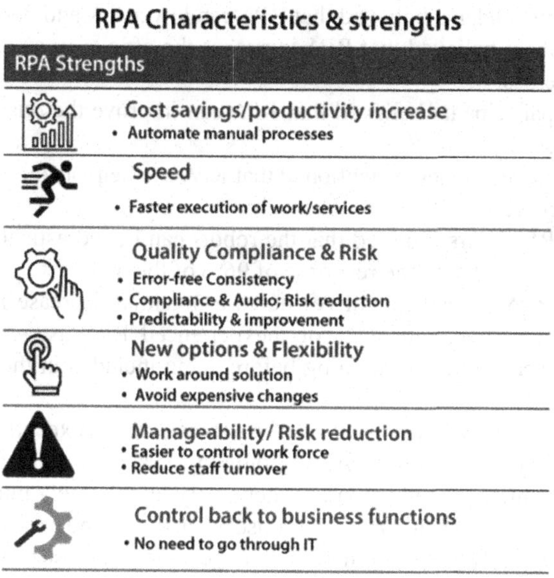

RPA Characteristics & strengths

FIGURE 17.5   Strengths and characteristics of RPA.

Source: https://www.tutorialandexample.com/rpa-interview-questions/

The strengths of the RPA technology are depicted in Figure 17.5 and further briefly explained as follows:

Most of the companies globally show increasing interest in RPA because of the strengths technology has. RPA is a new technology with an increasing number of applications. In other words, the number of users is increasing, and the users are happy with technology. The technology works faster, and all the expected benefits are being realized. There are no upfront costs associated with this technique. This technology barely affects the current IT world. The greatest benefit is that RPA has the flexibility to adapt to changing business environments.

17.6   IMPACT OF ROBOTIC PROCESS AUTOMATION AND ARTIFICIAL INTELLIGENCE

Bill Cline et al. (2016) stated that success in today's financial markets requires unprecedented levels of speed, accuracy, and cost-efficiency beyond what a human workforce can provide.

17.6.1   CAPGEMINI (2016) RESEARCH WORK

The Capgemini (2016) research report revealed the following research findings:

a)   According to 86% of participants, RPA can significantly cut down costs.

b) 86% of respondents believed that RPA can lower risk and boost compliance.

c) 86% of them believed that RPA increases the efficiency and performance of the processes.

d) 89% of participants believed that RPA can improve the quality of the work produced.

e) 91% of the respondents mentioned that RPA can help businesses save time on routine chores.

f) 84% of RPA users reported that the robots can help drastically reduce costs, when compared with the response of 96% of the nonusers.

g) 53% of RPA-trained executives noted a potential decrease in process complexity compared with 44% of inexperienced RPA users, suggesting that workers need sufficient training before being included in the RPA execution process.

h) Furthermore, it was disclosed that the success of RPA execution is determined by cost reduction due to RPA. Additionally, 65% of participants in the survey expressed that cost reduction is either a very or extremely important measure of success. More than 50% of RPA users stated that the goal of cost reduction is realized fully or more than their expectation. The survey also disclosed that 20%-50% cost reduction is achievable. Similarly, 58% of RPA users had experienced increased speed of the work processes and perceived as second most critical factor for the success of RPA implementation.

Capgemini further disclosed that companies of all sizes and irrespective of the sector or industry had expressed their intention that they would implement RPA in the near future. Additionally, it is revealed that firms that earn more than 1 billion Euros per annum intend to implement RPA in Finance and Accounting (F&A) function and Human Resource processes; on the contrary, business firms that have revenues less than 1 billion Euros per annum also have customer service on their agenda to execute RPA.

17.6.2   Deloitte (2017) Research Findings

According to a research report from Deloitte (2017), a majority of 400 companies had started adopting RPA and reported that their investment payback period is 1 year, on average, and the companies expressed that their expectations of cost reduction, accuracy, timeliness, flexibility, and improved compliance are met or exceeded.

17.6.3   Research Works of Lacity and Willcocks (2017)

Lacity and Willcocks (2017a) reported through their study that, among their previous 13 performed RPA case studies, the minimum 1-year return on investment (ROI) was 30%, while the largest ROI reached triple digits. Investment includes cost of software licenses, training, consulting, and developing RPA cases.

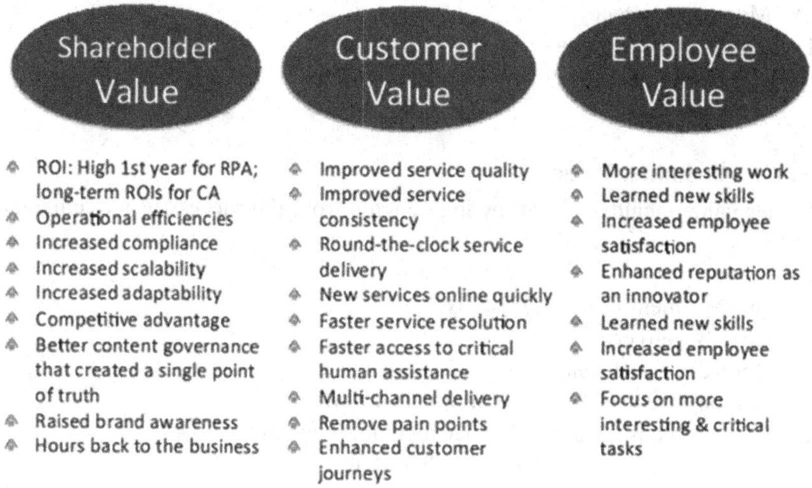

Shareholder Value	Customer Value	Employee Value
♠ ROI: High 1st year for RPA; long-term ROIs for CA	♠ Improved service quality	♠ More interesting work
♠ Operational efficiencies	♠ Improved service consistency	♠ Learned new skills
♠ Increased compliance	♠ Round-the-clock service delivery	♠ Increased employee satisfaction
♠ Increased scalability	♠ New services online quickly	♠ Enhanced reputation as an innovator
♠ Increased adaptability	♠ Faster service resolution	♠ Learned new skills
♠ Competitive advantage	♠ Faster access to critical human assistance	♠ Increased employee satisfaction
♠ Better content governance that created a single point of truth	♠ Multi-channel delivery	♠ Focus on more interesting & critical tasks
♠ Raised brand awareness	♠ Remove pain points	
♠ Hours back to the business	♠ Enhanced customer journeys	

FIGURE 17.6 The triple-win.

Source: Lacity and Willcocks (2017a).

The researchers had performed computation on savings in Full-Time Equivalents (FTE). They illustrate the concept with an example: a full-time employee takes 40 hours per week to finish a process and a bot (RPA) can perform the same process within 20 hours per week; then the savings in FTE earned by adopting the bot is 20 hours divided by 40 hours, or 0.5 FTE. Therefore, the saving made by adopting RPA would be 0.5 FTE per week, implying 50% of the human employee wages or salary can be saved. Lacity and Willcocks (2017b) further argue that successful adoption of robot or RPA reduces labor cost, and the work will also be processed in a standardized form, speedily, reliably, and with minimum or zero errors. All these merits will have a chain effect and result in more than the estimated savings.

Lacity and Willcocks (2017b) classified the benefits/value that adopters obtained from using RPA in three categories—shareholder value, customer value, and employee value. Theseare referred to as best practice organizations. The classified benefits are depicted in Figure 17.6:

A brief description of the three-dimensional (the authors describe this as "triple-win") benefits is presented as follows:

17.6.3.1 Shareholder Value

In addition to ROI, shareholder value is added by the following benefits:

a) More work with less manpower or reduction in FTE.
b) Increased compliance.
c) Increased scalability (in other words, enhanced performance with high operational efficiency).
d) Standardized, uniformed, and quality performance.

e) More transparency.
f) Competitive advantage.
g) New business and new market opportunities.

17.6.3.2 Customer Value

Customer value includes the following benefits from the successful implementation
of RPA:

a) Improvement in service quality.
b) Speedy delivery.
c) Zero-error performance.
d) Standardized services with more accuracy.
e) Work force is virtual and hence available round the clock.
f) Provision of new services quickly online.
g) Enhanced customer experience and satisfaction.

17.6.3.3 Employee Value

Employee value includes the following benefits from the successful implementation
of RPA:

a) No more of boring and repetitive tasks; instead, the employees will be
   assigned interesting work requiring creativity, emotional intelligence, and
   problem-solving skills.
b) More employee satisfaction.
c) Curiosity to learn new skills.

The three-dimensional benefits briefed above should be viewed as a smorgasbord
of the possible benefits and have been achieved by companies (those companies that
adopted RPA) as reported by Lacity and Willcocks. Best practice organizations were
able to extrapolate values from each of the three dimensions.

17.6.4 RESEARCH WORK OF IAN Sandholm (2019)

Ian classified the value of successful implementation of RPA into two major categories: direct value and indirect value. In each category, there are a set of elements
as depicted in Figure 17.7.

Direct value includes cost reduction, FTE savings, operational efficiency, scalability and flexibility, and employee experience improvements.

Indirect value is also called as the long run value or external value and refers to
the value obtained later in a casual chain. The researcher states that the indirect value
consists of the following attributes:

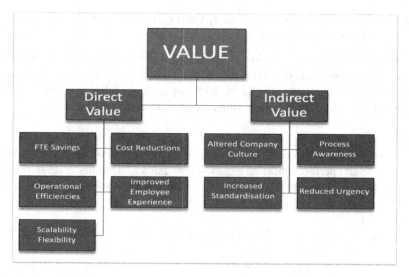

FIGURE 17.7   Successful implementation of RPA–Value.

Source: Ian Sandholm (2019).

a) Altered Company Culture

The business environment is dynamic and always changing. Based on the changes, the business firm has to shape itself to suit the changes to stay in the business. Accordingly, the required technology has to be adopted, and the required training should also be given to its employees to make a good fit for the new and high-end jobs to deliver the services to the clients up to their satisfaction. To accomplish this, all the changes required in the organization and among the employees with respect to economic, technological, social, and cultural aspects will be consolidated to make the business organization a successful enterprise.

b) Increased Standardization

RPA technology will perform the tasks in a uniformed and standardization; hence, product or service delivery will be the same quality without any variation for any number of times; the task is performed unlike in the case of human employee performance.

c) Process Awareness

As for a human employee, there is a possibility of human error as far as process awareness while performing the service repeatedly but not in the case of bot or RPA technology, as it works mechanically based on the rules. RPA implementation makes the employees learn the new process, which is knowledge gain for them.

d) Reduced Urgency

Once RPA is implemented, there is no urgency of further process development.

17.6.5 RESEARCH WORK OF HINDLE J, LACITY M, WILLCOCKS L, AND KHAN S (2018)

Blue Prism is the market leader in enterprise RPA and the creator of the term "robotic process automation." They recently collaborated with Knowledge Capital Partners to assess the deployments of their clients. With respect to the following parameters, the survey was held, and the research results are also presented briefly:

a) Scalability
   Scalability is defined as "the degree of flexibility with which the platform can cope and perform under an expanding workload." The survey result revealed that 97% of the users (of Blue Prism) rated it favorably for its capacity to scale to handle new or increasing workloads.

b) Adaptability
   Adaptability is defined as "the degree of flexibility with which automations can be introduced into additional business processes or can be altered to accommodate new or changing process rules or data types." The survey result revealed that 90% of the users (of Blue Prism) rated it favorably for its ability to adapt to new or evolving process rules or data types.

c) Security
   Security is defined as "the ability to prevent unauthorized access to computers, software, and data of the platform." The survey result revealed that 92% of the users (of Blue Prism) rated it favorably for its ability to prevent unauthorized access to computers, software, and data of the platform.

d) Service Quality
   Service quality is defined as "the ability to deliver services that conform to user's/client's expectations of accuracy, speed, and responsiveness." The survey result revealed that 99% of the users reported that the Blue Prism platform had improved their service quality for their clients.

e) Employee Satisfaction
   Employee satisfaction includes the degree of comfort on the job, scope for learning, increasing interest to work with the platform, and more excitement while on the job. Additionally, 90% of users claimed that the deployment of Blue Prism robots increased employee satisfaction.

f) Ease of Learning
   Ease of learning is defined as the degree of easiness with which first-time users can also learn to automate tasks using the platform without any difficulty and confusion. Additionally, 80% of the users have rated a positive result with respect to the ease of learning factor.

g) Deployment Speed
   An organization's (users') average speed to RPA deployment is defined as, "the time required to configure, test, and launch automations into production and delivery." Additionally, 86% of the users were able to launch their automations in 6-8 weeks when compared with 5-6 months of industry's average.

h) Return on Investment

ROI is defined as the surplus of revenue over and above the total investment for every year in percentage. The survey results on 1-year ROI for the Blue Prism platform are very impressive and attractive. Overall, 61% of respondent users reported more than 25% ROI within a single year, and 33% of respondent users reported more than 50% ROI over the entire period.

i) Compliance

Compliance is defined as an organization's adherence to laws, rules, regulations, and guidelines relevant to the business and its ability to provide supporting evidence. It is revealed that 80% of respondents reported that implementing the Blue Prism tool had improved enterprise compliance.

j) Overall Satisfaction

The survey results show that the users' overall satisfaction with the Blue Prism platform was quite high; 96% of the respondent users rated positive and impressive.

17.7 BOTTLENECKS AND RISKS

The RPA adopter will face challenges, bottlenecks, or risks while implementing and practicing on the RPA platform. Any change initiated in an organization will be definitely resisted by employees and other factors. Lacity and Willcocks (2017a) also call them as potential obstacles, issues, bottlenecks, challenges, or any other term preferred to describe something going wrong in the implementation or practicing of RPA on business transactions. Lacity and Willcocks (2017a) identified eight risk factors: strategy, sourcing selection, tool selection, stakeholder buy-in, automation launch, operational/execution, change management, and maturity. All these are self-explanatory and further depicted as a chart in Figure 17.8:

Suri et al. (2017) reported the following mentioned reasons for the failure of RPA implementation:

a) Fear of loss of jobs on the part of employees
b) Ignorance of the meaning of RPA and possible applications
c) Lack of resources for RPA adoption.

17.8 CONCLUSION

The business world is fueled with extensive competition whereby every company seeks to grab the world of opportunities to grow—organically and inorganically—in value and volumes without geographical boundaries using the latest and innovative technologies. Outsourcing with automation has emerged as a golden opportunity to budding technological entrepreneurs (technopreneurs) to offer high-tech cost-saving solutions to business enterprises. Hence, automation technologies are in more demand because of many advantages that were discussed in the previous section.

FIGURE 17.8   Major RPA risks.

Source: Lacity and Willcocks (2017a).

REFERENCES

1) Aguirre, S., & Rodriguez, A. (2017), Automation of a Business Process Using Robotic Process Automation (RPA): A Case Study. In J. C. Figueroa-García, E. R. López-Santana, J. L. Villa-Ramírez, & R. Ferro Escobar (Eds.), Communications in Computer and Information Science. Applied Computer Sciences in Engineering (pp. 65–71). Cham, Switzerland: Springer International Publishing. https://doi.org/10.1007/978- 3-319-66963-2_7

2) Autor, D. (2015), 'Why are there still so many Jobs? The history and future of work-place automation', Journal of Economic Perspectives 29, (3), pp. 3–30.

3) Bill Cline et al (2016), 'Rise of the Robots', KPMG Report www.kpmg.com

4) Capgemini (2016), 'Robotic Process Automation–Robots conquer business processes in back offices', a study conducted by Capgemini Consulting and Capgemini Business Services.

5) Davenport, T., & Kirby, J. (2015), 'Beyond automation', Harvard Business Review, June, pp. 58–65.

6) Deloitte (2017), 'The robots are ready. Are you? Untapped advantage in your digital workforce', https://www2.deloitte.com/content/dam/Deloitte/tr/Documents/techno-logy/deloitte-robots-are-read.pdf [Accessed 9 May 2020].

7) Fersht, P., & Slaby, J. (2012), 'Robotic Automation Emerges as a Threats to Traditional Low-cost Outsourcing', The Knowledge Community for Global Business and IT Services, HfS Research, Ltd, www.hfsresearch.com

8) Gejke, C. (2018), 'A new season in the risk landscape: Connecting the advancement in technology with changes in customer behaviour to enhance the way risk is measured and managed', Journal of Risk Management in Financial Institutions,11(2): 148–155.

9) Hindle J, Lacity M, Willcocks L and Khan S (2018), 'Robotic Process Automation: Benchmarking the Client Experience', Executive Research Report, www.Knowledgecapitalpartners.com

10) Ian Sandholm (2019), 'Successfully Utilizing RPA', Master of Science Thesis TRITA-ITM-KTH Industrial Engineering and Management, Industrial Management, KTH Royal Institute of Technology, School of Industrial Engineering and Management.

11) James Manyika et al (2017), 'A Future that Works: Automation, Employment, and Productivity', McKinsey Global Institute; can be browsed at https://www.mckinsey. com /~/media/mckinsey/featured%20insights/Digital%20Disruption/Harnessing%20 automation%20for%20a%20future%20that%20works/MGI-A-future-that-works-Executive-summary.ashx

12) Lacity, M. C., & Willcocks, L. P. (2016), 'Robotic process automation at Telefonica O2', MIS Quarterly Executive, 15(1), 21–35.

13) Lacity, M. and Willcocks, L. P. (2017a),'Robotic process automation and risk mitigation: the definitive guide', SB Publishing.

14) Lacity, M. C. and Willcocks, L. P. (2017b), 'A new approach to automating services', MIT Sloan Management Review.

15) Lacity, Mary and Willcocks, Leslie P. (2018), Robotic process and cognitive automation: the next phase, SB Publishing, Ashford.

16) Mendling, J., Decker, G., Hull, R., Reijers, H. A., Weber, I. (2018), 'How do Machine Learning, Robotic Process Automation, and Blockchains Affect the Human Factor in Business Process Management'? Communications of the Association for Information Systems, 43 (30): 1–23.

17) Moray, N., Inagaki, T. & Itoh, M. (2000),'Adaptive automation, trust, and self confidence in fault management of time critical tasks', Journal of Experimental Psychology: Applied 6, (1): 44–58.

18) Parasuraman, R. & Riley, V. (1997),'Humans and automation: Use, misuse, disuse, abuse', Human Factors, 39, (2): 230–253.

19) Peter Hofmann, Caroline Samp and Nils Urbach (2019), 'Robotic Process Automation, Research Center, Finance and Information Management', The International Journal on Networked Business, https://doi.org/10.1007/s12525-019-00365-8.

20) Slaby, J. (2012), 'Robotic automation emerges as a threat to traditional low-cost outsourcing', HfS Research, Ltd., pp: 1–18.

21) Suri, V. K., Elia, M. & van Hillegersberg, J. (2017),'Software bots–the next frontier for shared services and functional excellence', In: Oshri I., Kotlarsky J., Willcocks L. (ed.) Global Sourcing of Digital Services: Micro and Macro Perspectives. Lecture Notes in Business Information Processing, 306, 81–94. Springer International Publishing.

22) Technology and the American economy: Report of the National Commission on Technology, Automation and Economic Progress, US Department of Health, Education and Welfare, February 1966.

23) Vagia, M., Transeth, A. & Fjerdingen, S. (2016),'A literature review on the levels of automation during the years What are the different taxonomies that have been proposed'? Applied Ergonomics 53, 190–202.

24) Venkat Atluri et al (2019),'Tech-enabled transformations: The trillion-dollar opportunity for industrials', September 2019, McKinsey.com

Index